101 Lies

1. I'll call you.
2. I love you.
3. You're the only one.
4. I've never felt this way about anyone else.
5. I've got to work late at the office tonight.
6. That's the best sex I've ever had.
7. You've got the most beautiful eyes.
8. No, I'm not married.
9. Sorry. I must have left my wallet and credit cards at home.
10. You just have to believe me when I tell you nothing's wrong.
11. I'm ready to make a commitment.
12. Except for a beer or two, I never drink.
13. My wife and I haven't had sex in years.
14. We'll get married *as soon as I* ...
15. I'll be home in twenty minutes.
16. It's not that I don't care—I just have to spend more time with my kids.
17. I've only slept with maybe ten women in my entire life.
18. I've been celibate since we broke up.
19. I could never lie to you.
20. I can still last all night.
21. I always use a condom.
22. I can help you get a great job in my company (field).
23. I haven't seen her since she and I broke up.
24. I tested HIV negative.
25. I haven't done drugs (smoked pot) since college.
26. The only sexual fantasies I have are about you.
27. No, I don't think your thighs (stomach, breasts, hips, etc.) are too big.
28. I'm too tired.
29. How could you think I'd be interested in her? She's your best friend.

30. When it comes to oral sex, I'm the best.
31. I've never had any trouble keeping an erection before.
32. It's you and me, babe—we'll make love all over Europe.
33. I'd never do anything to hurt you.
34. I want to grow old with you.
35. Believe me, my wife and I live very separate lives.
36. Our having sex won't change a thing between us.
37. Don't worry, I've had a vasectomy.
38. I'm going to leave my wife.
39. You're nothing at all like my mother.
40. Your being a different religion doesn't matter to me.
41. It doesn't bother me that you make more money than I do.
42. Even without sex, we'd still be friends.
43. I think older women are the most exciting.
44. I'm considered one of the top people (in my field, in the company).
45. What attracts me to you is your mind.
46. We'll split all the child care and household chores fifty-fifty.
47. Of course I don't mind that you didn't come.
48. I've never had an affair before.
49. You're the only one who understands me.
50. I've never been in therapy.
51. You're the best thing that's ever happened to me.
52. No, I'm not seeing anyone else.
53. I haven't thought about her (old girlfriend) in years.
54. How many times do I have to tell you I'm not having an affair?
55. Your career is as important as mine.
56. I promise you that I'll change.
57. I want us to remain close friends always.
58. My wife and I have an understanding.
59. You're wonderful; you deserve someone better than me.
60. I don't masturbate.
61. Let's be friends first.
62. When you walked through that door, I knew it was the real thing.
63. I'd like you even if you were a man.
64. It's okay to be good looking, but looks just don't mean that much to me.
65. The differences between us will bring us even closer together.
66. I spend everything I earn on you and the kids.

67. No, I never said that.
68. You make me feel like a kid again.
69. I'm going out with the boys (to the gym, to the office).
70. I'll move wherever you want.
71. Of course I'm not bored with you.
72. As soon as I finish this project (get a promotion, a raise, make partner), we'll …
73. You've got more sex appeal in your little toe than my wife's got in her whole body.
74. It wouldn't be you and me anymore if I used one of those.
75. Let's pool our assets—whatever is mine is yours.
76. I still find you just as attractive as the day I met you.
77. Divorce is the farthest thing from my mind.
78. Sure, I'll watch the kids.
79. It's not just the sex I want, it's being close to you.
80. We'll be spending a lot of time together when I retire.
81. You're the only reason I've worked so hard.
82. If I didn't have all this work, you know I'd go with you and the kids to your mom's.
83. No one's ever turned me on like you do.
84. My boss says there's nothing to worry about.
85. I'll never tell …
86. Relax; she's just a friend.
87. This is just a temporary separation until we get things worked out.
88. Your hair (dress, outfit) looks fantastic.
89. It was just sex—it didn't mean a thing.
90. Of course I'm listening to what you're saying.
91. Come on in and we'll just cuddle for a few minutes.
92. No, I don't think you're fat.
93. You're the woman I should have married.
94. I'm going to be focusing on my work for a while now.
95. I guarantee you, I'm not the father.
96. Your having kids has nothing to do with my not wanting to get married.
97. I'm not ashamed of the way you talk (look, act, etc.).
98. It's nothing personal; I just don't like sharing my living space with someone.
99. This time I'm really serious.
100. Honestly, honey, it's just for the guys—none of the wives go to the conference.
101. I'll always take care of you.

101 Lies Men Tell Women

Also by Dory Hollander, Ph.D.

The Doom Loop System:
A Step-by-Step Guide to
Career Management

101 LIES MEN TELL WOMEN

and Why Women BelieveThem

DORY HOLLANDER, Ph.D.

HARPER

NEW YORK • LONDON • TORONTO • SYDNEY

HARPER

Grateful acknowledgment is made to reprint lyrics from "It's a Sin to Tell a Lie"/Billy Mayhew. Copyright © 1936, 1952 WB Music Corp. Copyright renewed. All rights reserved.

A hardcover edition of this book was published in 1995 by HarperCollins Publishers.

HarperCollins books may be purchased for educational, business, or sales promotional use. For information please write: Special Markets Department, HarperCollins Publishers, Inc., 10 East 53rd Street, New York, NY 10022.

First HarperPerennial edition published 1997.

Designed by Nancy Singer

The Library of Congress has catalogued the hardcover edition as follows:

Hollander, Dory.
   101 lies men tell women : and why women believe them / Dory Hollander. — 1st ed.
       p.   cm.
   ISBN 0-06-017125-1
   1. Deception.   2. Truthfulness and falsehood.   3. Man–woman relationships.   4. Interpersonal communication.   I. Title.
   BF637.D42H65   1995
   305.3—dc20   95-23268

ISBN 0-06-092812-3 (pbk.)

11 12 13 14 15 ❖/RRD 30 29 28 27 26 25 24

To the truth-teller in each of us

CONTENTS

ACKNOWLEDGMENTS

I like to think of myself as independent. But when it comes to writing a book, like living a life, we have many opportunities to accept guidance and see how the suggestions and views of others spur us to achieve far more than if left to our own devices. Often the question isn't whether or not we *can* go it alone, but whether we're smart enough to acknowledge and learn from the cumulative wisdom of others. So I feel pleased to have accumulated a certain indebtedness in writing *101 Lies*.

To whom am I indebted?

First, to all the people I interviewed—both the liars and those lied to. Their stories and insights gave me a heightened degree of empathy that I hadn't anticipated prior to hearing their compelling stories and capturing their words, feelings, and reflections. As this book unfolded, the collective and individual experiences of these men and women guided me to refine and reshape my thinking about lies men tell women, particularly the whys and wherefores. It was their genuine desire to understand why they lied or were lied to—or both—that helped me persist throughout two breakneck years of full-time consulting and writing. And it was what I learned from them that gave me the courage to let this book develop a voice of its own. Although I couldn't get each of their full stories into print, their words and insights and the lies they told or suffered have greatly influenced the tone and direction of each page of *101 Lies*.

Second, I am indebted to many, many researchers in psychology, sociology, and sociobiology. As background for my own research on the lies men and women tell each other, I relied on the body of knowledge their scholarship has created. I am also indebted to the many research psychologists who have performed hundreds of laboratory experiments on the topic of deception and related areas. In particular, the contributions of Paul Ekman on lie detection and Bella DePaulo on the nonverbal aspects of deception have helped me gain a better understanding of what we as psychologists know and don't know about lying. I also want to acknowledge three decades of groundbreaking work by gender-role theorists and researchers. While not always specifically referenced, this body of gender research forms the underpinning of much of my thinking on how differences in male and female socialization, from birth onwards, evolve to influence the ways in which men and women lie to each other, as well as most everything else in our lives. And among evolutional psychologists, whose writings I find fascinating, I want to single out the work of David Buss on the evolution of desire, which created many "ahas" for me as I thought about the evolutionary and adaptive role of the lie in our personal relationships.

Third, I am indebted to my good friend, companion, and colleague Dr. George Salamon, who helped me interview the men and women quoted in this book. In chapter after chapter, more than his time, he has contributed many ideas that have helped me refine my thinking, and he has been my supporter through continuously hectic twenty-hour days, as well as out-of-town life and work in a string of cities. Beyond surviving the occasionally uncomfortable scrutiny of a psychologist who is writing about the lies men tell women, George has also managed to concede a point or two when pushed to the wall. From the book's inception to its completion, George has worn many hats as my sounding board, informal editor, and, in its last days, even proofreader.

Which brings me to the rest of my "editorial board." I have been blessed and abandoned by three fine editors at HarperCollins— Nancy Peske, Betsy Thorpe, and Susan Moldow. Belatedly (alas), I learned that the top lie that editors tell authors is, "No, of course I'm not going anywhere else." Still, even after leaving HarperCollins, Nancy Peske acted as the freelance editor of *101 Lies*, and her interest in and commitment to the book have certainly made a difference in crafting the finished product. Betsy Thorpe, my second editor, wins the flexibility and goodwill award for her evenhanded treatment of shifting schedules and deadlines and for her calm and supportive style. And Susan Moldow, who has left me twice now, gets high marks for being the first to recognize the value of the concept of *101 Lies* and to bring the book into HarperCollins. I wish them all well in their new positions.

I want to acknowledge also my old friend and agent, Bruce Wexler, who has been with me through some tough times and whose insights, editorial savvy, and support were invaluable to me in producing *101 Lies* and, before that, my first book in 1991, *The Doom Loop System—A Step-by-Step Guide to Career Management*. Bruce has served as my outside editor, trying to keep me on the path of writing everyone's hands-down favorite book on lies.

I'd also like to thank my friend Betsy Walker for reading the finished manuscript and for her suggestions. And then there are my many clients, both corporate and individual, to whom I am indebted for their genuine interest in *101 Lies* and their acceptance of the intensely focused time and energy this book's deadlines required. And there is Max Millon, the president of the Relationship Center in St. Louis, Missouri, who generously helped me gain access to volunteer research subjects as part of my St. Louis sample.

Last, but never least, as they would remind me, should I be brazen enough to forget, I am indebted to my two staunchest supporters and toughest critics: my children, Sam Blumoff and Rebecca Hollander-Blumoff. Special thanks to Rebecca for her insights and eagle-eye proofing and to Sam for his unrelenting finish-line perspective. They are anchors of sense and stability in an increasingly crazy world.

INTRODUCTION

WHY A BOOK ON MEN'S LIES?

When I was growing up, my father used to tell me, "Never trust a liar." Being a good daughter, I carried this piece of generational wisdom with me throughout my girlhood. Still, I couldn't help wondering why my father chose to share it with me, his youngest daughter. It just didn't make sense. After all, why would anyone *trust a liar*?

But over the years, I began to see my father's point.

As a psychologist, I kept bumping into women who had been lied to by the men in their lives. As a career coach and corporate consultant, I saw lies in the business world harm the unsuspecting. And along the way, I ran into more than a few whoppers myself.

For a while I just filed the stories in my head. But later on, when I began thinking about the cumulative weight of the stories I had heard and my own experiences, I saw a recurring theme. No matter how heinous or outrageous the lies, women wound up blaming themselves rather than the elusive and often fast-disappearing liars.

They had trusted liars.

Sure, they were furious at the men who deceived them, but somehow many of them felt their own behavior or attitude had set the stage for the men's lies. No wonder a residue of hurt and anger lived on in these women's lives to cloud trust in their future relations.

I also worked with many men who talked about their lies to women, but few agonized over them. Some men even boasted about their ability to fool the women in their lives, or their uncanny, espionage-like ability to keep their intentions secret. While the women I worked with told me about their personal distress and anger over lies in their personal and work relationships, few men did. More often they brought up their own or someone else's lie as an interesting aside or an afterthought as we worked to solve some other pressing problem.

Gabe is a good example of this. He'd been working with me to effect a major career move to another city in the Northeast. We'd been strategizing this fast-tracker's career plans for about six months and had finally scored the big win we had been hoping for. He had it all—the offer, the salary, the title, the power curve he wanted so badly.

When I asked Gabe about the logistics of his move, he talked about how long it would take him to terminate his house lease and to pack up and hit the road. Probably less than three weeks.

He was on a very short tether.

Then the bombshell hit. "Oh yes, by the way," he added offhandedly. For me, "by the way" is usually a tip-off that something important that has been hidden is going to pop out, so naturally I perked up. Gabe explained that he had been living with this absolutely wonderful woman for a little over a year, and did I happen to have any advice on how to break the news to her, since it would mean the end of the relationship. And, "by the way," she'd also have to move all her belongings out of his place on pretty short notice, since it was his lease and she couldn't afford to maintain it. And then came the aftershock. Yet a third "by the way." Since he hadn't actually mentioned his job search to her, this would be all brand-new information.

I was stunned. Until then, Gabe had never mentioned that there was a woman in his life, much less one who expected that their relationship would lead toward a long-term commitment. He needed to tell her all this immediately. But, despite my coaching, Gabe waited to tell her until the week before the move. Why? Well, because it was easier. Because it fit his agenda, his timetable, his limited willingness to tolerate conflict and disharmony. To Gabe it made sense. Why should he ruin their last weeks together? If he was upset over waiting so long, I sure couldn't discern it. Was it a lie or, as many men put it, the far less harmful "not tell"?

Whatever we label Gabe's tactic, I'm sure the woman in Gabe's life didn't see it through the same laissez-faire lens he did. As she hurriedly packed up all her things in the two or three days following the announcement of his move, it's a fair guess that she wasn't saying, "What a surprise! What a guy! Gabe did the right thing by not telling me he had one foot out the door. It made our last couple of weeks together so much more blissful."

So why did I write this book on the lies that men tell women? I wrote it for Gabe's erstwhile housemate and all the women like her. So they can begin to bullet-proof themselves against the next and the next "not tell." So they won't be blindsided time after time. So all those women with their own Gabes will be able to talk more frankly about how lies and "not tells" affect them, and bring the issues of truth and honesty out of the dark into the sunshine. And so men like Gabe can understand how their blatant self-interest harms all the women who trust them and how it wreaks havoc in their lives.

I wrote this book to help open a franker dialogue between men and women about why we lie in the privacy of our homes, in our beds, at work, and in our public lives. This isn't easy for either gender, since we often fear the consequences of our own honesty as much as or more than the consequences of our partner's lies. But my experience is that no matter how uncomfortable you are, if you stay open and stick with honesty, you'll make just enough progress to bring about change.

Then there's something else to keep in mind. Most of us are still learning to deal with the taboo-laden, politically correct environment of the 1990s. Here we face many paradoxes when it comes to relationships between men and women. We've come a long way from the feminist stance of the 1960s, 1970s, and 1980s, when women abhorred any inference that men and women might differ from each other. Today we're far more willing to accept that men and women differ along more dimensions than upper body strength.

Yet we're still circumspect when it comes to bringing to the table any gender differences that seem negative or that have hurtful consequences. We want to make everyone right, so no one feels at fault. The result? The gender dialogue we desperately need is being strangled by the noose of political correctness. One of my hopes is that *101 Lies* will do its part in freeing up that dialogue—with your participation.

HOW MY INTEREST IN LIES GAINED MOMENTUM

The seed of the idea was planted many years ago when I was asked by a corporation to write a self-defense manual for women in sales. Here was a group of young, highly ambitious women who went out on the road by themselves for long stretches at a time, mainly in isolated rural areas. Although what I then knew about self-defense wouldn't have filled a thimble, I did know what it was like to travel by myself and thought the idea of the manual was a reasonable one. And I liked the prospect of women knowing how to defend themselves.

What I didn't anticipate were the strong objections of many men and women. Some people said it was protectionism—that women didn't need any special manual or treatment. Others argued that this approach directed too much negative attention to women's difficulties, and that this could hurt women—that it was best to leave these matters alone.

But the women on the road loved the idea of a self-defense manual, so I wrote the guide. And their overwhelmingly positive response stuck with me.

Over the years it has struck me that most women are out there "on the road" in their personal lives as well and could use a self-defense manual of another kind. I kept hearing women pour out their tales of trust and deception in love and work. I listened to their shock and disbelief that the men they had cared for would lie to them about their background, marital status, intentions, commitments, and the other women in their lives. And as I listened and heard the same patterns appear again and again, their stories began to strike a hauntingly familiar chord.

I recognized both a characteristic *set of lies* and *set of responses* to men's lies. And I began to realize that if women could see this pattern and realize the part they play in an invisible but debilitating dynamic of deception, they could spare themselves considerable pain and stop wasting precious time and effort. But it would be a challenge because here self-defense wouldn't be against unknown muggers, rapists, and thieves lurking in unfamiliar terrain, but against the very men closest to them, the men they had put their trust in—their dates, lovers, and husbands.

Most of us sense what feels safe and what doesn't. We intuit who's trustworthy and who's feeding us a line. But as time passes we forget. We train ourselves to disregard the early cues, to be ever so reasonable, to be relentlessly polite. We end up smiling, no matter what we're actually feeling, papering over our best hunches and reassuring ourselves that we're just fine, thank you.

But the funny thing is that we don't truly forget our hunches. We remember them *after* the hurt, *after* the betrayal. The discrepancies between what we intuitively know and what we tell ourselves jar us into obsessively replaying the details in search of the lost truth. Eventually our foresight catches up with our hindsight. We finally recognize what we knew to be true all along.

In the pursuit of connectedness, we forget that being nice or polite is usually far less critical than taking care of ourselves and avoiding or surviving threatening situations. Of course, disconnecting our sixth sense and short-circuiting its warning signs has some utility. This pushes us to take risks. Sometimes it works out well, but it also can put us in jeopardy.

When we ignore our internal warning signs that flash, *Proceed No Further*, it's like ignoring the suspicious actions of a potential mugger on a city street. We make ourselves unnecessarily vulnerable. When it comes to muggers or liars, hindsight is the great teacher as we sadly acknowledge, "I should have seen it coming."

As I thought about the themes that wind through women's stories of lies and liars, I remembered writing the self-defense manual. It highlighted dangers and reminded women that it's a good idea to stay alert and resist getting too comfortable too quickly. It emphasized how important it is to protect themselves in tough situations, how they can't count on anyone else to be looking after them. It described the specific clues and situations that might evoke reasonable suspicion. Then it offered general but not foolproof advice on how to deal with a host of disconcerting to potentially dangerous situations.

What, I wondered, if I were to write a self-defense manual for women that warned of a different kind of danger, the danger of men's lies? One that even smart, savvy women often don't see until after the damage has already been done?

I tried out the idea by talking to some women about it.

I said, "Hey, would you read a book called something like *101 Lies Men Tell Women*?" Their reactions were uniform. A smile, a laugh, and a quick "Sure. Just tell me where to buy it *right now*." Quite a few women editorialized, "Only 101? You're kidding. Why so few? Why not 1,001 . . . ? Let me tell you about the ones I've been told."

Then I talked to men I knew. I asked them the same question. Their responses? A few winced. "Oh no. Not another male-bashing book. Don't do it." Some said, "You should hear a few of the ones I've told." One man said, "Lies! The biggest mistake I ever made was telling my wife the truth right before our wedding. She's never let me forget it." And quite a few said in all earnestness, "101 lies? How are you ever going to find that many?"

TALKING TO WOMEN AND MEN ABOUT MEN'S LIES

The research plan was hatched. I and my colleague Dr. George Salamon interviewed sixty women and thirty-five men in four cities (Phoenix, St. Louis, Chicago, and Washington, D.C.) about their experiences with lying and being lied to. Most of the people interviewed answered my newspaper ads asking for volunteers to talk about trust and deceit in personal relationships. Some responded to a letter that asked clients of a dating service to volunteer for a research project. A few heard me give talks and offered to be interviewed, and a couple of volunteers worked in organizations I consult for. A few were recruited through lawyers, and I even interviewed two women I overheard talking about lies in a coffee shop to see if their stories were any different from the others I had heard. (They weren't.) Another four people were interviewed as part of an initial pilot study to try out the interview questions, get feedback on them, and determine the best order for the questions I asked in the interviews. These people came from various walks of life—professors, homemakers, lawyers, actors, bureaucrats, filmmakers, business people, scientists, teachers, secretaries, factory workers, and the ranks of the unemployed. They were racially and ethnically diverse and came from a wide variety of socioeconomic backgrounds.

What these men and women told us in structured interviews that lasted anywhere from one and one-half to six hours became grit and grist for this book. (You can read the actual questions we asked men and women by flipping to the Appendix at the end of the book.)Their stories are real. The names and places I've used in the book are not. I have changed them as well as a few identifying details (like number of children, specific occupations, and geographic areas) to protect both the guilty and the innocent from being recognized.

The ninety-five people we interviewed told engaging, often poignant stories of lying and being lied to. Some stories were hilarious. Many were heartbreaking. Some people were reflective, others cocky. Some wept as they spoke of their hurt and anger. But everyone had a story to tell. Some had many. From the youngest (twenty-one years old) to the oldest (seventy-two years old), the people we interviewed agreed that lying was part and parcel of American life. Yet few relished it when it intruded into their closest relations. There were only a few exceptions. These expressed pride in their expertise as skilled liars. But even these virtuosos of deceit lamented the havoc that their lies had brought into their relationships, and a few voiced their hope for a fresh start. Some of the people I interviewed have even written me to say how talking about their own and others' lies changed the way they think about lying and how that has firmed their resolve to lie no more.

Others, sure they had been lied to, were even surer that they'd never been the liars. The interview format seriously challenged this belief. Nearly every question about the lies the other sex had told was also asked in reverse. So, for example, after being asked about

the lies a man or woman told you in bed, you as the interview subject would then be asked about the bedroom lies you had told the
other sex.

By the end of two or three hours, many of those in the lied-to-
but-never-lying group were stunned by the degree to which they too
had been dishonest in their personal dealings. Thinking and talking
about your own lies pave the way for insight. One man, a thirty-
something single engineer, said, "Verbalizing makes my lying more
concrete; I find it harder to deny." At the end of a lengthy interview,
a recently divorced woman put it this way: "I ended up moving
from thinking men's lies are so different to thinking they are really
the same. You showed me that I lie in ways similar to my ex-
husband." Then she added, laughing, "But all my lies are justified."

Which leads me to two important points. First, this book is no
moral primer. My intent is *not* to define right and wrong, or to tell
people what they should or should not do in particular situations.
Instead, let's begin a genuine dialogue between men and women
about their experiences in lying and being lied to. My personal
belief is that honesty, coupled with empathy, good timing, and tact,
is the best policy. But our relationship with the truth and others'
views of it is something we all have to grapple with and resolve in
our own ways.

Second, I do not believe, nor do my data support the conclusion,
that men are the only liars—that only men tell lies to women, and
not vice versa.

Men lie. Women lie. Neither sex has any corner on shading the
truth. But my data and other findings do suggest that men tend to
lie more and with more devastating consequences for the other sex.
What's noteworthy here is that the differences and even the similarities between men's and women's lies are packed with information
we can use to develop more satisfying relationships and to avoid
toxic ones.

On the pages ahead you'll find example after example of the
absurdity and pathos of the lie in personal relations and discover
how crazy we are in our never-ending pursuit of connectedness.
You'll hear the different stories that men and women tell about trust
and relationships. You'll be privy to the ordinary and outrageous
lies, the half-truths and concealed truths that men have told and
that women have believed. The ninety-five men and women interviewed gave us the gift of their rich, often painful learning. Some of
their experiences may come uncomfortably close to who you are and
how you live your life.

IN SEARCH OF THE 101 LIES

What about the 101 lies? The ones at the front of the book. How did I come up with such a list? Were the lies chosen for being the most outrageous? The most harmful? The most frequent? Actually these and several other factors influenced which lies made the final cut. I wanted a list that accurately captured the deceit, manipulation, creativity, machismo, and everyday flavor that emerged from the interviews I conducted for this book. Most of the lies that are listed have several variations, and you'll find them in each chapter, often in the form of direct quotes from the men who told them or the women they were told to. I wanted to strike a balance between these kinds of lies so that we wouldn't end up with 101 versions of the ubiquitous "I'll call you" lie.

The first thirty-five lies on the list of 101 lies each represents a different category of lie most frequently mentioned by the men and women I interviewed. After these top thirty-five, the lies are listed without regard to frequency, to give you a sense of the diversity of the lies men tell.

How you use this list is up to you. Could be you'll find this list of 101 lies good for a chuckle or a quick "aha" of recognition. Or you may want to use this list to ask yourself and your friends which lies you've been told or have told yourself.

BEFORE YOU GET TO THE LIES

This book is meant first to promote new and early detection of the many shapes of men's lies and women's reactions to them. Second, I hope that I have created enough understanding and empathy for why people lie to allow both women and men to openly acknowledge their own as well as the other person's lies and to confront and discuss them matter-of-factly.

Lies come in many forms, and not all are excusable. Some are particularly mean-spirited. Some are habitual. Recognizing that, I want to help women who meet up with dangerous and outrageous liars to recognize the species, cut their losses early, and move on. Among those interviewed were at least five self-acknowledged or "recovering" habitual liars (including one female) who shared the tricks of their trade while cleansing their consciences.

What about you? Whether you're male or female, the lied to or the liar, I'd like you to walk away with:

- Greater awareness of the fact that men lie to women much more than most of us acknowledge.
- The realization that you are not alone in being lied to or in lying.
- An ability to analyze your own lies and your reactions to lies you've been told. Your analysis can help you understand why men and women lie to each other when telling the truth would be just as good.
- New strategies for coping with our relationship lies, other than a typically female silent avoidance or a typically male defensive denial.
- Added insight into your own behavior and that of the men or women in your life, which comes from a better understanding of how and why we lie.

Understanding lies and liars is the first step. Understanding ourselves and our reactions is the second. The third is developing a don't-go-anywhere-without-it self-defense plan. All this won't be easy, but it is worthwhile.

I once heard an old Bedouin saying that seems to capture the age-old dilemma of wanting to trust while needing to defend:

Trust in God, but tie your camel.

It's a challenge. How do we keep our faith in the goodness of people, respect our hunches, and defend ourselves against hurtful lies and liars *before* suffering damage? And how do we do this without becoming discouraged or bitter?

Coming to terms with ourselves as well as lies or liars may require what one of the most honest writers of our century, George Orwell, called the "power of facing unpleasant facts." But once you do, you'll come out stronger and saner.

Part 1
ANATOMY OF THE LIE

Chapter 1
Men Lie: They Just Do—So Why Do Women Believe Them?

He lied about everything—his age, his race, his education, his family, his girlfriend. He thought I'd like him better if he were Hispanic. He said his father was Cuban, that he lived in Miami, that everyone in his family had a college degree, that he had attended American University. He said he was twenty-two when he was only seventeen, and that the girl at his place who was slamming everything around was his cousin—when she was really his girlfriend.
—Twenty-six-year-old single female medical records technician

To cover my absence over the weekend I can make up just about anything and make it believable. That my father is in Austria and I have to meet him there 'cause my mom is ill. Or sometimes I just leave it mysterious—and say, "It's my family."
—Twenty-eight-year-old single male entrepreneur

I told a woman I needed her, knowing that the way I needed her was different from the way she interpreted it. To me she was a research subject, not a significant person in my life.
—Thirty-nine-year-old divorced male aeronautical designer

If I'm confident and I believe what I say, if someone else judges what I say as a lie, it doesn't really matter, I have the freedom to stray from my statements. I say I'm going to a friend's house, but I go to a book-

*store. "I'll be up to bed in ten minutes" then not show up for two
hours.*
—Forty-seven-year-old married male management consultant

"Men lie, they just do." So says Madonna during police questioning
in her 1993 movie, *Body of Evidence*. The *New York Times* movie
reviewer noted that this one crack generated more laughter and
agreement than any other line in the movie. On the strength of this
comment alone, I saw the movie and heard the line spark a rousing
chorus of agreement from the otherwise subdued women in the
audience.

Why? Because men lie—they just do.

Is this too harsh a judgment? Is it just another instance of male
bashing? I think not. The fact that men lie hardly condemns all men
as dangerous liars. Men's proclivity to lie varies remarkably. Some
men are bizarre and outrageous liars who lie for sport and profit.
Others are occasional liars who dissemble on demand in response to a
specific situation. Some indulge mainly in the garden-variety lie—the
little whites, the fibs, the embellishments. And some don't lie at all.
They are the pathological truth-tellers—the devotees of scrupulous
honesty. Most men fall somewhere in the middle of the spectrum.

Although women are willing to acknowledge a full range of lies
and liars, when it comes to their own personal lives, they seem to
confine their awareness to the lowest end of the liar's spectrum.
Unfortunately, too many women aren't prepared to recognize either
the lie or the liar until both have become history. Why have a blind
spot for men's lies, especially in an intimate relation? After all, a
blind spot for anything spells trouble. But when you trust someone
you shouldn't just because you feel that skepticism and romance are
an odd couple, you set yourself up for deep disappointment. Trust
has to be earned. And when you give your trust away too easily and
too fast, you become a perfect mark for anyone who chooses to act
unscrupulously.

An Epidemic of Lies

We don't have to look too hard for evidence of the lie.
Newspapers give us a daily readout on the astounding, near epic
proportion of dishonesty we tolerate. "Panel Censures Brooklyn
Judge for Lying" proclaims a *New York Times* headline as I write
this. The honesty of our president and Congress is called into question time after time. The nervous jokes on late-night TV about

whether President Clinton inhaled the now infamous joint or about how many steaks and potatoes Dan Rostenkowski actually downed at taxpayers' expense linger in our minds as disconcerting markers that even those in our highest offices lie.

Reluctantly, we adjust our expectations downward. Not even our cultural idols escape. Now it's the lovely Princess Di who is allegedly lying in some new scandal. Tomorrow it's a clergyman or a community leader. Or perhaps a neighbor. We grow weary.

Even as we watch television, well beyond "Oprah" and "Donahue" and the talk show circuit, the lie reigns supreme. A Supreme Court justice's veracity is under attack by a highly credible accuser—fellow legal scholar Anita Hill. One or the other is a liar. There's no way out. The polls show the public believes him. A year later the pendulum shifts and we believe her. The truth is, we're not sure what to believe anymore.

The boundaries between liars and heroes merge and blur. Is Oliver North, introduced by Ted Koppel on "Nightline" as "an accomplished liar," a scoundrel who told lies and got away with it, as some allege, or was he a hero defending his country? The nation splits on whether O.J. Simpson is a lying and brutal murderer or the all-American sports hero and star of TV commercials we have let into our living rooms and our hearts. Will we trust to the end, no matter what, or risk sifting through the evidence looking for truth rather than perception? We divide and bicker among ourselves.

Surrounded by public dramas, we find it hard not to take sides. Fascinated, we watch as the facts unfold and are endlessly reinterpreted for us. We struggle to make sense of how people we expected to trust could disappoint us like this.

There's an epidemic of lies, and like it or not, we're caught in it. Fact is, *the lie* is as ordinary and American as apple pie. Ordinary and volatile. As we attempt to separate fact from fiction, hope from reality, we're not so unlike the woman who can no longer deny her lover's or husband's or boss's private lies. She struggles to weave the emerging strands of evidence into an acceptable tapestry of truth and falsehood so she can go on living with him, loving him, and trusting him—even in the face of mounting evidence to the contrary. Why? She wants to believe the best of him. She's afraid to start all over again with someone new.

But at least the public lie is something that we can keep at arm's length. If Oliver North can lie his way out of anything, as a former CIA official once noted, that's the government's problem, not ours. We're spectators, not participants.

The private lie is far more unsettling. It comes at us on our own turf. You can't wipe it from your mind by putting down the newspaper or clicking the remote. The private lie is in our face, violating the sanctity of our own nest—the place where we live, where we let our guard down.

Private Lies Men Tell Women

Almost every woman who's ever tried her luck at the dating or marriage game has heard one or another version of these top-of-the-chart lies:

> *After a delightful dinner spent sharing the stories of your lives and your hopes, he tenderly kisses you on the cheek, looks you in the eye, and says, "I'll call you."*

Truth: For him it's a well-worn parting volley that merely buys him enough time to retreat into the safety of his own life. Don't bother to check your answering machine on the hour for his message. You won't hear from him again.

> *It's clear he's attracted to you. He keeps telling you how beautiful you are, and that feels nice. He can't keep his hands off you. You're flattered. But when he confesses, "I love you," you're a little unprepared for his sharing his feelings so soon. The sex is heartfelt.*

Truth: For him it was curiosity and conquest. "I love you" is no more than a passkey to your affections. He'll never go out with you again and he may even cross the street to avoid you—should he see you first.

> *He seems preoccupied and less attentive than ever before. He's been making near monthly trips to Syracuse to visit a supplier. You have your suspicions. But when you confront him, he flat out questions your sanity. He sighs heavily and says, "Trust me. There's no one else. You are the only one."*

Truth: He's been having a long-distance affair for over a year with a married woman who works for the supplier. Everyone in his office knows about it. People trade Syracuse jokes as soon as his phone rings. When he says, "You are the only one," could he mean you are the only one who doesn't know about his infidelity?

Maybe all this sounds a bit overstated. After all, how typical were these men's and women's experiences? Read on and decide for yourself. Look back to your relationships and personal history for clues. You probably have already encountered the lie in more than one of its many seductive forms. There may even be a new one awaiting your reluctant attention right now.

But Why Would He Lie to *Me*?

Pollsters and academics may debate the frequency, type, and intent of men's lies versus women's lies. But just knowing that one in five of us can't get through a single day without lying doesn't help us *understand* lies. When we get right down to it, lies don't feel very academic. They feel personal, very personal. The lie hits us where we live, love, and trust. Even though few women like to believe they are gullible, when you care about a man, you want to trust him. And why shouldn't you? Why would someone you care about purposely lie to you? To *you*, who truly believes you would be just as happy with the truth?

Most of the women I interviewed were anxious for answers. Not surprisingly, all had been lied to by one or more men in their lives. One was bilked out of more than $100,000 of her savings by a fast-talking liar who called her the "love of his life." Another had become pregnant by a man who had assured her he was sterile. Yet another wound up having a long-distance relationship with a supposedly single charmer who turned out to be married, and an embezzler to boot. Some women got herpes from men who claimed to have been celibate. One woman found that the mysterious charges her loving husband had run up on their MasterCard were for the exclusive services of prostitutes.

Most were luckier. They endured the ordinary, not the extraordinary, lie. They were only stood up for the symphony or a trip to Santa Fe, not at the altar. They were told they were the only ones, when there were actually one, two, or three others. They were told he was leaving his wife, when he was really building an addition to his house and planning a family vacation to Bermuda. They were told he was at a business meeting, when he was really down at the bar belting down a couple of scotches.

For me, the most important *why* has little to do with the men themselves. Rather, it has to do with why so many women are determined to understand *what makes the liar tick.* Why not focus instead on *why they suspended their own good sense and reasonable doubt to believe him?*

Why is it that so few of these bright and competent women sought—or better yet, demanded—help in *protecting themselves* from all the hurt and humiliation of the lies they had suffered?

I have no single answer. But there are clues and patterns that come from carefully sifting through what women and men say about lies and lying in relationships. Three possibilities stand out.

First, woman after woman told me she had believed a man's lies because *she had given him* no reason to lie to her. "Why would he lie to me?" she asked. "We're good friends. I accepted him just as he was." In other words, it made no sense that a man would bother to lie when the truth would have done quite nicely. He didn't have to lie to get her acceptance.

Second, many women seemed to have a major perceptual blind spot for *lies they wouldn't dream of telling him,* but that men had far less trouble inflicting on them. It's the "I wouldn't dream of lying about that, so why would he?" syndrome. It's simply outside their experience. One woman after another told me that they took men's statements at face value because they had no reason *not to trust* these men. These women often used their own internal standard of basic honesty as the benchmark for gauging a man's honesty. As one forty-year-old divorced woman noted, it never occurred her to that men would lie to her about their backgrounds, their jobs, or their romantic lives because she had never lied to them about such things. Those assumptions made it a stretch for her to question or evaluate the honesty of new men in her life. Confusing informed self-defense for cynicism, she was duped again and again, dooming herself to be sadder but no wiser for her experience.

Third, some women hold a *just world view,* in which we get what we give. So he lies? She thinks there's probably a reason for it. She links his past lies to a particular woman who mistreated him, rather than to a pattern of his behavior. Maybe his former wife was a nag, a pest who didn't appreciate him. Someone who gave him cause. She won't. These women have no trouble understanding that a man they love will lie if treated badly. But since they won't treat him badly, they think they can throw caution to the wind. Their relationship is the exception. Or so they believe.

It's easy to see how problematic these approaches are. If you aren't expecting him to lie to you and then he does, it's far harder to detect. Then when you finally catch on to his deception, you *may look to yourself, not him, for the reason*. The result? Self-doubt. He's off the hook and you try harder—with him or the next and the next man. The why of the lie is admittedly complex. But how we explain it to ourselves may be both complex and often just plain wrong.

But Not in *Our* Relationship

It's easy to let your natural guard down. You're convinced that even a confirmed liar isn't likely to do his dirty work in a relationship with you. Perhaps you know he lies at work or to avoid someone who calls that he doesn't want to talk to. Maybe he fudges a bit about his finances or what he does with his time. No matter. You say, "Go ahead and lie, but just don't lie in our relationship."

Such thinking shows a tacit acceptance of the pervasiveness of men's lies in relationships, but not in *this* relationship. You think this relationship will be different because you are involved in it. You hope that if you make it attractive enough for him to tell the truth, he won't be able to resist. So you avoid laying down the law and telling him in no uncertain terms what is and isn't acceptable by your standards. You figure all you would accomplish is making it harder for him to be candid. You fear that when you set boundaries around his freedom, even reasonable ones, you'll merely invite him to lie.

Women stick to these beliefs because they get a payoff. The compelling illusion of personal control offsets the fact that they may have precious little control, particularly when dealing with a liar. Could it be that he lies simply because he lies? Because that's part of who he is in his relationships with women? Not because his ex-wife or last woman friend treated him so much worse than you will?

Most women I talked with, reeling from the consequences of lies in past relationships, didn't see themselves as particularly stern or vigilant taskmasters. Rather, they saw themselves as good, easygoing partners—tolerant, flexible, empathic. By their own standards, they didn't deserve these or any other lies. What they deserved was total immunity from the pain of betrayal. To their surprise and dismay, they didn't get what they expected or had bargained for. His behavior, it turned out, was far less contingent on theirs than they had imagined. He is who he is. Even the power of their love couldn't change that.

How is it that even women driven to despair by men's lies in previous relationships manage to convince themselves that the whole phenomenon of lying was limited to one or two particular relationships? They assure themselves it won't happen again, attributing their last wrenching experience to their own behavior, or to that specific liar. They miss the obvious patterns that spring from the different agendas men and women pursue, and from the ways in which men and women have been socialized and have come to view each other.

Don't misunderstand. I'm not saying that stereotyping all men based on a single or even two or three bad experiences is a good idea. It's not. That would be unfair and unduly cynical. Staying open to the fact that there are decent and honest men who don't lie at the first hint of conflict is important. So is remembering that even among men who lie, some will lie "small," in ways that don't create instant heartbreak or cataclysm.

Not resorting to overgeneralization gives us a chance to hit our own reset button at the beginning of any new relationship. We can pack away any learned skepticism we've picked up along the way until we happen to need it again. That's a reasonable and adaptive strategy—to a point. But there's a point where this strategy keeps us from clearly recognizing the patterns that could make us wiser.

Trapped in Their Own Gender: Why Women Ask Why?

We all operate from our own frame of reference, using who we are to understand others. So it's natural to ask, "If I wouldn't do this to him, why would he do this to me?" The snag here is that being locked into our own point of view is an ineffective way of predicting other people's behavior. Why? Because other people don't see things the way we do. They see things *the way they do*. Who *they* are is not who *we* are, particularly when *they* are men and *we* are women.

What most women say they want is to trust the men they share their lives with. To believe that they're special. Many women don't like to acknowledge the lie, because it calls into question their hope for a safe and trusting world. That leaves them feeling vulnerable. But even when they do acknowledge the fact of the lie, they frequently don't take their knowledge to the next step of doing something about it. Have you ever noticed how seldom women take a truly hard line or the aggressive action necessary to protect themselves? As if acting in their own behalf is ignoble? Like the women I interviewed, many women *subvert themselves, and eventually their relationship, by pushing hard to understand the reasons that men lie.* Rather than recognizing patterns and tuning in to the symptoms of the lie, they play the good sport. They take it on the chin, and then try to learn whatever they need to somehow fix the problem.

This is a noble but inherently flawed effort. Maybe that's why in many circles "good sport" has become a euphemism for "loser."

Have you ever convinced yourself that if you only had the facts, if you only understood *why* he told you the lie, that you could turn the situation around? That you could then show him how his lie was an uncalled-for betrayal damaging to both of you? That then he might never do it again? *Harry, listen, I think we need to talk about why you acted like you were going to a board meeting when you were really seeing Marge. You didn't have to lie to me, when you could have just as easily said you wanted to have a couple of drinks with Marge. I wouldn't have minded that, but I do mind the lie. Why did you tell me that?*

If Harry is like a lot of men, he won't respond the way you had hoped. He'll deny your allegation altogether, or start by minimizing the situation. Then he'll get angry, attacking the facts you presented, or he'll astound you by responding with another excuse or a brand-new lie that puts you off and infuriates: *My God, Joan! Can't you give a guy room for a little spontaneity? The board meeting was called off when we got there, and you know if I called and told you I was going to have drinks with Marge, you would have thrown a fit. I was protecting you. Give me a break!*

The reasons for his lie could be simple—to avoid unpleasant consequences. Or complicated and well outside what makes sense to you. The reasons could be buried deep in his unexamined assumptions and expectations about how men and women are supposed to treat each other. His lies may spring from an intricate weave of his personality, values, fears, and self-interest, a weave with a pattern far, far different from your own. His lies may be spurred by hidden conflicts around his needs for privacy and personal freedom versus your need that he be accountable to you.

Whatever his reasons, one conclusion is clear. *He is not you. He* has a different history. *He* has been raised with a different set of expectations that guide him as a male in our culture. Quite possibly, he holds a different set of expectations about communication, sex, romance, marriage, and the value of relationships in general. Chances are he sees things, including honesty with you, in a different light. Sure, his world and yours overlap. But it's a mistake to assume that they're the same.

Of course, there's nothing wrong with your wanting to understand the why and wherefore of his lies. If such understanding reflects your curiosity or wanting to know him better, go for it. Why not do your share to help bridge the understanding gap among people, the gender gap between women and men? But if understanding the why of his lies is your strategy to change him, forget it. You have bought into a time-consuming and ultimately losing proposition. He's no lump of clay, and you are no Pygmalion.

Real change will come when you focus on yourself—not on changing him. Real change comes when you are willing and able to stake your claim on what you are and are not willing to live with. Just remember to let him in on it.

But it's up to you to decide whether you want to play by your own or the liar's rules. The payoff comes when you can open a frank dialogue with the men in your life about lies that men tell women. You can use the examples on the pages ahead to talk candidly about the effects of men's lies on women and of women's lies on men. In short, you can begin to have honest talk on the subject of lies and lying and how it affects both of you.

Living with the lie is something we talk about far too seldom outside the soaps and the courts. Most of us insist on acting as if everything's fine, even when we all realize it's not. Ignoring or failing to confront the everything's-fine myth is one of the biggest lies of all. In fact, as you read this book and take a close look at the many faces of dishonesty in all phases of relationships, it's hard not to be shocked at the number and range of lies people have learned to live with.

Living Under the Shadow of the Lie

Many women live in the shadow of the lie. It's a life governed by fear and uncertainty. They're like people living under a volcano. In the shadow of the volcano, acute awareness of every tremor and sound is a reasonable survival skill. Your life depends on it.

Living in the shadow of the lie is no different. But what we anxiously scan, look, and listen for is any sign of the molten, unexpurgated truth. Why the truth? Because here, the lie is the given. The lie is business as usual. It provides the reassuring hum of daily life.

Relative to what it hides, the lie can seem surprisingly civilized or even friendly. Truth is the scary part. For those of us who live in the shadow of a well-concealed truth, the lie comforts and frames our world. Most of us have been here or will be here at one time or another. When the truth is unbearable, we deny its danger, whether it be unprotected sex with a promiscuous lover who claims to be faithful or the failing health of a spouse who insists everything is just fine. It's amazing how easily we learn to turn down the volume on our own inner rumblings—the ones that are trying to alert us that something's going awry.

The lie and its sidekick, the unwelcome truth, cast a perennial double shadow on personal relationships. This is what one woman said after calling off her wedding because her fiance lied about the number of times he had been married: *"Even after I moved in with him there were lies and suspicion. I was always looking for clues that he was lying. After three years I knew he was having an affair. I asked him if he was hiding something from me. He said, 'I can't think of anything.' I was miserable. He was doing what he always did—lying."*

She discovered that looking for clues was an unfulfilling and all-consuming, full-time job. One that sapped her energy, raised her anxiety, and eventually left all parties feeling frustrated and unhappy.

Even when both people in the relationship adapt to the lie, the clear and present danger is that the truth will still surface. And when it does, you'll hear woman after woman say:

- "Why didn't I trust my gut?"
- "I looked the other way even when I knew something was wrong."
- "By believing him, I was the one who wound up living the lie."
- "I gave away years of my life."

Getting out from under the lie calls first for awareness, then for courage. Accommodation is the easiest path to the peace and security many of us crave. But when we do that we're only tricking ourselves for the short term. In the long term, everyone loses. Living with the lie, particularly the serious lie, eventually robs us of our energy and self-respect. And it may put us in emotional, mental, and physical jeopardy as well.

Sure, it's tempting to look the other way, to deny what you don't want to face. To put off for tomorrow or next week what you can't face today. And of course there's something to be said for carefully and deliberately choosing your timing, your tactics, your turf for the eventual confrontation. But as you read the chapters ahead, you will be immersed in the evidence—evidence that strongly suggests that relationships riddled with lies consume our peace and well-being, only to leave us wondering, months or decades later, why we gave our power and time to the liar rather than to our own best interests.

Chapter 2
How Men and Women Play the Lying Game

There are lots of different and dangerous truths: truths that wound, truths that clarify, truths that can make enemies. Why tell the truth when it can hurt you?
—Forty-one-year-old married male management consultant

Men are put in a position of responsibility. If they don't fulfill that, men think women will think less of them, so they tell lies.
—Thirty-seven-year-old married male government worker

Lying doesn't bother me, that's part of it . . . I don't inquire about lies because I don't want them to think I care.
—Thirty-year-old single male bond trader

When a man lies to me I feel like he's made a judgment about me: that I'm not intelligent, not perceptive, not a good listener.
—Twenty-four-year-old married female production manager

Men lie more because they like to be free. Women lie to constrict them, put boundaries around them.
—Twenty-six-year-old single female banker

Men are socialized so that less importance is placed on the relationship. This gives men more license to lie.
—Forty-seven-year-old married female personnel manager

How many times have you lied today? Did you bluff on a job interview? Exaggerate something? Make yourself sound more together than you really are? Did you tell someone who called that you were hurrying out the door, when really you were sitting down to a freshly brewed cup of coffee? Or perhaps you lied about something more serious. Did you deny responsibility for something you did? Hide your true feelings? Insist something didn't matter that you cared about deeply?

The average college student reportedly lies twice a day. Some studies suggest that the average American lies 13 times a week, while others estimate 6 to 7 times per day. Why should you or I be any different?

When it comes to lying, don't bet on men having a corner on the market. We all lie some of the time. Often it feels so natural, so absolutely right to lie, that we don't even register that we are lying or that the truth might do just as nicely. How does this happen?

For starters, think back to your own parents and what they told you about lying when you were growing up. Even more revealing, consider how what they told you squared with what you actually saw them do. For most of us, childhood is a time of confusing mixed messages that also apply to our budding codes of honesty. For example, although my own father told me never to trust a liar, my mother maintained that if you told a lie and crossed your fingers, that lie didn't really count. Which was true? As kids, how are we supposed to know what is real or what to believe?

Parents across many cultures routinely teach their children some version of "Thou shalt not lie," only to have their children catch them in the act of lying to each other or to their own children as well as to strangers. All this is confusing. Even though you know you're not supposed to lie, you keep getting messages like:

- Tell your true feelings or what really happened and you'll get punished.
- It's not nice to hurt anyone's feelings.
- If you don't have anything good to say, don't say anything.
- It doesn't pay to upset people unnecessarily.
- It's okay to lie to protect a friend.
- Always play to win.

As kids we learn that the consequences of being honest may land us in deep trouble, whereas the consequences of lying get us off the hook. That early learning can become a powerful guide for what we do as adults when the going gets rough.

Gender learning—what we learn as children about who wields power and who relinquishes it, about how men and women are supposed to act in personal relationships—adds yet another critical dimension. The blueprint of gender lays out expectations for how we as women and men should treat each other and communicate. The lie itself is a powerful form of communication. It puts up invisible boundaries where we least expect them and falsely comforts us when comfort is the last thing we should be feeling.

Like it or not, gender is a major force in shaping our lives and there's no reason to think that it won't also shape our lies. If men's and women's lies go their separate ways and you don't know it, you can bet on the resulting miscommunication causing your relationship to go its separate way as well.

Understanding how men and women differ in the way they play the lying game is far more than an interesting exercise. Identifying the patterns of gender differences is a survival tactic—one that helps you build trust while avoiding heartache.

Men and Women: Different Faces on the Lie

In a world where men and women hold different views of what's important to them, even the smallest of frictions can quickly escalate and transform love into war. The likelihood of one partner lying to another intensifies when their goals and agendas clash. This is even more likely when one partner has a hidden agenda or seeks to gain control in the relationship.

Where does this propensity for misunderstanding come from?

Men, more than women, have been raised to value the rational over the emotional, active control over receptivity, actions that lead to winning over discussions that lead to understanding, and the meting out of impersonal justice over compassionate caring. Women's patterns of relating are often forged in childhood through close and bonded relationships with mothers or female caregivers. Women then transfer these bonded relations to peers in adolescence, and to mates and families in adulthood. Women, far more than men, have been socialized to value connectedness, relationships, and communication.

Even though men and women share many values, abilities and traits, our differences also dictate how we approach even the smallest of challenges and transactions. Some researchers suggest that the result is tantamount to men and women living in subtly different cultures where every communication between them requires translation to be accurately understood.

The lie has much to be said for it as an effective way of fooling enemies and helping us survive with our lives intact under treacherous conditions. But in close personal relations the lie can be a serious liability that estranges us from each other. Yet many men and women are loath to give up their lies. Why? Because of the short-term pay-offs: more control and freedom to do what they please, more success in avoiding conflict and punishment, and more opportunity to pursue self-interest.

Yet the downside of the lie is daunting: isolation, reduced intimacy, lowered capacity for empathy, self-deception, and, ultimately, emptiness.

For many men, the lie is just another useful tool, a convenient way to get from here to there. But for many women the lie lingers as evidence of serious betrayal of trust and a failure to connect.

The differences are often striking. Consider this benign, but telling rationale for lying to women given by a forty-four-year-old divorced male engineer: *"I lie to preserve the interaction for a while to see if anything is there. Sins of omission help you avoid beginning an interaction with brutal honesty: nice to see you today and—by the way—you really should try another hairdresser. Lies are geared to maximizing gain."*

He sees the lie as a pragmatic way to establish a temporary relationship. For him it's the truth, what he calls "brutal honesty," that causes problems. Given this, it's not surprising that the way many men defined and discussed what is and is not a lie in male-female relations seems detached, even transactional, compared to the highly personal tone taken by women. These men often defined the lie with the flat affect of someone explaining the inner workings of a steam engine. If you were to tune out the words and listen only to their tone, it would be difficult to tell that they were talking about anything even remotely related to intimacy and trust.

This does not necessarily mean that lies have less impact on men. Consider this twenty-four-year-old man's response to the question, "What's your gut reaction when you know you've been lied to?": *"There's a horrible emotion that big lies elicit. I feel dread, sleeplessness, agitation. I feel crushed and hurt. But if I pieced the whole thing together, took circumstantial evidence and made sense of it, I feel good that I pierced the lie."*

He describes a lie's immense effect on his well-being and ability to function. But then he immediately moves into a problem-solving mode that lets him fix it by putting the jigsaw puzzle together. He regains control by gathering evidence and making sense of what was incomprehensible in his pain. Solving the problem restores his sense of personal efficacy. Logic, investigative data gathering, hypothesis generating, and bringing closure to what happened all rescue him from despair. What he doesn't talk about is the relationship itself, a subject women analyze at length. Nor does he speak about his own naiveté, where he went wrong, and whether or not to forgive and forget or to confront—all issues woman after woman address.

Such provocative differences between men's and women's approaches to the lie and their reactions to being lied to pave the way for the area we'll explore next: the differences between the lies men tell women and the lies women tell men and how each gender interprets and responds to them.

Round One of the Lying Game: Men's Lies, Women's Lies

I asked each of the men and women I interviewed to tell me about the *very last lie* they had told a member of the other sex. "Tell me about the very last time" something happened is just the kind of question that behavioral researchers love, because it produces thoughtful answers that are especially resistant to fudging. It is extremely effective at pulling out what someone actually did or said, rather than eliciting a shallow array of opinion, hearsay, or stereotype.

Go ahead and try it yourself. Think about the *very last time* you lied to a member of the other sex. Once you remember something, the instance becomes startlingly clear. You recall precisely what you said, what you felt, and why you felt compelled to lie rather than tell the truth. You can probably recollect the other person's reaction, how you felt about it, and whether you had regrets. Because it's your own lie, you're not way out on a limb, making inferences about what men or women lie about in general.

These are exactly the kinds of rich responses I got from the men and women I interviewed. A sampling of their "last lies" appears in the boxed quiz below. All I have done is disguise whether the teller is a man or a woman by substituting the gender-neutral name Pat for the real names of the people involved. Except for this name change and the masking of a few personal pronouns, these are people's unedited verbatim replies.

As you read each one, see how good you are at guessing which lies belong to women and which to men.

GUESSING WHICH "LAST LIES" ARE MEN'S AND WHICH ARE WOMEN'S

Man Woman   The Verbatim "Last Lie"

___   ___   1.   "I neglected to tell Pat that I was still playing the field. I said, 'I'll give you a call,' but then I didn't."

___   ___   2.   "I lied about what a great lover Pat was."

___   ___   3.   "At the movie theater, when I was with Pat, I saw the best friend of the person I was dating secretly last summer [while in a relationship with Pat]. Pat asked me, 'How do you know each other?' The friend and I both lied about how we happened to know each other."

___   ___   4.   "I met Pat at a party. I was overzealous about describing my job, what I did. Then I expanded on it. I said I had traveled places I'd never been, did things I'd never done."

___   ___   5.   "In the final days of the relationship, I was feeling depressed, and lied to Pat about getting professional help for my depression."

___   ___   6.   "It was in a work situation with my boss. I said I hadn't thought about the opportunity to perform in theater when I had, in order to keep the stage manager seeing me as selfless."

___   ___   7.   "One month ago. I didn't want to do it [continue the relationship]. I had dated Pat two or three times. I told Pat, 'It's not you, it's me.' But it was Pat."

___   ___   8.   "When I had been seeing Pat for a brief period of time, someone I had known earlier and who was unavailable became available. We had a brief sex tryst. I hid this from Pat."

___   ___   9.   "In a telephone conversation twelve days ago with a person I have a romantic interest in, but not a lot of emotional energy for, I adopted a general flirtatious tone that was disingenuous."

___   ___   10. "It was a polite lie—about Pat being good company when Pat fell asleep on the couch."

___   ___   11. "About Pat's behavior at the New Year's Eve party—not telling Pat I was pissed off."

___   ___   12. "We were having sex when I said I wanted to spend the rest of my life with Pat."

The Lies Themselves

Look at your own responses to these lies. What led you to think a particular lie belonged to a woman rather than a man or vice versa? What does that say about your expectations of the way men and women behave together? What stereotypes do you detect in your thinking about men's and women's behavior? Are any of these potential self-fulfilling prophecies? Sometimes our unexamined assumptions act like a lens that colors and distorts our interpretations of what's happening.

When you went through this list and guessed whether it was a man or woman discussing the particular "last lie," you were also bringing into play your own set of gender-based assumptions, hypotheses, and intuitions. Some will be accurate, some not. They are based on your own personal set of experiences with the other sex, as well as what you've absorbed along the way about how men and women interact in our culture. So whether you are right or wrong in your guesses, you can learn a lot about your own thinking and assumptions here.

Which were men's and which were women's lies? Check your guesses against the reality. Here are the actual genders of the liars:

Men's last lies were: Lies 1, 3, 4, 5, 8, 9, and 12.

Women's last lies were: Lies 2, 6, 7, 10, and 11.

Do men's and women's lies reflect a different set of unique markings, values, and priorities for each gender? Let's take a closer look at the lies themselves, as well as the reasons people give for telling them, and see what we can find out.

Men's Lies Under the Microscope

> Lie 1. *"I neglected to tell Pat that I was still playing the field. I said, 'I'll give you a call,' but then I didn't."*

"I'll call only you."

This beauty is a hybrid that seamlessly combines two common lies that men tell women, "You're the only one" and "I'll call you." Both drive women to distraction. First, implying that *she is the only one* or *neglecting to tell her that she is not* lands in the top three of men's most ubiquitous lies according to the women I interviewed. Second, this man's parting sally of promising to call with little or no intent to deliver wins an even higher rank in the liars' hall of fame.

The "I'll call you" lie evoked a litany of protests from the women I interviewed. Why? Because they took his "I'll call you" as a literal representation of his genuine intent to maintain the relationship, rather than as the throwaway male parting ritual that it is. To men, "I'll call you" no more mirrors his intent than "See you later" mirrors a person's real intent to see someone later that evening. The result? Your disappointment followed by his bafflement at your disappointment.

When I asked Mark to tell me what he had at stake here in lying rather than in telling his date the truth, he replied: *"The lie gave me an option to keep Sylvia interested in me. While I made up my mind, she wouldn't start looking for someone else. The benefit was that she might become important enough for me to continue the relationship."*

We might say that Mark had adopted a shopper's paradigm. He'd put his date on temporary hold, like so much merchandise, while he made the rounds to see what else was available. How she felt about it wasn't considered. His being in control and having all his options open to him was what counted.

Lie 3. *"I saw the best friend of the person I was dating secretly last summer [while in a relationship with Pat]. Pat asked me, 'How do you know each other?' The friend and I both lied about how we happened to know each other."*

"Relax, she's just a friend."

Here Joe becomes a party to a cover-up lie that implies "There's no one else." This lie is merely a more defensive version of the "You are the only one" lie that plays out teetering on the edge of discovery, just a prayer away from being caught in or near the act.

Luckily Joe had the collusion of his secret lover's best friend, who quickly recognized the precariousness of Joe's situation with his steady. Taking the role of social facilitator, she quickly offered Joe a gracious out—that, indeed, they were both mutual friends of a fictitious third party named Bob.

Perhaps what is most interesting here is not Joe's willing participation in the lie itself, but his response to the close call and his reasoning about his lie. First, he admitted he had been nearly speechless, panicked at the unexpected encounter with the friend. Then he had been totally relieved to realize his girlfriend remained "in the dark about my relationship with the other girl." Joe also confessed, "I felt no guilt."

When I asked if Joe had planned to lie, he took my question beyond the incident, saying, "Absolutely. I openly hid the relationship, everything. If she had found out it would have been mass hysteria, possibly a breakup, a complete shattering of trust."

Then something remarkable happened. Joe began to angrily berate himself, not for his infidelity, but for not being a more accomplished liar—as if the ability to lie swiftly, smoothly, and well was some kind of required core competency. He felt inept because he hadn't been quick-witted enough to initiate the lie. He had merely taken advantage of the opportunity to cover his tracks that his secret lover's friend had provided. Frightened at being found out, he'd been saved not by his own cunning, but by the silver tongue of his secret lover's girlfriend. He was one-down and this embarrassed him.

"I can lie extremely well. I did it with my parents and all through high school. But I don't lie to my friends." Who are the friends Joe doesn't lie to? "The guys." Hmmm. For this young man, "friends" and women appear to be two mutually exclusive categories to be treated quite differently. *Us* and *them*. His code of honor—no lies to friends—extends to the *us's*, but not to the *them's*. Dividing the world into *us* and *them* helps the liar justify his lies to anyone who is different. Lying is okay, as long as it is to *them*.

Lie 4. "I met Pat at a party. I was overzealous about describing my job, what I did. Then I expanded on it. I said I had traveled places I'd never been, did things I'd never done."

"Big man at the office."

This lie is pure unadulterated image management, self-serving PR. Mike adopted the marketplace lie of telling and selling—doing whatever it takes to close the deal. In this case Mike saw himself, not Peggy, as the commodity being traded. And as a commodity, Mike felt seriously below par. His intent was to sound fascinating ("like I wasn't a total homebody"), which for Mike meant career success, travel, worldliness—all that he was not.

Mike was surprised at how easily the lies "just came out of my mouth." What's worse, the woman to whom he was selling this highly fictitious version of himself bought the whole story. As he put it, "She was really interested in me. She grilled me about all the details. I could answer some of the questions 'cause of the details my boss [whose life he was really talking about] gives me."

The problem here became this man's unexpected success in repackaging himself as something he clearly was not. Mike's morning-after regrets were purely pragmatic. Now, how could he have a relationship with her and keep up the act? Suppose they ran into his boss, or someone who knew who he really was? His stress mounted. When he called Peggy the next day to apologize and reveal his true identity, she was shocked. She wisely took a step back and refused to accept a date with him. Later they began to go out, but every time Mike made a pronouncement, Peggy would probe suspiciously, "Is that really how it is?" And Mike still harbored fears that she would meet the people whose lives he had so generously borrowed from.

He realized his oversell had doomed the relationship and bailed out.

> Lie 5. "In the final days of the relationship, I was feeling depressed, and lied to Pat about getting professional help for my depression."

"Protecting himself from the truth."

We tend to think this is a woman's lie because it deals with depression and conflict avoidance—topics typically designated as women's turf, even though we all know men who have been depressed and who avoid conflict. But actually it's a man's lie, and not an atypical one. It centers on getting him off the hook and out the door without discussing his problems, communicating his feelings, or exposing his vulnerabilities. Edward realizes the relationship is over. Even worse, he believes that Marcia can't put up with his depression in the final days. His sense of self had taken a direct hit.

When asked if he had planned to lie to Marcia, Edward said, "No. I lied because it got me off the hook, like all lies. Faced with the situation I was in, it was *the only way out* of the situation. So I said 'I'll get some help.'" Edward saw himself in a helpless, one-down position that he couldn't reverse by talking to Marcia ("No matter what I did, she had made up her mind that she was going to end it anyway"). In the world he framed for himself, giving her more information would only put him at greater risk, causing him to lose even more ground to Marcia.

Marcia held the power of termination here. Edward had none. His only remaining power was determining how to exit and protect himself from further rejection. Rather than owning up to his problems or reconnecting with Marcia by discussing his hurt and anger, he retreated to a less personal, less exposed position. He philosophized, "It's a perplexing fact of life that the truth hurts. People are not ready to deal with the truth." Although he seemed to be talking about Marcia here, he later commented that Marcia "had made up her mind to end the relationship and had lied about her intent to do this," cryptically adding, "I prefer to be spared the pain from women." It's very likely Edward was talking about himself being spared from his own pain and not being able to deal with the truth himself. But without a gift for mind reading, who would ever know?

Does he have regrets about his lie? "Yes," he answered, "I always have regrets about not telling the truth, but I am pleased I handled something without causing people pain." Even though it seems that he was more protective of himself than of Marcia, in Edward's mind, at least, he had reasserted himself as being the one in charge. In part he had regained power by withholding information and putting one over on her. Yet he also feels he has retained a protector role, shielding Marcia from whatever pain the truth might cause her.

> Lie 8. "When I had been seeing Pat for a brief period of time, someone I had known earlier and who was unavailable became available. We had a brief sex tryst. I hid this from Pat."

"Yeah, I was a lout. But it's all her fault."

Here's a classic lie of entitlement. Andy had just started a promising relationship with Lisa when a woman—previously unavailable because she was involved with someone else—resurfaced somewhere out there in his peripheral vision. Too bad Andy had already agreed to Lisa's request for sexual exclusivity. Rather than pass up a promising opportunity, Andy the hunter acted as if it were business as usual, when in fact he had set out for a brief "sex tryst" with the tempting new opportunity.

What's striking here is Andy's offhand analysis of the situation. When asked what was at stake in hiding the brief sexual encounter from Lisa, Andy laid it out: "The relationship! She would have nailed me, trashed the relationship." By not saying anything to Lisa, he captured the best of two worlds—enticing sexual adventure and a steady, trusting girlfriend.

Did he have any remorse? At first, Andy took full responsibility. "No. Once you do something wrong . . . it's wrong. I was a lout." But then Andy immediately erases his blame and guilt in one fell swoop by repackaging it and pinning responsibility for his lie on Lisa by adding, "Expectations that it's going to be an exclusive relationship is a lie that women tell themselves." So his lie became *her* fault. Could it be that after trying on the consequences of the lie, he discovered he didn't like how they fit? So he told himself a new story that shifted the blame to *her* alleged beliefs, glossing over *his* real actions.

> *Lie 9. "In a telephone conversation . . . with a person I have*
> *a romantic interest in, but not a lot of emotional energy for,*
> *I adopted a general flirtatious tone that was disingenuous."*

"Don't get me wrong, I'm only pretending."

Some lies are flirtatious, even playful, following the unspoken laws of social etiquette. They are the feel-good lies—one part fact, two parts fiction—that require minimal effort, contain little malice, and mislead more than they deceive.

Hal's last lie was pretending to be more emotionally invested in Wendy than he actually felt. A single young man in his late twenties, Hal said what he had at stake in hiding his weak libido was "the continuation of her affection" and the avoidance of "an unpleasant phone conversation." He confesses to having "little emotional energy" for the late-night phone conversation. Then why did he call her? Turns out, he didn't. In the brave new world of male-female relationships, many men as well as women get prospecting calls from interested parties. As Hal put it, "She initiated the call. She served, I volleyed." But why bother with pretense? Why not just tell the caller you're too tired to talk right now or you're watching your favorite TV program?

Hal reasons that eventually there might be something in it for him, for example, "the expectation of future sex or romance." So for Hal it's a no-brainer. Why not opt for the allure of intimacy at a safe distance with minimal demands, little immediate cost, and no risk of rejection? On the other hand, Hal knows that he would have felt more emotional energy if he rather than Wendy had initiated the call. But why scotch his chances of scoring with someone who shows an interest in him? As Hal reasons, it's more of a strategy than a lie. He has no regrets.

> **Lie 12.** *"We were having sex when I said I wanted to spend the rest of my life with Pat."*

"I want to spend the rest of my life with you—just kidding."

How can a man get a woman's attention? Tell her he wants to spend the rest of his life with her. That should do it, particularly if he can convincingly whisper this in a moment of tender sexual intimacy. If she's in love with him, or looking for a permanent relationship, it's normal for her to feel affirmed, reassured, happy. Yet the happily-ever-after lies ("I want to spend the rest of my life with you," "I love you," and "Forever") are among the more common lies men tell women and women believe—for a time.

Brad, a forty-five-year-old lawyer, in bed with Helen, whom he had been seeing for five months, gratuitously expressed all these sentiments. When I asked him why he chose to tell Helen this particular lie, he shrugged and said, "It was what she wanted to hear." No, he didn't plan it, it "just came up." For Brad, promising "forever" was a way to create the right mood, not unlike arranging a candlelight dinner or playing romantic music. His goal was to increase Helen's commitment to the intimacy of the moment, to get her excited. It was part of a sexual ritual that, Brad had discovered, produced the right results.

Did Helen know it was a lie? No, but Brad predicted she certainly would catch on "down the road" when nothing more permanent materialized. After all, Brad had traveled this road before. Why are women so vulnerable to this lie? The initial problem many women have is not wanting to believe that a man they care about would lie to them about this. So they react to this genre of lie with stubborn naiveté. They say, "I didn't know that he would lie to me about *that*," or "How could he?" The "Tell 'em whatever they want to hear" lie, spoken in a vulnerable moment, just before quietly slipping out a back door into obscurity, leaves a wake of skeptical, and often angry, women in its path. The promise of forever can be a deeply hurtful lie.

Women's Lies Under the Microscope

Are women's lies any different? As you read through the next set of women's lies, keep in mind that women tend to place greater emphasis on the intent of a lie, as well as its potential for harm, than do men.

> **Lie 2.** *"I lied about what a great lover Pat was."*

"You're such a great lover."

Is it a lie or required sexual etiquette? That depends on both parties' expectations and past experience. But most women I interviewed saw this as one of those expected, ho-hum lies to soothe faltering male egos. Although no man I talked to complained about unwarranted bedroom flattery, a number of women identified "making men feel good about themselves" and their sexual performance as among the three most common lies women tell men. One man noted that the last time he realized he had been lied to by a woman was when he heard from Lana, a former lover, that Sue, his current love, had told her how lousy he was in bed. His reaction? "I was pissed: it affects the ego." But his interpretation of events didn't allow that he was indeed a lousy lover! Rather, he reframed Sue's critique of his lovemaking so Sue is merely saying this to "get back at Lana." In the face of evidence to the contrary, he still managed to exert enough spin control on the facts to keep his ego intact.

Still, isn't dishing out unjustified sexual flattery playing a loser's game? You made him feel good, but what do you get out of it? He thinks he's great, you know otherwise. By perpetrating the polite fantasy of the great lover, all you do is take your own short-term losses and in the long run make everyone's sexual satisfaction less likely. Telling your partner what you want sexually, and, at minimum, refraining from praising what you don't, makes a lot more sense.

> **Lie 6.** *"I said I hadn't thought about the opportunity to perform in theater when I had, in order to keep the stage manager seeing me as selfless."*

"What a good girl!"

Is it okay to be ambitious, to do what it takes to advance your career or personal status? Joanne wasn't so sure. When Matt, her boss, asked whether she'd considered performing in the theater rather than designing stage sets, Joanne denied her own personal career preference "to cover my intent for personal gain." In Joanne's mind admitting self-interest to her boss would compromise her virtue. Why lie about something so important to her with someone who could help her? "Because I don't want him to know that I want to get all I can from the theater. He sees me as a selfless individual with honesty and integrity. If he knew I was thinking of myself, he'd think I was less honest, had less integrity." She lies to protect the idealized image of her as a selfless, noncompetitive "good girl" that *she thinks* he holds. She believes that "if he really knew who I was, he'd think less of me."

In adopting this approach, Joanne puts herself in a powerless position with her boss. She hides who she really is and what she really wants, steadfastly denying her own ambition. This self-defeating lie could stop her career growth in its tracks and keep her in a subservient role, even while her boss seems ready enough to recognize her potential. True, Joanne might be scared or she might feel underqualified. But by hiding behind this ruse, she'll never find out if she's got the right stuff, and she's less likely to get all she wants from the theater.

Lie 7. "One month ago. I didn't want to do it [end the relationship]. I had dated Pat two or three times. I told Pat, 'It's not you, it's me.' But it was Pat."

"It's not you, it's me."

Victoria, at age thirty, was ready to settle down. But from her perspective Syd, the new man in her life, lacked the right stuff for the long haul. Too bad, since Syd was clueless. And as long as he kept asking her out and she had nothing else to do, she would go out with him.

When Syd asked Victoria out for the fourth time, she finally turned him down. An awkward moment to slug through, but so far so good. Then she lied. She ended her turndown with the classic disclaimer—"It's not you, it's me"—falsely reassuring Syd and placing blame for the ending on herself, not him. But as Victoria wryly added in the interview, "It *was* him."

So why did Victoria lie? On the surface this lie was pure noblesse oblige—the polar opposite of the more typically male lie of entitlement. Victoria found it hard to assert herself by turning down an interested guy simply because she didn't care for his company. Somehow, he is entitled, she is not. She underscores her reluctance to lie here by saying, "I didn't want to do it." But weighing her reluctance against Syd's demands for more contact, Victoria chose to exercise her right of rejection.

She took the dominant position of ending the relationship, but then immediately stepped back. She felt compelled to wrap her assertiveness in self-denigrating language that put her in a one-down position. In her mind, she was helping Syd save face and avoiding an even more unpleasant conversation.

Was Syd grateful to have his feelings spared? Not at all. According to Victoria, he was "angry, snarky." He closed the conversation by snidely glossing over the fact that she had just ended their relationship. Instead, he offered her an inversion of the standard male getaway line "I'll call you." He told her, "When your schedule clears, call me."

Syd walked right past her message and reasserted his control. Her lie more likely enraged than fooled him. But if he deals head-on with the rejection and pursues what really went wrong, he's likely to hit the unwelcome truth—that it probably *was* him. Several men I interviewed said that when a woman isn't interested in pursuing a relationship, they would prefer that she lie, saying she had met someone else. Losing a competition to another man allows them to exit with honor.

Endings are awkward for everyone. We'll look at lies of ending in more depth in Chapter 11, where we discuss how men orchestrate the final and often bitter ending of a relationship. The problem is that most of us have no prescribed script for gracefully ending relationships. We don't know how to do it without causing pain to the other party. Fact is, both sexes have trouble with endings. Breaking up, even after three dates, is hard to do.

> **Lie 10.** "*It was a polite lie—about Pat being good company when Pat fell asleep on the couch.*"

"My, what an absolutely delightful casserole this is."

Here we have a boilerplate version of the polite social lie nicely reconfigured for relationships. The casserole tastes suspiciously like bits of smoked shoe leather laced with catsup and stewed in a panoply of unrecognizable gray veggies, but you smilingly compliment the host on its splendid texture, presentation, and taste. These polite lies are the grease of casual human interaction where what counts is moving ahead uneventfully, glossing over minor differences in taste and perspective, and not engaging in a critical or offensive way.

The problem here is that this convention of superficial accommodation that allows us to say one thing when we really mean another begins to run amok when we apply it to intimate human interaction.

In this instance, Susan was not at all happy that Larry fell asleep on her couch after the concert. She was looking for some private sexy time with him. Instead, Larry turned out to be a boor. His actions told her she wasn't worth staying awake for. Embarrassed, he offered his apology. But Susan, rather than taking this as opportunity to set some mutual expectations about how and when they spend time together, chose to act like the perfect dinner guest. She glossed over his infraction. She reassured him he was terrific company anyway. At best, by not telling him what she wants, and reinforcing his undesirable behavior, all she'll get is more of the same. ("Since you liked that casserole so well last time, I made another one just like it for you.") At worst, by stifling her simmering irritation—which will probably break out later—she's let him know that she isn't trustworthy.

Lie 11. "About Pat's behavior at the New Year's Eve party— not telling Pat I was pissed off."

"Read my mind."

This type of concealed truth is a "not tell" that avoids even a hint of confrontation. And it is more typical of the women I spoke with than of the men. It swallows anger and then hangs on to the residual resentment that follows when he predictably fails to understand that anything went wrong.

The problem here is that Robin hides her aggravation with Ron all too well. Hidden, it doesn't disappear. Rather, it lingers to create distance between them. She discussed Ron's behavior at his New Year's party in painstaking detail with every one of her women friends who were there, and a couple who weren't. By concurring that his drunken carousing was entirely out of line, they each help Robin justify and maintain her anger.

So why didn't she just tell him? In Robin's mind he should have known flirting with other women and acting foolish upset her. If he'd paid a little more attention to her and a little less to everyone else, she would have had a better time. For Robin the success of the evening was defined in terms of their relationship, *not the party*. As a result, she's felt hurt and sulky, and more than a little afraid that, if he knew, he would trivialize her feelings. But Ron *did not* and *will not* read her mind. He figures, if she was upset, she'd tell him. So for him it was business as usual, just another uneventful New Year's party. The distance between them grows.

What These Lies Tell Us

First, men's and women's lies reveal a lot of similarities. Most of us want to preserve a view of ourselves as good people, so we put a positive spin on our own words and deeds. Given this, it's no surprise that both sexes see their lies as more protective of the other party than of themselves.

But the men interviewed listed nearly twice the number of reasons for their own lying as the women listed for theirs. What does this mean? Men may see and use the lie as a far more versatile "power" tool than do women. Men appear to use the lie more adaptively than women for short-term victories, to avoid confrontation or being caught in something and to solve problems. Fewer men than women mentioned agonizing over the impact of their dishonesty on their partners. In fact, many men seemed to separate the lie from its impact on their partners or to minimize its potential damage.

When we look at the actual lies that men and women discuss telling or being told by the other sex, women's lies were more often protective of the other person's feelings or the relationship, whereas men's tended to be protective of their own freedom and autonomy. In the twelve "last lies" we just looked at, the woman was more likely to lie to preserve a relationship or as part of a protective role. She wrongly assumed responsibility for something ("It's not you, it's me") to avoid offending someone with a more straightforward assertion of her own preferences or her anger. She glosses over the uncomfortable to soothe a friend's fragile ego or keep a relationship humming. While a man may also lie for all these reasons, he appears more likely to do it strategically—to win, to gain an advantage, or to avoid negative consequences, like a woman's anger.

The twelve "Pat" lies we just discussed highlight striking differences in how men and women play the lying game. Suppose we ask men and women to define the lie. Do you think we'll find the same pattern of differences in their thinking that we found in their stories?

Round Two of the Lying Game: Defining the Lie

Something makes him look bad. Say he has too much to drink and you drive him home from the party while he sleeps it off. The next day in addition to his hangover, he suffers instant memory loss. He demands accusingly, "What do you mean I had too much to drink? Don't you remember I've been sick for days with the flu?" You ask yourself, "What's going on?" Is this a lie, selective memory loss, or pure ego? And whatever it turns out to be, will the two of you ever sit down together to figure it out?

Most women don't confront a partner's lie until quite late in the game. Early on we do almost anything we can to avoid recognizing and confronting the lie. We make excuses for the liar or duck the L-word with a bevy of face-saving euphemisms—bluff, fib, disinformation, fabrication, misrepresentation, exaggeration, prevarication, spin-control, impression management, misrecollection, shading the truth, secret. Why not stop beating around the bush and call a lie a lie?

We avoid calling a lie a lie for a lot of reasons. Women seem more reluctant to square off with a partner on the issue of dishonesty than men, not wanting to hurt his feelings or be impolite. Ironically, women avoid calling a lie a lie for many of the same reasons that men lie: to avoid anger, to save the relationship, to hold the ugly truth at bay.

But part of the problem is semantic. We each define what *is* and *is not* a lie differently. We think we know what a lie is until we're challenged. When we confront the liar, he acts like we're crazy and says something that makes us wonder how we ever could have thought him a liar. He's so convincing we question our own senses. Could it be that men and women apply different standards to defining the lie in personal relationships?

Try defining the lie yourself. What is a lie? Say your definition out loud.

Did you say that a lie is something untrue or inaccurate? Did you add that an untrue statement is a lie whether or not the teller knows it to be false? This impersonal, black-white definition of the lie was favored more by the men than the women whom I interviewed.

Suppose you considered a lie a person's intent to deceive someone? Then your definition was more like that of the women. More women than men thought intent to deceive, not a factual deviation from an objective truth, defined a lie.

Men Define the Lie Impersonally

The men I interviewed stripped the lie clean of its intent to harm and its devastating effect on another human being. They used neutral rather than emotionally charged words to define the lie—words that, for the most part, ignored the impact of the lie on its human target. You could easily imagine their worry-free definitions of the lie in a consumer fraud manual or courtroom. Here is a sampling of how men defined a lie:

- "Something not true"
- "Something that's unreal"
- "Evasion of truth"

Even among the sixteen percent of men who said a liar's intent to deceive was important, their definitions exposed only the detached neutrality of a career diplomat:

- "An intentional readjustment of the truth"
- "A deviation from fact, intentionally misleading toward an end"

When we look at how dispassionately these men defined a lie, it's easy to forget there are real flesh and blood humans on the other end of the lie, suffering the consequences. Only two of the men I interviewed defined a lie as an untrue statement that affected someone else.

In fact, one third of the men transformed the lie into a "half-truth," or an "omission of important information" *before* tackling a definition. One man put a heroic spin on the lie by defining it as "a form of problem solving that gets everyone off the hook." Ironically, he was one of the men who included human suffering in his definition, but with an unexpected twist! He pointed out that the lie causes pain, but only when the "the truth gets out" and "wrecks the solution." For him the truth, not the lie, was the troublemaker!

Women Define the Lie Personally

Enter women, enter a different lexicon, a different way of seeing the lie. What the men overlooked, the women zeroed in on. The intent of the liar and the impact of the lie on its target were exactly what nearly half of the women I interviewed considered most important in defining a lie. Women measured the seriousness of a lie by the pain it inflicted, not by how much of a deviation it was from a material fact. Consider these definitions:

- "Something that hurts. Something that is not true that hurts me—an excuse for not telling the real story"
- "Any untruth that has consequences that hurt or injure someone else"

Some women, like men, saw lies as mere technical violations of an impersonal truth, but most talked about the damage the lie had wrought in their own lives and how they felt about it—even as they defined the lie.

Do You Swear To Tell the Whole Truth?

When you testify in a court of law, you "solemnly swear to tell the truth, the whole truth, and nothing but the truth, so help you God." You then face a dilemma. You're also instructed to answer *only* what is asked! How are you supposed to do both? This same dilemma holds in our relationships. Do we hold to an implied oath to tell all, "the whole truth," or do we answer only what our partner is savvy enough to question us about and strong enough to hear? If we tell all, we may risk losing our partner's affection or even our relationship. But if we answer only the specific questions our partners ask, are we lying in principle by holding back other critical truths?

Suppose your partner omits to tell you that he had a drink after work with an attractive new co-worker. You feel hurt, like he tried to put one over on you and you let him know it. But instead of offering an explanation or apologizing, he acts genuinely outraged that you would equate his withholding the truth with lying. He swears he would never lie to you, *but you still feel lied to.* For him it was a harmless "not tell." For you it's a suspicious and hurtful omission that casts doubt—in short, a lie.

Who is right? Are you justified, or is he?

On the issue of whether concealing the truth is a lie, men and women split. Even where they seem to agree, a closer read of their answers shows them to be miles apart. When I asked people "Is concealing the truth a lie?" that question stumped a lot of people.

Most men saw nothing wrong with concealing potentially damaging information from their wives and lovers, as long as they didn't lie overtly. But seventy percent of women were just as sure that a "not tell" was a bonafide lie.

If you think this sounds like trouble, you're right. When a man conceals something important from a woman, he's less likely to see himself as lying than she is. As long as he hasn't materially misrepresented the facts he figures he's home free. One man put it this way: "If it hasn't been said, how can it be a lie?" Or he may take a classic "Ask me no questions, I'll tell you no lies" approach. So when a woman asks and he lies, he sees his lie as her responsibility, since she was the one who insisted on questioning him. In his mind he remains blameless. But in her mind he intended to deceive her and his omission followed by his lie hurts. For her this *sequence* is likely to constitute a lie. Consider how certain these women are that concealing the truth is a lie:

- "Concealing is a lie . . . 'Do you miss her?' 'No.' Of course not, 'cause he was seeing her. It was a technical truth. He was concealing that he was seeing her."
- "Yes . . . Acting *as if* is also a lie. Leading you to believe they are more into the relationship then they are is a lie."
- "Concealing . . . that's deception. Not being totally honest is gray . . . it's a lie."

Now take a look at the responses of the men who *also agree that concealing the truth is a lie,* but who nonetheless qualify their answers or limit concealing the truth as a lie to the narrowest of "only if" conditions :

- ". . . I know the truth and I am purposely evading it. 'What kinds of magazines do I subscribe to?' '*Time, Newsweek, Playboy.*' I wouldn't say *Playboy.* Is it a lie for me to conceal the third one? . . . *I've said nothing that's not true. But I haven't answered the real question.*"
- "It's a lie only if you're specifically requested to tell the truth."
- "It's a lie only if it's concealing a material fact."
- "If they don't ask, I don't have to tell."

Some men find the principle of telling the whole truth an unreasonable intrusion, like the young man who asked me: "Do you have a right to keep your 'thought crimes' private, or do you have to admit them like actions?" Most women glossed over technicalities. If a concealed truth created harm and misled, they said it was a lie. Even the few women who thought concealing the truth was *not* a lie still managed to consider intent and outcome. They speculated on the damage a concealed truth, *while still not a lie*, might cause to the relationship:

- "If what you tell is completely true, but you don't tell the other part . . . it's not technically a lie, but you could use this to act deceitfully."
- ". . . If your intent is not malicious, then it's not a lie."

Some, like this woman, couldn't keep their specific fears and ambivalence about discovering an unwelcome concealed truth out of their definition: *"Deep down I know he lied all along and I don't want to know. Should we probe partial truths? Should we ask 'Why didn't you call me back?' Then when he says "'cause I fell asleep,' should I ask 'Alone or with someone else?'"*

As the person lied to, we are constantly weighing our discomfort with the lie against our discomfort with the truth.

Round Three of the Lying Game: Responding to the Lie

"I don't really want to believe I've been lied to. Then I feel kind of naive."
—Thirty-five-year-old married female sales representative

Suppose someone you care about lies to you, but not successfully enough to fool you. You feel reasonably sure that this person has played fast and loose with the truth. How do you react?

HOW YOU RESPOND TO THE LIE

---

1. **Deny**: Tactfully look the other way; pretend it never happened.
2. **Blame yourself:** Search deep inside yourself to see if you gave cause.
3. **Confront**: Angrily demand the facts, nothing but the facts.
4. **Stew**: Work yourself into a tizzy, endlessly ruminating about the lie.
5. **Chuckle**: Find the lie amusing, have a good laugh.
6. **Discuss**: Demand an immediate heart-to-heart to get to the bottom of it.
7. **Terminate**: Kick this person out of your life.

Although men and women do all of the above, based on my interviews and other research findings, a woman who has been lied to is more likely to deny the lie (answer 1), blame herself, not the liar (answer 2), endlessly replay the circumstances of the lie (answer 4), or want to discuss what happened (answer 6). A man lied to is more likely to confront the liar (answer 3), find the lie amusing (answer 4), and/or terminate the relationship (answer 7). Welcome to Round Three of the lying game, where men and women approach both the lie and being lied to from the perspective of their own gender.

What's happening? Men and women approach the lie in a way wholly consistent with how they've been raised. Without acknowledging the gender roots of our actions, we play out roles that we've come to believe are appropriate to being a man or a woman in our culture. So when a man is sure he has been lied to, his sense of masculinity dictates that he avoid losing his power and dominance. To save face, he can minimize the hurt of the lie, either by laughing it off or by taking the role of the wronged party. Whatever he does, he's unlikely to obsess over the lie or blame himself. That would only push him down lower in the power hierarchy. More likely, he'll blame the liar and turn the situation to his advantage. Like any other wronged party on the Court TV channel, he restores justice by seeking damages. But power, not money, is the pay-off. The liar has provided him the chance to exert the masculine right to an honorable defense. In short, his male role dictates that he become the guardian of justice, not the relationship. So when you lie to him, don't expect him to politely smile and look the other way or endlessly agonize over his complicity in the lie. More likely, he'll put the relationship second to restoring power and equity.

A woman lied to responds with a different agenda. Even when the lie is hurtful, she's more apt to put the lie in the context of what is important to her—preserving the relationship. Forget threat and angry confrontation. She'll smooth things over by politely overlooking the lie or by struggling to make sense of it, no matter how vile or incomprehensible the lie first seems. If there's a hidden reason he lied to her, she'll wonder, "Could it be me?" More humiliated or shamed than angry, she may keep asking herself what she did to cause this perfectly decent man to lie to her. No matter what the outcome or how angry she eventually becomes, she'll probably blame herself, rather than the liar. She may even swallow her first surges of anger, opting instead for discussion and forgiveness. After all, she has learned her feminine role: to be the guardian of the relationship. Restoring justice comes in a sorry second.

When I asked women why they believed the lie in the face of compelling evidence to the contrary, one after another offered preserving the relationship as the answer. This squares with the groundbreaking work on gender differences in moral reasoning by Harvard psychologist Carol Gilligan in her 1982 book, *In a Different Voice*. Gilligan details how women come to prioritize connectedness and relationships, whereas men prioritize their separateness and the pursuit of justice.

Obsessing Over Being Lied To

Which sex obsesses more about being lied to? Women were the hands-down winners. Nearly all the women interviewed (an amazing ninety-seven percent!) admitted to obsessing over the lie in all its grisly detail. Some mulled the lie over for weeks, even months after the event, trying to fathom exactly why it had happened, as if the replay would release some essential but still hidden truth. They reconstructed the lie "to see if there was a thread of truth in it" or if there was any evidence that "maybe it's my fault." Like latter-day alchemists, they struggled to convert the incomprehensible and hurtful lie into a comprehensible nugget of value.

Take Gina, a twenty-six-year-old married property manager, who laughingly said, "Obsess? I even can remember specifically what I was wearing and where I was sitting at the time of a lie. I can't bury it. *I want to remember the specifics so it doesn't happen again.*"

Thirty-five percent of the men claimed not to ruminate over the lie. A number said their main response when a woman lied to them was amusement. Interestingly, not a single woman mentioned finding being lied to by a man funny! Len, a twenty-three-year-old single information systems manager, said he didn't mind being lied to by a woman, adding, "It's moxie when a woman doesn't tell the truth." Among the under-thirty crowd in particular, the men I interviewed tended to see women's lies (and their own) as creative, sexy, and challenging.

Blaming the Liar or Blaming Ourselves

When someone lies to her, Marla, a law student, says that she feels "self doubt, that something's wrong with me" and "disgust" that she's "so dumb, naive." She blames herself. Marla is just twenty-five years old, but another ten or twenty years of experience don't seem to derail many women from singing the "what did I do wrong?" song when they're the ones victimized by a lie. Benita, a thirty-seven-year-old secretary, berates herself for being older but no wiser when it comes to the lie: "I kick myself whenever I'm lied to. How could I have been so blind? Not seeing it sooner." Then she wistfully adds, "Maybe I'll be wiser next time."

Then there's the thirty-three-year-old accountant who caught her lover of six months in bed with his "platonic friend" and blamed herself, not him, for her humiliation: *Did I pick the wrong people? Do I believe people because I want to? Did it just happen? . . . What might I be doing? It's not just coincidence that someone is lying to me on this subject. What role do I play? I want to know so I can regain control and not be subjected to this a million more times in my life.*

Even among the over-forty crowd, many women felt like Sally, a forty-five-year-old divorced sales clerk, who started out talking about her anger at men who lie, but ended up turning her anger for being duped on herself: *I feel angry when I'm lied to. I just want to pop them and say 'why did you have to lie'? Why didn't you give me a choice by being honest? I can't believe anything they say after that. I feel like a failure. Why did this man lie to me? Do I have anything written on me that says, 'You can lie to me'?*

Forty-year-old Dawn is another good example. She became pregnant by a man who told her he'd been divorced for sixteen months from a woman named Sara. After he broke off the relationship with Dawn, saying "We're getting too close . . . and I'm not ready to settle down," she decided to go to city hall to check his divorce papers. Finding none, she located a copy of his marriage license. Confronted, he confessed that he was still married to Sara. How did Dawn react? By beginning "to doubt myself, my ability to judge someone's character . . . I became withdrawn."

Few men blamed themselves for being the victim of a woman's lies. Only one man interviewed, compared with more than a dozen women, assumed blame for being the victim of a woman's lie. When men got angry over being lied to, they seemed to have little trouble either blaming the woman or terminating the relationship. A single male physician described his tactic of telling a woman he catches in a lie "to call me in two weeks—I have too much work to be around."

Even men in secure, high-trust marriages may be secretly trigger-happy when it comes to terminating the relationship. Jack, a forty-six-year-old operations manager, says he is married to a woman who never lies to him. But, he adds, if he ever found out that his wife were lying, he would act swiftly and decisively. He "would confront her and end the relationship." Not a single woman I spoke with offered such willingness to terminate a relationship on the basis of a single lie. At least not before ruminating about it for months and trying to understand it from his point of view.

Breaking the Deadlock of the Lying Game

Men distance themselves from the lie, letting it go, seeing it as amusing, or terminating the relationship. Women absorb the lie right into their core, obsessing about the lie's why and wherefore, blaming themselves for being victimized, feeling one down, and trying to put the positive spin of understanding on a hurtful deceit. Whether lying or lied to, a man more typically seeks to assert or restore his power and autonomy. A woman more often is ready to tackle whatever it takes to keep the relationship going.

How can we break the deadlock? The challenge is in overcoming the classic mismatch between men's and women's reactions to the lie. That mismatch begins and ends with each gender trapped in its own perspective.

The solution begins with each gender breaking out of its own perspective to understand the lie from both the other person's *and the other gender's* point of view. Women and men can effectively change the unwritten rules and outcome of the lying game by learning from each other. After all, we all have a lot at stake. Without breaking through the inherent mismatch between men and women as they play the lying game, disappointment and confusion will continue to reign on both sides of the lie.

Men need to take a hint from women and tend the relationship as well as seek power and dominance. Men also need to value connectedness enough to pay attention to the effect of the lie on the trust they are building with their partners.

Women can take a clue from men, by more forcefully asserting their power, protecting their own rights, and restoring equity through confronting the liar. Women also need to get comfortable telling how the lie affects them—placing responsibility for the lie on the liar, not on themselves.

The first step in this process is to understand how men play the lying game and how you react. On the pages ahead we'll tackle men's lies in their many forms. Let's start with lies at first sight— the flirtations and lines that enhance who he is and that draw you into his world.

Part 2
LIES AS HOOKS

Chapter 3
Lies at First Sight

A couple of months ago at the bakery, a man claimed we went to high school together.
—Thirty-three-year-old married female accountant

*They always tell me how young I look. How attractive I
am. . . . maybe they do mean it.*
—Forty-year-old single female office administrator

*I was in Las Vegas and this guy came over to me and said, "You're
really doing well, would you like to be my lady luck when I play
blackjack?"*
—Thirty-seven-year-old divorced female interior designer

*It doesn't really hurt anything. It prolongs the thread being
woven. . . . If I'm flirting with someone and she says, "How many
sexually transmitted diseases have you had?" and I say "Six," it
won't further the relationship.*
—Twenty-five-year-old single male account manager

They don't have to tell me lies or lines. I'm just interested.
—Thirty-two-year-old married female medical technician

Lies at first sight run the gamut from mild flirting to flagrant
makeovers. Maybe you think you've heard them all. Maybe you've
even believed a few of them. Lies at first sight aim to flatter, reassure, and impress you, *before* you know the facts. But they're hard
to counter because they feel so right in the moment. They appeal to
our magazine-prepped, sugar-coated fantasies of how a man and a
woman are supposed to act in those first few breathless moments.

It's all too easy to forget that lies at first sight are designed to
hook you into something you may neither expect nor want! One thing
you can be sure of is that they are not random events. They function
as seductive remnants, leftovers of the mating rituals in the animal
kingdom. Lies that hook soften the edges of your natural skepticism,

leaving you more receptive to and interested in the person who uses them.

At a time when you don't know much about the stranger speaking his lines, these lies are a crafted fiction that color your impressions and attract you to him. The danger? They can feel like harmless flattery when they're outright deception. Or the less risky reverse. You mistake his harmless puffery for something far more sinister, missing out on someone you might really like. Naturally, it takes two to make lies at first sight work. Keep in mind that how much you're willing to believe what you've been told by this stranger depends as much on *who you are* as on *what he says*.

Sometimes lies at first sight seem instant ego-boosters. Who wouldn't love them? At the supermarket a man you've never seen before makes your day when he whispers to you in the checkout line, "You have the most beautiful hair I've ever seen," or "I can't believe someone as young as you has two grown children!"

Sometimes lies at first sight are disarmingly self-disclosing. Your heart goes out to this man. Just before he makes his big move on you at the office Christmas party, he confesses: "I've really been burned by women. You're the first woman I've felt attracted to since my divorce."

Sometimes lies at first sight pose as purely factual information about the liar. You're not sure why this man you've just met on the train is revealing the intricacies of his shopping habits or geographic history, but there it is: "I buy a new BMW every other year," or "I grew up on a two-thousand-acre ranch about 150 miles from here." But since you figure he has no reason to lie to you, why doubt him?

Sometimes lies at first sight are just time passers. They do no more than help you both fight boredom at a friend's wedding, or while away a disappointingly rainy afternoon at a beach resort.

Often, they should send you running.

If he says he doesn't drink, then orders a bottle of wine before dinner; says he's never been married when you've heard he has custody of the kids, realize that your guardian angel is working overtime and head for the nearest exit. When his self-promoting patter doesn't square with his behavior in the first round, this man has done you the supreme favor of showing his cards early, well before you've bet the ranch. Since his exit was the designated finish line of the relationship anyway, realize that in bailing out early all you've done is beat him to the punch.

It pays to take a long, hard look at these hooks before getting reeled in.

It's also useful to remember that not all lies at first sight will inflict harm. Even when the intent is to mislead, there are lies and then there are lies. Flirtation can be great fun if you see it for what it is and, more important, for what it is not.

Yet even benign flirtation can exact a toll. In an age when political correctness and sexual harassment at work are beginning to spill over into the world of romance and personal life, that toll now may be levied more often on men who ignore these dimensions than on women.

Other lies at first sight? There are the old-fashioned and much maligned lines—alternately amusing and irritating—and in a more pernicious vein, there are the sometimes hilarious, sometimes devastating frog-to-prince lies that let him literally be too good to be true. We'll look at the frog-to-prince lie in the next chapter.

Let's begin by looking at two of these early relationship lies—flirtations and lines—what to make of them and what to do about them.

Do Flirting Rituals Foster the Lie?

It's an age-old romantic come-on— a smile, a gesture, your eyes meet. The room heats up and everyone else fades from view. By flirting he telegraphs his genuine interest in you. You do the same. When it's reciprocal, two strangers move across a room into the same cozy space. Anything feels possible.

Blame it on our programming. Like other mammals, both sexes of our species innately use certain looks, gestures, and innuendoes to signal their interest in courtship to an attractive mating partner. We want the target of our signals to notice us, make contact, show interest, impress us, and make us feel good. We want to get close enough to make a go–no-go decision and either close the deal or leave and try all over again with a new prospect.

Part fun, part animal kingdom, the ritual of flirting gets results.

So far so good. But suppose neither of you is quite as interested or available as you would like to have the other believe. Think about your own experience with flirting. Was there a time when flirting felt too good to be true—and it was? So, when and how does flirting become a lie?

Flirting: Different Agendas, Perceptions, and Expectations

How we define what's innocent and what's dishonest depends on what we expect to happen. Consider Webster's definition of flirting:

To play at courtship. To act the lover for sport.

—*Webster's New International*
Dictionary, Unabridged Second Edition

If both of you agree that the flirtation is pure sport, no problem. But if he is playing for sport and you are playing for real, flirting can move from harmless play to potentially harmful lie. In other words, if you perceive his casual comment that "this is the best conversation I've had in years" to be true, and he perceives it as idle bar talk, you're likely to be hurt when he fails to call and feel you've been lied to.

How can we possibly know someone's intentions when all we have are the scant cues of a first meeting? What another person intends takes time to discern. Without destroying momentum, you have to decide. Are you dealing with a playful event? Is his only intent to amuse himself (and possibly you), or does his flirting signal his real willingness to take your budding interest to the next step? You can't know until you get a little closer to the flirt, and therein lies the danger.

Men and women can harbor very different perspectives about what's at stake at first blush and what a good outcome will look like. When she thinks a good outcome is a lunch date next Sunday to get to know each other better and he thinks a good outcome is wild and wanton sex that night, it's easy for both parties to feel confused. Too often anticipation, not realization, turns out to be the name of the game. And only you can protect you. So caveat emptor!

In the Mind of the Beholder

He acts as if you're the only one in the room who matters. His lively eyes are riveted on you, his conversation is sexy. Sparks fly. His manner exudes chemistry of the highest order. But is his exaggerated and perhaps foreshortened interest in you a lie or a social art form? It's all in the mind of the beholder.

Whether you're dealing with a successful flirtation or an offensive lie depends on how in synch the two of you are on these aspects of the flirtation:

- Playfulness
- Pretext
- Parity
- Political correctness

Playfulness

Say your encounter is a savor-the-moment event. You create sheer man-woman fun that may lead nowhere at all. You both could be married to someone else. No matter. Once you leave the train station, you may never see each other again. Still, in the moment, you tacitly agree to ice all that. Your eyes lock. For the next fifteen minutes life as you both know it recedes. You construct some fetchingly evocative dialogue that exudes sexy and mutual appreciation. Then when the moment is over, it's over. You both knew it was all foreplay, no action. No problem, no hurt, no lie. A good time was had by all.

Pretext

Let's face it. There's often nothing earthshakingly genuine about flirting and the lines two strangers use to strike up a conversation, except for the fleeting interest two people show in each other. That's where pretext comes in.

In the magic of the moment the two of you conspire *to act as if the disingenuous is genuine*. You tacitly agree to hold reality at bay. You act as if the two of you are the most fascinating people in the world. Your lives could grace the pages of *Vogue*. You are Bacall, he is Bogart. Your partner is worth your total attention, and you're worth his. In part, pretext involves *shading who you really are*, and spotlighting your best, most witty, and creative self. You both unabashedly embellish your accomplishments. Even though you were fired from your job and your marriage is on the rocks, you act as if you've got everything under control. Or maybe you step away from all that and invent an altogether new persona. You may even *pretend to have a future together*, although you both understand it's strictly in the moment.

Forget authenticity—pretext is strictly *faux*. But since the flirtation is ephemeral, it's just good fun.

You might even use pretext to *invent the circumstances* to initiate and keep the contact going. You fake being lost even though you grew up two blocks away, or you politely inquire about how much soap to use in the laundromat when the directions are clearly printed on the box. Or you ask someone to take your picture although you know full well you have no film in the camera (a technique recommended by Jill Jillsen in her book *Flirting*). All is fair, even the little white lies—for now.

Again, as long as neither of you loses sight of the fact that you're just pretending, these flirtations aren't likely to metamorphose into lies.

So where does the problem begin? It starts when two people differ on the sticky dimensions of *parity* and *political correctness*. Then a flirtation can move quickly from innocent fun to misleading lie. When parity fails to kick in and/or political correctness defines the backdrop for flirtation, lines, or other early relationship hooks, then trouble, not romance, becomes the order of the day.

Parity

Parity means similarity. The two of you share the same viewpoint. Parity at any stage of a relationship happens when both of you either tacitly or explicitly agree on what's going on, so there's built-in reciprocity. For example, in a flirtation, privately you both know this encounter is playful—not even commitment to a date, much less happily-ever-after. You both realize you're not really all that irresistible or fascinating. You both recognize that a good part of what's being said in your encounter is pure hype, exaggeration, or pulp fiction. What you both agree on poses no problem.

But suppose one of you has a different understanding of what's happening. Goodbye parity, hello confusion. At the end of the evening one of you will feel duped. He says he had a great time. You say he recklessly misrepresented himself, his intentions, and his interest in you. But accusations can go either way, depending on which gender's expectations were violated. He just as easily can feel misled, if you were the one leading the charge.

In the 1990s we're also likely to mix lack of parity with political correctness.

Political Correctness

Take a dash of male flirtation (he appreciatively looks you over), a few complimentary male lines ("You're so beautiful you must be a model"), and mix with new, tougher standards for gender-neutral, nonsexist behavior.

What do you get? A powerful formula for instant miscommunication and lasting trouble. Perhaps his intent is to make playful verbal contact with you for a few minutes, constructing the pretext of total interest through a line, come-on, or embellishment. If he naively assumes parity will automatically kick in, his plan can backfire big time. His playful intent may have an altogether different and none too pleasant outcome. If you don't choose to operate by his rules, you may see his actions as assumptively insulting and "non-PC." If you don't see his "playing at courtship" or "acting the lover for sport" as legitimate or appropriate to the setting, you may interpret his "hitting on you" as disrespectful or intimidating.

If this happens in the workplace, up the ante tenfold. Is it charming banter or is it sexual harassment? Not surprisingly, just as men and women differ in their definitions of what constitutes a lie, men and women differ in their recognition of what kinds of flirtation and come-ons constitute sexually harassing behavior.

You complain that his looks and sexual innuendoes create a "hostile work environment." In the workplace this may give you enough cause to file a complaint with the Equal Employment Opportunity Commission (EEOC). He's aghast. In his mind, he was just playing at the sport of love, nothing serious or intimidating! More and more, I am hearing men complain about how they have to self-censor those charming lines and innuendoes over lunch with a woman for fear of being seen as non-PC or, much worse, as harassing. And more and more I am hearing women make charges of sexual harassment in response to unwelcome and repeated sexually charged innuendoes. Sometimes these charges are based on male-female dialogues that would have been widely appreciated in the romantic movie comedies of the 1940s, but are seriously out of place and inappropriate in the workplace of the 1990s. Times clearly have changed. And using "I was just flirting" as a hasty cover-up for an intent to embarrass or disempower a woman is a lie that contributes to the confusion, making women angry and making flirting a potentially dangerous, high-stakes game.

Parity Is the Operating Rule

Once you know how to do it, distinguishing flirtation from lie is a piece of cake. When you and he see flirting in the same playful way, you agree on its appropriateness to the situation and you're in "sync" on where it is or isn't going. No one is likely to point an accusing finger at the other person as a liar or anything else. You have parity.

But when one of you sees flirting as playful sport and the other sees flirting as serious relationship building, you have trouble. The more serious one is likely to feel duped or betrayed. Truth resides in the eye of the beholder, and here each beholder sees a different truth.

Let's take a closer look at an example from the interviews of how the operating rule of parity plays out.

The Impostor: A Playful Pretext for Every Occasion

Wes loves to flirt, but you'd never guess. Now fortyish, happily married to a woman he adores and settled in the suburbs with a couple of kids, he seems a little on the shy side. What most people don't suspect is the imaginative inner life Wes harbors and how it breaks out now and then in harmless flirting, with a bit of flair. Master of the playful pretext, Wes flirts by making up preposterous stories about himself. To cover his shyness, he flirts by becoming an outrageous impostor.

Flirtation 1.

Take the international business trip, for example, when Wes was still single. He passed the hours flirting with the attractive woman who sat next to him on the plane. This is what he told me: *"I make up stories all the time. I told this woman I was a prince from some country in Europe. I was being very serious. The game was to see how far she could push me without breaking me. We went out to dinner and kept playing it. She played with me. I never saw her again."*

What did she do? She laughed appreciatively and bought into the game.

Even now Wes doesn't know how much, if any, of the story she believed. He's pretty sure she didn't believe it, but his uncertainty made the game interesting. He knew he was playing fast and loose with the truth, but the questions she asked about what royal life was like suggested she didn't really care much about the truth of his tale.

Two travelers in time and space meet. He tells a preposterous lie. She recognizes it as being only for fun and signs on. She appreciates the absurdity of his story, adds a dash of her own humor, and challenges him to be even more creative. Like two dancers, each aware of the nuances of the other's moves, they realize it's only a dance. He's leading, she's following, and that's okay. They mirror each other's routines and enjoy the fleeting instant.

The operating rule is clear to both. They both know it's just pretend and suspend disbelief *for the moment*. They have parity. Their mutual recognition of pretext and playfulness makes the pretense work.

Although we don't know the woman's side of this situation, Wes ended up feeling good about the evening. Both parties were playing with the same set of operating rules. The encounter led nowhere. It was an end in itself.

Flirtation 2.

Now consider Wes's other story, the one that backfired and that he still talks about more than fifteen years after the event.

When he first entered law school, he went alone to a university-wide get-acquainted dance. Not knowing anyone, he wound up drinking beer by himself, feeling socially inept. A woman he was standing near asked him where he was from, and what he was doing in Chicago.

As Wes put it, *"What I was doing was mundane, boring. What I said to her was an experiment, a probe. I created an outrageous situation, something ludicrous enough to be obviously false, but that had some ring of truth to it. Something that compelled her to react in some way. Basically, it was an opening line that got out of hand, then lost its steam."*

At first, Wes felt she wasn't his type—"too plain, not too appealing, too much jewelry."

But as she prodded him about his background, the playful impostor and possibilities emerged.

"I said my father was Halston, the famous dress designer. She said, 'Oh, your parents are Mr. and Mrs. Halston?' I said, 'No, they are Halston and Mrs.—my father doesn't let anyone call him mister.' I went on and on, until I got bored. But she was mesmerized. I should have picked a better topic. She didn't want it to end. I went to the bathroom. She followed me."

At this point Wes realized his flirting partner was not in the least playful. She was seriously star-struck, hooked on his son-of-celebrity status. She wanted the total *National Enquirer* scoop on his famous father. He wanted out.

She mistook his pretext and playfulness for an earnest sharing of information. They had no parity. What happens next is telling: *"I waited a few minutes, then I opened the bathroom window and crawled out to avoid her. I was literally relieved. When I walked around the corner of the building to my car, there she was. She said: 'I waited for you outside the bathroom.' I lied to her: 'I took a long time.'"*

Wes's playful flirtation backfired because she totally missed Wes's impostor spoof and Wes didn't have the wherewithal to come clean or clue her in. As he put it, "I wasn't skilled enough to be polite." He wanted to end the dialogue. She wanted to continue it. He ducked the moment of truth by crawling out a window. Then, confronted, he lied to cover his avoidance!

If you have parity, then playfulness and pretext may lead some-where—or not. But without parity, playfulness and pretext mislead.

Lines or Lies?

When men toss out lines to hook you, the line must dangle the right kind of bait to attract the right kind of catch. So what consti-tutes a line will be anything *he thinks* will attract you. Unfortunately, he's likely to offer his line at a time when he knows next to nothing about you. The result? He reaches deep into his tackle box packed with whatever glittering lure his past experiences and assumptions tell him women will go for, when he would be better off relying on more natural bait.

The line he'll use may be disingenuous—outrageous flattery, pretentious chivalry, complete fakery, or an insincere promise. It's natural to think a flattering line is all about us, but no matter what the line's content, when you get right down to it, his line reveals far more about him, the speaker, than about you and your effect on him.

When you pay close attention, his lines tell you a story. They expose a lot more than he bargains for about who he is—his insecu-rities, his fantasies, and his hopes. His lines may even paint a star-tling picture of how he views women.

Test it out. Think back to a relationship that started with him throwing you a line. It doesn't have to be some fabulous movie-script come-on. Let's face it. An occasional line is charming; most are pedestrian. Real-life lines just aren't that exceptional.

Once you remember the line, think about what it tells you:

- Did his line focus attention on you or him?
- Was it flattering or insulting?
- Did he portray himself as rich, talented, or moving in the right circles?
- Did he offer you something he thought you wanted without checking it out?

Compare the lines you've heard with this garden assortment taken from the ninety-five interviews.

YOUR LINE RECOGNITION SCORECARD

Name That Line

1. You're the best!

"How'd you manage to get all the brains and the beauty?"

Focuses on how beautiful, smart or talented you are.

2. He's *so* impressed.

"You're going to law school! I'm impressed."

Lets you know the impact of your beauty, intelligence, or
accomplishment on him.

3. Anything you want, he's got it.

*"I've got a fabulous house on the lake, there's a job opening at
my firm."*

Offers complete one-stop shopping and he's got it all.

4. He's the best!

"I'm a brown belt in karate and I go to law school at night."

Extols his own virtues *ad nauseam*.

5. Stick with him for sexual delight.

"I can make you feel like a real woman."

Talks hot and sexy to get you in the right frame of mind.

6. He's ready for commitment.

"You're the kind of woman I'd like to grow old with."

Says he's open to forming a serious relationship.

7. Him too! Your interests are his interests.

"Yeah. If it's not classical music, I just turn the radio off."

Molds himself to fit your real or imagined interests.

8. He's a nonmaterial guy.

"Community service is far more important to me than money."

> Misrepresents himself as altruistic, PC, or materially challenged.
>
> 9. **Bait-and-switch is his game.**
>
> *"Would you mind if I came in for a minute to use the bathroom?"*
>
> Uses pretext to get foot in door, then escalates or switches tunes.
>
> 10. **Someone else made him do it.**
>
> *"My friend really likes you, so he sent me over to meet you."*
>
> Quickly abdicates accountability for own actions.

The Lines

What are men's most common lines? They follow fairly predictable themes. Mostly they extol your unique virtues of appearance, personality, or intelligence ("I love your smile," or "You look so young, so attractive," or "I love your accent," or "You must be a model"). Or they tell what they hope will be a compelling story about them—even if it involves exaggerating, misrepresenting, or glamorizing who they are, what they do, what they offer.

The first kind of line is based on the idea that flattery will get him somewhere. Too bad it's the instant variety, based on too little or no data. So he says, "You must be a model," simply because you're tall and thin. The second kind falsifies or bends the truth to impress or mislead. All "I'm a photographer" or "I'm a rock musician" may really mean is that he owns a camera or sings in the shower. Some lines make grand promises without intent to keep them. So his "We'll travel around the world together" may actually turn into a little weekend trip together—*if you pay for it.*

Sometimes lines are quintessentially playful, simply pure fun and games. Or they may skip playfulness altogether, reflecting a kind of yuppie "hurry sickness." This is the feeling that everything must come to fruition in the moment and that the relationship from initial sizzle to happily-ever-after must occur in an uninterrupted heartbeat.

Check your own experience and prepare for what's ahead with these lines from the scorecard.

You're the Best!

- "I've been watching you all night. Your eyes look so soulful, so terribly sad. I feel like we've met somewhere before."

- "I love your smile. It lights up the room."
- "You're so intelligent, so interesting, you must be a writer."
- "You're gorgeous."
- "I'll bet you're a trainer at a health club."

Well, who doesn't want to be adored? These lines give you instant adulation. They hook into our natural hunger for appreciation. Even though "You're the best" lines seem nauseatingly superficial in hindsight, they hold promise on two fronts.

On the first, if they target a real asset (your eyes *are* soulful, your smile *is* outstanding, you graduated *magna cum laude*, you *are* a knockout, a jock, etc.), these lines show he's attentive to the limited facts he's able to cull by observation. Even better, he's adept enough to use them to break the ice.

On the second front, these lines tell you he's willing to focus on you, rather than himself, in the first round—always an excellent sign! Even if his "You're the best" lines wildly exaggerate your beauty or intelligence, they tell you he's willing to place you at the center of conversation. This has promise.

But pay close attention to what comes next. If he discloses nothing about who he is, even when you pointedly inquire, back off. He may be hiding something you'd really rather know—like his being married or just in town for the night. In this case, "You're the best" hooks and conceals.

Are these lines really genuine lies? Because they're so complimentary, it's hard for most of us to tell. We hope not! Even when "You're the best" lines make us squirm, they may not be lies. They may reflect our discomfort at encountering a man's unrelentingly positive focus on us, or a sense of being judged intrusively by someone who barely knows us, A forty-two year-old accountant found the attentions of a new man in her life difficult to accept. She said, "*The first time I met the guy, he went on and on about how fascinating I was. It was flattering, but too much positive created a negative. I said thank you, but I'm not that great.*"

Other women take this incredulity one step further. When a stranger offers "You're so intelligent," they balk. They refuse to be assessed. As one woman said, "Who the hell are you to tell me that! We just met."

One thirty-five-year-old married woman summed up a lot of women's feelings when she said: "*Maybe it* ["You're so beautiful, a wonderful person"] *wasn't a lie. I see things cynically due to my experience. I don't want to be a sucker again. I take it with a grain of salt. I watch to see how fast they press for intimacy.*" Sadder but wiser, she's still willing to suspend her disbelief, while exercising due caution. Not a bad starting gate position.

He's *So* Impressed

- "I'm really impressed with what you're trying to accomplish."
- "I'm quite interested in your dissertation research."
- "I love women who wear outrageous hats."

"I'm so impressed" lines offer a slight but important twist to "You're the best." What they add to the party is *his reaction* to what you've just said or to some unique aspect of how you look or present yourself. The positive is that by managing to get both of you in the same sentence in an upbeat way, he shows you that he's an equal opportunity guy. When he intersects his interest with something special about you, there's room for both of you from the first moment.

The downside? When his lines have a fawning quality or his reaction makes you uncomfortable, something else may be at work. He may be flashing his need to identify with an accomplished woman to take the heat off his own lack of direction or achievement. If he gets you talking about your dissertation or your job, he won't have to say a word about how unhappy he is with his own station in life. It's still too early for you to know, but if you opt to stick around for a while, you may want to check this out. How satisfied is he with his own accomplishments?

Anything You Want, He's Got It

- "Are you creative? I have a great entry-level job open for you in marketing."
- "How would you like to come out to my fabulous house on the lake one weekend?"
- "I'm a dress designer and I'm looking for a model for my new line."
- "I have a friend with a plane. We can fly over Yosemite together."
- "You like to travel? I'll have my travel agent arrange for a theater weekend in London."

Maybe they're true, maybe they're not. Maybe these lines are just the 1990s quick and dirty version of the traditional wine-her-and-dine-her routine. One thing's for sure—the "anything you want, he's got it" lines give you plenty of warning. This man feels the surest way to your heart is with tantalizing *material* bait. He'll offer anything he can think of: jobs, perks, trips, services, and opportunities. Because he sets himself up as the giver and you as the taker, he's the one who owns the toys, holds the power. "Anything you want" lines present unmistakable evidence about what he values most: control and resources. So watch out. Even if his promises are real, he may see you as yet another asset to be bought and traded.

What if his promises are false? They tell you a different story—a story about the extremes he believes he has to resort to in competing for the attention of a woman like you—or any woman. Don't for a minute think this reflects on how you are presenting yourself. Many men I interviewed told some variation of this forty-five-year-old married man's comments on his elaborate lines: *"About 65 percent of the time I don't feel attractive to women, so it's important for me to be the aggressor. I have to use ploys to get women. They just wouldn't want me on my own."*

Too bad many of these men will never find out if they could have been accepted on their own merit without the help of their elaborate props and promises. Consider the line that suggests he might have an enticing job offer for you. That actually happened to Molly, a twenty-six-year-old single woman in Chicago. Molly told me a man came up to her at a bar, asked if she was creative, and then "suggested a job offer I would die for." He got her attention *and phone number*. Molly commented, "He strung me on for several weeks and asked me for dinner. I just wanted a job. Finally, he never called back." His line was fairly successful in capturing Molly's interest—at least until she figured out it was a ploy. Then she felt deceived. The problem here is that he set himself and the budding relationship up for defeat. His line gets her interested in the phantom job, not him. Had he set up the encounter differently, perhaps they would be seeing each other now.

Keep in mind what the man who uses this type of line is not doing. He is *not* spending his energy finding out what mutual interests you have that might lead to the next steps of real relationship building.

He's the Best!

- "I'm a lobbyist. I know all the movers and shakers on the Hill."
- "I just finished interviewing for a job and I'm negotiating a $250,000-a-year salary, plus a great bonus."
- "I'm the best. You won't find any better."
- "I'm a reporter for *Rolling Stone*, and my friend here is a lawyer."
- "I do high-level security work for the government."
- "I go big game hunting in Tibet."

C'est moi! When the first and the last words out of his mouth are "I" and "me," you know he's hell-bent to impress and you're only the latest casualty in the series. "I'm the best" is by far the most common male line men *and* women talked about. Most of these "I'm the best" lines are sheer hype and invention. They tell you he's internalized the view that "the man who dies with the most toys wins" as a standard for judging himself. Now he's using this standard as part of a high-pressure sales pitch to get your attention. These lines and the peacock strut that goes with them are standard male courtship and mating rituals. The question is merely one of degree.

To convince you he's a catch, he's trying to position himself as high as possible in a hierarchical model where status and power define his worth. He believes that any general resources he can call up, like money, job, family status, and adventure, will boost his position in the pecking order and make him a more attractive catch for you.

Glamorizing work is probably the most popular impression-management ploy. If what he does for a living defines him, upping his job status increases his market value. The hyped-up resume has become to the courting ritual what fake IDs used to be for the under-age drinking crowd—an entry card. As one single twenty-nine-year-old man noted, "I always overglamorize where I work. I say I do high-level security work for the government when the reality is I work in a warehouse." How common is this? And what happens when he is discovered?

Let's count the variations on this theme. Some men use a fake or overblown work status just to establish contact. Then they 'fess up. For example, after grabbing her undivided attention in their first five minutes by dropping senators' names, the Washington, D.C., lobbyist with the glitzy connections on Capitol Hill came clean. He confessed to being no more than a drab and dusty researcher, iso-lated in his lab. The twenty-five-year-old target of his misinforma-tion took it all in stride. She said, "I'm dating him . . . it didn't bother me. It amused me." But from her viewpoint and from that of the many other women I've spoken with, job pretense or other self-enhancing hype wasn't necessary, either.

Why do men use such outrageously self-promoting lines when simply showing sincere interest in a woman would go down easier?

Michael summed it up in four words: "I am so boring." For Michael, the self-aggrandizing line provides instant rescue from oblivion. In a fairly anonymous setting like a bar, it allows him to pretend to be all he is not—daring, wealthy, prestigious—without fear of being caught. In short, the line allows him to get away with creating a new identity without fear of reprisal. Michael's personal best? "In Switzerland I told one girl I met that I had climbed the Matterhorn, since there was no way she could check it out."

Some self-promotions are plainly gamy or macho exercises in male bonding. When two Mutt and Jeff pals spend a Friday night offering themselves as a fraternal twin "two-fer" to every woman who looks their way, they're not looking for a relationship. They're creating tall tales they'll brag about to the boys over a beer the next afternoon. As one of the twosome using the *Rolling Stone* line told me, "We did it as a joke to see how effective we'd be if we lied." No harm was intended. It was a guy's game. The intimacy was between the two of them. They gave little or no thought to the effect of their line on the woman they were scamming.

Stick With Him for Sexual Delight

- "I can make you feel like a real woman."
- "I care about you."
- "I'll give you an orgasm every single time."
- "Do you like oral sex? I love oral sex."
- "I've been celibate for three years."
- "I had the most erotic dream about you last night."

Sexual come-ons are among the oldest lines in the book. As lines go, too often they're *prêt-à-porter*—prepackaged and overprac-ticed—strategies for getting results. That casually seductive phrase he drops at first meeting may have been mimed for hours in front of his bathroom mirror, long before he caught his first glimpse of you from across the crowded room. When it comes to women, he's in sales. And why not? According to many of the men I interviewed, sexual come-ons still work wonders. Even at their most provocative, these outrageously seductive lines can hook your fantasies. That's why the sexual come-on is "section 1A" of his marketing plan to a targeted demographic area of one—you. If only one in fifty women is going to fall for his line, the next forty-nine no's get him that much closer to a yes.

Listen to how this worldly twenty-three-year-old single male thinks about the timing of his contrived and well-worn "I care" line. He says, "I don't lie to get women into bed. I say 'I care about you' two weeks before we have sex. It's a different kind of lie." And according to him, it gets the woman.

Why are these lines so successful when so many are hackneyed and easy to spot? Are women fools? Or is this what we like?

For starters, sexual come-on lines tell you in the first three minutes what this man has on his mind—sex, sex, and *more* sex. As you speak together, it's easy to imagine his visualizing making love to you. He isn't distracting you with any prattle about his accomplishments or possessions. His obvious interest in sex gets you thinking about sex too—with him as a possible partner. That's a lot more than any of the previous lines have accomplished.

How successful are these lines? Consider that even the man who said he was celibate did well with his line. Marie, a thirty-year-old single account executive, was fascinated. She said, "He was a box I couldn't open; he said he was very religious." No man had ever used that approach with her before. As with more successful lines, she wasn't sure whether it was a lie or genuine. She took his words as a serious challenge and invited him out. But later she wondered if it was a code phrase for being gay or HIV positive. Still, she slept with him, or attempted to. Turned out he couldn't hold an erection. The line worked, but he didn't.

What about the "I love oral sex" gambit? It's a surprisingly common approach, usually followed by a polite inquiry as to whether you enjoy oral sex too! At least one man using this line lamented his deprived state by pointing out, "My wife doesn't enjoy oral sex." His sexual come-on was his unmet desire to perform cunnilingus on an appreciative woman! Since this wasn't bedroom talk but first-meeting dialogue, most women dismissed this approach as an unsettlingly personal but vacuous line.

One woman who told me she loves oral sex volunteered that men often pop the "Do you enjoy oral sex too?" question. But she continued, *"They say they really like it, when they really hate it.*

They just use it as a come-on. Then when it's time to actually do it, if they do at all, that's not how they feel about it at all."

Still it's hard for the uninitiated to tell—is this true preference or ruse? One thirty-five-year-old single women told me she took a man's "I love oral sex" line as a true statement. Later, she recategorized it as a lie. Why? Because after becoming sexually involved, they rarely engaged in oral sex. Despite his implied promise, he balked. Confused, she reasoned that if he had been telling the truth, then something must be wrong with her. She didn't confront him directly, but managed to bring up the topic. His answer confirmed her worst fears. She was mortified when he said her "pubic hair was too scratchy." Then she mulled it over and got angry. "If he really loved oral sex all that much, and my pubic hair was scratchy, he would figure some way to do something about it." The relationship ended. Did he really love oral sex as much as he had proclaimed, or was this man just paying initial "lip service" to get her into a sexual relationship with him?

He's Ready for Commitment

- "I'm looking for a serious long-term relationship."
- "I'm newly single and I want you to help me celebrate my divorce."
- "Hey baby! I've been watching you and I'd like to go out."
- "I was married to a wonderful woman who got hit by a drunk driver and killed."
- "You're married? Well, I'm married too. We just won't tell them about us."
- "I had a fight with my girlfriend."

His line touts his availability like a primitive mating call. You are touched by how open he is to getting involved with you.

Your error. Often *nothing* could be further from truth than his availability.

Look at what this forty-four-year-old married man, who repeatedly had scored with his earnest "I'm looking for a serious relationship," said about his favorite approach: *"I lied from the first meeting about being interested in a serious long-term relationship. I learned this worked from trial and error. What women want is that you commit your heart to the relationship. This got me where I wanted to go. I don't think about the pain. I'd get tired of it, then get rid of the woman and the pain would go away."*

Chilling words for most women!

Even the most innocent line in this group, "I've been watching you and I'd like to go out," turned sour when twenty-eight-year-old Alice, who spent the last month dating the man who spoke it, discovered a picture of him with his very current wife and two kids.

Sometimes the availability line moves into a more deliberate lie-at-first-sight category. Kristin, a thirty-five-year-old woman, met an interesting widower who told her a wrenching story: *"He told me he'd been married to a wonderful woman. She went out to buy groceries and was killed by a drunk driver."*

She had no qualms about going out with him or going up to his apartment. Once at his apartment, she suspected something wasn't right. "When I went to his apartment, it was a blank slate." There were no mementos or evidence of his wife anywhere. Later her cousin, who knew the man, spilled the beans. This man's poor dead wife was alive and well. The only truth he offered here was his wish to be free of his wife.

What about the "I've had a fight with my girlfriend" line? Even if this man is really available—relationally and emotionally—the timing is wrong. But Marlene's experience is probably typical. Despite what Jack said, he hadn't really had a fight with his girlfriend Jody. So when his good buddy Marlene believed him and let him into her apartment to talk him through it, the only real fight she encountered was their own, as she battled him off and threw him out.

Him Too! Your Interests Are His Interests

- "I'm really interested in Latin dancing."
- "I love to walk in the woods too."
- "You run? I'm training for a marathon."

You've just met and already the two of you seem like a perfect match. Maybe a touch too perfect. How is it that this man you barely know has the exact same interests, has read the same books, and loves to walk at five in the morning just like you?

Easy. Because he has just made it all up. He got you talking about yourself. Then he listened carefully to what you said and reinvented himself in your image. As one forty-two-year-old divorced man said, "I stretch what we have in common, stretch my intellectual knowledge."

So he says he's interested in Latin dancing, but on closer inspection he can't do a two-step and thinks a Latin dance is something you attend—like the Russian ballet. One forty-year-old woman stockbroker in a rocky marriage said, "My current husband kept saying we had a lot of things in common, that he was athletic too, how much he liked to walk." She took it at face value. She married the guy! At the very least, she figured she'd found a life partner for all her favorite activities. After they settled in, she discovered that he hadn't gone for a walk in ten years, that he wasn't in the least athletic, that the karate he'd taken had been a decade earlier. Making matters even worse, they didn't enjoy the same kinds of movies or books either. Belatedly, she discovered the self-defense rule for the "your interests are my interests" line—test it before you invest in it.

He's a Nonmaterial Guy

- "I'm not materialistic. I'm a social worker."
- "Yeah, I'm in law school. But I'm going to do public interest law."
- "I'm a volunteer for the Humane Society."

He sounds so selfless, so PC. Here's a man with the dedication of Mother Teresa and the social conscience of Karl Marx. Sick of slick yuppie acquisitiveness, you're touched by the sweet appeal of this man's altruism. You can imagine the two of you working together on an Indian reservation or joining the Peace Corps. In a funny and appealing way, it's real romance.

This is just how newly divorced Michelle felt when she met her nonmaterial guy—Mr. Social Worker. Here was a man whose values she could respect. But she did a major double take when her self-denying guy, whose "entire aura had hooked me," drove off into the sunset in his brand-new Mercedes-Benz. Disappointed, she wondered why a man would so downplay his assets in the first meeting. Why not just say who he is and let the chips fall?

Why do some men do this? Maybe it's for your sake, maybe not. Could be he's pumping up his credibility by giving voice to his idealism, as much for himself as for you. Could be his trumped-up altruism reflects an internal struggle between his ideal and real selves. Or perhaps it's just a way to present himself as socially responsive and sensitive, rather than the conniving opportunist he really is—simply because he thinks you'll spring for it. The problem is, it's still too early to make a judgment call.

What do men say? Most often, according to the men I've interviewed, the intent of their money-isn't-important routine is plain old self-protection. This may come as a surprise to you since you've only just met him, but he's already protecting himself and his megabucks from *you*. *You*, not capitalism, are the enemy. You and any other woman who might want to take his toys if you only knew he had them! Maybe he has been warned that women won't be able to love him for himself if they see those glittering assets first.

This is the strategy a thirty-nine-year-old investment banker told me he uses when he meets a new woman: *"I lie 'down,' not up. I tell them I'm a cashier at Target [a discount store]. I use my pickup truck, not my town car. I feel that a lot of women are attracted to men for materialistic reasons."*

Or maybe some stereotyped vision of woman as gold digger dances in his head. Consider how this forty-four-year-old lawyer viewed his reversal-of-riches tactic. When it came to hiding assets, he was master from day one: *"It seems like the right thing to do. I don't like calling it lying . . . I shade things about money. I don't tell them how much I earn, my savings. . . . Financially, I don't want them to get the wrong idea—that I'm independently wealthy, that they can be dependent on me."*

Whether it's a line, concealing the truth, or an outright lie probably depends on when, how, *and if* his full disclosure occurs. If he proclaims his nonmaterialism too loudly or too often, take note. In the meantime, it pays to take a wait-and-see attitude. His early and extreme earnestness may be a better indicator that he is lying than frankly playful irreverence.

Bait-and-Switch Is His Game

- "Would you mind if I came in for a second to use the bathroom?"
- "I'll come over on my day off and fix your computer."
- "I have this huge tank of unbelievable tropical fish. Why don't you come up to my place and I'll show them to you?"

We've come to expect bait-and-switch in the supermarket or on our friendly shoppers' network, but here it is alive and well, smack dab in the middle of your private life. So watch out.

Bait-and-switch lines often start slow and easy. That way you don't put up any defenses against them. A line or slogan lulls you into accepting a request or action at face value. Then, just as you agree to what seems like a perfectly reasonable request, in kicks the "switch." It's as if he's saying, "Now that I've got you, I'll up the ante."

I overheard the first bait-and-switch routine ("Would you mind if I came in for a second?") while I was sitting in a coffee shop idly waiting for an espresso. Two young professional women were animatedly discussing their experiences with the men in their lives in an unmistakable "Can you believe this one?" tone. Because I had just finished eighty-five interviews, their conversation naturally caught my attention. So I asked if I could interview them. A few days later this is what Gina, a twenty-eight-year-old newly married real estate agent told me about what she and Gwen had been discussing: *"When my boss dropped me off at the end of the evening, he said he had to come in to use the bathroom. Then he said he wanted to see how my bedroom was decorated. The next thing out of his mouth was 'My wife is so boring.'"*

It's classic. He uses a ruse to get his foot in the door like any street peddler hyped for a sale. Once inside he ups the ante, escalating the relationship by degrees. Having reached the sacred temple—Gina's bedroom—without Gina sounding an alarm, he leaps to phase two of the plan—"My wife is so boring." Now, although Gina laughs about this publicly, it is clear that she is distressed about it privately. First, this is her boss, so professional boundaries aren't being respected, and the outcome could be damning no matter what she does. His bait-and-switch tactic puts her at risk. Second, since she was engaged and soon to be married at the time, she felt her personal boundaries weren't being respected either. Third, whether she's naively or tacitly colluding in this rolling sequence of increasingly suggestive moves, Gina is now in harm's way. She justifiably feels in emotional jeopardy. He has pulled her into "their secret."

What about the other bait-and-switch lines? What they share in common is providing the pretext of a legitimate reason either for getting into a woman's private quarters or for getting a woman into the man's private quarters where, away from the fray, his hidden agendas can unfold.

He says he'll come over to her house to fix her computer. It sounds like an act of generosity. What's wrong with that? Plenty, according to Susan, a twenty-seven-year-old married communications training guru. Susan was talking about none other than her best friend's husband, who "comes over to my house during the day on the pretext of fixing the computer, but really to make a pass at me." Although Susan makes a big show of rebuffing Hal's pass, she confesses that she has secret fantasies about him. This compounds the problem.

How does the glaringly obvious "Come up to my apartment to see my tropical fish" (or "my etchings," "my new electric guitar"— fill in the blank; you know the drill) fit into this picture? Craig, a forty-year-old investment analyst and the man who volunteered the tropical fish bait-and-switch line, attributed it to his best friend (noting he never had to use lines to get women interested in him). Why use such a worn-out old come-on? Easy. Because it works. Listen to his explanation: *"You meet her and you know she's interested in you, but she can't just have instant sex with you. She doesn't want to feel like a slut or a whore. So you have to have some guise with spontaneity attached to it, so it doesn't seem planned and she can feel good about what you're going to do."*

Bait-and-switch is usually based on his assumption that both you and he want the same thing. In his mind, his job is to provide you the face-saving line that allows you to do what, if you were really honest, you'd want to do anyway—usually, to have sex with him. In the first two instances I've discussed, the women involved were emotionally ambivalent about the men who were baiting and switching. This is key, because bait-and-switch requires your ambivalence to succeed. Without your openness to whatever he has in mind, the bait-and-switch technique has no power other than being a minor nuisance in the total scheme of things.

Someone Else Made Him Do It

- "This is embarrassing. I'm playing a game of truth or dare and I'm supposed to get your phone number. Can I have it?"
- "I'm on a mission of mercy for my friend who really wants to meet you but is too shy to come over himself."

You are the most appealing woman he's ever seen. But this man can't approach you under his own steam. Even though he desperately wants to meet you, he won't take responsibility for his impulse to make contact. *His ambivalence*, not yours, gets in the way. "Someone else made me do it" lines are usually harmless enough, but don't forget to ask yourself what this man is telling you about himself. In the first line, a twenty-something man in a college bar is signaling that he's uncomfortable with getting to know you as more than another drinking buddy.

This line is no show-stopper when it comes to relationship start-ups. Still, in the next phases of getting to know each other, why not stay alert to other ways he may duck his own feelings or pass responsibility for them to someone else? Forewarned is forearmed.

Macho or "Non"?

Many men have "attitude" about the line. For them the line is neither fun nor sexy, but glaring evidence that they don't feel good enough about themselves to flaunt who they really are. Some men I interviewed reacted with righteous indignation to the idea that they might need a line. Here is an assortment of disclaimers I heard from men on their reliance on the line:

- "I can make up an opening line, start conversation anytime, anywhere. What I am is pretty good and I don't have to lie about it."

    —Thirty-two-year-old single male
- "I haven't had to do that [use a line]—not for a while.".

    —Forty-two-year-old single male
- "I have not used a line with a woman. I go after them."

    —Thirty-five-year-old married man
- "I'm completely without guile, I'm too nice."

    —Thirty-eight-year-old single male

These men view needing a line to meet interesting women as evidence of nonmacho weakness. The men who reveled in their lines were a different breed. Contrary to what I would have guessed before the interviews, these were the more obviously romantic or creative men. A few had memorized lines from vintage movies that they delivered with tongue-in-cheek bravado. Several gave unusual lines, like the one this twenty-six-year-old single sales rep felt was his most successful: *"I say I'm into cloud watching, storm watching. Women are fascinated by it. They like men who are dreamy, sensitive to minor things, appreciative of aesthetics."*

Other men, like this thirty-seven-year-old single computer technician, declared that they had liberated themselves from the line and felt good about it: *"In the past I said I learned to dance well when I didn't. . . . The most emancipating thing about being honest is that all the horrible things I know about myself, others don't see as so horrible."*

So the debate continues. Is the line a lie, a self-deception, or a creative act? How we see it determines how we manage it.

How to Manage the Flirtation and the Line

He's interested. He flirtatiously volleys a line into your court. He says, "Haven't we met somewhere before?" You immediately rate him low on originality. You know it's a classic Cary Grant–style line because you heard it on the old movie channel last night. It's your move.

What to do? You can brush him off or treat him with suspicion. But if you're interested, why do that? The flirtatious guy can be an otherwise honest person, having some fun, wanting to meet someone like you, and using the flirtation and the line to signal that in a serious world increasingly governed by work and getting ahead, he's looking for a playfully nonplatonic, nonwork relationship. What you do next depends on you, how you feel, and what you want.

If you're in the mood, laugh—to show him you know it's just a game. Let him know you have a sense of humor. Say something mildly skeptical or deliver matching repartee. If he tells you that he is a twin, but you see that his designated twin for the evening clearly came from a distinctly variant genetic pool, you might smile and disingenuously say, "You must be putting me on." Treat it as an opportunity for a witty ten-minute interchange, not as a soul-baring session. If he tells you that he's Halston's son, compliment him on his originality, rather than pumping him for the details. Try being playful while reserving your healthy skepticism. If you're in the mood, see his creative bent as the evening's entertainment. But don't confuse a flirtation for romance, or a line for heartfelt conversation.

Remember, even though it's play, he's revealing who he is by what he chooses to present to you and how he does it. Even though he doesn't intend to, he'll tell you a lot about himself. This is solid information that you can pull up later for review. Consider yourself both a participant *and* an observer in the repartee and see what you can find out. At the very least, view it as an opportunity to sharpen your observational and lie detection skills.

Get a handle on what he is accomplishing with his line. As you talk, ask yourself these questions:

WHAT TO ASK YOURSELF ABOUT HIS LINES

- Which types of lines described earlier best fit what he's doing?
- What exactly is he misrepresenting or overstating?
- Is his opening patter based solely on him, his job, his talents, and his status?
- Has he allowed space for you in his hype, or is it all about him?
- Is he matching who he is to who he thinks you are?
- Is he offering you something that he probably can't deliver?
- Is his zeal for your talents and attributes flattering or outrageous?
- To what extent is he telling you what he thinks you want to hear?
- Is he consistent in his storyline?
- What is he really telling you about himself?

After you've considered the lines he's tossed your way, put whatever he is doing in the context of what *you* want, whether it's for the next twenty minutes or for the next twenty years. You are the gatekeeper here. So what happens next depends in good part on what you're willing to let happen. Even if it's only for the moment, you're in charge of how you spend it.

Here, in the flirtation and the line, the play's the thing. Whether it's fact or fiction is often a question of degree. Still, even playful beginnings provide you with a telling behavioral snapshot of who this man is. It's a preview that you can go back to later, if the relationship gels, that lets you take a fresh peek at how he treated you when he had very little at stake. It provides an early benchmark for his general relationship behavior.

What follows? Only slightly beyond the flirtation and its companion, the line, lurks the potentially misleading frog-to-prince lie. If he aims to develop a relationship with you beyond your early banter, he'll want to make himself look good to you, *very good*. To make his mark, he might resort to frog-to-prince lies. These sometimes hilarious, sometimes devastating lies literally let him be too good to be true.

Frog-to-prince lies are the focus of the next chapter.

Chapter 4
From Frog to Prince

As he fell to the ground, however, he was no longer a frog but a prince with kind and beautiful eyes who . . . now became her [the princess's] friend and husband. And he told her how a wicked witch had put a spell on him and how nobody had been able to set him free from the well but she alone, and tomorrow they would go to his kingdom together.
—From the "The Frog King, or Iron Henry," *Grimms' Fairy Tales*, translated by Lore Segal, 1985

When we hear the frog-to-prince story as children, we learn a powerful and compelling lesson of transformational love that shapes our expectations of what is possible throughout our lives. The hope and promise of the archetypal fairy tale finds its place among our most ingrained, unspoken expectations.

Do you remember the famous story?

The princess's favorite golden ball falls deep into a well, causing her great unhappiness. Distraught over the loss of her golden ball, she accepts the cheeky proposition of a repulsive little frog who lives in the well. He says he will retrieve her ball, but only in exchange for certain favors. What he demands is outrageous: a close relationship in which the princess will love him best, play with him, and let him be her dearest friend; and allow him to sit at the table with her, eat from her plate, drink from her cup, and sleep with her in her bed. Without fully considering the implications of her promise, the princess quickly agrees to these conditions. Besides, not knowing she is a character in a fairy tale where anything can happen, she reasons that it's highly improbable that a disgusting and slimy frog could ever be friends with someone like her. Of course, she misjudges the single-minded tenacity of the ugly little frog. To her chagrin, after retrieving her golden ball, the frog holds her to her promise—as does her father the king. As the story unfolds, the nasty little frog unrelentingly escalates his demands for intimacy based on her promise to him.

Which Path to Princedom?

How does the fairy tale end? If you're like most people, you remember the story ending with the princess kissing the frog, who then turns into a prince. Together they ride off to his golden kingdom.

A nice but inaccurate ending.

The actual ending of the Grimms' tale is laced with the princess's rejection, conflict, and anger—precisely what most men fear. The princess, none too pleased by the frog's insistence that she keep her promise, balks at taking him into her silky bed. When the frog threatens to tell the king, the princess responds by angrily flinging the frog against the wall. Then, as he falls to the ground, the miracle occurs—he is instantaneously transformed into a prince. So even though the frog encounters angry rejection rather than acceptance, we arrive at the same place: the happily-ever-after ending as the couple rides off together to the prince's kingdom.

In both endings—the popular kiss and the considerably more tense flinging of the frog—the ugly frog is transformed into a prince through contact with the princess's true emotions. We learn a powerful lesson. We learn that expressing our genuine feelings of either loving acceptance or honest outrage can transform even a commonly repulsive and nasty creature into a prince.

But, as we'll hear again and again from the stories of the men and women I interviewed, contact with a woman's real emotions of love or anger—or contact with their own true emotions—is the one thing many men will go to the ends of the earth to avoid.

The Frog-to-Prince Lie

Go to any singles bar, or any professional convention where men congregate in large numbers, whatever they might be—accountants, physicians, lawyers, engineers. Tune in to random snatches of conversation between men and women. It doesn't matter whether the men are young, old, single, or married. You can bet you'll be treated to the steady croaking of a chorus of bullfrogs. Each is singing louder and deeper to attract the attention of potential mates.

Maybe you don't think of men in this way—most women don't—but you'd be amazed at the number of men who freely admit that this is precisely the way they *talk* and *act*.

The way these men talk and act is what the frog-to-prince lie is all about. This lie is about overcoming ordinariness. It's about getting the edge on a whole chorus of competing frogs by flashing ever more dominance, more intelligence, more potential, more wealth, more resources, more availability—or more of anything else that is the latest valued currency in the dating and mating market.

You are probably safe in assuming that down deep he's fairly sure he's no prince. Still, that's the last thing he wants you to know. So he turns to the frog-to-prince lie to help him pose as your prince.

Listen to how this forty-two-year-old married consultant builds himself up to outdo the competition: *"My colleagues say I'm a habitual liar, but it's a marketing thing: what's the best way to market yourself to a woman? Do you accentuate the positive or deal outright with the negative? How should I behave in a situation to uphold the highest level of integrity I can? Without harming the other person, how can I present myself in a way that doesn't let the competition eat my lunch?"*

Here's how I define the frog-to-prince lie :

Any outright lie or set of intentional misrepresentations that glamorize who he is, and that he believes will make him look more desirable in your eyes.

Like his choice of lines, the particular frog-to-prince lies he chooses are revealing. What and how he distorts depends directly on who he really longs to be, and—if he has much sense—on what he believes you long for him to be.

To make himself look irresistible to you, he'll embellish whatever he can, just to grab your interest and reduce the chances that you'll reject him. His past history, his present situation, and his future potential are all fair game for his subtle or not so subtle misrepresentations.

How does he pull it off? Over dinner, he busily cobbles together bits and pieces of fact and innuendo. He is transforming himself from frog to prince long before the first round of drinks arrives. If he's an extroverted charmer, he'll weave his new identity as he speaks, as amazed at his own precocious inventiveness as you would be—if only you knew. A fifty-three-year-old divorced commercial real estate manager told me about a man she met at a singles dance who offered her a quick menu of princely options, including celebrity access: *"He said, 'Why don't you come to Las Vegas with me? I'm a personal friend of Wayne Newton's.' He also told me he lived in a big house on the side of a mountain. Later, I found out he lived in some little place."*

What does a man believe it takes to be a prince? For some the answer is easy: whatever they're not. Consider this twenty-nine-year-old single and conservative pin-striped banker who apparently felt obliged to be Mr. Super Macho Hero to get a woman he had just met to notice him: *"I told a woman I was a bodyguard, that I had a gun. She was intrigued. She was excited, she wanted to believe it. I would like to be someone like that."*

Others feel obligated to create the mystique of sexual adventure. Haven't experienced it? Flaunt it anyway! This thirty-five-year-old married city administrator augmented his past with phony orgies: *"I lied to Margo about the time I was in college. I told her I was part of the drug culture, I embellished and made up stories about orgies."*

A man's ready ease in taking indecent liberties with his identity, occupation, finances, sexual history, or whatever makes it a challenge for a woman to differentiate fact from fiction, prince from frog.

In fact, when it comes to meeting the right man, there's a popular saying among women:

> You've got to kiss a lot of frogs.

Why? Because we can't tell the frog-prince from the frog-frog until we get close. *Very close.* That takes time and effort. It also shifts the advantage to the frog. And let's face it, what frog wouldn't use that advantage?

After all, his overarching mission isn't self-revelation. It's to win your attention and out-croak the competition. Unlike lies as masks and evasions (which we'll discuss in the next chapters), where men can easily rationalize that they are lying to spare a woman pain, to protect her from an unwelcome truth, or to soften the blow of a hard decision, the frog-to-prince lie is conspicuously self-promoting. Its sole intent is to lead you into believing that he is something he is not—that he's no frog, but your very own prince.

Beware the Lie That Offers What You Wish For

Before we look at the ten most frequent kinds of frog-to-prince lies, there's a simple principle you ought to know. It's called *synchronicity*. Whenever a man's frog-to-prince lie works its magic best, you'll encounter a stunning correspondence between the lie he tells and the virtues you're seeking. You want it? He makes you think he has it. That's the essence of synchronicity. The conditions are ripe for you to believe the lie that convincingly fits your expectations.

The process is not unlike going shopping, except it's much less intentional. You decide what you want and then go out on a search-and-find mission. You shop around until you find a rough approximation of what you're looking for. You pay careful attention to all the ways that item matches your wish list. Then on the spur of the moment you decide to buy. Once you've committed to buy, you put your blinders on and ignore all the ways the item doesn't fit what you were looking for. It's not until long after the urge to buy has cooled down that you glumly realize you're stuck with something all wrong—like a navy-blue version of the black suit you really wanted.

Attending to attributes that match what we want to see, while overlooking those we don't, is called *selective attention*. We all do it. It's natural for people to pay exquisitely close attention to whatever matches their preconceptions and to ignore what doesn't.

The problem is that most women have a soft spot in their hearts for men who exhibit certain predictable attributes. The false prince knows this and plays to his audience. If you don't know it too, you will be fooled.

So begin your self-defense by perusing the following lists of factors women are most likely to see as desirable in men, gleaned from my own and others' research. Decide which match your own list of most coveted attributes.

You can rate each statement's importance to you on this ten-point scale:

1 = This is no hook for me.

5 = I can take it or leave it.

10 = Hang on to this one!

TRADITIONAL AND NEW WAYS WOMEN DEFINE THE PRINCE
___

Rate how important each factor is on a 1 to 10 scale.

1. Outstanding Material Resources

___high-income player
___has a stash of savings

___owns all the latest gadgets and possessions
___sports a new fully paid-for car
___owns a big house
___has other material resources I deem important

2. Prestige

___holds an important job
___lives in the "right" neighborhood
___comes from a well-known family
___has significant accomplishments
___is on the path to fame and fortune
___has whatever else strikes me as prestigious

3. Career Aspirations

___is seen as mover and shaker who's making it
___is on some path to outstanding career success
___has impressive plans for successful, prestigious career

4. Intelligence/Cleverness

___oozes intellectual horsepower
___displays worldly knowledge, is informed
___appears well-educated
___has the right degrees (M.B.A., J.D., Ph.D., M.D.)
___sounds smart about whatever I think is important

5. Masculinity

___visibly asserts himself
___flexes his intellectual or physical muscle
___acts as if he could beat off any competition
___shows general macho behavior
___looks as if he would serve and protect

6. Willingness to Commit

___sends strong signals that he's unencumbered
___says he's ready, willing, and able to commit to new
   relationship

7. Sexual Accountability

___has had zero or few current or immediate past sexual
partners
___is totally believable about his steadfast adherence to safe
sex
___wants a monogamous sexual relationship
___has a heterosexual orientation

8. Health

___is currently free from contagious, sexually transmitted
diseases
___levels with me about whatever he's got

9. Sensitivity

___is in touch with his feelings, as well as his positions on
issues
___is able to communicate his feelings to me
___is sensitive to my feelings and positions on issues

10. Honesty/Character

___what he appears to be is what I will really get
___his word is good
___what he omits to say doesn't misleadingly conceal

Whichever factors you've given the highest ratings reflect what
you value most. Your ratings provide a quick guide to your own soft
spots. That makes it easier to figure out which frog-to-prince lies
will be likeliest to hook you, since these lies display precisely what
you are looking for. For example, if you view a man's readiness to
commit as critical, you're more likely to be taken in by claims that
he's looking for a serious relationship. If an inquiring mind is high
on your most-wanted list, someone who boasts the right degrees and
flashes his intellect will hit your soft spot. By being aware of the
preferences that make you vulnerable to certain kinds of lies, you
stay a step ahead of synchronicity. Otherwise the principle of synchronicity is more likely to work in his favor when he tells you what
you are predisposed to hear.

Regardless of what you are looking for, what's important here is that you know your own vulnerabilities. These soft spots are also most likely to become your blind spots—precisely those areas of synchronicity where who he *pretends to be* perfectly fits who you *want him to be*. It is what you seek and most long for that predisposes you to believing the wannabe prince and to suppressing your skepticism.

Try Sitting on His Lily Pad

Put yourself in his place. Take Robb, who isn't wealthy, has an average IQ, and would much rather continue to watch "Beavis and Butthead" than stretch his intellect by acquiring an M.B.A. When it comes to sex, he's a bit of a gadabout. Still, he wants to attract you for a quick romance or even a longer relationship—as long as he remains free to philander.

Even though he acts like a couch potato, when it comes to knowing what women are looking for in a man, he's no dummy. By some feat of osmosis, he and his friends have managed to commit your shopping list, chapter and verse, to memory. They know it even better than you do. He's all set to hook you.

Then he faces reality. He looks in the mirror and confronts a distressingly ordinary frog whose challenge is to croak louder and smarter than the rest.

What "smarter" may mean is taking a step or two back to listen for a while. Then, like this thirty-five-year-old single computer programmer, he selects the right answer—telling a woman whatever he thinks she might want to hear: *"I learned that women like to hear certain things, for example, 'No, I'm not seeing someone else.' But I am having sex with someone else. The woman's interpretation has to do with exclusivity. Technically she's asking the wrong question. Or women like to hear that you're on good terms with old girlfriends. So I talk about my old girlfriend in glowing terms. Or that you haven't had sex for some time, that you hadn't been in a sexual relation. So you lie about sexual encounters. You keep the casual ones hidden."*

But you do not have to believe these frog-to-prince lies. While empathy is generally desirable, unfounded trust is not. So let's begin to cull out his frog-to-prince lies, to understand that many of his claims are mere mating signals, not affirmations of his honesty and goodness.

As one sadder but wiser woman I interviewed reflected: *"When it seems too good to be true, it usually is. There's what I call 'paralleling'—whatever you like, he likes too. The purpose of paralleling is to ingratiate the man to you. He makes you think you're starting*

something special, a special connection, but what he's doing is help-
ing create the right conditions for immediate sex."

What he calls "telling them what they want to hear" and what
she calls "paralleling" are really alternate ways of looking at
intended synchronicity. It's time to acknowledge that even though
his immediate goal may be casual sex, he wants you to believe he is
a prince and to respect him—at least until dawn's early break.

Top-of-the-Chart Frog-to-Prince Lies

It pays to get on a first-name basis with the most common types
of frog-to-prince lies. Even though the list below won't capture them
all, it will ground you in the basics. Compare these top ten categories of lies with the factors you rate as most important in defining
a desirable man. Which fit yours most closely? Remember that
wherever there's a close correspondence between your ideal and who
he pretends to be, you are more likely to be vulnerable to his frog-
to-prince misrepresentations. Which ones have "gotcha" so far?

THE TEN MOST COMMON TYPES OF FROG-TO-PRINCE LIES

1. Lies About Money

"I make a great salary. I've got the Mercedes paid off."
"I made a lot of money on the stock market. I live off my
   trust fund."
"We'll go to the most exclusive restaurants."

2. Lies About Prestige

"My great-great grandfather was the first mayor of this
   town."
"All the men in my mother's family attended West Point."
"I'm going to run for Congress some day."

3. Lies About Career

"I'm getting a big promotion next month."
"I'm going to law school in the fall."
"My new play will open in New York next season."
"I'm a physician."

"I have my own business."
"I work for the CIA."

4. Lies About Intelligence

"I'm a member of Mensa."
"I was valedictorian of my class."
"I'm working on my Ph.D."
"I never study for my exams."

5. Lies About Readiness for a Relationship

"I want to be in a relationship."
"I'm tired of one-night stands."
"I want to get married and start a family."

6. Lies About Sexual History

"I've never had a sexually transmitted disease."
"I tested negative for HIV."
"I've had sex with only two women in the past year."
"I always practice safe sex."

7. Lies About Sensitivity

"I belong to a men's group."
"I love to write poetry."
"I'm in touch with my inner child."
"I consider myself a feminist."

8. Lies About Availability

"I'm single."
"I'm not seeing anyone right now."
"I'm getting a divorce."
"I broke up with my girlfriend."

9. Lies About Interest in Casual Sex

"I want a long, long relationship with you."
"I'm a one-woman man."
"You'll never get rid of me."

10. Lies About Honesty and Other Values

"I'd never lie to you."
"I'm not a liar."
"Spirituality is important to me."
"I live by the Golden Rule."
"What you see is what you get!"

Which are the most common of the common? Two stand out above the crowd: occupational and marital makeovers.

If what a man does for a living defines who he is, a whole lot of men are redefining themselves. Among the women I interviewed, nearly one-third talked about men either enhancing or flat-out lying about what they did for a living. Once upon a time he had a subscription to *Psychology Today*, so he calls himself a media psychologist; he gave to United Way twice last year, and now he's a community philanthropist. Believe it or not, an entire army of impostors are fighting for your tender loving attention. Who are they? They could be anybody, and that of course is the problem! The drabbest of clerks or bureaucrats can transform themselves in a single convincing phrase into the most glamorous of pilots, designers, actors, sportscasters, lobbyists, or CEOs.

The second most common makeover, marital status, is more problematic. It might not matter to you if he is a baker or a surgeon, but you might think long and hard about getting involved with the married father of five. Marital makeovers are almost always instant and proceed in only one direction. He transforms himself from married to single as he speaks. He rationalizes his metamorphosis with a litany of "why nots." Since he's only been married a year—what the heck—*why not* say he's still single? He has just separated from his wife, so *why not* say he's divorced? True, he may wish he were still single or newly divorced, but when he puts that Band-Aid over his wedding ring, *why not* say he's gone too far?

A Less Obvious Reason for Frog-to-Prince Lies

Once you recognize the pattern and shape of his frog-to-prince lies, you're ready to understand the reasons behind them.

We've already discussed how men use frog-to-prince lies to hook you into a relationship. Among the ninety-five men and women I interviewed, 50 percent of the men and 60 percent of the women independently volunteered that men lie most frequently and predictably at the beginning of the relationship when they want to impress you.

But frog-to-prince lies serve another purpose well beyond hooking you. That purpose is rooted in who he is. It is more personal than interpersonal. Some men use frog-to-prince lies to help narrow the gap between the real and the ideal—who they *really are* versus who they think they *ought to be*.

The Problem Is Inside Him

The war that's raging is really inside him. This comes as a surprise to a lot of women, because many a man who feels that his real self doesn't measure up to his ideal self looks more like a prince than a frog—at least on the surface. He may even sport most of the attributes on your hit list. He looks and acts just like the women's magazines say a desirable man should: bright, ambitious, reasonably educated, financially secure, employed, sensitive, handsome. So what's wrong?

The problem is internal. Often, no amount of objective achievement will help him overcome it. For reasons that probably stem from his childhood, his original family situation, and the effect of unrelenting and unrealistic expectations about what it takes to be a successful male, he doesn't feel good about himself. When the gap between his real and ideal self feels vast, he has a serious problem. He hasn't measured up to his own tough standards, never mind yours.

Down deep, he feels like a frog through and through.

From his vantage point, it's obvious to him that you would see him as lacking too—*if you only knew who he really was.*

The objective truth of his achievements or attractiveness is irrelevant to him. In fact, for some would-be princes there is a paradoxical effect: the more he accomplishes, the less likely he feels loved for himself. At the same time, he relentlessly compares himself to others who seem better and brighter and more successful. Under these conditions even a well-educated and prestigious contender for your affections could feel woefully inadequate when it comes to distinguishing himself from all the other contenders for a woman's love.

Sometimes this leads him to the lie.

As one pragmatic and still single thirty-four-year-old male engineer put it: "I lie about anything where an honest approach would make me appear ineligible."

He'll do anything just to make sure you don't throw him back into the well with all the other frogs. Why? This same man later added: *"I lie to avoid rejection ... due to lack of security about whether I will be accepted and loved for myself."*

His job is to convince you *both* that he's no frog. But oddly enough, it may be a lot easier to convince you than himself.

The sanest way for you to view all this is that his frog-to-prince lies are truly *his* problem. They defend him against the bleakness of his own reality. The sad paradox is that when he fools and wins you over, it only convinces him even further that no one could love him for who he really is.

These lies also communicate a powerful message. They tell you that:

Whoever he eventually turns out to be, he's not all that comfortable with it.
And no matter how much you like him, you probably shouldn't be either.

Spotting the Frog-to-Prince Lie

Many women are naive about the degree to which some men will embellish or transform their identity when the truth would have done just fine. The trick is to stay alert to the possibility of the frog-to-prince lie and other lies without turning unduly cynical.

So the next time you hear what you think might be a frog-to-prince lie, don't just shrug it off. Instead:

- *Let it sink in.* Mull it over a bit, wonder about it.
- *Relate the lie to what you value.* Consider whether he is lying about something you believe is an important attribute.
- *Check for selective attention.* Ask yourself whether you are paying attention only to those things he says that match what you are looking for.
- *Pinpoint his pattern of lies.* Use the checklist that follows to think about the specifics of what he might be lying about in his past, his present, or his future.

These techniques help keep you focused. They also help you assess your own reactions so you can begin to develop a self-defense strategy. Frog-to-prince lies range from the mundane (several women told me men had lied about their eye color by wearing colored contact lenses; their height and weight; even their shirt size) to the deadly (criminal history, sexual history, health, and marital status).

Sometimes these early relationship lies seem so sweetly desperate that you're inclined to forgive them, when in fact they are merely the first in a whole series of lies built upon lies. That's what happened to Marisa in her relationship with Saul, who eventually proved to be a highly skilled con artist who captured her time and cash. Note how, even after the fact of lost time, faith, and money—and despite her raging anger—she still extends him the benefit of the doubt and grants him sympathy, not justice: *"Saul lied about his age—he said he was forty-nine; he was fifty-three. I found out when I saw it on his driver's license six months into the relationship. I'm sensitive to people's insecurities—not to their lies. He lied to protect his self-esteem and because he thought I was younger."*

It's easy to overlook the small stuff in the drama of the moment or with someone you long to trust. Use the following checklist to counteract the deadly joint blinders of synchronicity and selective attention. Or to refresh your memory about the enormous range of events, places, facts, and intentions that anyone can fudge at will. Feel free to add categories from your own experiences that aren't on the list.

CHECKLIST FOR SPOTTING HIS FROG-TO-PRINCE LIES

His Past	His Present	His Future
___where he grew up	___where he lives	___where he plans to live
___his family history	___whom he lives with	___his family commitments
___schools he attended	___his educational level	___his educational plans
___his past earnings	___current earnings	___future earnings
___past wealth	___current finances	___financial ambition
___where he has worked	___where he works	___his career plans
___children fathered	___children responsible for	___desire for children
___marital history	___current marital status	___intent to marry
___sexual history	___his current sexual partners	___sexual exclusivity
___his medical history	___his health/fitness	___how fit he'll become
___what he has achieved	___his accomplishments	___his ambition
___where he's traveled	___his adventures	___his wanderlust

Red Flags to Watch Out For

As you think about early relationship lies, watch out for these red flags:

- He misrepresents his marital or relationship status.
- He distorts his current situation—job, residence, friendships, etc.
- He creates a string of lies about basic personal statistics: his age, height, weight, ethnicity, nationality, citizenship.
- He tells gratuitous lies that seem to serve no purpose whatsoever.
- You catch him in a series of contradictions about his past or current personal or professional circumstances.
- He makes statements about your future together that strike you as premature or extreme ("I want you to move in with me," or "I'm going to buy you a diamond necklace").

If any of these flags pop up, conduct your own thorough investigation. Refuse to be misled by his words. Look past his words for the facts and data that support or refute them. No matter what the actual facts of the situation turn out to be, they are much friendlier close up than the lie. Over and over again, it's what you *don't* see that will hurt you. Think of yourself as your own private eye. Public records like marriage licenses, birth certificates, and divorce decrees are available to you at city hall. If you're seriously hooked on him and very suspicious, check it out.

The good thing is that unless he's very smart and very well practiced, you'll probably catch him in the act of deceiving you. Whether it takes a month, a year, or more, eventually you will catch the frog who pretends to be a prince, *because the one thing he truly can't make over is who he really is.*

The question is never *whether* you'll catch on, only *when.*

Far better to invest time and effort at the front end of a relationship then after you've bet the ranch on elusive "vaporware" that never materializes.

Gender and Deception

Frog-to-prince lies aren't hard to spot once you know what to look for. In a 1991 study, psychologists William Tooke and Lori Camire asked 110 male and female university students to rate how often they had used eighty-eight different deceptive tactics, from bragging "to make myself seem better than I am" to "sucking in my stomach when I'm around members of the opposite sex."

What they found was revealing. In male-female relationships, men more often than women used deceptive strategies that involved acting as if they had more resources than they actually had, and as if they were kinder, more sincere, and more trustworthy than they actually were. But how effective were these deceptions?

Frog-to-Prince Deceptions That Work

These same psychologists asked a new group of 116 university men and women just how effective the same eighty-eight deceptive acts were in increasing their own sex's desirability with a partner. Men rated the early relationship deceptions they used most often—the tried-and-true—as most effective. This suggests men feel their current deceptions do the job. Men felt most effective with women when they misrepresented:

- How sincere or kind they were.
- How macho they were.
- How well off they were.
- How intelligent they were.
- How sensitive and vulnerable they were.
- How much they cared about a woman when they really didn't.

What about women? Don't they use a separate but equal form of the frog-to-prince lie? Yes, but with a striking difference!

Women's Frog to-Princess Lies

Women's chief deception with men was *making themselves look better than they really were*—more physically attractive, taller, thinner, tanner, younger, sexier. So women's most frequent frog-to-princess lies create a facade of makeup, false fingernails, and slimming vertical stripes, while men's most frequent ones create a more varied deceptive patchwork of material resources, readiness for a relationship, and a mix of attitudes, behaviors, and "masculinity." These differences are as informative as they are astounding.

They sound a warning about what men's frog-to-prince lies are and are not. Unlike women's early dating deceptions centered on using makeup and clothing to make themselves look prettier, sexier, and thinner, men's frog-to-prince lies are neither small cosmetic shadings nor nip-and-tuck enhancements. They're often major surgery. They're not "I want your attention" flirting routines either. Although these frog-to-prince lies may begin with a line or two, they're not likely to end there. When lying is an effective way to achieve goals, it becomes one more tactic to use as needed.

Which among women's frog-to-princess makeovers actually worked? Not much sizzle here. Women rated their benign, nonverbal deceptions—like wearing makeup, wearing tight clothing, attractively fixing hair, acting more feminine—as their most effective tactics with men.

When it comes to impression management, it appears that men may prefer words and actions to hook, while women dabble in the visual—makeup, clothing, and magazine-like femininity.

Vive la différence? Perhaps. But how does it play out? Of course we know that many women rival and occasionally surpass men in their ability to misrepresent, distort, and obscure the truth. Still, for these early dating deceptions, what are the most serious repercussions of masquerading as a blond when you're really a brunette, or as flat-stomached jock rather than exposing a bit of flab? Suppose your cleavage *is* augmented by a Wonderbra. How does that square with his saying that he's interested in you when he's not, or that he's sensitive to the issues you care about most, at least until the end of his conversation with you?

Why Women Believe the Frog Could Be a Prince

So he's a frog. You've caught him. Turns out he's not single. He's quite married with three kids, a fourth on the way, a house in suburbia. What else? Okay. He's not a vice president, but he does work in the executive cafeteria. And by the way, he's not studying for his Ph.D. in psychology after all, but he has been in group therapy for six years. All lies that women I spoke with were told!

Pretty obvious and relatively easy to spot! Then why do women get reeled in by the frog-to-prince and other early relationship lies?

The Allure of the False Prince

The odd thing is, even after a woman has figured out what the frog is up to, she may still forgive him. Why? Because even though his identity is pure cotton-candy fluff, sugar-spun gossamer lacking substance, he has made her feel so very special. He has allowed her to be part of his glamorous life—however fictitious it may be. In turn she gives him special dispensation.

Why? Because the false prince is often a no-holds-barred charmer. Since his goal is to convince you he's no frog, he manages to do all the things that real princes are supposed to do. For many women this constitutes seduction of the highest order. He is a romantic who notices what you're wearing, your new haircut. He writes you notes and cards. He remembers the first month anniversary of your meeting, sends you flowers, chocolates, and gifts. He makes you laugh before he makes you cry.

And then when you do find out, you fall prey to the message of the Frog King fairy tale, that every frog could be a prince waiting for the princess to release him. But you stop short of throwing him against the wall and letting him feel the power of your rage over his lies. Even if this prince isn't quite what he's made himself out to be, you convince yourself that you and only you can help him on his journey toward princedom.

Too bad, because alchemy will sound like kid stuff after three months with this man. You will join the long line of women recounting a litany of regrets—"If he had just told me the truth," and "I wasted nine years of my life with a man who lived a lie," and "I just wish I'd never met him."

So let's reinforce our understanding of the frog-to-prince liar by repeating this mantra as many times as required: *Frog is frog is frog.*

What to Do With a False Prince: Rochelle's Story

How tempting is the frog-to-prince charmer? Even smart women who should know better can be taken in.

Rochelle, a lovely, single twenty-eight-year-old corporate manager, wanted my advice. After a three-year-long dry spell of finding no one she wanted to date, she fell for a coworker. Although Larry wasn't in her department, they worked on a joint project in the spring. He'd asked her out for a drink and they'd spent the evening laughing and talking. He was interested in all the same things she was: dancing, music, working out. As she described this man and her obvious pleasure in his company, I felt delighted that she had met someone who was interested in her. Still smiling, I asked, "So, what's the advice you're looking for?"

"Well," she said, "before I went out with Larry I asked a few people about him. I got the usual 'great guy.' They also said he was going through a divorce and that his wife had custody of their two little girls. I found out he lived in a cute little house in the suburbs.

"When we went out, I asked him how old his kids were. He bristled. Said he didn't have any. Was engaged once, never married. Now it was my turn to do a total double-take! Of course, I couldn't tell him I'd been snooping. So I said nothing, but I've had this knot in my stomach all week. After we finish talking I'm going out to dinner with him at this great place. And I'm still excited about him, but something's wrong.

"You're probably going to say that I always find a reason for breaking off a good thing. Should I let go of the whole thing about his wife and the kids? They *are* getting a divorce."

I asked if she'd checked with her original sources to be sure that she'd gotten everything right, and that they were talking about Larry.

"Are you kidding? You bet! The next morning! I said, 'You made an awful mistake about Larry. Or were you just teasing me? He doesn't have any kids, he's never been married, and he lives in a little apartment in the city, not a house!' My friend in his department said she'd met his wife and kids at the mall. He even had pictures of them on his desk before the divorce. He told everyone he was renewing his lease on the house.

"Dr. Hollander, should I just forget it and see where it goes, and just have a good time?"

What would you have advised Rochelle?

The bleak truth here is that Larry breached her trust *when he didn't have to*. By doing that, he revealed that whatever his internal battles might be, he's unlikely to share them. Merely owning up to his marital status and fatherhood constituted a major challenge. What Larry overlooked is that our actions boomerang to find us again and again.

Even though Rochelle now knows Larry is lying to her, she doesn't get angry. *Instead, she copes by doubting her own judgment.* The idea that a colleague would lie about having children is alien to her. She can't imagine why he would hide a wife and family when she wouldn't reject him just because his marriage failed. But once she recognizes his lies, instead of questioning him, Rochelle questions herself. She wonders if it's unreasonable to expect unadulterated truth from her wannabe prince. She genuinely wants to pursue this relationship, yet his lie sticks in her craw.

So, how should it end? Again, what would you advise Rochelle? Here is what I told her, "Rochelle, neither of us knows why

Larry lied to you. But he isn't lying about his shirt size. He's lying about who he is. Being attracted to him won't overcome that. If it would, you wouldn't be here asking for advice. Liking merely allows you to connect, to see what else you have in common. Next, you need to find out whether Larry is a man you can trust. And here, Larry's already showing his true colors, waving the proverbial red flag in your face. Forge forward and what will you get? A couple of nights in bed with a liar? Falling in love with a liar? Ask yourself if this is what you want in a significant relationship. If not, slow down. Ask yourself hard questions about what's important to you. *Forget about changing him.* Even if you succeeded, a layer of residual distrust will cloud the relationship as it progresses. In the heat of battle you'll both shade the truth now and then. And when that happens you'll flash back to how this man gratuitously lied to you over the first round of drinks.

"If you're going to see Larry, enjoy the food, music, and conversation. Then talk straight. Tell him flat out that you don't believe him. Tell him why. Watch what he does. If he hangs on to his story, check one last time with his coworkers. Then you'll feel confident you've done the right thing. Look him up in last year's telephone directory and see where he lived then, what his telephone number was. If it's a different number, call and see who answers.

"If he says, 'I didn't want you to know about my wife and kids 'cause I didn't want you to think less of me,' discuss how you *both feel.* Then if you're satisfied, proceed. *But with caution.* Maybe he's telling the truth; maybe he's telling you what you want to hear. Only time and careful observation will tell.

"If he is lying, walk away. Don't look back. Consider yourself lucky he showed his hand early. Suppose you fell in love with him. What would you get? The major heartache that comes from loving a gratuitous liar. You don't have the power to change *this* frog into a prince. Frog is frog."

Defend Yourself: Somebody Has To

What can you do to protect yourself from a man who presents himself as better or different than he is? Plenty! Develop a series of self-defense strategies that protect *you,* not him. Start with the list of suggestions that follows. Refuse to proceed with blind trust. Remind yourself that trust has to be earned. Realize that even though self-defense is necessary and important, you still may resist it. Why? Because early in a relationship the last thing you want to do is play Sherlock Holmes. You'd rather have delightful romance and runaway fun than crack the case! But why be a patsy for the predictable frog-to-prince lie? Why find out too late that you've fallen in love with what's not, and won't ever be?

Instead, be level-headed and curious. Ask probing questions about everything he says in the early stages.

If you feel that investigating the facts or challenging the lie is too unromantic, tuck into your data bank this twenty-six-year-old single charmer's approach to truth-in-packaging related to his sexual history: *"I had a minor STD from a prior relationship. In the early stages of a relationship, I wouldn't tell a woman that. I'm not being overly paranoid; I'm just looking at self-interest. I want to establish the possibility of getting the relationship going and not making myself a leper for something one in five sexually active people have."*

He and others like him have no problem at all looking after their own self-interest, even when it's at your expense. Why not ensure your own self-protection? When it comes to your relationships, who is watching out for you and your best interests?

A thirty-seven-year-old married woman I interviewed told me, "In the beginning, it's hard to tell they're lying because you trust them. You start questioning in the middle." But by then, of course, it's often too late. You took the bait. To prevent this, why not adopt the following self-defense strategies?

A FEW FROG-TO-PRINCE LIE SELF-DEFENSE STRATEGIES

What to Do

- Make it your rule to take nothing at face value.

- Ask factual questions like a reporter gathering data.

- Ask to meet his friends and family, see his dog.

- Meet him at his office, and show up early.

- Check his phone number, his address in the white pages, the company where he works.

- Call him in the morning, midday at home.

- Note any synchronicity between what you want and what he presents.

- Tell him you hold him accountable for what he says.

- Track and confront any and all inconsistencies.

- Recognize when he is self-promoting and see it for what it is.

- Tell him your standards for honesty and trust, and see if he adapts to them.

- If a pattern of lying continues, together seek professional counseling or end the relationship.

What Not to Do

- Sweetly trust the word, above all else.

- Listen politely and soak it up.

- Let him keep you isolated from people he knows.

- Meet him only on neutral turf—a museum, the dock.

- Don't take his number, have him call you.

- Assume he isn't living with anyone.

- Accept whatever he says as reflecting him, not you.

- Take a "whatever" laissez-faire attitude.

- Overlook inconsistencies, make excuses for him.

- Conclude he is terrific and see it his way.

- Silently go along with his program and wait to see how things turn out.

- If a pattern of lying continues, commiserate with your friends.

From Fairy Tale to Real Life

What lessons can we learn from frog-to-prince lies? The fairy tale gives us a powerful paradigm for change. *Communicating genuine emotions creates a powerful opportunity for change.*

We also see how many frog-to-prince lies are fueled by men's fear of rejection. The possibility that a powerful woman might cast them back into the well scares them. But at the same time they also crave intimacy and connection. Their lies may be a strategy for addressing this dilemma. *Frog-to-prince lies allow them to distin-*

guish themselves, forestalling a woman's rejection and temporarily winning her attention and admiration.

Women face a different dilemma. Do they search for a prince who displays all the valued attributes on their wish list, keeping guard against misleading synchronicity and frog-to-prince lies? Or do they accept a lovable but ordinary man who presents himself and all his flaws more honestly? Making sane choices is a challenge when a man offers a woman what she finds most attractive. *After all, she is far readier for genuine romance than for the detective work required to find out how genuine he's been about himself.*

In this scenario it's easy to see how honesty and truth-in-packaging become the first casualties in a long, long list.

How the Fairy Tale Might Play Out

Consider how this tale might play out. He hides who he is so you will love him and so he can hide his shame at being a frog and not a prince. You innocently wind up loving the fake prince and his *image* of success and macho virtue, not the real thing. By presenting himself as a prince, he wins your conditional love. Unfortunately, maintaining that love requires a cascade of supporting falsehoods. These lies protect both of you from the truth *and* from the intimacy. Both of you lose.

As the relationship unfolds, some discovery is inevitable, evoking a stream of excuses, disappointment, and discontent. Fairy tales teach us an important lesson. Both love and anger are powerful and engaging emotions that create the potential for enduring intimacy. Posing and pretending to be what we are not creates barriers and distance. Men who cloak themselves in a mantle of false grandeur or accomplishment, or in an alternative identity, wind up avoiding truth and intimacy. They may be loved, but not for who they are.

The alternative is to recognize frog-to-prince lies at the outset. To lay aside any hope that you can rescue the frog-to-prince liar and transform him. The more likely outcome is being stuck with both a frog and a liar! His past behavior is the best predictor of what's in store for you. A princely conversion, no matter how much you might wish it, isn't likely. You either have to accept him as he is and work with that or put him back in the well and move on.

From Hooks to Masks

Lies as hooks enhance and attract. The flirtation, the line, and the frog-to-prince lie bring a man and a woman close enough to see if they want to take the relationship to the next step. But once you're close enough to establish the intimacy you both seem to have wanted, something else may kick into gear. While lies as hooks enhance who he is to attract and draw you in, lies as masks hide and distort who he really is. So lies as masks create distance and reduce intimacy, while appearing to do just the opposite. Unlike either lines or frog-to-prince lies, lies as masks are far more difficult to spot and can prove far more malevolent to your relationship.

The next section discusses lies that mask and what to do about them.

Part 3
LIES AS MASKS

Chapter 5
Masquerade

Most men get women into long-term relationships—get them interested—by not being themselves. Then they find out it's not you. You're not as wealthy, funny, or you do something different. I present a non-lying picture of me. I go where I like to go, not pretending.
—Thirty-one-year-old divorced male political analyst

I can lie at any time or stage of the relationship, depending on my need to prevent disclosure, keep control, and avoid traveling down a path I'm not willing to go down. My lies help maintain the facade I want to present.
—Forty-three-year-old married male management consultant

Self-disclosure doesn't fit with my priorities.
—Twenty-nine-year-old single male law student

A mask hides. It flashes a misleading facade to the world that throws friend and foe, self and others off course. The mask's deception may be intentional or unintentional, pernicious or innocent. But since intimacy requires both knowing and being known by another human being, the masked man (or woman) is condemned to fail.

Lies often evolve into masks rather than begin that way. We learn early on that who we are isn't acceptable to our family, our friends. Or we find that we don't measure up to some cultural ideal that prescribes how a boy or girl is supposed to look or act. So we pull down the shades and lock the door on who we really are and go forth into the world, lying to conceal our secrets. Sometimes we just lie to others. Sometimes we guard our secrets so well that we begin to lie to ourselves.

In relationships, some masks that men wear are extensions of the hooks they use to snare women with the glittering lure of the line or a transformational frog-to-prince lie. When he tells her he's a banker (and he's really a teller at a bank), he might see his lie as harmless and temporary. He rationalizes the lie as a technical truth. After all, he does work in a bank, doesn't he? He assures himself, "I'll tell her the whole truth when she gets to know me better and understands who I am." But you know what? The longer he lets the lie go undisturbed, the harder it becomes to reveal the truth. What begins as an ephemeral boast or transient bit of hyperbole hardens into something unexpectedly permanent, into a comforting mask that he can't or doesn't want to remove.

The result? What you hear and see may be nothing at all like what you eventually get. The lie as mask hides his feelings, his motives, and his thoughts. It eventually may feel so natural that even he has trouble peeling it away.

Both men and women wear masks. Even though our focus is on men's lies, in this chapter we are going to discuss the masks each gender wears. Identifying the masks common to each gender helps us to see how masks subtly prevent intimacy and foster lies, even in our closest relationships.

The Kissing Cousins: Hooks, Masks, and Evasions

There are many kinds of lies and many ways to sort them. One way is to look at lies according to three functions they serve in relationships: hooks, masks, and evasions. We've just looked at lies as hooks, and we're about to discuss lies as masks. Later, we'll get to lies as evasions. What do these lies have in common, and how do we tell them apart?

What lies as hooks, masks, and evasions have in common is one overarching aim: To make *him, not you,* the gatekeeper of who gets to know the truth.

You can accurately identify the three kissing cousins of hooks, masks, and evasions when you begin to realize that each type of lie hides a different aspect of who he is in relation to you:

- The *hook* pulls you closer by offering you a variety of wish-list items that he thinks top your most-wanted list.
- The *mask* disguises who he is, what he feels, and what he thinks.
- The *evasion* makes his actions inaccessible to you so he can do whatever he wants far away from your scrutiny.

All effectively keep you in the dark, but not out of harm's way. Sometimes lies as hooks, masks, and evasions overlap and seem so similar that you can hardly distinguish one from the other. None of this makes deciphering his lies easy. So how are you supposed to figure it out? Let's have some fun sorting hooks, masks, and evasions by looking at the three little words that men and women ranked in the top three lies men tell women.

Deciphering the Biggest Lie of All

> *Be sure it's true, when you say "I love you."*
> *It's a sin to tell a lie.*
> *Millions of hearts have been broken*
> *Just because these words were spoken.*
> —FROM THE SONG "IT'S A SIN
> TO TELL A LIE"

He says, "I love you." For most women hope and trust dictate that when a man says, "I love you," he means it. And *sometimes* he does. But, unfortunately, as too many women have learned, "I love you" can often be the biggest lie of all.

Consider these three look-alike lies, "I love you" and two variations.

Which do you think is a hook? A mask? An evasion?

- Lie 1. "I knew I loved you from the moment you walked through the door."

- Lie 2. "I love you."

- Lie 3. "You know I still love you."

What's the difference? Among these three, the only difference is in his intent, which isn't apparent in the moment. How could you possibly know? Only by understanding the context and circumstances of the lie and doing some serious investigating. Let's get a handle on how to untangle the three "I love you" look-alikes.

Untangling the Look-alikes

Lie 1. "I knew I loved you from the moment you walked through the door."

Lie 1 is a hook.

Intent: To pull you closer in and keep you there.

As lies go, "I knew I loved you from the moment you walked through the door" is a hook. It takes its undeserved credibility from the myth of love at first sight, which romanticizes the magical instant you meet. His lie seduces you with its fairy tale mimicry. A bit of romance paired with your expectations allow him to effortlessly use this hook to draw you closer and reassure you. When this lie comes too early, long before either of you could possibly know who the other is, you can bet he knew no such thing when you walked through that door. Maybe he lusted after you. Maybe he thought you looked open and friendly. Or, less flattering, maybe his gang merely designated you the pick of a so-so litter at that particular event.

Your best short-term strategy is to view this hook as harmless. See it as a form of revisionist history in the service of your budding relationship. Consider that this hook derives its power from his skillful reading of your needs relative to his own. He's betting you want to be seen as stunningly attractive, special, and sexy. And, oh yes, he hopes to coax you into seeing him as fabulously smooth, romantic, and charming. That's the beauty. The lie as hook works to literally pull two total strangers together. Its sole intent is to attract you. The problem here is that you could be so eager for love and a relationship that you forget this hook's normal composition is 60 percent hype and 40 percent testosterone. If he's this fast and forward in his profession of love *before he knows who you are*, chances are it's worked for him before or he doesn't care who you turn out to be after the first night.

Much later in a relationship, after you've been together awhile, he might use this same lie ("I knew I loved you from the minute . . . ") to build a shared past and create your own romantic mythology. While still untrue, this self-serving mythology ("I remember the first time I saw you. I knew I loved you from the minute . . . ") becomes an effective hook that reinforces your feelings of being special. It holds the two of you together. Of course, just to complicate things, let's not forget that there are a few truly romantic souls out there who genuinely believe in love at first sight, and for them, this statement is no lie.

Lie 2. "I love you."

Lie 2 is a mask.

Intent: To cover what he's really thinking or feeling.

Like a lot of seductive lies men and women tell each other, even when "I love you" is a disappointing lie, it temporarily grants you something you sincerely, perhaps even desperately, wish for. That makes you less likely to challenge the mask of "I love you."

Too bad his "I love you" lie covers up the fact that what he is feeling is lust, not love, or perhaps that he's really feeling precious little. When "I love you" is a mask, it allows him to conform to what he believes a woman wants sexually: a sincere declaration of his feeling. That way he is doing the right thing, gaining your acceptance by giving you what *he thinks* you want to hear.

The fact that "I love you" can also easily be a truth adds to its tantalizing ambiguity and increases the stakes. This creates a dilemma. How to tell the truth from the lie?

Maybe he says "I love you" in the middle of lovemaking. You relax and bask in feeling loved. You don't realize that lasting love is not what's on his mind at all.

According to the men and women I interviewed, "I love you" is one of the most common lies that men tell women. In another study reported by David Buss in his 1994 book, *The Evolution of Desire*, over 70 percent of college-aged men said they exaggerated the depth of their feelings to have sex with a woman, and a stunning 97 percent of college-aged women said they had personally experienced this in their relations with men.

Sherman, a forty-two-year-old never-married information systems consultant, says his own "I love you" lies are just hooks to "get a woman into bed." He remembers his first lie to a woman being "'I love you'—to my first girlfriend." Why did he lie about being in love to a fifteen-year-old girl? Because "I wanted to get past first base and hit a home run." Since he grew up Baptist, he learned that "you only have sex 'cause you love each other, so I say 'I love you' as a tool to open doors."

But once he's into her bed, Sherman says he stops the lies. Why? Because he no longer needs them: "By then you already know you're going to reach your goal." Then a funny thing happens as we talk. Despite what Sherman has just said to me, he completely contradicts himself, noting that he *often lies once he has a woman in bed*, "just to make them more excited—by saying things like 'I love you' or talking during sex."

And despite his declaration of love, he confesses, "I had no compunction about fulfilling my urges with other women. My hormones were talking. After a while we both knew 'I love you' was a lie. It was a pattern I had gotten used to, and *it was so successful, I just kept on using it*."

Sherman's initial hook had become a mask. It was successful, it got him just what he wanted, and it was so effortlessly comfortable he couldn't just toss it away.

Sherman's lie is no anomaly in this. His intent, like that of many men, is to get a woman sexually excited to increase his own pleasure, and he's learned somewhere along the way that "I love you" is the magic key that unlocks her passion. So for Sherman, "I love you" is part hook, to draw the woman into bed with him. It's also part mask, to hide his detachment from his own and her emotions as well as his real motive (heightened sexual pleasure), which is light years away from the intimacy he promises.

It's natural for most women to draw the conclusion that a man's freely volunteered "I love you" reflects what he sincerely feels ("we'd been dating; there was no reason not to believe him"). To you, the three little "I love you" words may feel sacred enough that you don't want to doubt or test the limits. But for him "I love you" may be anything but sacred. He may even say "I love you" to cover his guilt over lusting after another woman, or over having sexual fantasies that you have no place in.

Of course, sometimes "I love you" means just that. And when it does, it's wonderful. But when it doesn't, his words are a deceitful mask that hide what he really thinks and feels.

Lie 3. *"You know I still love you."*

Lie 3 is an evasion.

Intent: To shroud his actions so he can do whatever he wants free of your scrutiny.

You notice how cool he is toward you. How what used to charm him now only irritates. You could cut the tension between the two of you with a knife. So you ask, "What's going on?" He showers you with reassurances punctuated with, "C'mon, sweetheart, *you know I still love you.*" Maybe he does, and maybe he doesn't. But when this statement is a lie of evasion, it's what *he doesn't tell* about where he's going and whom he's seeing that's the critical missing piece of information. By telling you what he thinks you want to hear, he hopes to cover up what he's really doing with his time and his life, and anything else that he thinks you'd either dislike or interfere with. The evasive lie buys him freedom to do his own thing and set his own course.

Recognizing Hooks, Masks, and Evasions

Sure it's confusing. Lies *are* confusing. Try thinking about it this way. The main difference among these lies is *intent*. But when you first hear the lie, you won't be able to figure out what his intent is, at least not right away. That takes time and observation. What are you supposed to do in the interim?

Get familiar with the most common hooks, masks, and evasions, and the reasons men give for them. See if you can identify them in novels and movies. Get some practice. Use this knowledge to think more critically about what's happening in your own relationship. Take a step back and listen to the dialogue. Ask yourself what these lies conceal or disguise. Let yourself be curious. Get more information. Probe what's happening as you watch the scenario unfold. The circumstances around the lie will help you decide. Listen closely to the experiences of other women too, and without becoming unduly cynical, see what you can learn that may save you unnecessary grief.

Even though you may not know his intent, what he is lying about will have real consequences, from the trivial to the life-threatening, that could affect your trust, your relationship, and your health.

When Masks Become a Habit

The lies we tell each other in relationships are rarely one-timers. Nor do the lies we're told appear one day and disappear the next. They are deeply rooted in who the person telling the lie is and has been. Of course, lies also reflect the situation and what the liar has to gain or lose at this point in the relationship. But his lies usually have far more to do with who he is than with who you are. It's easy for the lie to become a way of life.

Our friend Sherman says that when it comes to lies, he's a lot like a social drinker. He explains, "I only tell 'social lies' to women so I can be perceived positively—until something better comes along." Sherman uses the lie to hold his place with the current woman and hedge his bets while shopping for a better buy. But then he suddenly demonstrates the seductive nature of the lie as mask when he adds, his voice cracking with emotion: *I'm not sure that my lies stop when I find the right person.*

The problem Sherman has encountered here is that once his lies get going, they develop a life of their own. He feels like a spectator. It's as if the lie, not Sherman, has taken charge while he looks on.

Even though Sherman sounds as if he is addicted to lies, these lies began innocently enough. They were convenient hooks that bolstered his image to make him appear attractive and resourceful enough to enter into a relationship with a desirable woman. But once he finds his best buy, his ideal woman, how does he suddenly turn off the lies to expose who he really is so he can connect with her?

The question is: How do any of us who lie, or who have been lied to, stop the music? How do we stop the lying?

Jeremiah, a thirty-five-year-old married agency administrator, is a master at using lies "to draw the person in and create intimacy and interest." But once he gets closer, he encounters a new problem. The hook he used so successfully is replaced by a mask, "a protective shell," that refuses to fall away as he moves deeper into the relationship. Jeremiah talks about the secrets he routinely keeps from women in his life, saying: *"I don't like to be questioned about my past, my background. Women have a tendency to ask questions about my background. I like to build a protective shell around me so I don't get hurt. Instead, I end up hurting other people."*

His mask, like many we will see in this chapter, is two parts omission and one part commission. He hides himself by silently fending off intrusions into his inner sanctum. He stops just short of using smoke and mirrors to distort and disguise who he is. By wearing the lie as mask, Jeremiah protects himself from being known and judged, and *ultimately from being loved.*

Does he fool the woman he is hiding himself from?

Jeremiah thinks not: *"They know immediately. She says, 'There are a lot of things you're not telling me. Only you know the whole story.'"* But what Jeremiah misses, perhaps intentionally, is that at this juncture in the relationship, she is inviting him to reveal the whole story. Jeremiah can choose to tell the truth and risk being vulnerable to get closer. Or he can deny his omissions and preserve the comfort of the status quo.

What does he do? He shifts his mask from omission to outright commission by choosing denial: *"Of course, I maintain that I've told them everything."* He adds major insult to injury by lying to her about concealing the truth she already knows is there. So Jeremiah's lie isolates him from the woman who wants to come closer. But at the same time it wins him privacy and safety. Whether he's aware of it or not, he has traded the possibility of intimacy for the lonely certainty of control. He has joined the masquerade.

The Masquerade

There are times when we all hide our face so no one will ever find us. Men are not alone in this. But which masks are the most common ones that men and women wear in relationships? Here are eight common masks men talked about wearing in their relationships with women.

THE MASQUERADER'S BALL 1

The Most Common Masks Men Wear

1. The Mask of Stoicism

"I wasn't in touch with my feelings. I was denying the truth. I was just covering up my feelings more and more and stuffing myself in my own shit."

"I present myself as the strong silent type, reticent. In truth, I would rather not say and be thought a fool than say and be confirmed a fool."

"I'm not open about my true feelings on a topic. If I open up and tell my true feelings I may have to invest more time in the situation than I really want."

"I hide my feelings. How I feel about them, my reactions to their actions, openness."

2. The Mask of an Impermeable Past

"I won't tell any details about me, my past."

"I avoid telling anything the other person perceives as wrong. The past has no bearing on the present; it shouldn't matter."

"I don't tell political secrets, what happened in graduate school, radicalism, the number of jobs I've had. Women don't like it, aren't accepting of such a history."

3. The Mask of "Everything's Fine"

"I honestly tell them everything's fine when it's not."

"I hide how I actually feel about something; say that something's okay, not a problem. I do this mainly to avoid confrontation."

"When she touches me she can be a little rough. I say nothing. I don't tell her do it this way or that way. Instead, I
say, 'That feels really good.'"

4. The Mask of Financial Secrecy

"Any time I have someone over to my place, I shuffle my
bank statement in my drawer. Marge asked me about my
finances. I'm tight-lipped about finances. I see it as dangerous information."
"I hide my assets ($400,000) early in the relationship
because I don't want women to judge me on this basis."
"I have a total concealment of financial information and a
total fear of rejection 'cause I'm not wealthy enough."
"I don't perceive myself to be as socially desirable as others
are, so I attempt to overcome this deficiency by not talking about finance or wealth."

5. The Mask of Sexual Prowess and Revisionist Sexual History

"I feel I have to flaunt my sexual prowess. I know it's bullshit, but I have to keep the momentum up."
"I lie about having more experience than I really do. It's a
macho thing, that a man who's attained my age should
have more experience than I've had."
"I lie about the number of women I've been with. I get it
down to double digits."

6. The Mask of False Commitment

"My lie was that I wanted to spend the rest of my life with
her."
"I'd marry you in a New York minute."
"She asked if I had met anyone else. I said no, even though I
had, because I was in an awkward position. She thought
we still had a chance of getting back together."

7. The Mask of Sobriety or Abstinence

"I omitted to tell someone I've been in trouble with the law,
that I was arrested on DWIs. It would tarnish me, give a

negative view, so I'm pretty good at covering them up."

"I was smoking pot when I told a woman I was dating I quit. I was smoking behind her back for four years."

"The first time that I met her I told her, 'I used to drink a lot, but I no longer do.'"

8. The Mask of Honesty

"I don't lie, but I don't tell her the truth either."

"I'm honest in my relationships. Sure I tell women 'I love you' and 'That's the best sex I ever had,' but it's exaggeration, flattery—I don't see them as lies."

"When we first starting going out we established that it was critical that we be open and honest. Now it's not so much a lie as a 'not tell.'"

How do you feel when you look over these eight masks and the quotes that describe them? Perhaps you've already encountered the masks on this list and the real faces behind them. What sense do you get of the men behind the masks?

Years ago when I was still in graduate school I heard a discussion of a study that looked at how men and women felt when they put on their business suits and went forth in the world. It seemed men felt that their suits were like armor. No one could see through their drab gray flannel to their imperfections and frailties, or to judge them.

Women took a different view. They felt that the clothing they wore was near transparent. Instead of hiding them, it revealed them, along with all their imperfections. Even dressed to the hilt, they remained vulnerable.

The lies as masks that men don seem much like their business suits—an opaque psychological armor. These masks permit men to present an impenetrable face to the world and to those who wish to love them. They effectively block your perceptions of his true intentions, feelings, and past and current situations. So it's likely that he feels freer from discovery behind his mask, more effectively hidden than you would. What does this suggest? That the average man may be more audaciously confident, more secure in flaunting his masks to the outside world than a woman might be.

And why not? His masks have high payoff. They afford him the convenience of avoiding all that unpleasantness that comes from spending time and effort explaining himself to you. He is spared

from dealing with your upset, your need to confront and understand his attitude or the relationship. To paraphrase a line spoken
by the wolf in the Little Red Riding Hood story, his masks are "all
the better to avoid you with, my dear." A man's impenetrable mask
insulates his power and puts others on notice at the same time that
it protects him. As one man, a thirty-two-year-old single aeronautical engineer, said: *"Do I need to place myself in a situation where
I'm vulnerable and the other person is angry at me? Am I secure
enough to do this? . . . Rejection is a very big thing for me."*

It's easier to shut down. Beneath the powerful macho mask of
stoicism and an impenetrable past may lie his real fear of your
anger and rejection.

There is another downside to the various masks he has gotten so
comfortable in. They distance him from examining his own anger.
They leave no room for him to touch the emotional soft spot of his
own vulnerability. His impenetrable masks keep him from being
exposed to himself as well as the outside world. Sure, they make him
inaccessible to you. But often they make him inaccessible to himself
as well. His masks hold both *self-awareness* and *intimacy* at bay.

The Masks Women Wear

Women wear masks too. If they were identical to men's, we
would have instant understanding of men's lies as masks. But we
can't assume that women's masks will be the same as those of men.
As women talked about their own secrets and their own lies to men,
I deciphered many differences, as well as a few similarities, in the
masks each gender chooses. Compare the following six masks the
women I interviewed said they used to protect, conceal, and disguise
themselves in relationships with men.

THE MASQUERADER'S BALL 2

The Most Common Masks Women Wear

1. The Mask of Positive Thinking

"I walk and talk strong but inside I'm very fragile. I hide
    that I'm afraid of men, that I don't date."
"I hide my dysfunctional problems so I don't appear vulner-
    able."

2. The Mask of Sexual Inexperience

"I don't tell them how many men I've been intimate with, so they won't think badly of me. It's not accepted today that women are sexually active."

"I lie about previous sexual activity 'cause I'm afraid that they would judge me too harshly."

3. The Mask of a Normal Family Background

"I hide that my mother was an alcoholic. It's embarrassing."

"I never talk about my mother's manic depression. That we were homeless for two years when she couldn't hold a job. Everyone thinks I had a normal childhood."

"I don't disclose what I'm not proud of, like growing up in an alcoholic family. I don't make everything perfect. I tell some of the truth, but leave out details. I don't want to tell horror stories right away."

4. The Mask of Sexual Excitement

"I pretend to have orgasms to keep our relationship going."

"I lie about what feels good. My husband has a huge ego; he feels like he's God's gift. I coach him, but I hate to tell him the truth during the act. I don't think bedroom lies to reassure him are harmful."

5. The Mask of Nonvictimization

"I hide that I was date-raped and had an abortion after the date rape."

"Five years ago I was raped. I told no one—eventually my sister . . . When you tell you get picked apart. Suddenly you're a promiscuous woman. You're on trial."

6. The Mask of Financial Savvy

"I never talk about the money I spend on clothes and gifts. I act as if I spend next to nothing on my wardrobe so it's a nonissue. I hide my purchases from him and how

> much they cost. I feel embarrassed that I feel embar-
> rassed."
> "I hide that my family borrows money from me. Or I say it's
> only $25, when it's really $50."
> "I hide my income. I cover up 'cause I live in a prestigious
> place I can't afford."

The differences between the masks men and women wear in personal relations are striking. While men's masks often function to block any emotional readout, women's masks substitute a happy rather than blank face for their internal anxiety and fear. The women I talked with were more likely to put a positive spin on a host of less than ideal thoughts, relationships, and personal histories. Many women papered over a dysfunctional family history with a warm and inviting storybook "truth," whereas men simply sealed off their past and moved on. As men seem to protect themselves from being known, women seem to protect themselves from being classified as needy, different, or flawed.

Just as many women dress to minimize their physical imperfections, they also act stronger and more optimistic than they feel, pretend their original families are happier and more normal than they actually were. They avoid disclosing their past or present victimization even to those closest to them.

Like the heroines of those old girl-next-door films of the 1940s and 1950s, many women present themselves as being sexually inexperienced, but nonetheless responsive and ready to be shown the ropes by the right man. And many women strive to appear financially savvy, lest they be seen as inept, easy marks, extravagant, or gold diggers. Even among the women accountants and business owners I interviewed, several reported deferring publicly to their husbands' flawed financial judgments, while privately watching over the checkbook and hiding assets. And married women in particular seemed uncomfortable admitting that they had spent any money on themselves—their appearance, their wardrobe, or their general well-being.

Women's masks reveal that we are more likely to be embarrassed by not measuring up to some ideal standard. Many of us adapt and contort ourselves to match what we believe a man expects. Never mind that this approach moves us to compete with many unrealistic, airbrushed expectations. Never mind that we're likely to feel that our masks are transparent, allowing all the world to view our imperfection.

The Man Behind the Mask

*I lived with him and didn't know he was a closet drinker until one day
in his bedroom I pulled open a drawer and a bottle of vodka rolled out.*
—Forty-two-year-old single female medical assistant

Sometimes his masks work. But what does this mean? That we
fall in love with the mask, and not the man behind it? Then when it
is over, we ask who and what was it that we really loved. And we
wonder why he chose to wear a mask rather than let us know him.

Beneath our masks are the secrets we keep from ourselves and
from those close to us. Because men and women grow up with different sets of expectations about what it takes to be accepted, successful, and loved, we have some secrets that differ as well as some
we share. He keeps his secrets, and you keep yours.

It's no news flash that an abundance of men struggle with
awareness and communication of their innermost feelings. Men may
have learned how to cloak their feelings of hurt, tenderness, and
caring so automatically that hiding these feelings doesn't even seem
secretive to them. What's more, as both men and women of the
1990s are fond of noting, some men become extraordinarily successful at hiding that they have *any feelings at all.* For these men the
mask of stoicism has worked all too well. They hide their joy as well
as their insecurity. Unfortunately, the only emotion some men have
been socialized to express is their angry aggression.

It isn't that men *don't* have a full range of feelings. Quite the contrary! It's that all too many men have declared the more vulnerable
and emotional aspects of their lives forbidden terrain to themselves, as
well as to you. Because they are locked out of their inner lives, it's
easy for them to place the measure of their worth on the outer world
of success and performance—and make a career of neglecting a
potentially rich inner world of emotions and self-awareness.

So it comes as no surprise that men's most common mask of
choice isn't the happy face. Rather, it's the rough-hewn mask of stoicism. As one thirty-seven-year-old single graphic designer put it:
"*My secret was* that I had feelings, *that I was not impregnable. It's
a big male secret: the stoic gender role.*"

The mask of stoicism encourages concealing the truth and dis-
courages openness and intimacy at every stage of a relationship. It
represents a major "disconnect between him and you, *and* for himself." Honesty becomes moot.

What secrets do women hide beneath their masks?

Beneath the Happy Face: Her Secrets

Only you know exactly what your secrets are, but sometimes by understanding the secrets we keep from men and why we keep them we gain insight into the secrets they keep from us. What can we learn from our own secrets? The ones listed here may or may not be yours. But they can help you begin to focus on whatever you habitually mask in your personal relationships.

When I asked women and men to talk about the secrets they had kept from the other sex, a whopping 45 percent of women's spontaneously discussed secrets were about negative feelings, undesirable thoughts, and personal fears! Some of the things they hide are:

- Negative feelings about their bodies. ("I'm embarrassed that I hate some parts of my body, so I don't talk about them.")
- Depressed or angry thoughts. ("My little black shadow thoughts about wanting to hit the car with the obnoxious bumper sticker . . . If they knew they would think badly of me. *I've made a career of being happy*.")
- Interesting thoughts and ideas. ("I hide little trivial things like the theories I'm forming in my head, because he may think I'm stupid.")

The Secret of an Unsmiling Face

I try to be as positive as I can. I worry that people might not think I'm as nice as I am.
—Twenty-four-year-old married female creative director

Have you ever noticed how many women draw a smiling happy face alongside their names? What's so great about a happy face? For one thing, happy faces don't threaten anyone. For another, studies show that men find a woman's open and friendly appearance sexy. Should that happy face drop off for an instant, fear not! Someone will urge you to put it right back on, regardless of the events in your life. Think of all the times you have been implored to "smile!" by a man you hardly knew. Studies continue to show that women and girls smile more than men. That smiling face may be part of women's good-girl persona in the world, a socially acceptable way of appearing far more together than they feel. Check it out yourself. A tight smile that involves the mouth, but not the eyes, may serve to safely mask a woman's anger. Why would a woman mask it? Because an overt display of anger, while often stunningly effective in getting an issue out on the table, may also be censured and labeled as unfeminine, inappropriate, or even a sign of PMS or emotional instability!

The Secret of an Imperfect Family

While men tend to disguise themselves by putting an airtight casing around their feelings and by presenting a sketchy past stripped clean of damning detail, many women take this whitewashing one step further. They parade the guise of the perfect family. This mask conceals difficult and defining personal histories, often with secrets involving an alcoholic parent, a sexually abusive relative, or a financially draining family relationship. These are issues that none of the men I interviewed mentioned as something they kept secret. Why? Certainly not because men don't have them. Rather, it's because over the course of their lives many women stay more closely involved in relationships with family members—even dysfunctional ones—than do men. The result? These women identify more fully with their family's problems and fear guilt by association. And because women may be less valued in their own right—apart from their original family—that endows the original family with more clout as a reference group.

The Secret of Victimization

The women I interviewed also talked about another distinctive set of secrets that distinguished them from the men: the painful (and often shame-inducing) events of rape, coercive relationships, and abortions they hide behind the comforting mask of a perfectly ordinary and uneventful life. Although many men also have abusive family histories and relationships, these experiences tend to be more common among women. Among the sixty women I interviewed, seven talked, sometimes haltingly, about their secret of having been raped and how difficult it remained for them to expose this part of their past to the men in their lives. Several others discussed being abused as children as a dark secret they still couldn't bring themselves to talk about. How common is this? According to various estimates, as many as one in four women report personal histories that include rape, molestation, or abuse. And as many as one in two have experienced incidents of sexual harassment in the workplace. That's a lot of women! Yet, it is also estimated that fewer than 5% of women report such experiences to authorities. When these traumatizing experiences affect so many women, why do we keep them hidden? Could be that many women, all too familiar with the blame-the-victim mentality that vilifies or rejects those who speak up, fear to open their own personal baggage for view.

The Masks We Share

Where did men and women share similar secrets? Men and women both revised their sexual histories, although most often in differing directions, and both hid some part of their financial dealings from their dates and their spouses.

Secrets of a Revised Sexual History

Men and women shared similar secrets in the area of past sexual history. It looks as if both men and women fudge in whatever way is convenient for them, doctoring the facts in ways they believe will improve how they look to a partner. Whatever the truth might have been, both genders don the conservative mask of more moderate past sexual activity whenever a long-term relationship is in the offing. But there are clear differences. Over and over, women tend to fudge in the direction of fewer partners, whether the encounter was a serious commitment or a fling. They revise their sexual history downward toward an idealized standard of female naiveté and inexperience. For men the pattern is less clear. The closer to zero his actual number of partners is, the more likely a man is to ratchet it upward. That leads some men to greatly exaggerate the total number of sexual partners lurking in what they hope will be seen as their colorful pasts. But today a professed Don Juan may be more effective in snaring admiration at the neighborhood bar than in a prospective sexual liaison. Since the rise of AIDS, boasting of sexual conquests has become an increasingly risky tactic. Boasting of too many partners, whether you are male or female, has become a relationship-halting negative.

Of course, there are still plenty of exceptions. Take the newly divorced woman. She's afraid of scaring off her first postdivorce lover when he finds out he is number one in her dating reentry lineup, so she may abandon a standard of postdivorce naiveté by pretending he's not the first. Then there are a surprising number of women without any sexual experience or lasting relationships who resist disclosing this. Trish, a thirty-year-old divorced screenplay writer, masks the fact that she's "not had many serious relationships, but many superficial ones." Or consider Gwen, a thirty-two-year-old single public relations account executive: *"I keep secret from men the fact that I have never maintained a relationship for more than seven months. This seems to terrify men. When they say, 'Tell me about your past relationships,' I don't want to . . . I feel bad."*

The purpose of these nondisclosures is to avoid frightening away a new prospect by seeming too flawed, potentially dependent, or chronically passed over. If these women don't tell, they don't have to explain why. Another exception is the man with a gargantuan number of sexual experiences. He may minimize the sheer number of encounters and move himself to a more user-friendly level—say six to eight relationships. In an age of AIDS and sexually transmitted diseases (STDs), men are just as aware as women that experience with too many sexual partners flashes a highly undesirable promiscuity rating to potential lovers. And of those I interviewed, five men but only one women admitted to wearing the mask of abstinence and sexual health to cover the secret of serious STDs.

Secrets About Finances

I went out with a rich girl. I pretended everything was fine financially when I was having the worst year I'd ever had. I was starving myself so I'd have $200 in my pocket when I'd go to lunch with her. I had every bit of cash I had in my pocket! I was ready to spend my net worth over lunch!
—Thirty-year-old single male sales manager

Conventional wisdom dictates that, whatever the reality, men pretend to earn more while women pretend to spend less. Fact or fiction? Here's an instance where conventional wisdom got it mostly right. According to the men and women I interviewed, more men keep their earnings secret and more women keep their spending secret. Pretending to be more financially successful than he really was topped women's lists of men's money lies. Whether he's asset- challenged or rolling in money, a man's likely to protect himself from being found financially lacking or becoming a target for a gold digger.

But it's more complicated. Ten of the women I interviewed reported that their "financially successful" guys turned out to be inveterate "moochers," eager to let the woman in their lives help finance their new pick-up truck or put her credit card to work. Literally the poorer for their experiences, several women belatedly learned that their men did what many companies practice: they flaunted their assets and concealed their debts. As one man confided, "I don't tell them I'm $300,000 in debt the first time I meet them."

What about women? Rather than wearing the mask of financial success, women tended to hide their financial naiveté and veil their vulnerability as an easy mark. Among their money secrets were old and uncollected loans to former husbands, fiancés, lovers, and family members. One woman hid that she had stolen money at her husband's request to support his drug addiction. Other women concealed that they were living above their means. When it came to spending patterns there was a real gender difference. Many married women affirmed the old stereotype of the wife who reduces the price of her purchases to close-out specials. These women wouldn't dream of telling a partner what something really cost. With men hidden costs were there too, but rarely for additions to their own wardrobes. Rather, they hid expenses incurred for affairs with other women, a second full-time relationship, and for a host of attention-grabbing addictions like alcohol, drugs, gambling, or prostitutes. Like fifty-four-year-old Gordon, now divorced, who "secreted away several thousand dollars," then denied he had done it. Why? "Because it was my money, my right. But it was money I was using to conduct the affair." Or like thirty-five-year-old Lief, whose creative euphemism for his gambling losses of $200 a night was "negative purchases." And then there were the men who admitted to squirreling away funds in hidden accounts in preparation for an anticipated but still unannounced divorce somewhere down the pike.

In those relationships where the power/money dynamic was reversed so the woman was the chief breadwinner, the results were often predictable. With the tables turned, men, like this now divorced twenty-nine-year-old, sometimes lied about their spending while women lied about their assets: *"I was hiding cash and purchases from my ex-wife. She likes to control all the money, every cent. I worked two jobs. My wife kept track of all the money coming in. I had to justify anything I wanted to buy. I started keeping extra money I made to buy things. If I tell a new woman this, she will ask, 'Is he going to do this with me too?' So I don't tell."*

This is what thirty-six-year-old Hannah said about her husband's penchant for hiding his new gun purchases: *"I manage the checkbook and lie about the available money, since if we have money he keeps buying more guns."*

Wielding power and lying about money seem to go hand in hand, overriding gender differences on the way to the bank. The partner with greater earnings and power is likely to be more secretive about personal finances. But in a world where women can expect to earn 35 percent to 40 percent less than men in the workplace, receive fewer promotions, and hit a glass ceiling mid-career that keeps them from reaching the top, it's still safe to predict which gender will lie about what.

Why We Wear Masks That Hide Our Secrets

The secrets we hide dictate the masks that we wear. But why do we keep them? Although men's masks may not look like ours, they wear masks in their relationships for many of the same reasons we do. The mask, after all, provides a multipurpose defense that works for both sexes. We both hide secrets and wear masks:

- To give us a quick cover, an image, that shades and smooths down our rough edges. (Our worst fear: We'll be seen and rejected as bizarre, crass, or generally undesirable.)
- To help us feel more in control so we can get what we really want. (Our worst fear: By showing our true selves, we'll lose control and forever be losers in love and life.)
- To afford us privacy and let us conceal our darkest secrets. (Our worst fear: If they knew who we really were, they would go screaming into the night.)
- To let us sidestep our real feelings and vulnerabilities. (Our worst fear: Were our true feelings to be known, no one would love that quivering mass of uncertainty and fear we know too well.)
- To cover up the absence of genuine feeling or involvement. (Our worst fear: They will learn that at the heart of things we are more shallow and empty than we appear.)

The fact is, we all have parts of ourselves that we feel uncomfortable with or ashamed of. But does this have to doom us to relationships riddled with secrets, masks, and lies?

Is Masquerade What We Really Want?

In the beginning there are expository lies: lies of packaging and marketing; you try to package and market yourself as effectively as you

*can at initial contact. These are lies around who you are, what you
do. You shellac over your vices. But these lies are exposed up front as
you get closer. You can only do it a little. Otherwise, when exposed you
have to cut and run. Later lies are lies of convenience so you can keep
traveling as you want. Not that I'm Joe Move Maker, but if she asks
where were you, I might say I was doing something else, when it was
boys' night out.*
—Twenty-five-year-old single male entrepreneur

If men and women are engaged in a masquerade that dresses
each gender in different costumes, this raises serious questions.
What price do we pay individually and collectively for hanging on
to this ritual? Is it just the way things are, or can we break through
our masks to achieve greater honesty and integrity in our relationships?

When we first meet people we parade our best selves before
them. We're afraid to let them see who we really are in any depth.
That's normal. Both men and women fear rejection and hurt with
good reason. That's the root fear that sparks the frog-to-prince lie.
But there's far more to this than fear of rejection.

We want new people in our lives to see us as we'd like to see
ourselves. A singles get-together or a first encounter is a lot like a
Mardi Gras, where nearly everybody is disguised in the mask and
costume of an ideal self they hope others will find admirable.

Why bother? Because, at first blush, *we feel closest to people
who see us as we prefer to be seen*, not as who we really are. In the
heat of the moment, we want to trick ourselves into believing in a
better, more gentle us. When a man and woman both see each other
through rose-colored lenses that closely match the other person's
ideal self, the outcome is quick and easy intimacy. But it is also a
form of risky fiction that has a short shelf life.

The Fear and Relief of Discovery

Why is that? If our masquerades get us quick and easy intimacy,
why throw out our rose-colored lenses? If they worked then, why
not now? Because as time passes, our masks begin to detract from
our intimacy and create a whole new level of tension.

The less comfortable we are in our own skins, the greater the
discrepancy between who we really are and who our masks portray
us to be. As our relationship progresses and the layers of masks we
all wear begin to peel away, we fear discovery. Stress mounts as we

work harder and harder to keep our disguises intact. Sometimes maintaining a false self creates so much strain that we pack it all up and head for the hills, where it's a relief to just relax and be ourselves again.

But if there is an accomplished liar under the mask, he or she faces a problem of a different type. The liar doesn't know how to pack it up. Remember Sherman, who said, "I'm not sure that my lies stop when I find the right person."

Here's the rub for Sherman and all the others like him. Once we are established in an ongoing relationship, research on this topic reveals that we much prefer our partners to see and accept us in ways that match our *real* selves—how we really see ourselves *without the masks*. We can no longer bear to be loved and admired for what we aren't, for what we can't possibly deliver on. If we're uncomfortable in our own skins, we want our partners to accept us like this and love us anyway. Even virtuoso liars, out of touch with themselves, crave affirmation for what's underneath the mask.

So if we see ourselves negatively under the mask, a partner who evaluates us too positively doesn't affirm us at all. This discrepancy just adds stress to our lives. We feel compelled to disguise who we are—even on our home turf—by keeping the mask in place. The greater the discrepancy between who we are and who we've presented ourselves to be, the more we feel compelled to act in ways contrary to our nature. Maintaining the lie as mask takes more energy and effort and begins to feel wrong. Being vague about all manner of detail, emotion, and behavior becomes a way of life. Then, as time passes, it becomes harder and harder to strip away our masks to expose our secrets and who we really are. We wind up at odds with ourselves and with our partners. We have left the realm of honesty and intimacy for the performing arts.

As we evolve in our relationships it helps to remind ourselves that:

> We are most intimate with the partner whose view of
> us matches and affirms our own.

To Mask or Not to Mask?

What can we learn from all this? You might try looking at it this way. At their very best and *in their most benign forms*, when lies as hooks and masks appear early in the game, they create possibilities. They let us suspend our natural wariness and mute the harshest, most negative criticism we use to judge ourselves and others. When we put our best foot forward, we give ourselves more leeway to be accepted. And when others put their best foot forward, they give us more room to accept—even if erroneously—a highly imperfect, but still perfectly lovable partner. Being hypercritical too early can inhibit this process.

The problem here is that the serious liar is counting on this suspension of judgment. That's what allows him to conduct his business of deception, undetected. And that creates serious caveats for you. At the same time you want to stay open to possibilities, you will also want to be alert to the likelihood that *what you see may not be what you get*; that, as an old children's rhyme warns, "Things are never what they seem, milk will masquerade as cream."

Later in the relationship, masks begin to interfere. It's inevitable, desirable, and even critical that his mask and yours begin to slip. Then you both become more transparent to each other, easier to read. This gives you a chance to understand and accept the other person for who he really is. And in the best of all worlds, he too will accept you for who you really are. This process holds both your feet firmly on the path to intimacy.

But when lies as masks stay put as the relationship progresses, they are a mere surrogate, a place holder for the real person hidden behind them. As any relationship deepens, our lies as masks halt acceptance and emotional intimacy in their tracks.

In the next three chapters we'll see how lies as masks do their complicated work. In our relationships we each wear many masks, some simultaneously. We won't discuss all the masks men wear in relationships. Instead, we'll focus on three common masks that seriously affect sexual intimacy, commitment, and harmony. We'll consider two familiar places: first the bedroom, to see how his masks play out in the sexual arena, and then the living room, to learn how his masks create the illusory comfort of false commitment and a falsely reassuring sense that everything is just fine.

Chapter 6
Lying in Bed

It's the old cliché. Men use love to get sex, women use sex to get love.
Men come out the better.
—Twenty-three-year-old single female editor

My lie was not telling her I had a doctor's appointment to get checked
for STD—human papilloma. I told her I had to be somewhere else,
stuttered, got red-faced guilty.
—Twenty-six-year-old single male sales rep

The bedroom is where we shed our clothing and many of our
defenses. Since we allow ourselves to feel most vulnerable here, it's
no surprise that any breach of trust feels distressingly treacherous.
In addition, there are increasingly high stakes for some bedroom
lies, such as "I haven't had sex with anyone for over a year," "I test
negative for HIV," and "I've never had herpes."

Of course, not everyone "lies" in bed. Nearly one-fourth of the
men I interviewed felt that the bedroom was where *they were least
likely* to lie. While these same men might have lied to their mates
and lovers about where they had spent the afternoon, their interest
in an attractive new neighbor, and the size of their bonus last
month, *they felt far freer to be honest in the bedroom*. It was as if
they felt they didn't *have to lie* in bed. Of these self-proclaimed
honest lovers, a few pointed out that since their usual lies were
aimed at getting a woman into bed, why would they lie once they
had her there? As one of them put it, "Sex is a time of honesty."
And for a couple of the men, it was only during *sexual intimacy
that they never lied to a woman.*

But many men had far less trouble shedding their clothing than
their masks. And many women I interviewed corroborated these
stories with their own experiences.

What are these omnipresent masks? There are the ones he wears
to get into your bed, the ones he wears to stay in it, and the ones he
wears to beat a hasty retreat.

Lies That Get Him Into Your Bed

> *"I love you."*
>
> *"You have a great body."*
>
> *"I've always wanted to sleep with a model."*
>
> *"It would be a great honor to sleep with you."*
>
> *"Sex with my wife is so boring."*

They were saying what they thought they had to say to get to sleep with someone, saying what they think I want to hear. But I hear it as a lie.
—Twenty-eight-year-old newly married female property manager

Men, like women, lie about their sexual experience to ingratiate themselves, to make themselves more attractive as sexual partners, and to measure up to whatever ideal standard—studly or sensitive—plays in their heads. For some men this means dramatically playing down the number of sexual partners they've had. For others it means grandstanding, bragging about their real or imagined sexual prowess, the pleasure they'll give you, or how sexually enlightened they are. For some this translates into falsely holding out as bait their readiness to commit to a relationship, just as some women falsely deny their own real interest in a long-term relationship to enhance their desirability. And, perhaps scariest of all in the 1990s, for some men this means staunchly denying the sexually transmitted diseases they'll carry into your life, and, perhaps, beyond to *your* following partner.

The masks that men wear to get into your bed reveal as well as hide. Once you learn to recognize them, they are a veritable guide to the stereotypes that the masked man uses to judge himself as well as you. A man's masks tell you about whatever he thinks will tip the scale in his direction, whether for a luscious afternoon delight or for a longer-term liaison. They also can give you a quick peek at which factors he thinks *his masculinity* and *your femininity* ride on.

But, even knowing all this, chances are you'll stumble across a surprise or two in the bedroom. Ask Donna.

The Lie of Sexual Innocence: Donna and Garth

This is Donna's story of her first love and the masks he brought into her life nine years ago. Today Donna is twenty-five years old, married, and successful in her work as a corporate trainer. When I asked Donna about the first lie she remembered a man telling her, she leaned back and sighed, "I was still a virgin." Back in her high school days when she was just sixteen years old, she'd dated Garth for four months. He was one year older and they were in love. Donna decided to let him into her bed. The experience was very romantic: *"It was very special. I loved him and he loved me. We decided we were both going to have our first sexual experience together. We went to a hotel and he brought candles, we took a bath together. It was totally sensual and experiential. He told me I was the first person he had ever slept with. It was so sweet."*

She looked up, continuing, "And it was absolutely false."

Donna had no idea anything was wrong until the next week when her girlfriends were playing truth or dare at a slumber party. They said, "Donna, we hate to tell you, but . . . " and laid it on the line. Her romantically exquisite experience was no more than a carefully staged lie by a two-timing Casanova with substantial and widely known sexual experience.

When I asked her why she believed Garth's lie, her answer encapsulated what I had heard over and over again in various forms from the sixty women I interviewed, and from hundreds of private clients: *"I believed him with all my heart. He'd never done anything to produce doubt. I'd gone out with him for four months. I'm a very trusting person. He said he loved me and I believed him. I wanted him to be my first, and I never even conceived that any deception was occurring."*

Donna didn't have a suspicious bone in her body. Not then. Besides, lying about his virginity was hardly the typical male lie a young woman might be scanning for. So it was easy for Donna to make one of women's most predictable errors—believing the words he tells her—the very words she most wants to hear from him.

How did Donna feel about the lie? Nine years after his lie, as Donna relived the discovery of his deception, her words poured out: *"I felt crushed, betrayed, shocked. I denied it, and then I got madder and madder. I could've killed him. I went home. I stewed about it. I wanted to go into a hole and hide myself. I went into myself. My world exploded when I found out he had planned and woven a deception. I never talked to him again."*

This seventeen-year-old man had created a false first sexual experience for Donna that she would carry with her for the rest of her life. Even though the experience itself had been wonderful, the tenderness and sweetness of the romance and the sex were then ruined by the knowledge that she had been duped and scammed. What she had innocently participated in was the scheme of a budding con artist. Going back to high school the next day, she was humiliated. It seemed everyone knew the truth about Garth except her.

Her eagerness for a romantic first sexual experience and her willingness to unquestioningly believe the liar gave her a legacy—a sexual history that still pains her. And a lesson in duplicity that proved hard to forget.

Donna wanted him to be her first and wanted the event to be special to him too. She didn't recognize the synchronicity he had created with his "me too" lie, predisposing her to believe him. Donna made another common mistake beyond giving too much credence to words. Like women of all ages and from all walks of life, *she confused liking with trust.* Sure, she liked this young man. Liking someone is obvious and immediate. You realize you like someone in the first few minutes. Donna had not yet learned that:

Trust is a fooler. It takes time and has to be earned.

In trusting someone simply because she liked him, Donna ended up trusting a liar, and she got burned.

But why would a young man hide his sexual experience and disguise himself as a virgin? Why go through such an elaborate setup and ritual? Since she believed they loved each other, the ritual probably wasn't necessary for Garth to hit the jackpot.

Masks serve a lot of purposes, like maintaining an image, getting us what we want, helping us avoid vulnerability and anger—but the main one is to disguise who we really are. In this case, the mask worked. Donna had no idea with whom she was really sharing her bed.

Initially, Garth's lie of virginity was a hook. It drew them closer together. Maybe it was a game—a response to a dare from his friends. But once the plan began to unfold, he didn't know how to stop the game and come clean. The successful hook had been transformed into a mask that had hardened and that he couldn't easily peel off without upsetting the plan. Left wearing his virginal mask once they were in bed, he saw how much their first sexual experience meant to Donna. *Garth didn't know how to tell her the truth without hurting her,* so the mask stiffened and remained securely in place. Later he rightly feared her anger and rejection if she discovered the truth.

Garth didn't tell a woman who trusted him the truth. Her

friends did. The outcome was hurt, anger, and finally rejection. Garth gained an evening in bed with a beautiful young woman who loved him, but he lost the relationship. He left Donna, whose biggest mistake was trusting him, with a gratuitous legacy of humiliation and distrust in the wake of emotional intimacy. She walked away with a new and unwanted notch in her belt, one she still carries with her: the notch of skepticism and distrust.

Even though the specific mask of virginity may seem more typically a woman's lie, several men I interviewed volunteered that they too had lied about their virginity. What insight can we gain from hearing their side of the story?

The Mask of Sexual Innocence: Ted and Lisa

This is Ted's experience. When Ted first slept with Lisa in college she was his fourth sexual experience. He was her first. But Lisa gave him the impression that she thought she was his first. So what's a guy supposed to do? Easy. "I lied and told her, 'You are the first.'" But Ted, unlike Donna, did not take the lie as a defining moment. In fact, in talking about the incident, he trivialized it by repeatedly downgrading his deception to white-lie status.

But he did lie.

Why was it so important to Ted to appear inexperienced? Was he trying to put one over on Lisa? Not from Ted's point of view. As Ted tells it, he just was being a gentleman. He willingly wore the mask of virginity for Lisa's sake, because he "wanted to be close to her," because he "had strong feelings toward her." He said he hoped for "closer intimacy."

But when asked how he felt about deceiving Lisa, Ted immediately changed his tune. He blew it off: *"I had no guilt at all. It was something I said for myself."*

Hmmm. Apparently it wasn't for *Lisa's sake* that he lied after all, but *for his own!* When I asked Ted what, if anything, he would do differently, the second part of his answer was a first-class eye-opener: *"I think I'd let her know she wasn't my first woman. I wouldn't give her power over me."*

Ted made an awfully quick trip from intimacy to power. Why?

For Ted, wearing the mantle of virginity allowed him to create a fantasy of closeness, because that was what *he* wanted. She didn't ask for it. Lisa's virginity provided no more than the backdrop, a setting for the event. Later, after the end of the relationship and with hindsight, Ted had no trouble replacing his focus on tenderness with more traditional concern for power. As he reflected on it, presenting himself as a virgin diminished his power in the relationship. After all, it put both partners on equal footing, when in fact they weren't. He had more experience. By denying this, he had handed her the power chip—and afterward suffered macho regret. When sexual innocence and sexual bravado go toe to toe, could it be that the man who chooses the lie of innocence will eventually feel the loser? Ted's innocence was a lot like a retail store's loss leader that lures at the start, but slashes profits at the end.

The Lie of High-Octane Sex

This mask is the polar opposite of the mask of sexual innocence. He flaunts his sexual prowess on the assumption that every woman longs for a skilled lover. This mask is often more of a promise than a reality, but it has its appeal. He confesses to you about his high-energy sexual appetite on the first date. He touches your neck erotically when he helps you on with your coat. No matter what he looks like, this man is convincing because he's letting you know he thinks about sex with you all the time. He tells you his dreams and his fantasies and puts you in them. Then he demands to know yours. He is exciting.

The lie here isn't the interest or the promise. It's the reality. Once a relationship is established, he may be all bravado with little sustaining reality. No matter what happens, his identity depends on your telling him that he's the best. He's counting on you to help ward off his doubts and insecurities, and that could be a full-time job requiring the doting attention of several women. So watch out.

Lies of Sexual Experience

Is it socialization or is it testosterone? No one can say for sure, but we do know that men consistently say they lust after more sexual partners than do women. And men also report having more sexual partners year by year, lifetime by lifetime, than do women.

No matter where you look, the data are the same. According to a survey reported on National Public Radio and written up in the *Washington Post*, the average American woman has had three sexual partners while the average American man boasts eleven. Other behavioral studies report that over the course of a lifetime men say they would like eighteen sexual partners compared to women's paltry four or five. In the same vein, a large-scale national survey of

1,347 men and 1,418 women (*The Janus Report of Sexual Behavior*, published in 1993) found that more than twice the proportion of men (39 percent) to women (16 percent) reported having had thirty or more sexual partners. On the high end, 18 percent of men relative to only 7 percent of women reported sixty-one partners or more. And at the very high end of one thousand partners or more, although the numbers are small, men outnumbered women three to one.

Who are these partners? For men they might be anyone. According to some studies, college men are more likely than women to see sex as a desirable possibility with partners they've known less than a week. For many men, women they've known less than an hour is okay too, thanks. What about college women? Caution is the order of the day. They say they're more inclined to consent to sex with someone they've known for five years and to feel neutral at best about sex with someone they've known only six months. But try asking them about consenting to have sex with someone they've known less than a week and they'll balk. Someone they've known an hour? Forget it. Of course there are plenty of exceptions. And, surprise! A lot of men claim to be one!

What does any of this have to do with masks? Just think about it. How could the average man have eleven partners to the average woman's three, unless a very few women account for huge numbers of partners, the so-called slut phenomenon. Or, unless, as *Washington Post* columnist Henry Dunbar slyly notes, both men and women are lying in opposite directions about the number of sexual partners they actually have had. So men ratchet the number up and women crank the number down. And the truth is somewhere in between.

Maybe it's just another case of our brave new world rife with sexually transmitted diseases and AIDS, but in my interviews, both highly experienced men *and* women tended to adjust their number of sexual partners downward when talking with a "prospect." The exceptions were a small number of especially inexperienced thirty-somethings of both genders. These sexual rookies harbored considerable embarrassment about their abysmally low- to zero-frequency of sexual partners. The women I spoke with tended to shut down, avoiding discussion of the topic altogether. Consider Marcy, a thirty-two-year-old single account executive with near-zero sexual experience, who said, "I just don't disclose how many sexual relations I've had. Otherwise I'm pretty open." Or good-looking and fast-talking Gina, whom men repeatedly and mistakenly identify as an easy sexual mark: *"I keep secret the number of people I've slept with. I've only slept with six. Everyone assumes it's a lot more. They think I'm lying. Since it starts a conversation I don't want to have, I stopped telling."*

In contrast, several inexperienced men I interviewed simply fudge the facts, like Craig, who tells women, "I've been with someone sexually when I haven't" and is still hoping for the "big break." They viewed their lack of sexual experience as an embarrassing secret to keep from women. More frequently, men lied about the sheer numbers of sexual partners they had. This is what Earl told me: *"Sure. I lie to women about how many partners I've had. I underestimate by a lot—maybe 90 percent. I try to find a line where it's still believable. Where they know I'm not a virgin, but I'm an experienced and caring person. They may not believe it, but it's better they don't buy the lie than that I say a truth that disturbs them. My lie tells them that they have a low chance of sexual disease. It tells them that they're special. When it comes to number of partners, I won't tell the truth, except with my male friends."*

Just in case you're wondering, Earl is no forty-five-year-old Romeo. He just celebrated his twenty-third birthday.

The moral of the story here seems to be that you can't really trust his numbers and he can't trust yours. That means your only refuge is falling back on the stats. And the stats, even though they too rely on self-report, are clear in this regard. Most men will have and admit to having far more sexual partners over the course of their lifetimes, both before, during, and after marriage, than you will. You may encounter the exception. But more probably, like our friend Donna, you'll be fooled.

The Deadly Lies of Safe Sex and Sexual Health

No. He is not sterile and he has not had a vasectomy. He is not celibate and the herpes cream tucked in his briefcase is not there for his roommate. If you believe these or any number of other lies men earnestly offer just to get you to have condom-less, unprotected sex, stand in line behind the many trusting and anguished women I've interviewed who said things like:

- "It didn't occur to me that he could be lying." She is discussing her pregnancy after her first boyfriend told her he was sterile and there was nothing to worry about.

- "He lied about practicing safe sex, when he couldn't hold an erection with a condom on for one full minute." Her evidence here is that as soon as he puts a condom on, he loses his erection. "He should have said, 'No, I don't practice safe sex, *but I should.*' I wouldn't have slept with him at the time. I would have taken him to be tested to see if he was HIV positive. Six months later I went and had the AIDS test. People are irresponsible sexually."

- "My ex-boyfriend had herpes, but never told me all the time we were sleeping together. My whole world fell apart. I was angry and frustrated . . . I told him, 'It's a complete betrayal, a deception.' *Why couldn't he talk to me, be open?*"

A man's herpes or HIV status understandably comes up time after time as issues women fear men lied about. Women lament men's too quick, too pat answers to what they believe are life and death concerns about safe sex and a man's sexual history. One woman told me she suspected the man she'd been in a relationship with for two years was seeing other women. Her main concern? Safe sex—not jealousy. Refusing to use a condom, he deflected her pleas for safe sex with this chilling put-down: "Do you think you're the only one whose life is important here?" What was chilling about his put-down? First, his deflection twisted her legitimate health concern into a selfish act where she saw herself as the only important one. And second, it tacitly acknowledged other women, while putting her at the mercy of *his* judgment about whom *he* deemed "safe" for the unprotected sex he preferred.

Many of my single and newly divorced female clients tell me they are celibate. Why? Not because they can't find a man, but because they can no longer bear to deal with the hassle of determining his sexual history and his health status, or getting him to wear a condom. They have given up and have opted for health over uncertainty.

Safe sex was rarely an issue for the men I interviewed. If anything, their most clearly avowed goal was to avoid condom use, even though it defied common sense.

A thirty-seven-year-old single draftsman described his bedroom talk as "a means to an end, to get what you want." He said: *"My major lie is the message to a woman that being unaware of what you are doing is good for the experience. She says, 'This is happening so fast.' Then I say, 'Don't worry about it. Trust your feelings. Go with the moment.' But my message to the woman is a lie."*

What does he want? "Just to keep the momentum up and avoid condom usage." Safe sex? For him, that's seemingly a nonissue.

Why? We each have secrets. We know precisely whom we've been with, exactly what we've done, and how much at risk we've put ourselves. Our partners—particularly new ones—can't access our information. They have only what we choose to tell them and their own hunches to guide them.

Yet many men continue to subscribe to the old school of thinking that most women are safe because they are more sexually chaste and will exercise more caution. Or that women won't lie to them. Is all of this plain old testosterone singing a persuasive if deadly love song? Or is this merely a male take-the-hill mentality combined with a lack of empathy for their partners?

Marty's story is a good example of a man whose own agenda precluded his partner's safety. A single thirty-two-year-old actuary, he really liked Jill. He'd dated her for six weeks, "then the relationship got heavy. It snowballed and got really passionate, physical. But she was a virgin, so we didn't have intercourse." Nonetheless, they were spending five nights a week together.

Maybe the relationship would have been physically consummated with more time and tenderness, but Marty had been planning a three-month-long trip to Southeast Asia, so off he went: *". . . all the time writing her letters, telling her how much I'm missing her. How I want to consummate the relationship. In the meantime I'm having sex while I'm away. Being an ex-dude I say, 'What the fuck, I'm a young person.' I'd planned this trip way in advance of meeting her."*

Marty has a fine adventure and comes home to Jill, who is eagerly awaiting his return. But there is an immediate hint of trouble: *"She asks me, 'Have you been good?' I say, 'Yes. I haven't had sex with anyone.' Lie! . . . Then she's telling me about her fear of AIDS, that she has a cousin dying of it."*

Jill, as it turns out, had a conversation with Marty's mother, who knew about his "sex with a couple of people on the road."

Why didn't Marty just level with Jill and tell the truth? Sexual urgency was the culprit: *"I wanted to be honest, but if I were honest I would have to wait six months for an AIDS test. So I lied. I find it hard to believe, but that's the truth. Anyway, if I told her I had slept with a prostitute, she would have broken up with me."*

From Marty's perspective, he was damned if he lied and damned if he didn't.

At this point, Jill got even. She held out the gift of her complete acceptance and love if only Marty would be honest: *"Jill volunteered, 'Honesty is everything. You have to tell me who you are so I can love who you are.' So I told her I slept with someone else."*

Then she abruptly withdrew her promise of acceptance. *"She said, 'The fact that you could lie to me means I'm out. That's the end . . . ' She nailed me so precisely, by reading me so well, that I had to step back and look at myself. I realized I really did hide my true intentions . . . I came to realize what scum I am/was to all these women. We spent the next year as friends. We slept together without sex."*

So Marty didn't get what he wanted, but still managed to learn something from the experience. What he'd do differently is to "be much more up front about intentions." He'd say, "I'm going away and I probably will have sex while on the road."

But how he felt about it was a different matter: *"I'm bitter. She forced me to bail out. I also realize she's a basket case. I don't know why we are still friends."*

· Was Marty justified in either stance? After all, he wanted to do his own thing when he was on the road. And that's what he did. But when he came back, he took for granted Jill's sexual chastity and abstinence while he was in Manila and Bangkok. He was the wandering Odysseus and she the faithful Penelope. He assumed she had waited for him.

Once back in the fold, foremost on Marty's mind was sleeping with Jill that night, rather than waiting six months for the results of an AIDS test. Marty's sexual needs were running the show. To get her in bed, Marty was perfectly content to put Jill at risk, even though she let him know she was nervous about the threat of AIDS. She tried to trigger his empathy by talking to him about her cousin who was dying of AIDS. Eventually she tricked him into the truth by falsely holding out the bough of unconditional love in exchange for honesty—and got even. Even though Marty had lied, it didn't occur to him that Jill could lie too.

Maybe she concluded that if Marty really cared about her, he had an awfully funny way of showing it, behaving with callous indifference to her health and safety. If a long-term relationship with Marty was what she wanted, Jill won the battle of getting even, but lost the war. If she wanted an enduring relationship with someone she could trust, she won both, since she gets to try for a new relationship with her health intact. It looks like Marty, not Jill, is the loser here.

Lies That Keep You in Bed, at Least for a While

"I love you," "I've never done this with anyone else," and "You're the best" all fall into the more generic category of "Tell 'em what they want to hear" bedroom lies. As lies go, these are highly efficient dual-purpose masks. He may have used one or more of them to get you into bed. And since they worked so well to *get* you there, he'll keep bringing them out again in order to *keep* you there—at least until he's ready to move on.

The dilemma is that even when what he's doing seems transparent or off-putting, it's not always a mask. Sometimes what he does and says is the genuine thing. How do you separate the real gold from the fool's gold? It takes an awful lot of prospecting to tell the difference. Even then, an experienced prospector might err once in a while in the direction of fool's gold. And so can you.

One answer to this dilemma is patience and a willingness to wait him out. If you can just wait long enough, you'll be able to separate what's real from what's not. Generally, the masks he uses to keep you in bed will not survive the test of time or a committed relationship. These masks take so much energy and create so many problems that eventually he will find it a huge relief to end the relationship and take off his stultifying mask—at least until the next time. Once you move beyond quick and casual sex into a more stable relationship, his fraying mask—and the absence of real feeling—send signals that should trigger your distress. Then you can decide to work on the relationship or move out of it.

How do lies designed to keep you in bed work their wonders? Let's go back to the most powerful and often most hurtful lie of all—"I love you," the mask that can transition you into bed, keep you there for a time, and, as it drops away gradually, boot you out.

When "I Love You" Is a Lie

The "I love you" mask is so ubiquitous that some cynical women automatically substitute "blah, blah, blah" as soon they hear the words. We've already talked about the three look-alike "I love you" lies in the last chapter and how these three important little words can be seductively used as hooks, masks, and evasions. They can represent the truth of the moment or the truth forever. But when a woman takes them for the real thing and they're not, they hurt.

Who among us hasn't wanted to find and build a life with someone we can love and who will love us in return? But many of women's worst fears in personal relationships center around the use and abuse of "I love you." As they should. Why? Because most of us know women who have given years of their lives to men they truly believed loved them, only to find that they were sadly mistaken. They tread a bitter path to knowledge.

How does it happen? Most women know that a man might say, "I love you" to get her into bed. But once they are there, why would a man keep saying, "I love you" if he doesn't? Most women I spoke with found the false claim of "I love you" in an ongoing sexual or serious relationship to be an altogether unacceptable breach of trust.

Gina, a twenty-eight-year-old married property manager, was particularly vehement on this point. Gina was ready and waiting when I asked her about the last bedroom lie she had been told. She instantly reeled off the litany of lies that I listed at the start of the "Lies That Get Him Into Your Bed" section. Then she added more thoughtfully: *"Two months into the relationship at a pretty shallow level, he screams out 'I love you' in bed, like what you'd read in some magazine . . . I say, 'Why do you love me?' He says, 'I was just wrapped up in the moment. I thought it was the right thing to do.' But he doesn't love me or even know me. They say what they think women like to hear. One man told me he loved me all the time. Then he jilted me for a med school student."*

What would Gina prefer him to do? Again a quick response: "Nothing. I don't want him to say, 'I love you' in bed."

Margaret, a thirty-five-year-old married office manager, showed even less good humor. She told me about a man she had been in a relationship with for nearly four months. He'd said he loved her and she believed him. Then, when he met someone new, he sprang the bad news. "Margaret, I don't love you. It was just fun and good times." According to Margaret, he added insult to injury by hammering in yet another disclaimer—that "his love was never true to begin with." That ended the relationship, but not the pain. Margaret was "really bitter for a time" as she saw him coming and going, happy and involved with other women.

Then she began to get it. *"He was repeating his pattern with lots of other women. His cycle was four months. I could predict it. Maybe he did me a favor in ending it."* This man had a clear and recognizable pattern that anyone who watched him could discern. All you had to do was watch. Too bad that each woman he hit on couldn't learn from the experience of the woman before her. Even understanding that this was his problem and his pattern, the experience left Margaret wondering why he would take something as serious as "I love you" and "throw it around so loosely." Echoing the reactions of many women who have had similar letdowns, Margaret wishes men would reserve these three words "for the real feeling."

Some men agree. One man in his late twenties, who by his own admission repeatedly fails to live up to his personal credo that "honesty is the best policy," says that he nonetheless still considers "I love you" sacred. In fact, he says it's the only thing he never lies about.

Most men I interviewed concurred, at least in principle. Remember Sherman, who said he only lied to get women into bed, not once they were in bed? But he then turned around and contradicted himself in the next breath, saying he lied about "I love you" to get a woman more sexually excited.

Some men expressed regret at having misled a woman about their feelings and intentions. They said things like "I wish I had been more mature. I would have refrained from saying, 'I love you.'" Or they sidestepped responsibility altogether, putting the blame for their betrayals elsewhere, saying, "If I had just come from a different family background I might have been more truthful."

But many men I've talked with offered no apology. Why should they? They rationalized that they used the "I love you" lie because "it's what women want to hear" (a theme men will repeat ad nauseam), and because it keeps the relationship going, even if just for the short haul.

To many women "I love you" feels sacred. It's a code phrase reserved for long-term commitment, dedication, and devotion. It means someone cares enough to put aside his or her own wishes and desires to cherish those of the partner. When women believe the words "I love you" and feel the same way, a whole string of assumptions cascades from these three little words.

Whatever associations love has for each of us, most of us cherish the idea of committed love. Maybe we even see it as a panacea. But sometimes even love isn't enough of a buffer against temptation. As much as we may long for it, we also crave our autonomy. This natural ambivalence often makes us especially vulnerable to a breach of trust. As we try to keep up with our partner's evolving needs for our quality time, economic support, satisfying sex, family participation, and emotional sharing, we get increasingly frazzled. We long to be carefree—maybe even single. Fantasies or sexual desires that had gone underground now clamor for our attention. At one point or another in any relationship, both partners may secretly wish to be free of the draining constraints of their commitments.

The man or woman who craves sexual freedom, unfettered autonomy, and unaccounted-for time may start lying, both in bed and out. Then it's easy for our "I love you" lies to escalate from mask to more dangerous evasions, as we'll see in Chapters 9 and 10. For now, let's return to the lies as masks we use in the bedroom.

The Lie of "Before You, Nothing"

It sort of makes you wonder. He's thirty-five or fifty-five years old yet he makes it seem like you are the only woman with whom he's ever been emotionally involved. "Sure there's been sex," he offers, "but never like this." Is it possible? And why would he bother to lie about his own past experience?

Eli is a fifty-five-year-old think tank analyst, handsome, articulate, and engaging. Yet when I asked him, "What secrets do you keep from the women in your life?" he surprised me by saying, "I hide my sexual intimacy with women from my past." Why? Because he anticipated their reactions and wanted to head them off at the pass. This is his explanation for lying about past sexual intimacy: *"It would create a black cloud over the existing relationship. She'd ask me, 'Do you still have desires to have sexual relations with that woman?' Then of course you reassure them. But it becomes an issue you don't want to deal with."*

So it turns out that Eli is not embarrassed about his past intimacies. He just has no commitment to revealing any truth that causes him inconvenience or discomfort. Why? His current love may guess it, but having interviewed Eli, I know it. Eli is a man who leaves many blurred endings behind him. He rarely shuts a door to a past relationship. His companions from the past still write and phone him, even after a lapse of years. Eli, like many men, uses the undefined ending as a way of hedging his bets against any lean seasons ahead. His present is peppered with women who still call and write in hope of renewing their relationship.

So, no, Eli doesn't want to talk to you about his past sexual intimacies. Of course he doesn't. That would let you see your own probable future as woman number twenty-two or thirty-six on his preprogrammed call dialing system.

Eli is not alone in this. Many men are secretive about other women in their lives—past and present. Twenty percent of the men I interviewed kept friendships and sexual relations from the past under tight wraps. They hid these relationships because, like Ralph, a thirty-seven-year-old East Coast attorney, they "felt that the current relationship feels threatened by them." But Ralph then added an interesting insight: that revealing past intimacies "would create more conflict than there should be." So his mask served to keep the new relationship going by helping him avoid a woman's probing curiosity or anger. Note how Ralph couches his remarks in a flatly impersonal business-memo tone, using phrases like "the current relationship," and "create more conflict than there should be." He easily could be discussing a new customer relationship or a conflict on his project team. Where are the real women in these relationships? Ralph's choice of words may expose a telling mindset—in which women are seen more as interchangeable widgets than as real flesh-and-blood people with feelings and personalities. That places one more barrier on the road to intimacy, and makes women all the easier to lie to.

Some men hang on to lies about infrequent intimacy for altogether different reasons, like embarrassment, prudishness, or shame. Hank, a thirty-one-year-old political lobbyist, doesn't "consider it proper to discuss past sexual relations, because she'd want to know what I had done." And Tim, a thirty-year-old bond trader, hasn't told anybody that he slept with a woman twenty years older than himself, a total stranger who, as he phrased it, had "cold called" him at work, probably mistaking him for someone else she had talked to at the brokerage. After meeting this stranger for lunch, he arranged to see her at the home of a friend for an afternoon of uninhibited sex—and, oh yes, he did use a condom. Even though he really liked the intrigue and the idea of it, he explained why he would never tell anyone: *"I haven't told anyone. I feel it's not normal. I feel some shame. That girls might think it's weird to go off with a woman twenty years older than me."*

For Tim, erasing this adventure from his sexual resume allows him to maintain the aura of respectability he thinks he needs to hang on to his relationships.

What these men have in common is a discomfort with their own sexuality and past choices they believe detract from their current or next intimate relationship. Perhaps, if a woman knew, she would ask embarrassing questions, expose long-buried feelings, see him as too strange, or feel less special herself.

Many men automatically apply their own template of "shoulds" and "oughts" to their sexual relationships. Some of the milder "shoulds" and "oughts" are expressed in male ritual masks of sexual etiquette.

The "Harmless" Ritual Lies of Sexual Etiquette

Men's bedroom lies? Oh yeah, you mean the "ravers." They're overly flattering, overcomplimentary about my body. But since I really want to believe it, I'm not really sure even now if it was a lie.
—Forty-year-old single female sales clerk

Miss Manners surely would approve. These socially correct lies run the gamut from "You're not fat," to "You're pretty," to "I don't like big breasts," when you have just pointed out that your breasts are small. Can you believe this man waxes ecstatic about your stretch marks and, yes, even those sweet little purple tributaries running down the hills and valleys of your cellulite-laden thighs? Gazing deeply into your eyes, this man informs you, who have never intentionally exercised more than ten minutes a week, that "you have the legs of a dancer."

Now you know for sure he's lying. But he wants to make you feel good. He wants to make you feel less self-conscious so you both will have a rip-roaring time in bed. The funny thing is that sometimes his reassuring patter truly scores him grand success.

So what's the big deal? For some women taking their clothes off with a lover, particularly a fresh one, constitutes a singular act of courage. They kiss sexual arousal goodbye as their relentless and scathing internal critic takes over. The internal mantra goes like this: too fat, too flabby, too much stomach, not enough bosom, buns of jelly. If his polite lies restore confidence, what's the harm?

For some women, none. Take Cindy, a twenty-eight-year-old secretary. She reports that she loves it when men say "how happy they are with my body just the way it is." Men, she admits, probably tell her "what I want to hear in the heat of the moment." She assumes they know how "self-conscious and insecure" she really is. When I asked her what she would prefer men to do instead, Cindy said she wouldn't change a thing: "I like to hear it. Keep on lying."

Or take Lill, the forty-year-old sales clerk who labels her zealously overpolite lovers the "ravers." She never gives a man a hard time when he tells her she has perfect breasts ("I don't," she adds). On the whole, Lill thinks sexual etiquette is "*very* nice." Still, she struggles to understand it, reflecting that it may have nothing at all to do with her, that "maybe it's a turn-on for him to be verbal about my body." Sometimes she lets herself believe her ears ("Maybe he's so crazy about me, he really thinks I'm beautiful"). But even Lill's generosity has an edge to it. When asked what she would prefer a "raver" to do instead, she offers him a new and improved script: *"It doesn't turn me on to have my body parts compared to other women's. Like, you are a '7.' I don't want him to say I'm 'better than average.' I would rather he say, 'You drove me wild in bed.'"*

Maybe the polite sexual lie doesn't harm, but it doesn't build trust either. Especially when early flattery fails to pass the test of time. When forty-four-year-old divorced Shelly first got into bed with Todd, she loved his lie that "I'm thin."

"I loved it. I was standing there naked and he said I was thin. I was heavier than I had ever been in my life, but I wanted to believe I was thin."

Eventually as they kept dating, they wound up going to Weight Watchers together. According to Shelly, "He knew I was self-conscious about my weight and confessed, 'I thought that was what you'd want to hear.'" Although Shelly managed to put a positive spin on it, it eroded her trust. She would have preferred that he had "not said anything."

Todd had committed no crime. He was just doing what a gaggle of men do in the kitchen, the living room, and the bedroom. He was telling the current woman in his life *what he thought she wanted to hear.*

"Tell 'em what they want to hear."

As we have seen, the "Tell 'em what they want to hear" tactic is one of the most widely cited reasons men give for lying to women in situation after situation. But sheer frequency of use doesn't make it right. "Tell 'em what they want to hear" can reflect a subtle attitude problem—a tendency to see women as objects to be placated, cajoled, conquered, and enjoyed. Or it can reflect a failure of empathy. At best, he and she are reading from different scripts, attuned to different rituals.

One thirty-two-year-old newly married banker confided that he really enjoyed "telling a woman who is not fabulously attractive that she is beautiful." But his instant makeover of the ugly duckling is neither classic Pygmalion nor strictly altruistic. Think of it this way: this man's a time and motion engineer of the bedroom. The big pay-off for his lie is that it "enhances performance." He literally gets more bang for his buck or, as he puts it, "more enthusiasm in the sexual act." Is the ugly duckling grateful, or does she feel used and abused? He's not sure because he's not thinking of her reaction beyond sexual performance. He responds by comparing himself to "a photographer saying, 'You're beautiful' to enhance the productivity of the photo shoot." For this young professional the motivation for telling her what she wants to hear is two parts power trip, one part intimacy.

What happens when a woman takes a "Tell 'em what they want to hear" lie at face value? Marianne's a good example. She's a bright thirty-four-year-old divorced sales representative, who had been thinking of moving from the West Coast to New York. Jack, the man she had been seeing, opposed the move and was trying to change her mind. "He called me twenty times a day." When she spoke frankly to him about her serious concerns over his excessive drinking and impotency, he reassured her, "Our sex life will get better when you get more comfortable with me." The night before he left on a business junket, he spoke the magic words, "I love you." And she believed them. Why would a smart woman like Marianne trust her future to an alcoholic with impotency problems—one who was working overtime to persuade her not to move beyond his reach? Here's what she said: "He told me he loved me, how much it meant to him if I didn't move to New York. *I didn't trust it, but I wanted to hear it.*" The result? She didn't move. But the relationship didn't either. The power of his words, working in perfect synchrony with what she wanted to hear, overcame her good sense. She wasted another year of her life, trying to rescue a man who continued to drift beyond her reach.

How do you defend yourself against this kind of lie? For starters, *if it sounds too good to be true, it probably is.* Ask yourself what it is that you truly want to hear, and compare it against what he is telling you. If the match is hand-glove perfect, allow yourself to be more curious, skeptical. Ask what he has to gain from telling you what you want to hear. If it is sexual or monetary gain, beware. Be prepared to laugh off or challenge any extreme compliments he throws in your direction. Just as you would think twice if he called you the unsexiest or the ugliest woman on earth, you might want to think twice if he tells you are the sexiest or most beautiful.

"You're the best."

According to the men and the women I spoke with, when it comes to sexual etiquette, "You're the best" was the hands-down winner for men's most common bedroom lie. Twenty percent of the women I interviewed spontaneously came up with "You're the best" as the last bedroom lie they remember being told, and 15 percent of the men I interviewed mentioned it as well. Several men said they had even planned out exactly how they would use this spurious phrase. For many men, "You're the best" is part of the ritual. They use it as skillfully as they can: to keep her, please her, and pump her up for the next round.

Sexually savvy women, on the other hand, award "You're the best" lies lukewarm to scalding reviews. As one woman deadpanned, "You are the best cow in the whole herd!" Some dismiss it as a piece of the pro-forma male-female sexual script. They rate it as being about as sexy as an exchange between two coworkers where the first says, "How are things going?" and the second responds, "Great!" It's pure social ritual.

In fact, this lie can backfire. Some women find it hard not to react negatively. One disgruntled and now separated thirty-five-year-old woman attributed her husband's saying "You're the best" and "Our sex is great" (when she knew better) to different standards, to gender-scripted behavior and to plain old "fooling himself." She also saw "You're the best" as an easy cop-out that let him meet his own needs without taking care of hers: *"In fact, it's totally predictable sex. I know where his hand will be and when at any exact moment. 'Get on, get out, score!' When what I wanted was more cuddling."*

If this seems a bit harsh, let's revisit an older, wiser Donna, the Donna who had been duped on her maiden voyage by Garth's just-kidding virginity. Newly married Donna called "You're the best" a "stupid lie." *"We've all heard it before. It's bullshit. They all say, 'You're the best.' They think saying it elicits an outgoing assertive response from the woman they have in bed, that she will really go for it. It's part of their ritual. In reality it's an implicit patronizing comparison."*

Donna, rather than being flattered, resents being compared with other women, and suspects "You're the best" is more manipulative and self-serving than gracious. Joan, a twenty-five-year-old single woman, takes this reasoning a step further. She finds "You're the best" to be "both off-putting and impersonal. It sounds like something someone would tell a clone, what they think you would want to hear, a cliché." Joan doesn't want to be placated or treated like an object. She'd rather hear a man say something intimate about the two of them. Even something as prosaic as "I'm enjoying my time with you."

Why do so many men rely on such a pedestrian and inept compliment? The men I talked to saw this lie in an altogether different light: less routine than a thank-you, more personal than politely holding open a door, but much less scurrilous than a lie. Carl, forty-three years old and divorced after ten years, summed up a certain male attitude to the issue. Carl told me in all earnestness that " 'You're great,' 'I love you,' 'That's the best I ever had' are just exaggerations. *I don't see them as lies.*" Carl believes women "*like to hear it*" and that these "exaggerations" "*create a mood.*" Does he plan to use these "exaggerations"? Carl doesn't hesitate: "Yes. I do. I really want to say it."

What happens if a naive and uninitiated woman takes these harmless feel-good lies at face value? When she realizes that his "heartfelt" compliments were just ritualistic lies more grounded in a sexual how-to manual than in their personal intimacy together, she's likely to feel embarrassed and foolish. After being told that she's the best, she may think that they've got something special going—only to run into him with someone else the next day or a couple of weeks later. How common is this? Even women in their forties and fifties made the mistake of believing "You're the best," "I love you," and "That was the greatest sex I ever had" were harbingers of exclusivity and an ongoing relationship. Whoa. Slow down. No way. Not yet.

Best advice? Remember that the polite mask of sexual etiquette can spawn lies that are meant for his benefit more than for your own. From his perspective, it's to his advantage if you are boldly unselfconscious. That gives him the pleasure he believes his compliments ensure. If this works for you too, let it be. All's well. Could be he's just a generous, polite soul. Just don't mistake his polite lies for the real thing or the cornerstone of a permanent committed relationship. The real thing takes time and testing. All you have here is protocol. Style, not substance.

The Hidden Houdini Mask

When it comes to sexual intimacy, some men are veritable Houdinis of the bedroom. Once they draw the curtains and lock themselves in, they put all their energy into freeing themselves. Now you see them, now you don't. Their disappearing acts are often legendary. Ask the boys down at the bar any Saturday afternoon.

It's hard for these Houdinis to forget, even for a moment, where sex and the profession of their love might lead them. These men are stand-in Romeos with the obsessive inner turmoil of a full-blown commit-a-phobe. Sure, he acts interested, but even as he's caressing you and telling you how soft your skin is, his half-closed eyes remain focused on the door. What he hides from you is that after the sex, his main obsession is getting out from between the sheets. This leads him to any number and type of lies. For him, like other commit-a-phobes, the lie becomes his wormhole to freedom.

Some Houdinis use the mask of pleasant agreeability to get into and out of your bed with a minimum of emotional involvement and personal pain. This mask is more utility than pretension, since it's worn only from the time of entering your bedroom to the time of exiting, allowing him to pass through as efficiently as possible. Chances are, you won't get to know this artful dodger very well, since he's agile and well-practiced when it comes to saying goodbye without looking back.

Philip, a twenty-six-year-old graduate student, wears the mask of the hidden Houdini all too well. If only they knew in advance, his escape route tactics would distress, not disarm, many of the women he charms. Philip earnestly leans forward to explain: *"From the beginning I try to keep the end in mind—and that's always getting out. The second time I sleep with a girl, she asks if I will go to Mass with her. I say yes. But I have no intent to go, especially if some good pro football or something is on TV."*

How does Philip explain his avoidance of a serious relationship to himself? *"It's the path of least resistance. Say whatever is best at the moment, then get Machiavellian later to get out of it. I ask how do I get out of this with the least amount of pain, complexity, and tears . . . I am conditioned to respond positively to women's requests, need, and desires. I try to avoid meeting family members."*

Yet, in the next breath, Philip talks about yearning to settle down, finding the right woman, beginning a family, moving into a house in the 'burbs with a white picket fence. This young man's fantasy life is all caricature, without a real flesh-and-blood woman in the picture—no one to make demands, to connect with emotionally. What went wrong here? Did Philip watch too many Doris Day films on the old movie channel or is he lying to himself, the women in his life, and us? Chances are he neither sees nor listens to himself or his own contradictions.

One thing's for sure. Philip's opportunistic view of intimacy is overlaid with picture book stereotypes that box him in, even in the act of lovemaking. No wonder he wriggles like a Harry Houdini emerging from a straitjacket at the first mention of church, family, or permanence. He has created his own lock-box.

Knock 'Em Dead Honesty—No Mask, No Kidding

A man who tells the truth should keep his horse saddled.
—Russian proverb

So here's the killer question. How open and honest do you really want your partner to be? Do you want to know his secret fantasies, what he is really thinking as you make love, how he truly reacts to your dimpled thighs, to the sounds you make or don't? Do you genuinely want to know why he was too tired when you initiated love-making last night? Or is the mask he's wearing just fine, thank you, and *please, please* keep it in place?

One tactic that men and women use to keep a relationship on track is the pact of honesty. Married couples agree to tell it like it is before they get married, or after the first infidelity. Dating couples agree to it because they're tired of the lies, the letdowns, and the anger. Even a man who is cheating on his wife may insist on honesty with his lover as a way of creating greater closeness than he has in his marriage, where fiction du jour stands in for truth. While his wife thinks he's playing golf or squash, he's sequestered away at the local motel of choice with another woman, who, unlike his wife, knows just where and who he is.

But for many men and women honesty has its drawbacks. In conversations with dozens of men, one theme thundered out. I labeled it "the trouble with honesty." Honesty, as many men tell it, creates far more serious consequences than do lies.

Consider Nick and Chuck. Their stories illustrate how burden-some honesty sometimes feels to men, and the effort and delicacy it requires.

Nick sat in my office. His face had turned a blotchy pink. I'd just asked him to tell me about his last bedroom lie. He'd already gone on record with me, telling me he didn't lie to his wife. When he first started dating Lynne ten years ago they struck a deal "that it was critical we be open and honest." Nick was one of a dozen men I interviewed who started out saying he'd rarely or never lied.

I prodded him a little, saying, "You're pretty red for a guy who says he doesn't lie." He smiled, then told me what was on his mind, justifying himself as he went: *"It wasn't a lie as much as a 'not tell.' It was a lie of omission, not commission. It was about a domination/submission sexual fantasy that didn't include my wife. I bent, not broke, the bond of trust between us by not including her."*

I pushed a little harder: "Was telling each other every thought you had part of the bargain you struck?" Nick ignored the probe. *"The problem is that I've been using the adult computer bulletin board. I logged on to it and now I have a secret life. It wasn't a planned lie because I found the computer adult bulletin board by accident and just logged on to it. She doesn't know the extent to which I have conversations about sexual fantasies. I haven't issued full disclosure. I violated a cornerstone of our relationship. It's not a critical violation, it's a technical violation."*

Nick was torn between his commitment to unequivocal honesty and his new and satisfying secret life on the adult computer bulletin board. Still, he rationalized it as an unplanned rather than a planned lie, as a "technical" rather than a "critical" violation. In his mind he had violated only the letter, not the spirit, of the law.

I asked why not come clean and confess the truth to Lynne? His answer was thought-provoking and thoughtful: *"I feel I have more fantasies than Lynne does. In sex, I lead, she follows my lead, so I feel I have more potential for being judged for thinking something. It's like an argument from Catherine Mackinnon that if a person fantasizes about rape, they are a rapist. I protect myself from that kind of judgment by keeping my thoughts secret. I stay in control, comfortable that I'm not interjecting something into our relationship that will undo what we have. I fear that I could screw up the relationship and that she might leave me. This is a whole area of gray. I have to figure it out internally. Is it more important to pursue something or to let it go? I fear she would think, 'My God, you're on the fringe of things, I reject you,' that Lynne will see me in a different way. It could change our relationship."*

Nick cares about the commitments he's made to Lynne. Yet honesty has now become a mask that hides his secret life—a life that gives him sexual pleasure without his wife's knowledge or participation. His covert activity on the computer adult bulletin board doesn't seem to do any harm. Maybe Dr. Ruth would even say it might help his sex life. But his fear of discovery and rejection are getting in the way. It impedes the flow of honest and straight communication from him to Lynne. It walls off whole parts of Nick's personality in ways that create a chilly distance where there had been none. Nick worries about what Lynne would think of him if she knew. The problem is that by leaving his thoughts secret, he is ducking his fears and creating an unnecessary barrier to their intimacy. Even worse, he is confusing his sexual fantasies with the betrayal of trust his "not tell" signifies. Will she be angrier with him for playing out his sexual fantasies on the bulletin board or for keeping them secret, and so betraying their agreement?

Nick's shame and fear has transformed their pact of honesty into a hypocritical and constrictive mask. As he hides behind it, both he and Lynne become victims of what would appear to be a victimless crime of sexual talk on the adult computer bulletin board.

Then there is Chuck, a thirty-two-year-old business manager, in an altogether different situation, also involving honesty. Like Nick, he too had agreed to a full disclosure agreement in his relationship. Chuck and his girlfriend Jennifer had agreed to tell the whole truth, "no matter what." Chuck took that to mean that he literally had license to "be *really* honest with her." So one night after they had been drinking together and were making love, Chuck "detected an odor that shouldn't have been there." Without hesitating, he honored his commitment to full disclosure: *"I told the truth about something very personal: her vaginal odor. I suggested a douche."*

The result was nothing Chuck wanted. Jennifer was "highly and immediately offended." Whatever her personal hygiene issues, Chuck was never again privy to them, since the relationship ended. Of course, this incident was probably one contributing factor among many, but here's Chuck's postmortem: *"I was embarrassed by what I had said, but I was too prideful to say I was sorry. I was truthful, but wrong. I should have refrained from oral sex and not said anything."*

It was a delicate situation. And one that comes up more frequently than we think. What is the best way to manage it? Is there a best time or way to bring up vaginal odor or any other uncomfortable disclosure? Chuck held to the letter of his agreement of full disclosure, to an extent that clearly exceeded whatever Jennifer had in mind. Then he took full disclosure one step further. Gratuitously, in the middle of sex play, he became Jennifer's medical adviser by recommending that she douche.

Perhaps Chuck got carried away with the heady freedom that honesty granted him. That in turn taught him what every nonliar who hopes to be effective eventually learns—the power of timing. The truth has many moments and many shapes. Contrary to popular opinion, it doesn't have to be brutal. The trick is to imbue the truth with genuine empathy and caring for the other person, and not treat it like a hot potato. As offended as Jennifer was in the moment, there's a good chance she would have forgiven Chuck if he had persisted in pursuing the relationship. Unfortunately, Chuck's embarrassment got in the way. He distanced himself, and the relationship came to a halt.

So back to the original question. How open and honest do you really want your sexual partner to be? Honesty, like deceit, has its liabilities. What both stories illustrate here is that a pact of honesty is no quick fix for the complex challenges and problems that arise in any relationship. Still, caring *and* frank discussion will almost always be better for a long-term relationship and the individual than the lie. But that takes reasonable communication skills, good judgment, and a modicum of courage on the part of both parties. It requires that you listen and respect his intent to talk openly about difficult issues, even if you don't like what he is saying, and that you both acknowledge that while this is difficult it is preferable to the lie. *If* that is what you both believe.

Honesty that works calls for dedication, deliberate effort, and thick skin. For many men and women, the lie is the quick and dirty substitute of choice. Which brings us to another issue—the masks women wear in bed.

The Masks That Women Wear in Bed

Do men and women differ in the way they lie to each other about sexual matters? The reality may be elusive, but both men and women seem to agree that *women lie less* in the bedroom. Among the ninety-five men and women I interviewed, both genders thought women told fewer bedroom lies than men. *Nearly half of the men I interviewed didn't think a woman had ever lied to them in the bedroom!* That's a solid vote of confidence for women's honesty. Yet among the women interviewed, who knew precisely whether and how often they'd lied and to whom, only 25 percent said they didn't lie in bed.

What about the 75 percent of the women who did lie to a man in bed? Which masks did they wear? Here's the pattern that emerged from the forty-five women who admitted they'd lied in bed.

FOUR MASKS WOMEN ARE LIKELY TO WEAR IN THE BEDROOM

1. The Mask of Sexual Fulfillment

This turned out to be the number one lie. Among the women I interviewed, one-third lied about enjoying sex, about being sexually satisfied by their partners, about what feels good, and about having orgasms. Faked orgasms lead this pack of lies.

What Women Said They Lie About in the Bedroom

"I fake orgasm all the time. One guy always asked. He was good in bed, but thought it was important that I have an orgasm every time. I don't have to have an orgasm every single time. But I didn't want to hurt his feelings."

"I faked having an orgasm. I told him I liked having sex with him, but I wasn't really excited."

"I lied about orgasms. I told him I had one when I didn't. To make him feel special. I'm not sexually intimate with a lot of people."

"I lied about orgasm because Ed tries so hard. He says it's not important, but I lie to make him feel good. Also he loves oral sex. I don't. I was abused as a child with oral sex. I lie about liking oral sex."

2. The Mask of Sexual Etiquette

Fifteen percent of the women interviewed talked about their polite lies of complimenting him on his penis size ("It's so big"), his body ("You have a great body"), or his prowess ("You're the best"); or minimizing his impotence ("No problem"). But sometimes, lurking behind her accommodating mask is pure vitriol.

What Women Said They Lie About in the Bedroom

"That he's the greatest. His last girlfriend made him feel inadequate. He had no ego on sex. To get it on a regular basis, I had to build it up."

"At a time of impotence. I say it doesn't really bother me—no problem, but it does."

"When I say something in the bedroom, it must have a grain of truth in it. So I say I love your eyes, shoulders. My lies are lies of omission. I lie by not telling him his dick is too small, undersized, that he doesn't know how to kiss, that he is an inept lover."

"I say things that make them feel good—that everything was great when it really wasn't; blunt honesty in the bedroom is not good for relationships. But dishonesty may backfire if everything isn't right. You want them to stop, but then they say: I thought you liked it."

"Mine was the 'It's so big' lie. The sex wasn't good. After sex, I didn't like the person. I didn't want to be the one to say you're not good in bed, you have no personality, and you're not good-looking. So I commented on his size."

3. The Mask of Legitimate Avoidance

Excuses, excuses. Over 10 percent of the women interviewed wore the mask of "I'm too tired," "I have a headache," or "It's a bad time of month." (Given that 33 percent faked orgasm and/or lied about being satisfied and interested in sex, the real question is why the percentage of excuses is so low.)

What Women Said They Lie About in the Bedroom

"I would lie not to have sex. 'It's a bad time of month.' Anything to buy time."

"I never told a man he wasn't good in bed, although a lot weren't. One guy I lied to wasn't able to have an erection that I liked. Not strong enough. To avoid him I told him I had an itch and had gone to a health clinic. They told me I had an infection."

4. The Mask of Innocence

Very few women lied about the number of previous relationships they'd had, what they had done in those relationships, or the last time they'd had sex. A few covered up a seamy or tempestuous past.

What Women Said They Lie About in the Bedroom

"I like to suggest things I liked from previous relations. But I say it's something I heard or read about, like being tied up, or like tantric sex. I see if they are open to it. I don't admit I've ever done it. I get positive results. They ask: 'Have you ever done this before?' At this point, sometimes I say yes, sometimes no."

"Scott asked me if I had slept with anyone else after we broke up. I said no, but had slept with another ex-boyfriend. Why? Because I knew we wouldn't get back together and I didn't want him to hate me."

"I keep secret that I did work on a phone sex line for three weeks. And that work is a complete lie—'I'm home alone, I'm five-foot-eight, and I have red hair.' Not."

What's most striking here? That one-third of the women interviewed said they lied to men about their level of sexual interest
(high), their enjoyment (you betcha), and their orgasms (yes, yes,
yes). The fact that one-third of their lies dealt with pretending to be
sexually satisfied is telling, particularly since they had not been
asked whether they'd lied about their sexual satisfaction. Despite
their faux sexual interest, very few of these women said they made
up excuses to avoid sex.

Yet when I looked at who reported using excuses to avoid sex,
nearly all the spurious excuses were generated by women who
reported faking orgasms. Listen to this thirty-five-year-old secretary,
now separated from her husband: *"I concealed my discontent, feigned
orgasm—because otherwise he would keep things up and I wasn't
stimulated. It was painful. I lied just to get him off of me. I made
excuses, all the old standbys: I'm about to get my period, I have a
headache, I'm too tired."*

Apparently, some women avoid sex as much to duck relentless
pressure to feign excitement as for reasons of low sexual satisfaction.

But not all women who faked orgasms used excuses to avoid sex.
One sexually discontented wife in a troubled marriage reported her
lie was "Let's have sex every night" so "he would stay in the marriage." She was committed to doing whatever it took to keep the
marriage intact. As you might guess, her effort failed and they
landed in divorce court.

Overall, it appears that women did what they thought they had
to do to be viable, convivial sexual partners—even when there wasn't
a lot of sexual pleasure in it for them. Even in the 1990s, decades
after the "sexual revolution," many women still find it difficult to
honestly tell a man what *they* really like, rather than go along with
his sexual program.

Interestingly, not a single man interviewed mentioned excuses
for avoiding sex as a typical woman's lie. But several men targeted
women's too innocent presentation of themselves as a lie. Even here,
though, how some men reacted to learning of a lover's rich past sexual experience may hold a surprise or two for those women who
cling to the mask of false sexual innocence.

Consider how Tim, the thirty-year-old single bond trader, reacted
to discovering his girlfriend's secret sexual exploits: *"We went out for
two years. Catherine acted like everything we did was the first time
she'd ever done it. She'd spent a semester in Barcelona and had gone
out with this guy there. One day when I'd borrowed her car, I found
a tape he'd sent her in her the glove compartment. I played it. They*

were having crazy animal sex. This tape was a user's guide to Catherine. I didn't confront her. No. I used the information."

Was Tim angry and hurt that he'd been duped? If so, he hid it well in the interview. Tim saw the tape as covert sexual intelligence. He took it as an opportunity and guide to new sexual adventure. How many women do you think would respond to a similar discovery in a similar way? Would you?

What Can We Learn From These Stories?

Sex can be casual or an expression of lasting love and commitment. But the masks we wear in the bedroom clearly apply to both partners and can surprise and hurt us at any stage of a relationship. Lies as masks make it difficult for anyone to know what's real and what's not, what our partners want and what we want. For example, sometimes we're not sure if we are seeking casual sex or a lasting relationship or if we want a particular sexual relationship to end or to continue. It's even harder to ferret out what *someone else* really wants, especially given that he may be even more confused than you are. But sometimes he knows exactly what he wants, and it's 180 degrees removed from anything you would remotely agree to, if only you knew too.

That's why it's especially important not to make assumptions or think a basic self-defense strategy will rob you of your ability to enjoy a relationship. Think of it this way: self-defense is an invitation to remember how important you are, not to become a cynic. After all, you might as well protect yourself, since your life and well-being depend on it.

So take some time to define your own sexual self-defense strategy. Use the "Sexual Masks Self-Defense Checklist" to remind yourself which self-defense principles to load into your holster before you get seriously involved with him.

SEXUAL MASKS SELF-DEFENSE CHECKLIST

---

1. *Learn the most common bedroom masks*—sexual innocence, experience, high-octane sex, safe sex, sexual health, "I love you," "Tell 'em what they want to hear," the hidden Houdini, etc.

   Ask yourself which ones you have heard him using. Identify a few. Sort through the information he's unintentionally giving you about who he is, his level of experience, his readiness for commitment, his sexual etiquette.

Remember the purpose of the mask is to conceal, so you'll be led to make the decision that is good for him, not necessarily for you. Avoid this. Instead, ask yourself what it is that you want.

2. *Resist being seduced by his sweet talk.* It's tempting, but remember they're just words. The more attractive his words are to you, the more likely you'll take them at face value. Instead shift your focus to his behavior.

Does he act like he's in love with you or is he just mouthing the right phrases?

Test his talk. Ask him to do something inconvenient for you. See how willing he is, or how caringly he turns you down.

3. *Ask him tough questions.* Challenge what he says. See what happens. Watch him to see if he contradicts himself. Notice any discrepancies in his answers.

Be impudent. Ask: "You mean you've always had safe sex? Every single time? Tell me about a time you forgot."

If you entrap him, it's not the end of the world. Why not have the conversation now without pain that you'd be having in three or six months anyway? You might even break ground for a high-trust relationship.

Watch for any patterns. Did he say New Jersey and then change to New York? Did he say he'd been celibate for a year and then change it to six months?

Talk to him about the discrepancies. Don't make life easy for him by making empathic excuses for him. See what he does. Regard it as an interesting experiment, like putting a smoke detector in your kitchen.

4. *Check him out with other women and with his friends.* What do they say?

Ask tough questions. What really happened when he left his wife?

How did he lose custody of his kids? How long has he worked there?

Why go in blind? Even if you don't like what you hear, the facts are the facts, and you still have the wherewithal to run for the nearest exit.

5. *Separate liking and trust.* Of course you're going to like him. He's literally doing everything he can to charm your pants off. Fine. But remember liking is chemistry—which isn't bad for starters, but it may not be enough. Trust has to be earned over time.

Don't make hasty decisions with potential for serious consequences based on chemistry alone. Give the relationship a little more time.

You liked him then, you'll like him later.

6. *Note if he protests his honesty too early, too plaintively, or too frequently.* Regard this as a poor predictor of real honesty, and a reasonable predictor of the mask of honesty (or a past problem with lying).

Pay attention to how often he proclaims that he's not lying even when you've made no accusation. Does he start sentences with "I swear this is true," or "You have to believe me," or "I'd never lie to you"?

7. *Memorize the "Tell 'em what they want to hear" principle.* Post it on your refrigerator door. The only way to beat this one is to know exactly what you most want to hear or believe. Remember how the principle of synchronicity can wipe out your good judgment to make you an easy pawn.

Compare your wish list with his catalog of proffered goodies. If the fit is too good to be true, assume it isn't and start over at the top of this list again.

The masks he wears in bed may reflect a wide range of macho posturing, gender stereotypes, and all-weather fears about dependence and commitment. These masks are rooted in the bedrock of who he is, not just in the times, the situation, or you.

It helps to remember that people's behavior is consistent and his pattern of lying is no exception. Once you get this simple fact straight, you can see how the lines and hooks he used to get you in bed correspond with what happens next. What he did yesterday and last week will be the best predictors of what he will do tomorrow—

and next week and next year. Change can and does occur, but view it as the exception, not the rule. Despite what some men say ("I never lie in bed"), when it comes to basic personality and values, very few men or women are virtuoso quick change artists in the bedroom or anywhere else. Who we are in a moment of sexual intimacy will reflect who we are the rest of the day, the week, and the year. The principle holds true for men and women.

This means that his early relationship masks will often be harbingers of far more durable masks that will continue to obscure who he is later. The result is to keep intimacy at arm's length. As we move from the bedroom to the living room and other areas of life, you are more likely to encounter a new set of painful foolers—false commitment and the "everything is fine" mask. We'll look at those next.

Chapter 7
False Commitment

She wanted a lifetime commitment. I told her I loved her in a moment of passion.
—Forty-three-year-old divorced male city administrator

I was pulling her in close when I really didn't want it. I wasn't proceeding with the relationship at all. I was lying to myself. I always considered myself first.
—Thirty-seven-year-old single male business analyst

He promised to stay married because that was our commitment. Then he left the marriage after all the lies. The relationship I married into was over ten years before the relationship ended.
—Forty-nine-year-old divorced female teacher

Commitment has given birth to many lies and has even spawned the term, "commit-a-phobe," the topic of many therapy sessions and jokes! Commitment is a powerful word with dual and ironic meanings. And it's a term that seems to evoke equally strong but opposite feelings in men and women. To be committed in a relationship is to feel emotionally and/or financially connected *and* obligated to someone. But more ominously, being committed also has the meaning of being involuntarily confined—as in a prison or mental institution. You bet there's irony here. For a number of men, and some women, the process of committing emotionally and financially to another human being propels them into relationship claustrophobia, and induces the immediate *feeling* of being involuntarily confined. No wonder that commitment and its avoidance inspire so many masks, misunderstandings, and all manner of lies.

How does this paradox of commitment play out against the backdrop of our own lives? Think back to the various commitments men have pledged to you over the course of your life. What's the very first commitment you remember a man making to you? It might have come from a father, an older brother, a relative, a teacher, a first boyfriend, or someone else. For me, it was my father promising that "God willing" (his favorite hedge), we'd vacation that long ago summer of 1950 at South Haven, Michigan, on the lake.

Once you start thinking about it, you'll encounter commitment at all levels—from the daily to the once-in-a-lifetime, from the ordinary to the sublime. The following checklist of a whole range of commitments will help jog your memory about commitments made to you, whether kept or broken.

A RANGE OF COMMITMENTS FROM THE ORDINARY TO THE SUBLIME

Kept	Broken	The Commitment
___	___	1. To pick you up somewhere, school, the airport, the hospital.
___	___	2. To return a borrowed book or videotape.
___	___	3. To attend a party you are giving.
___	___	4. To show up somewhere on time.
___	___	5. To show up somewhere.
___	___	6. To call you the next day, week.
___	___	7. To be responsible for birth control.
___	___	8. To make love a certain way.
___	___	9. To love and care for you.
___	___	10. To have an exclusive relationship.
___	___	11. To be honest.
___	___	12. To talk about feelings.
___	___	13. To tell you when the relationship is over, or if there's someone else.
___	___	14. To get engaged, married.
___	___	15. To have a monogamous relationship.
___	___	16. To start a family.
___	___	17. To be in the delivery room with you.
___	___	18. To be an equal child care partner.
___	___	19. To raise the children in a certain religion.
___	___	20. To support the family or contribute to family income.
___	___	21. To manage your finances.
___	___	22. To live in a certain geographic location.
___	___	23. To support your going back to school.
___	___	24. To spend time with the family.
___	___	25. To balance work and family time.
___	___	26. To stop drinking, using drugs, overeating, abusing.
___	___	27. To go to a marriage counselor, psychologist, get help.
___	___	28. To be your soulmate and partner till death do you part.

Pick a few commitments made to you that still seem important. Go back in time and think about how you felt when you first heard him make his commitment to you. Did you take him at his word without questioning his sincerity? Were you ecstatic, delighted, scared, doubting? What were your best hopes and worst fears? For example, I still can remember how my father's promise made me feel—the happiest little girl in the world. I could hardly wait for summer to come. However you felt, jot it down.

Now fast-forward to endings. Play out in your mind the details of what actually happened for each commitment. Suppose his commitments were false promises. Were you angry with yourself for believing him, and with him for lying to you, who so innocently believed him, the liar?

What do you think he really intended to happen, and how did it square with the outcome that is now permanently etched into your personal history? Was there some explanation that gave you solace or strength? In my father's case, he became seriously ill and couldn't go anywhere, but that didn't keep me from feeling disappointed and let down. What about you? Did you feel humiliated, abandoned, distraught?

How warily do you eye the next man who swears he'll call you, love you, marry you, be faithful to you, help you raise your children in your religion, or whatever else a seductive commitment might look like for you? And what have you learned from all your experiences here?

Our experiences are legacies that color our perspectives as we go forward into our next relationships. Commitments kept and broken are powerful teachers. But to take advantage of that learning and to take care of ourselves, we must be able to distinguish between a person's intent, and the many possible outcomes of that person's actions.

Recognizing the Difference Between Intent and Outcome

Intent and outcome are different beasts. At the time of a promise, his intent may or may not be sincere. But even if it is sincere, things change. He (and we) may leave a trail of unintentional disappointment in our wake. And no matter what our original intent, the outcome of our promises is what our partners, friends, and lovers are stuck with. So what he meant may be very different from what you finally get.

What if you had the power to look back at the promises someone makes at the start of a relationship, while seeing ahead to just how these promises played out months or years later? Truth would separate itself from deception in a heartbeat. The result? Where men's lies are the issue, every woman would be an instant winner. You'd know whom to trust and whom to trash! Your decisions would be informed by *his real behavior*, not his words.

Janus, the mythical Roman god of beginnings, could look forward and backward. Ancient Romans portrayed him with two faces back to back, so Janus could look in both directions at the same time.

Most of us have to earn Janus-like vision the hard way. It's called 20/20 hindsight. The only consolation is that the more experience we get, the better our chances for developing wisdom and judgment.

What would we see if we had Janus-like vision? We'd find commitments honored, people working hard to achieve harmony, dealing honestly with each other. We'd see auspicious and inauspicious beginnings and some happy endings. Interspersed we'd find all manner of lies and truths withheld. And we'd be stunned by the seductive power of those lies.

Particularly lies about commitment. After all, the promise of commitment sounds good because when it's authentic, it's wonderful. But for some men, commitment to a woman amounts to little more than target practice. When they hit the bull's-eye by falsely convincing you that they're genuine contenders, they take their winnings away. Some have bouts of conscience and eventually change their ways. But for others you're just another casualty along the way—someone they duped to get what they wanted. Too bad what they wanted was so very different from what you wanted.

But even for the willing, keeping promises made is no small challenge. The art of the kept promise is a dying craft. It demands being open to knowing ourselves and our feelings. It requires that we discipline ourselves to say no to other compelling and available options. And no matter how resolute our intent, remember things change—ourselves, our circumstances, our partner. So the outcome of our promises can turn out very different from what we intended. Let's see how this plays out.

Types of False Commitment

His lie? That we'll be together forever (or at least until I leave this apartment).
—Thirty-year-old single female sales manager

*His lie to me was that he wanted to travel farther down the path, that
there were other things he wanted to share, that he wanted further
intimacy.*
—Thirty-eight-year-old single female chef

His mask of false commitment allows him to move light years
beyond those first few quick trips to your bedroom into every other
area of your life, yet his true motives can be as artfully cloaked as
any Klingon warship on *Star Trek*.

What is he hiding and why? Let's begin by identifying the
masks of false commitment that women most frequently encounter:

THREE TYPES OF FALSE COMMITMENT

1. The Hollow Committer

Sure, he's committed himself to you—just don't ask him why.
Maybe it was timing. All his friends were pairing off, or he
just got tired of playing the field. Maybe he was too ashamed
to tell you he didn't know how he really felt or what he
wanted. You tell yourself it's just strong macho silence. But
the truth is, he's truly clueless, and in another fifteen years
when your kids ask him, "Why'd you marry Mom?" he'll
join ranks with all the other men shaking their heads in
wonderment and saying, "Seemed like a good idea at the
time," or, "Dunno. Beats me." And mean it! Unfortunately,
because his commitment was hollow from the start, it can
collapse at a moment's notice, leading to a devastating,
sometimes out-of-the-blue end to the relationship.

2. The Minimalist Committer

When it comes to relationships this guy's a master of the minimum. He's the consummate noncommitter. His energy may
be in his career, in the kids, in strutting his body at the
neighborhood gym, in other women. Wherever it is, it's
clearly not in you and in the relationship, but you won't
know that at first. Maybe he's angry and is holding back his
tender feelings to get even. More likely he's oblivious, and
probably no happier than he's making you.

3. The Opportunistic Committer

Here's the classic case. He tells you whatever it takes to get and
keep you involved with him, sexually, emotionally, even

financially. But he has no stable, lasting interest in you. Maybe you're a looker, a trophy date, a brain who can write his term papers, a hard-charging money-making machine, or just a good roll in the hay. You represent an opportunity for him to get something he wants or needs, and he's seized the day. Just remember it's over when he says it's over, and that's any time now.

No matter how a particular relationship actually ends, these masks of false commitment present serious breaches in trust between men and women. As often as not, these masks reflect that he may be as much out of touch with himself as with you. Years of holding his feelings in check have left him bereft of self-knowledge and insight, as he hides his true intent from you and himself. Trying to please everyone, he pleases no one, least of all himself. And years of trying to get into women's beds haven't given him the right set of social skills to make a convincing case that he really wasn't that serious, after all.

What's at the heart of these masks of false commitment? Harvard psychologist Samuel Osherson in his 1992 book *Wrestling With Love* is clearly onto something when he points to men's "attachment battles." According to Osherson, what this means is that in men, ". . . the desire to connect and the impulse to shun intimacy arise at the same time." Osherson rightly points out that paying attention to "men's wish to run away from relationships" causes us to "miss their attempts to connect." But the error of missing a man's intense battle with intimacy is both more common and more treacherous for the women in his life.

Focusing on men's attempts to connect
causes women to miss men's wishes to run away from relationships.

Men's "attachment battles" put an oscillating "I want you"/"I don't want you" face on their commitments that confuses and distresses many women. Scratch a little and you may find his ambivalence at the root of many of his lies of commitment and harmony.

Take these two men—Andrew and Jake. Let's begin by looking at their masks of hollow commitment.

Hollow Commitments: Now and Forever

Decades apart in age, and in different parts of the country, Andrew and Jake have something in common. They each used the mask of hollow commitment to hide themselves and their attachment battles from view. Each told a woman he wanted to marry her, then did just that.

You're probably wondering, did you read something wrong? Since when did proposing and making good on the proposal become a lie? Isn't that the way it's supposed to happen for millions of happy couples? When a man says he wants to get married and then shows up at the altar to say, "I do," how can this point to a commitment problem?

First, remember that the mask of false commitment is a fooler—one that most women, in what they hope are serious relationships, are predisposed to believe. He says, "Let's get married." She says, "Are you really serious?" He nods, and in a nanosecond she's at the bridal registry. After all, *he said it, he must mean it.* And because so many men are commit-a-phobes who regard the C-word with the same uneasy affection with which a thief regards a prison cell, a woman who hears those three little words, "Let's get married," may justifiably want to strike while the iron is hot—before his attachment cools off and he reverses himself.

Unfortunately, "Let's get married" talk, like "I love you" talk, is cheap, and often hollow. Believe it or not, despite the words he's spoken, he may not mean to imply genuine commitment. All declaring "I want to marry you" may do for him is help him temporarily gloss over having no clue at all about what he really feels or wants. Maybe he feels lonely in the moment or wants to be in step with his friends who are rapidly pairing off with the women of their choice. Maybe that's why he offhandedly checks the marriage box. In the moment, it seems like a good thing to do. But because there are two of you, that casual choice profoundly affects his life—and yours. Without thinking anything through, he lets himself be coerced into commitments he is not ready to keep emotionally. Why? Because they are not real. They are hollow.

How could something like this happen? It's hard not to feel some empathy for both parties. Thirty-one years after the fact, that's exactly what Andrew, a thoughtful and articulate man in his mid-fifties, pondered as we talked. Speaking slowly, pensively, he said: *"I was feeling strange pressures from her, her family, society, circa 1963. It seemed like the right thing to do. All my buddies were married, so it made sense. I didn't want to lose her. It was at her prompting and suggesting that there was a clear danger of her going away. But I never gained or regained any emotional commitment."*

Asked how he felt, he looks down and says, "I wished for some way out of it. I was aware I wasn't totally comfortable at the time. Gradually I realized that I didn't want to get married." The outcome: "We ended up getting married and divorced after eighteen years."

Andrew was caught up in the changing times of the sixties. As Barbara Ehrenreich observes in her 1983 book, *The Hearts of Men*, marriage was positive proof of maturity. The idea was "to build a working partnership" where you "overcame romance for a realistic conception of marriage" and "a mutual state of emotional maturity." The American male at twenty-three years of age did feel "strange pressures" to enter adult life by slipping into the breadwinner, husband, father role. Getting married was indeed considered the right thing to do. And Andrew was ripe for the plucking. An Air Force Academy graduate, he was used to doing the right thing, conforming to expectations, to rules. He made a promise and kept it. But what Andrew felt was really obligation and duty, not a commitment of the heart. He wanted to step up and be counted as a man, as an adult. Marriage, for Andrew, was just another rite of passage like graduation or a promotion, marking his arrival at the next stage. His feelings about what he truly wanted were as artfully hidden from himself as from his bride. Andrew's mask was emotional commitment where there was none. And eventually, as times changed, that hollow emotional void took its toll. Both Andrew and his wife eventually grew apart, had affairs of the heart, then divorced.

In Jake's case, his march to the altar began with an offhandedly impulsive remark. Jake, a film producer who now calls himself a recovering pathological liar, had been drinking and was oozing macho bravado. There he was in Tucson, moderately drunk and talking on the phone to his old college girlfriend in Phoenix, when these words sprang from his mouth: "If there's anyone I'd spend the rest of my life with, it's you." Jake wryly notes that although this lie took place over a decade ago, it was the last lie he got caught in, and caught he was: *Martha took it as a proposal. Yet I didn't want to get married. . . . She took the bus back to Tucson. She thought I had proposed. I went along with it. That was in March. I finished school in June and joined her in Phoenix. We got married in November.*

The shocker here is not that Martha mistook Jake's casual remark for a proposal, but that Jake went along with her version of it. He could have said, "Hey, I really care about you, but I don't know what I want. I'm not ready to commit." But rather than endure the embarrassment of the moment and the reality of his own ambivalence, he went along with her program. What on earth was he thinking? And how did the accidental marriage work out? You be the judge.

For starters, his quasi-proposal reflected and exacerbated the attachment battle Jake was fighting. Jake was deeply ambivalent and only dimly aware of why. He wanted to connect *and* keep his distance. And that's exactly what he did.

He began with the time-honored male tradition of "sowing his wild oats"—*with a vengeance*. Jake the condemned man, committed to a lifetime sentence with Martha, had only nine months of freedom before the door clanged shut. According to Jake, "There were four affairs I had between March and November, both in Tucson and in Phoenix." His commitment to Martha was a hollow mask, a sham—not a reality. But Martha couldn't see it. Her background dictated that "You're supposed to marry your college sweetheart." His proposal came "just as she was out of college, lonely . . . " Marriage to Martha didn't stop Jake's philandering. He continued to have new affairs after they were married and to lie about them, making excuses as he went. But Jake didn't have to sweat too much because Martha was the perfect complement for his escalating lies. As Jake put it, "Martha never questioned my lies. They were never extravagant, grandiose." Then Jake, the master of the lie, offers any wannabe liars a bit of gratuitous coaching: *"If you're going to lie, keep it simple and stick with the same thing."*

While Martha conveniently accepted her husband's statements at face value (providing another example of women's reverent belief in the power of the word over action), Jake was perfecting the artful craft of deceit.

Eventually Jake fell in love with one of the several women he was having affairs with, and left a thoroughly surprised Martha. Predictably, Jake took his lying ways and continuing ambivalence around commitment with him into his next two marriages.

Relationship-Stopping Breaches of Commitment

Breaches of commitment are serious. They involve reneging on a promise or agreement that both parties originally made as a cornerstone of the relationship. Breached commitments can be about anything of importance for a twosome: where they are going to live, whose job will come first, how exclusive their relationship will be, whether they will marry, have a family, save or spend their income, belong to a particular religion.

Why would someone make false and hollow commitments on such serious relationship-stopping issues? For the following reasons:

- *It was tactical.* Committing was the shortest and most expedient way from A to B, or to whatever else the committer wanted—sex, marriage, children, a home in suburbia. The false committer will think about what the commitment implies tomorrow, next month, or next year, which unfortunately for the relationship *will* eventually roll around.
- *It was mindless accommodation.* Agreeing amounted to more of an unreasoned "Okay, I can do that" than a Machiavellian "I'll agree now and change my mind once I get what I want." The agreement here amounts to more of an impulse to please than a real commitment. But it sets the stage for the eventual breach anyway, when the committer finally realizes the long-range implications of the commitment.
- *Things changed.* It seemed fine enough at the time, but after living with this commitment for a while and seeing how it played out in daily life it's clear that it was a mistake and "escape" now has become the internal watchword. This realization sets the stage for the commitment-breaching behavior to follow.

What's missing in these reasons? The attempt to openly say, "Hey, wait a minute. I made a mistake, I didn't think it through," or "I changed my mind" and to renegotiate the agreement. The party who has changed his or her mind acts unilaterally and precipitously to change the rules without saying so, endowing this breach with its devastating potential.

For example, at some point in a relationship or marriage, a couple decides either to have or not have children, or to have or not have another child. Even though both parties might not feel an equal commitment to parenthood, eventually they agree on a course of action and commit to it. Once they make a decision, the consequences are clear: to have procreational or purely recreational sex.

Madeleine and Ned ran into this issue. They'd been married seven years and had two children. But Madeleine at age thirty-seven wanted a third, and her biological clock was buzzing like an alarm clock. They "had talked about having another child," and Madeleine was sure "Ned was on the same wavelength." One night, after a brief argument, they were making love when: *"In the middle, he excuses himself. He goes to the bathroom and comes back. We sort of finish, but I notice that he's soft. I felt he didn't come. I ask him if he came, he says 'Yeah.' I then ask him if he's sure he came. He again says, 'Yeah.' The next day we're talking. I know he didn't come. Normally, I'd let it go. But I knew he was wrong, so I kept at it. Finally he said, 'All right, I didn't come . . . I don't want to have a baby. I went to the bathroom to jerk off.'"*

Madeleine was outraged. Now it was her turn to get mad. She wanted to be pregnant. Ned had withheld his sperm *and lied to her about it.* So she began by shaming him. "Now you're telling me because of a little argument you don't want to have a baby?" He backs down and agrees that they should try again. But the lie has crystallized some fundamental difference for Madeleine: *"After that I didn't trust him anymore. He too became withdrawn. The lie did us in. It punched a hole in our relationship."*

What has gone wrong? It's not that they disagreed. It's that Ned had gone along with Madeleine's program without really buying into it, rather than honestly telling her, "I don't know, I need to think about it. I don't really want another child." Then after agreeing to something that really mattered to Madeleine, he tried to put one over on her and to deny it. In a moment of residual anger, the truth broke out. Madeleine caught Ned wearing the mask of hollow commitment, and even worse, lying to avoid conflict, with all its distressing messiness. It's true—a heated discussion might have been uncomfortable. But if it had opened the door to real dialogue, it would have beaten what happened to their family. The lie was a symptom *and* a catalyst. They divorced two years later.

Minimalist Commitment

The minimalist committer might have plenty of heart and soul to offer. The problem is that he's not going to invest it in you or the relationship. Often, he will tip his hand early, failing to show up on a second or third date, making excuses to cover that he isn't even committed enough to pick up the phone when you call him. But if you don't understand it sooner, you will later. He's detached, often with a history of leaving women waiting and wondering. Except for brief moments of sexual connectedness, he's often lost the attachment battle and has opted for a sporadic series of easy-in, easy-out, low-energy, low-commitment relationships. No matter how promising he seems to you in the moment, eventually you too will take your place in the series.

His Minimalist Commitment to Leaving His Wife

He says he hasn't had sex with his wife for ten years; they don't sleep in the same bedroom, much less the same bed. She's an unreasonable shrew with equal propensities for anger and shopping. He's hired a lawyer, is transferring his assets to higher ground (that should tell you something), and is looking for an apartment. And, by the way, he loves you and wants to live with you as soon as he takes care of his finances, settles custody issues, breaks the news to his in-laws—whatever.

What he says he's going to do isn't as important as what he doesn't do. As time goes by, he doesn't leave his wife.

Tania could write chapter and verse on this minimalist's mask. She had no trouble believing how unhappy Al was in his marriage. She had known him for years: *"He's someone I've known a long time. I even had a romantic relationship with him back in high school. Now, twenty years later, he's still part of a gang of friends that go back a long way. About one and a half years ago I slept with him three times. When he said 'I'm splitting with my wife. I'm going home and packing my bags,' I believed him. He and his wife were having a lot of problems. They had a horrible relationship. I had heard him tell her he was going to leave."*

Why did Al tell Tania he was leaving his wife when he wasn't? Tania puts it in starkly simple terms: "He lied to get me into bed. He thought he was going to leave—but didn't have complete desire. He was depressed." The end result of all this was that "I got pregnant. But I didn't tell him the whole thing until after I had an abortion because [by then] I was seeing someone else."

So Tania continued to sleep with her old boyfriend and he continued to tell her he was going to pack his bags and leave his wife. Nearly two years later he is still with his "roommate" in an argumentative "conflict habituated" (as the sociologists call it) marital relationship.

Tania gets the good sport award. Asked if she has regrets, she says, "Yes, I wouldn't have slept with him if I had known he wasn't going to leave her." But then she adds, "I got him a job where I worked on the Monday after the Saturday I had the abortion. He didn't even know yet." He told her the same lie over and over, and she omitted to tell him one big truth.

To better understand this phenomenon, let's go back to Andrew, whose hollow commitment to marry his girlfriend thirty years ago resulted in a long-term marriage that spawned a couple of affairs by both parties. He also lied to one of the other women about his commitment to her. In this instance, Andrew became a minimalist, not a hollow committer, who carefully chose his words to assuage his conscience: *"I never said outright, 'Let's get married.' But told her I was going to divorce my wife and that 'we can then think about being married.' I did this so I could be comfortable with myself. Then my wife found out about the affair. The other woman was very unhappy, actively angry."*

When I asked why he thought she had believed him, Andrew's words reflected his mix of blame, remorse, and self-reproach: *"Why did she let herself be fooled? Because she wanted to be. . . . It still doesn't excuse me."*

Andrew has had plenty of time to review and reflect on the consequences his hollow commitment (to his wife) and his minimalist commitment (to his lover) have wrought. He recognizes that his habitual lies of choice are "I am committed to you" and "I want to marry you." He even adds that more recently: *"In two instances I have assured women that I wanted to marry them. It never happened. There are two women out there who don't trust me. They wanted to get married . . . I said to myself, 'This is a great woman to have a friendly great sexual relationship with, but not to spend the rest of life with.' . . . What I wanted was a whitewashed version of my former wife."*

Given his insight, what, if anything, would Andrew do differently now? *"I would still have the affair. But I would make it clear that it was an affair. I wouldn't make promises and commitments. I would be honest."*

So now at fifty-three years of age, with hard-won 20/20 hindsight, Andrew opts for honesty, since his "lies have proved too painful in the long run."

Like Al and Andrew, the minimalist committer is likely to be a fence-sitter when pressed to actually leave his wife. A few men I've talked with and quite a few women clients mention that hackneyed B-movie phrase, "I don't want to lose you," in these kinds of caught-between-a-rock-and-a-hard-place situations. Is this phrase a lie or is it the truth? I think this one has some earmarks of the truth. "I don't want to lose you" captures the minimalist's reality quite nicely. It's partly true. He *doesn't* want to lose you, but he doesn't want to put any effort into keeping you either. Andrew explained it like this: "I want to retain the person in my sphere, so I tell little lies with big emotional consequences as a means of keeping someone."

Men like Andrew may have the necessary decency and aversion to stop short of telling their lovers the big "I love you" lie. Whatever you represent to him—acceptance, comfort, freedom from his marriage, a fail-safe, a safe harbor, a mother—he values that and would dearly miss it for a time, should you get tired of waiting for him. Just don't expect him to do anything beyond expressing his fear of loss. His commitment to you, which includes leaving his wife, is truly minimalist.

Promised and Jilted: A Minimalist Story

Okay, if he didn't stand you up at the altar, why does it feel like it? He said sure, he'd meet you in New Orleans where you, your mother, and your brother were going to spend the week. But there you are, and where is he? No warning, no excuses, just a no-show. How common is this? I heard the theme of no-shows come up again and again, from failing to show up for dates, to failing to show up for weekends planned months in advance, to failing to be heard from again after the wedding gown is purchased and the priest stands ready. How many women have sat and waited, alone and stunned, for the man who wasn't there and never would be?

Gwen is one of them, and it still rankles her. In fact, some days she can't stop replaying the whole episode. At thirty-two, Gwen has the fresh good looks and open quality of the girl next door. It's especially hard for her to hide the cloudy hurt in her eyes as she makes light of the last time she was lied to by a man, Larry. "I was misled. Promised and jilted," she says. *"One guy I dated wanted constant companionship. By his behavior, he led me to believe he was more into the relationship than he really was. I thought he must really like me because he was spending so much time with me. If I give up my time for him, it means something. He told my friends he really liked me, but never said to me how much he liked me. The relationship was blissful till it crashed and burned."*

What made this promising relationship crash and burn? Knowingly or not, Gwen had raised the stakes on Larry's minimalist commitment. She wanted Larry to meet her mother, even though it required that Gwen travel halfway across the country to make the encounter happen. Too bad all Larry could hear were the doors to his cell clanging shut: *"We agreed upon New Orleans at a hotel. He didn't show up. I called him and he wouldn't take my call. Finally, it occurred to me that the relationship meant more to me than to him. He couldn't invest in it. He misled me by his behavior, not his words. Maybe he just snapped. The relationship was progressing and it definitely scared him. He snapped."*

Gwen was working hard to explain to herself what she still can't fathom. How could somebody she trusted, someone she was in a serious romantic relationship with, humiliate and blindside her like this, with her mother in tow? I pushed her on the point, asking her, "When was the last time you had talked to him?" Gwen shook her head in continuing disbelief. "I had *seen him* just ten days before. I sensed nothing wrong. I believed him 'cause I had no reason not to." Echoing herself, and hundreds of other women I've spoken with, Gwen repeated this phrase, her voice trailing off. "No reason not to . . . "

No matter what he had intended when he promised to meet her in New Orleans, Gwen was still carrying the real and painful outcome of his lie. I hated to ask, but it was important to know: "Gwen, how did his lie affect you?" Who couldn't empathize with her answer? *"I was horribly upset. I felt sick. I loved him. I haven't loved anyone since. My mother said, 'Maybe he was in a wreck.' Later, I called him . . . He couldn't talk things through. I just wanted to hear his side of it. Maybe he didn't want to disappoint me face to face. I don't know. I said, 'You jerk! You cad!' All he said was: 'I have a lot going on right now. You're right.'"*

If Gwen could play director and rescript that awful weekend, now knowing just how minimal his commitment to her was, how would she redo it? Gwen's answer is revealing: *"I'd want to have been let down slowly. I think of him now as a truly reckless person. I gave him the option—instead of coming to see me this weekend, it's okay if you don't want to. I gave him an out. If only he would have taken it, I would have had a clue. As it is, I still ruminate about it."*

Gwen is no dummy. She's a successful public relations account executive and strategist. She covered herself and him by giving him plenty of room to say no, to save face without causing her undue pain. The fact that he didn't take the option spoke volumes to subtle Gwen, used to reading between the lines. It told her he was serious, that he'd be there. It was inconceivable to Gwen that, were the tables turned, she would be a no-show for Larry. To Gwen that behavior would have been reckless. Gwen knows how to put herself in the other person's shoes.

But Gwen's patience and goodwill toward the men who had lied to her, like that of the other women I interviewed, showed signs of fraying as the interview went into its second and third hour. Whereas at first Gwen had wondered whether she was "disregarding important information," "not seeing the warning flags until too late," now she lamented as she listened to her stories, "Look at this ship of fools I have to deal with. I wish I could start fresh . . . I feel like I'm carrying too much baggage." Her despair and disappointment were beginning to turn to edgy anger. His "serious, but not deadly" minimalist commitment had left an imprint of bitter hurt. This man contributed his small share to making the chasm between the sexes a little wider. The next time Gwen expects to be less naive, more cynical. What was Larry's intent? Probably not what Gwen has taken away as the outcome.

Commitment-Lite: "I'll Call You"

Is it a lie or not? Here's a promise so minimalist that it splits men and women right down the middle. Ask the men in your life how seriously, how gravely they view the unkept promise to call a woman after a first date or a few months into a relationship, or at the end of a relationship. Then ask your women friends. See if you hear the same reactions.

Twenty percent of the women I interviewed named "I'll call you" as one of the three most common lies men had told them, but only one man put "I'll call you" on his list of men's top three lies to women. And among the women, another 25 percent spontaneously mentioned the "I'll call you" lie in the course of their interviews (compared with less than 15 percent of the men). Besides these sixty women I interviewed, I've heard hundreds of women complain about this broken promise. Sure, it's not in the same genre of hurtful lie as "I love you," but some women call it men's most common and irritating lie.

But it's a funny thing. Most men don't see it that way at all. Talk about minimalist! They don't even think "I'll call you" is a commitment, much less a lie. In fact, many don't think reneging on the promise to call you should even be taken personally! Some of the men I interviewed were outraged that anyone would categorize "I'll call you" as a lie of commitment. Incredulously, they asked me, "Do most women really expect a call after 'I'll call you'?" They argued, "It's just an expression. It doesn't mean anything."

Maybe not to *them*. But to most *women*, "I'll call you" is one of the most ubiquitous and confusing lies. If she said it, she'd mean it. So why doesn't he?

It seems like a relatively small commitment, compared to such biggies as "I'll marry you," "I'll make child support payments," or "I'll be monogamous." Yet it is a breach. When the unconsummated

"I'll call you" comes from a new acquaintance, it may not be surprising to the initiated, but it certainly is irritating. When the
unconsummated "I'll call you" lingers as the final remnant of a
longer-term relationship, however, it leaves even the most jaded
feeling sinkingly unsettled, anxiously waiting for the phone to ring
weeks, even months later.

Why? Again, women have a different relationship with words
than men do. For a woman, "I'll call you" is a statement of intent to
continue the relationship. It's shorthand for "I like you" and "I want
to spend more time with you." It's an affirmation with an obligation
tagged on its end. "I'll call you" leaves the channel open for greater
intimacy.

For a man, "I'll call you" is a lot like, "So long, it's been good to
know you and I've got to be drifting along." It's a quick exit line that
promises nothing and wants nothing in return. It gets him safely out
your door and back onto his own turf. Worse, from a woman's point
of view, it may be a painless way of closing things down.

For you it's a hint of commitment you expect him to keep. For
him it's just a minimalist phrase that guarantees his safe passage.

Opportunist Commitments

You've met someone new and you're open to seeing how things
develop. Whether you know it or not, you've made him an offer he
cannot refuse. Whatever you have or represent—beauty, brains,
body, sex, status, cash, companionship—it's too good to pass up.
But his intent is to take advantage of a great deal and then move on.
Maybe he tells you. Then it's no lie, just business between consenting adults. But often he doesn't tell you, even though he doesn't
need a crystal ball to see what's coming down the road. It's you who
will be caught offguard and seriously blindsided. While you're fan-
tasizing about the future, using your current bliss as the standard,
he's well into strategizing about how to let himself off the hook.
Chances are, he's already got a plan.

The Promise of Exclusivity

The promise of exclusivity is a false commitment that buys him
the freedom to do exactly what he wants to do without your knowledge. Sometimes the promise of exclusivity is also an opportunistic
facade that simply gets him from there to here, at least for a while.
It's more of a transaction than a commitment.

That's how Stuart uses it. Stuart at midlife is good-looking, self-assured, and full of flirtatious charm. He laughed at the thought of the first lie he'd ever told a woman—the knowing laugh of a man who'd told many a lie since: *"My first lie was, 'You're the most important girl in my life,' the lie of exclusivity, knowing full well that I have a little black book in my back pocket with twelve other names in it that I would call on Sunday morning."*

Stuart, like nearly one-third of the men I interviewed, subscribed to the "Tell 'em whatever they want to hear" school of male-female romantic relations. He lied about exclusivity because "I assume that this is what women in general want to hear—that they value exclusive commitments." What Stuart valued here was "sex, status, and having a girlfriend as my possession." Did she know his commitment to her was a fraud? Stuart blew off my question: "She knew it, I knew it, our friends knew it. Guys talked, girls talked. We just never came together."

Stuart had quelled his own attachment battle by routinely assuming a whatever-it-takes-to-close-the-deal approach—taking ownership and making a trade whenever it suited him. For Stuart, commitment wasn't personal. It was all part of a buy-sell game. In fact, when the relationship ended, that wasn't personal either: "She went away and she was replaced by someone else." Some names were crossed off the list and others added. Stuart liked keeping his options open.

Whatever You Call It—It's Just Temporary

*I concealed my feelings, my purposeful lack of communications, that
the relationship was a temporary thing, that I wouldn't have gotten
involved with her if she weren't moving. I wanted sexual fulfillment. So
did she. But she liked me more than I liked her. Rather than allowing
her to find out, I concealed the truth. I didn't say.*
—Thirty-two-year-old single male actuary

Oh yes. It feels like the real thing. He's interested and attentive. He's romantic and has plenty of time for you. Too bad you're not privy to the fact that the only reason he's involved with you at all is (pick one or more of the options listed below):

1. You both live in different cities.
2. He knows he's taking a new job in West Africa in two months.

3. You're moving to a faraway city in six months and told him.
4. You're both married to other partners.
5. It's a same-time-next-year arrangement.

For Marty it was option three. Marty, as you may recall, is the same Marty who went to the Philippines and Thailand, neglecting to tell his virginal girlfriend that he was also going on a sexual adventure. In the new situation Marty is still actively searching for an uncommitted sexual relationship, and this one seemed like a no-brainer to him. Courtney was moving to Oklahoma while Marty was tied to an East Coast home office, with no travel schedule on the horizon. Marty viewed it as an opportunity, a great deal for both of them. They'd both have a fine time, then say goodbye with no regrets. Marty was ecstatic. He lucked into a relationship where he could see the ending at the beginning. The only problem was that he omitted to let Courtney in on the arrangement.

The payoff for Marty was "keeping the relationship going on my terms. *Noncommitment.*" Marty claims he didn't plan to lie or mask his motives at all. At least not at first. Why should he? He thought they "were on even ground." Since she was moving, he figured she'd see it his way. Pity he didn't bother to let her in on it.

The problem was that geographic boundaries were irrelevant to Courtney. In an age of planes, phones, and faxes, what difference did two thousand miles make? As the relationship moved on, Marty began to see the light: *"I realized she liked me a great deal. She started calling me a lot. A couple times a week. Sometimes more often. She was crowding me a lot. But I didn't tell her."*

So Marty adopted the mask of commitment. He hid his discomfort and didn't allude to his plan for a hard stop to the relationship the moment Courtney left town. He went along with her terms, pretending that his level of liking roughly approximated hers, all of which was an opportunistic lie. Eventually, after considerable travail, Courtney got the real message and faded out of his life.

Marty's intent had been a temporary liaison and that's what he got. But Marty was not relieved. He retained both a residual sense of having done her wrong *and* anger about feeling guilty: *"I feel guilty about it. Is it a crime that she likes me more than I like her? Why did I have to feel guilty about it?"*

And with hindsight, he has some regrets: *"Part of me is not open and honest. If I had been more of myself, you know—this is how I am, take it or leave it—I would have been more comfortable."*

Marty was motivated by self-interest. So was Courtney. Had Marty communicated his real intent, then they would have been on equal footing and would have had a better chance to develop whatever was possible. The relationship might not have gone anywhere, but the outcome and effect would have been different. It wouldn't have ended with recrimination, guilt, and hurt.

Premature Commitment

It was only our first date, but I asked her, "Why don't you move in with me? It's a big house; I've got plenty of room and it's silly for both of us to be paying rent."
—Forty-four-year-old divorced male physician

Then I told her, "You said when we met last week that you wanted to travel around the world for a month? I've already called my travel agent. She's working on it."
—Sixty-five-year-old divorced male attorney

Then Bill said, "You'll meet my friend Harvey who I grew up with, and Charlie who's my business partner. In a month or so you've got to meet the kids." In a month or so, he stopped calling me. I never saw him again.
—Thirty-eight-year-old divorced female social worker

Some men seem predisposed to what I've come to call the premature commitment syndrome. They meet you and deem you well within the range of whatever standards they consider acceptable. You have the minimally required set of attributes. You are attractive enough, physically fit enough, smart enough, funny enough, talented enough, make a good enough impression. Maybe you're even an armpiece or a trophy, at the high-end of their range of acceptability. These men are not shoppers; they are deal closers. They are in a big hurry to put in their bid and close the deal. Often they are successful men in business, media, or academe, used to making quick decisions, getting what they want, then moving on. They lack a partner, a honey, and you fill the bill—or, at least, come close enough. For them, it's not so different from walking into a department store and, on finding a reasonable selection of oxford-cloth dress shirts, quickly picking out the acceptable colors in the right size and heading back to the office with their purchases. The whole exercise is impersonal and highly expedient and gets them what they need while the merchandise is available. They're only a step or two up on the scale from impulse buyers. But this time the purchase is you.

By driving ahead quickly and assuredly, these men often hope to bypass altogether the tortuous phases of getting to know all about you. They want to skip learning your moods and opinions, your needs and wants. In fact, they don't really want to spend time getting to know you at all. They'd rather possess you, or at least the idea of you. They're counting on their quick high bid to shortcut the process of getting them from here to there. So they commit prematurely.

Sometimes they act like it's a done deal, that you'll spend the rest of your lives together. As Gwen, our bright and attractive thirty-two-year-old single public relations account executive described it, "They forge a fake bond." They say "too much too soon" as if "we must get to know each other instantly . . . to be best friends by the end of dinner." When she went out with a man who informed her at dinner's end that "you are exactly the kind of woman I am looking for," she wasn't flattered: *He didn't know me. He just wanted a woman and I sort of fit. I felt like a widget. If not me, it would be the next woman. I was like a placeholder. I told him I didn't have the eagerness that he did.*

Gwen's insight got her off the hot seat of being his ideal woman and out of the relationship. A smart move.

The problem begins in earnest when a woman accepts the premature committer's early bid. These self-assured quick closers inevitably suffer an immediate and irrepressible case of buyer's remorse. Their attachment battles begin in earnest. Consumed with self-doubt, they fixate on your every real or imagined flaw. All they can think of is getting out and returning their purchase unopened.

What was a sure thing becomes totally unworkable. Expect to hear a million excuses. "My mother says I haven't met enough women yet." (His mother? He's a forty-five-year-old defense industry analyst!) "My ex-wife won't like you." (He never mentioned an ex-wife, and why should he care what she thinks?) "I can't make a commitment until the trouble at the office clears up." (What trouble at the office, and what does that have to do with your relationship?) Whatever excuses he makes, he's delivering a clear message: "I'm not even ready to buy a car, much less get married or have you move in or take you out for brunch." Or whatever else he has committed himself to. Expect him to call at the last minute to cancel your dinner date or your weekend getaway.

Don't fret. As in many cases of opportunistic commitment, nine times out of ten it's nothing personal. This man was predisposed to commit to the first woman he saw who fit the part. And then to back out. It just happened to be you. His behavior has absolutely nothing to do with who you are. In this case, *it is he*. So toss him back into the pond and find a different spot to fish from. And just in case it was personal, better to know it now than in six months, after you've loaded your furniture into the U-Haul to move to his place and given up your phone number.

Commitment as Retribution

Most commitments are breached because one party isn't fully committed, commits for the wrong reasons, or commits at a bad time. Any of these is enough to cause the break—and the heartbreak. Then there are stories in which commitments are broken and then used like a weapon to hurt the partner who caused the breach.

In this tale the deceiver is Donna, and it is Lance who seeks a calculated retribution. Donna, then eighteen years old, was engaged to Lance. They were planning to marry after he graduated from the Naval Academy in the spring. The summer before he had to leave for training, Donna worked as a camp counselor, and while at the camp she had a summer love affair. This is how Donna describes what happened: *"I never told Lance. I was writing him letters while making out with the other guy. I spent six days at camp, and went home the seventh day. I took my lover home with me Sunday so we could be together. We slept in the same bed, took a shower together. Then I saw my fiance's car in the driveway. He was asleep at the wheel in the driveway. He had driven all day and night to be with me. Lance and I had an agreement—no sex [with anyone else]. So I threw a blanket on the couch, bunched everything up, fixed everything up in the house. Then I walked out to get the paper. I faked it. 'Lance! Oh, I'm so glad to see you here.' I brought him inside. I introduced him to my lover saying, 'This is my boyfriend.' It was a covert lie. He never asked more."*

Lance did find out, but not until one year later. Although Donna had told him never to read her diary, he was alone at her house and "it was a temptation." He went through her desk, read it, and discovered the grisly details, chapter and verse, of her affair, the lover, the betrayal. This is how Donna describes it: *"He was in a dilemma. He had read my diary, betrayed my trust. I told him, 'Don't ever read my diary.' He read it and didn't tell me . . . Then he avoided me, he wouldn't be intimate with me. The following week he con-*

fronted me, laid it out. 'You want to know what's wrong? I read your diary.' Then I got mad. 'How far did you read?' 'I know about last summer.' I felt scared. My mouth was dry. I was sweating bullets. My heart was pounding. I was engaged to this man and he'd found out. I was an idiot that wrote it down. I thought, 'He's going to drop me. I'm going to lose him. How could he do that to me?' I sobbed, 'I love you. Don't leave me.' We talked about it. We tried to work it through. He said: 'I don't know you. I thought I loved you.' He didn't call me names or yell. He's a passive person. He was hurt and angry. But there was no emotion to it. "

In the midst of Donna's tears and his recriminations and confrontation, Lance remains the perfect officer and gentleman, showing no emotion whatsoever. He had incubated the hurt of her betrayal for a week before speaking. The mask of stoicism fit him well. They discussed Donna's lie. She made excuses, but couldn't explain her infidelity. It wasn't a rational event. They struggled and worked it out, or so Donna thought.

Wounded to the core, Lance sought retribution and justice. That's when Lance donned the mask of false commitment, but not one of the three types we have discussed so far. *His* was the mask of false commitment as retribution, a way to *restore his honor.* For six months he says everything's fine, while waiting for his opportunity to even the score: *"After Lance read my diary and discovered my lie in the last six months of our engagement, he perpetuated the lie that he still loved me, while planning to end our relationship as soon as he graduated from the Naval Academy. Then he broke the engagement without warning me."*

Lance kept the parting sterile and disconnected from his emotions. With a surgeon's coolness, he excised the relationship that pained him: *"Lance graduated from the Academy. Then he said, 'I'm not going to take you with me.' He sent me a letter two weeks later saying, 'I don't ever want to see you again. Keep the ring.' I called him. I was angry. Why was he playing with me? He said, 'I want you to finish college. I need some space.' But he came back to that issue."*

Donna took it hard. She thought of nothing else. Eventually she reversed the blame. She asked: *"How could he do this to me? I had a ring. I felt betrayed, humiliated. He hurt me. I was depressed for three years. He didn't think about my feelings."*

She told herself he was a jerk. She eventually married someone else. But if Donna had to do it over, she "wouldn't have cheated on him. He was my first true love and a fantastic man."

Donna's story blends all the elements of high drama and real life: commitment, broken promises, deception, betrayal, and revenge. At its core is the saga of false commitment and its power to wound. Lance—unlike the majority of the women I interviewed who didn't seek to even the score no matter how heinous the betrayal—sought to avenge himself. Donna's breach fueled Lance's well-hidden plan to get even. His words after discovering her infidelity and cover-up ruse were revealing. He told her, "I don't know you." He was right. He didn't, and she, it turned out, didn't know him either.

Too Good to Be True: A Mélange of Masks

What a prince! This man is attentive and charming, and adores the ground you walk on. It started with a line but then he delivered on it. He calls you from his car phone and in between flights, sends you loving poetry by fax and even e-mail. He can hardly wait to see you, has flowers delivered to you at work when he's out of town— which is often—and eradicates any residual doubts by buying you a lovely gold locket with an inscription that reads, "Forever." It's a fairy tale romance, too good to be true.

Rest assured. It's not.

You are part and parcel of his rich inner life that has broken out in what may be a first, second, or chronically recurring manifestation of a serious midlife crisis. He's fighting feeling old, tired, and disappointed with his life. He'll never accomplish his dream. You are part of the secret escape fantasy he has constructed to keep himself going from one to the other end of his day. This man could be a pathological liar or he could be seriously depressed. In fact, he could be both. With you he lies about commitment. When it comes to false commitment, this man pays off like a slot machine, where you get hollow, opportunistic, and minimalist commitments lined up in a row. And if you hang in there long enough with him, you'll find out he doesn't really mean *any* of them. While this is devastating, his lies to you are only half the damage. The rest of his "not tells" may be to the wife and family at home.

Let him go.

The Legacy of the Masks of Commitment

That men don the many masks of false commitment is clear. Less clear and more complicated is why. Oscar Wilde observed that there are only two tragedies in life. One is not getting what you want. The other is getting it. Somehow we manage to want what we don't have and reject what we do.

At the heart of this battle is our ambivalence about our need to be free and to connect. Some psychologists call this need to be distant *and* close the porcupine dilemma. Why? Because porcupines want to huddle close enough to share warmth against the cold, but then as they get closer they face each other's sharp quills—and push or are pushed away. Sooner or later such ambivalence tugs and pulls at men and women alike. But men's fierce attachment battles can be confusing to them and their partners, especially when internal conflict causes them to push toward commitment until it looks real—then back off. As commitment and connectedness become possible, some men discover what they truly wanted was freedom. But since he doesn't want to lose you either, once he's regained his freedom he doubles back, looking for you or a new version of you—the one that got away. The truth? He didn't want to commit, but he didn't want to give up anything either.

Faced with dilemmas about lasting commitment, many men find it more expedient to focus on what's right for the short term. They opt for appeasement rather than permanence. They tell you what they think you want to hear *and what you are most likely to be programmed to believe.*

In a professional and social community that values commitment to the family, he may view a serious relationship as an event that moves him farther along his path to success. His relationship with you may serve as more of a career asset than an emotional high. For him (and for many women) marriage and family may simply be "on-time life events." Everyone's doing it, it's the right thing to do at this particular time. If you happen to be within the range of what he thinks he wants, you become a generic and impersonal—not a personal and specific—choice.

In that case, his commitment is to a way of life, not to you. As his significant other, you may be no more than a temporary player in the drama of his unfolding life. This stage-set effect is compounded when a woman is also driven to commitment by similar needs (peer pressure, timing, fear of being alone, and wanting to start a family). But even when men buy into genuine commitment, many find they lack the critical communication and relationship skills they need to pull it off and negotiate the tough realities ahead. So they, and perhaps you too, fake it. This time the facade he creates is the mask of "everything's fine."

These everything's-fine masks avoid conflict, anger, and unpleasantness, while their wearers go their own way, undeterred. These facades win the happy twosome the right to *appear* harmonious at the price of real connection, discussion, and openness. Months or even years down the road, you'll be asking yourself, "Who was that masked man?"

The mask he wore so skillfully is the next one we'll discuss. The misleading lies of false harmony come as the logical aftermath and corollary to the lies of false commitment we've been discussing. And the emotional separation that the deceptive "everything's fine" mask spawns paves an ever-so-smooth path for the darkest lies of all—lies of evasion.

Chapter 8
When "Everything's Fine" Is a Lie

*Men never talk about their feelings. I'm sure they have them. I'm not
sure they can identify them. They deny they have them because they
don't want to be seen as weak.*
—Thirty-four-year-old divorced female student

*What they feel strongly, they don't tell. To avoid an argument they
would rather lie.*
—Twenty-eight-year-old single female purchasing clerk

*My husband lies because he doesn't want to deal with my anger. If I
get angry he doesn't understand, which is another little wedge
between us. But when I do find out, I'm more angry than when he
doesn't tell me. My wrath is greater.*
—Thirty-three-year-old married female paralegal

*He didn't want to hurt my feelings. He thought I'd get angry. He didn't
want to get chewed out. I'm not sure if he was protecting me or himself.*
—Twenty-four-year-old married female consultant

Scan the personals. You'll discover a hope chest of dreams for happily-
ever-after that range from an old-fashioned cottage for two to yuppi-
fied power alliances. From romantic walks together, to dancing cheek
to cheek on the veranda, to sitting peacefully by the fireplace sipping
brandy, to raising healthy and beautiful children together. Whatever
the dreams are, the ensuing realities are often more like daytime soaps
than days in the life of Prince and Princess Charming. Even in the
Grimms' fairy tales, after the prince and princess ride off together into
the golden sunset, the story mercifully ends, and we're spared the
tawdry tabloid accounts of the coming decline and dissolution.
  Once we commit to a relationship, lies continue to play their

role. Early on, flirtations, lines, and frog-to-prince promises helped draw us closer together. Then lies as masks kept us from knowing precisely with whom we were hooking up. But once committed to each other, we won ourselves another go at the brass rings of openness and honesty.

Too bad the masks don't peel away. Too bad most of us have no plan for forthrightly constructing the idyllic life we crave. But not having a clue doesn't keep us from trying. And conflict surely isn't what we're going to try for. Yet, ironically, conflict and resentment are often what we get.

Why? Neither men nor women deal very well with the jousting that breaks out when two people from different backgrounds try to achieve their divergent goals within the intimate territory they share. And in the process, women aren't the only ones who smooth and dodge conflict. Men often hide behind the mask of stoicism, pretending everything's fine when it's not. They act as if they have no feelings when they do. We all know women who complain that men won't talk to them about how they feel or about anything personal. Yet these same women preserve the status quo and assuage their hopes that all's right in their world by carefully scrutinizing every behavioral nuance, while ever so politely carefully looking the other way. When women ignore symptoms of trouble while men pretend everything's fine, the result is that no one tells and no one asks. False harmony is achieved at the price of the real thing.

Many men I interviewed insisted that everything's-fine lies were necessary. These men downplayed their business-as-usual lies as white lies or "baby" lies. For a man like this, the everything's-fine mask makes life tolerable because it permits him to enjoy habitual peace and quiet without having to explain himself. More to the point, these lies also shield him. From what? From your anger at being excised from the world of his real feelings. But you're not the only one cut away from his feelings. As often as not, he is too.

They Have Feelings Too, Don't They?

There have to be feelings. Men just don't talk about them.
—Twenty-three-year-old single female lab assistant

Men hide their innermost thoughts. Their emotions are what they keep secret.
—Twenty-seven-year-old divorced female nurse

I kept secret that I had feelings. Now I'm being excruciatingly honest.
It's difficult to be honest. I never know how I come across. I was being
detailed in my answers. When I fudged the truth, I thought I was con-
trolling the interaction but really it was all in my head.
—Thirty-seven-year-old single male computer graphic designer

A seemingly perplexed Sigmund Freud once asked this oft-quoted
question: *"What do women want?"* The question that perplexes
women is: *"What do men feel?"* For nearly one-fourth of the women I
interviewed, and hundreds of clients and students over the past fifteen
years, this is the question. And when it comes to men's lies of false
harmony, the right question has found the right target.

Louise failed to understand this question until a few years
after her divorce. She mistook the man she had married nineteen
years earlier—whose career she had gladly supported and whose
children she had borne—for someone she genuinely knew and
understood. What she belatedly discovered was that she had
known him far less well than the fictional heroes in the stories she
loved to read and pen. The man Louise had married became a
successful stranger. He fooled her so well that five years after the
wrenching dissolution of what she had believed was a stable and
committed marriage, she was still fitting together the pieces of his
identity, his liaisons, his lies. She was learning that he had shut
down and locked her out of his feelings long before the affairs and
the divorce.

Alternating between anger and despair, she observed that he,
like many men, had probably lied to fill the empty spaces where he
knew he should have feelings but somehow didn't. She realized that
not knowing what he felt made him feel inadequate.

His reassuring but utterly false facade was an expedient means
of hiding his uncertainty, confusion, and inner turmoil about not
knowing his own core. Masks of false commitment and false harmony are attempts to remedy a man's inability to articulate and
account for his own feelings, and that also puts him back into control.

I've worked with many men who valiantly risk digging deep
into the well of their own feelings—only to come up frustratingly
empty. Over and over I hear some exasperated version of "You
keep asking me what I feel, what I felt. *I don't know. I don't know
what I feel.*" It's been so long since they paid close attention to
their feelings that they can look their own feelings in the face and
not recognize what's there. To get some empathy for this, think

about the times when you have angrily denied that you are angry. Anger is in your blind spot, even as it spills over into your voice and your tensed muscles. Others can see and hear it, even if you cannot.

This denial is what many men say they encounter in themselves for a whole range of feelings. But why are so many men so uncomfortable with their feelings? Why avoid them? Some men do it because they believe emotions are for women, not for real men. They learned at an early age that big boys couldn't show vulnerability, pain, or uncertainty without fear of humiliation. I've seen men in their early twenties, still close to the battle of separating themselves from powerful mothers and asserting their maleness, so embarrassed by their emotional sensitivity that they make self-deprecating cracks like "Why don't I just dress in pink, like a girl?"

The stoic mask of "no feelings" may have worked well to distance him first from his mother and now from you. But for many men denial of feeling leaves a big void. They find themselves at a loss when it comes to quickly pulling their feelings out with the right tone, words, and subtle nuances feelings require. Many men, particularly in men's support groups, discover that allowing themselves to feel evokes a sense of powerlessness rather than strength. Discovering what they feel can be a daunting challenge.

According to marriage and family counselor John Amodeo in his 1994 book, *Love and Betrayal,* "Real communication is only possible to the degree that we can be open to what is really happening inside us." We could easily substitute the word "honesty" or "intimacy" or "commitment" for "communication."

Here's the kernel of the problem. If intimacy is based on openness and ability to access and communicate feelings, it will challenge many men. When intimacy, genuine feeling, and powerlessness come to be connected, openness pushes some men *far* outside their comfort zone.

Stuart, the midlife married consultant with the little black book, summed this up when I asked him what he lies about most: *"Feelings. I lie about how I feel about women, my reactions to their actions, their openness. [I lie about] lots of different and dangerous truths: truths that wound, truths that clarify, truths that can make enemies. Why tell the truth when it can hurt you? I lie to minimize my own pain. Better to be wounded early than badly in relationships with women."*

Lies provide a convenient shorthand for avoiding feelings and truth, an instant armor against the self and intimacy. And once lies lock in place as part of the landscape of a relationship, they help keep and widen the distance between the two of you as he defends himself against being known.

If you don't bridge the distance between you, the spaces that separate you harden over time. They become a no-man's-land, literally and figuratively. Nothing grows on this land, yet you continue to live there. Often one of you, perhaps both, act as if your relationship is still alive. But it may not be. All you've done is declare a cold peace.

When Peace Becomes a Stand-in for Harmony

Peace and harmony. Like love and marriage, peace and harmony are often spoken in the same breath. Yet peace and harmony can play out ever so differently. For many couples, like warring nations, peace simply signifies the absence or cessation of overt hostilities. And while that's a lot better than knock-down, drag-out warfare, it's a long way from harmony. Superficial peace isn't the real thing. It is a form of false harmony that leads to relationship-stopping complacency.

Harmony requires a deliberate and mutual openness and trust. It compels us to put the relationship first even when jobs, friends, children, and individual needs compete for limited air time.

For many men that feels suspiciously like work. To invoke that old cliché, "His home is his castle." And when it comes to dealing with unpleasantness and conflict, forget it—he already gave at the office. All he seeks is:

No confrontation. No argument. No conflict.

In fact, no display of real feelings either, whether friendly or hostile. When they come home, a lot of men are like medieval knights who, after battling dragons all day, just want to draw up the castle bridge and retreat. They feel entitled to a time-out from the world of stress and strain, from inquiring minds, from the relentless art of the deal—even if that means moving far, far away from intimacy with you.

So he opts for peace without harmony. Short of sheer make-believe, here are a few tactics and techniques he's likely to use as shortcuts. This fail-proof formula is gleaned from the experiences of hundreds of disengaged peace-at-any-price couples.

QUICK FORMULA FOR PEACE WITHOUT HARMONY

- Greet any "What's bothering you, honey?" questions with:
  - Silence.
  - Denial.
  - Quick change of subject.
- Avoid discussing any sensitive issues.
- If things heat up quickly, close down.
- When confronted directly, lie.
- Show no vulnerability.
- Stay too busy to talk.
- Give information on a need-to-know basis only.
- Pretend everything's fine, that it's business as usual, no matter what's really going on.
- If all else fails, pacify her with gifts.

These tactics foster only alienation. For the women who stay home, the inaccessible male they greet at the door may make them feel shut out. The many women who march out into the world and return to their nests at nightfall also seek a sanctuary free of the conflict and arguments of their work life. They want a world where they can be accepted and understood. But withdrawal usually isn't their path of choice. Both groups of women are likely to see the home as a sanctuary for meaningful rapport-building, not retreat. For them this means talking, discussing, and connecting.

So here we have it once again. A fundamental split in the way men and women communicate, so well identified by Lillian Rubin in *Intimate Strangers* and documented by Deborah Tannen in *You Just Don't Understand*. It's as if men and women have different models governing what constitutes their ideal daily relations, different agendas, and different underlying interests. So how do we get to harmony?

The Road to Harmony

Think back to the marriages you observed as a child. Who tip-toed around whom? How much anger and rage seethed under the surface of business as usual and everything's fine? How often did pure vitriol break out? Do you recall a family picnic or dinner when

you were an accidental witness to an unexpected outburst or a genuine *War of the Roses* between Aunt Sarah and Uncle Ben?

In your own long-term relationships do you opt for peace at any
price? Are smoldering tensions heating up under a deceptively conventional facade, or is there open hand-to-hand combat in the
trenches? How are two people supposed to deal with the inevitable
differences in opinion and values so that resentments don't pile up
until something sparks a damaging explosion?

For two people to achieve harmony over time they must agree to:

* Define harmony as important to the relationship.
* Share a vision of what harmony will look and feel like.
* Spend time talking to each other about what's working and
  what's not.
* Keep communicating, *especially* when it feels uncomfortable.
* Learn and apply strong conflict-resolution skills.
* Persist, not just in one or two ways, but *variously*.
* Devote abundant energy and goodwill to each other.

Sounds like work? No question. But it's work with huge payoff
for the long haul, work worth its weight in gold.

When Harmony Is the Road Not Taken

How does it happen that two people who care about each other
become alienated and avoidant? Many men and women go on automatic pilot when they enter steady and enduring relationships. They
paid their dues, and now they can relax. Couples cease attending to
what's really happening in the relationship, except to quell the
immediate crisis du jour. Of course, that doesn't mean nothing is
happening. While Rip Van Winkle slumbered, the world still turned
and time passed. Suddenly, one or both of you is jolted back into
awareness by some personal wake-up call. Maybe it's middle age
staring back at you from the bathroom mirror, maybe it's being
fired from your job "for life," maybe it's falling in love with someone refreshingly and tantalizingly new.

So what? If lies and the "peace" they ensure allow you both to
function and keep the relationship afloat, what's wrong with that?
Unfortunately, lies of agreement give comfort at the very moment
you both should be loudly sounding the alarm and discussing your
differences. Ironically, these reassuring lies ensure everything but
lasting harmony.

When "Everything's Fine" Ducks Uncertainty

Even if they aren't in touch with the specific feelings that push and drive their own behavior, most men know when something doesn't feel right. Sometimes this creates an uncomfortable under-current of confusion about what's really happening. But since the only way to resolve it is to delve into feelings and motivations that churn deep below the surface, they may opt instead for instant clo-sure. How? Instead of exposing and confronting their feelings and uncertainty, they may slap a mask of "everything's fine" over their doubt in order to restore control.

That's what Jeff did. At age thirty-seven and still single, he talks about his difficulty in ending his relationship with Amy, his first girlfriend in high school: *"My first lie was not being able to tell her that I didn't want to marry her. I was at the point of asking her to marry me and everything in my head was going 'Wrong, wrong.'"*

Jeff knew something was wrong, but he had a tangle of interper-sonal relations and feelings—his own and hers—to sort through. And what he was looking for was certainty and closure, clean solu-tions. Jeff gives a particularly thoughtful analysis of his difficulty in recognizing and coming to terms with his own uncertainty. *"The lie was that I refused to take responsibility for my own awareness. I had to feel in control. I was unable to say, 'I don't know where I want this relationship to go, but I want to find out.' It was too hard to tell her, 'I'm not sure you are the person I want to spend the rest of my life with.' My discontent was so strong and my ability to break off was so weak that I hoped she would do it for me, 'cause I couldn't."*

Jeff has said a lot here. He was locked into his overriding need to be in charge of the situation, to make the go–no-go decision, and to have unequivocal answers to dicey issues of emotional commit-ment. These needs aren't peculiar to Jeff. They are part and parcel of the male role in our culture. Nonetheless, his need for control and certainty backfired. When he couldn't attain either, he had no idea how to tell Amy the gray and murky truth about their possible future together. Jeff knew he had doubts, but he felt helpless to tell her about them. He hadn't a clue about how to deal with Amy's upset. When Jeff tried to break up, it seemed that Amy became so upset that he couldn't sever their tie. He was back at square one.

Even worse, whenever Amy rallied and started to date someone else, Jeff would pull her back. He didn't want her, but he lapsed into primal territorialism when anyone else did. Jeff's discomfort with his own ambivalence sent mixed signals to Amy. Eventually Jeff began to abdicate responsibility to Amy for the decision to pull out, getting madder and madder at Amy for not deciding. Fortunately, Amy got the message. She solved his problem. She broke off the relationship and married someone else.

Jeff's failing went beyond being unable to accept and discuss his own mixed feelings and his uncertainty. He was also suffering from a failure of empathy. Jeff had wanted Amy to take responsibility for his feelings and act on them, even though he was unable to walk in her shoes, unwilling to find out what she wanted. While his lack of self-knowledge and comfort were understandable, by not addressing it honestly he hurt Amy.

Of course, Jeff still has time to learn. As he gains more insight-producing experiences, he may be better able to balance his need for comfort with the honesty necessary for a trusting relationship. But Jeff isn't alone in this kind of behavior. It's hard at any age to sever ties with someone you like and are attached to. Men and women both know how difficult this can be. Some men refuse to take responsibility for their own feelings and, like Jeff, try to shift responsibility onto the woman for ending it. As one unhappily committed commercial artist in a thirty-five-year-old marriage confided, "Every day I pray that my wife will find a very rich doctor, fall madly in love, and be fantastically happy." Unfortunately, before she had that opportunity, he managed to find a very young student, fall madly in love, and be fantastically unfaithful. His wife, now in her sixties, is on her own.

When Feelings Are Hidden, Any Excuse Will Do

Some men are unable to tell the truth about their feelings. They'll use any excuse to initiate a major change in the relationship. The more serious the real feelings, the more trivial the actual excuse may be. Ruth, a fifty-five-year-old realtor, knows that drill all too well. The any-excuse-will-do scenario has happened to her several times. Once would have been enough. She'd been dating Isaac for a year, and the relationship seemed fine. They went to a real estate open house where they got a T-shirt that Isaac wore later that day to play tennis. In one of those normally mundane and uneventful incidents of daily life, Isaac asked Ruth to wash his T-shirt. She declined the invitation. Ordinarily that would be no big deal, but things began to heat up: *"He made a big deal of my not wanting to wash his T-shirt and walked out. I thought he was having a tantrum, but later I realized he was serious. He wanted to end the relationship. It seemed too trivial."*

It was trivial. What wasn't trivial was that he was interested in someone else. With hard-earned twenty/twenty hindsight, Ruth now realizes that Isaac was scouting around for a reason, *any reason,* to end the relationship. What she would have liked? Here it comes again: like thousands of women, she says she wanted the truth. Ruth wishes "that he would have told the truth, that he was seeing someone else, even if it hurt. I wanted to know the exact reason it ended."

Lying to Avoid Her Anger

Most of us know that the truth has a long fuse. Eventually it will light the darkness. So why bother to pretend? Why not just tell it like it is? These are questions that stump a lot of bright and perceptive women. The answers are complicated and idiosyncratic, grounded in the endless variations of personalities, relationships, and situations. But if I had to come up with a single answer, I'd bet on men's fear of evoking a powerful woman's anger.

This idea that men lie to duck women's anger often comes as a surprise to even the most perceptive of women, who believe men hold all the power chips and that confrontation and domination are the primary domain of the male of the species. Don't bet on it. Remember that every grown man was once a little boy, and that the majority of those little boys were raised under the close scrutiny and tutelage of a powerful mother with authority to shame and punish. From a child's viewpoint, this female authority could react in threatening, unpredictable, and fear-invoking ways. Equally daunting to a young boy is the problem posed in identifying too closely with this powerful woman who controls his life and being thought a mama's boy. That too could bring shame and humiliation. Finally, little boys, unlike little girls, also face the early and major hurdle of figuring out how to separate themselves from this strong and powerful mother, and how to bond with other boys and men. Then, following that separation, they spend years of childhood and adolescence figuring out how to keep tight boundaries around who they are (their identities) and what they do (their independence), in ways that tell the world that they are unequivocally "man," not "woman."

To do this, men have traditionally found their voice and established their identity and influence in the world outside the home,

outside personal male-female relationships. Men typically assert
their primary voice in the world of work and public life. If you want
to hear what that male voice in unedited form sounds like, tune in
any day to the voice of American talk radio. You'll hear the public
voice of men filled with opinion, passion, and zeal about issues that
skirt the personal. It is a voice of male bonding, but out there—not
close to home.

Women dominate the private world of relationships, a world full
of connections and attachments. It is in this private world that men
tend to feel the greatest discomfort. It is here that they are most
prone to shut down when their quick-fix solutions fail either to remedy the pain of their partners or to shield themselves from scrutiny.
It is here that women complain most vociferously about men's failure to talk, acknowledge, empathize, and engage with them emotionally. And it is here that men's lies and "not tells" about who they
are with the women in their lives feel so particularly treacherous.

The irony is that what makes women angry is men's failure to
talk straight and to connect, while women's anger is exactly what
men will lie and shut down to avoid. Clearly, we have here a Catch-
22 with major implications for male-female dialogue and truthfulness!

Let's look behind the mask of "everything's fine" to see how this
Catch-22 eats away at intimacy.

When "Everything's Fine" Hides His Shame and Anger

*I honestly tell them everything is fine when it's not. I keep secret the
things I believe to be hurtful or disappointing to my partner.*
—Jake, a thirty-five-year-old married male film producer

You remember Jake, the self-declared recovering pathological
liar? He's now on his third marriage and a veteran of twenty-plus
affairs. Number one among his most frequent relationship lies?
Without the slightest bit of self-consciousness, Jake says: "I *honestly*
tell them everything is fine *when it's not.*" Then parenthetically he
adds, "One of the reasons I was a such a good liar is because I didn't
really lie—I just didn't tell the whole truth."

Jake readily admits he has trouble confronting his own and his
wife's anger. He tells us that, only the night before we spoke, he told
his wife, Christy, that he was too tired to make love. The truth was
that "I didn't want to make love. I was really angry at something
she had done that day."

The lie, the mask of "too tired" for sex, was punishment because Christy had jumped at him for not putting a cover on one of her CDs earlier that day.

But even though Jake has made working on his problem with lies and the truth a first priority with his wife, as soon as she asks him directly whether he is angry, his resolve to be honest crumbles. His knee-jerk response is "no." More than likely, under Jake's veneer of anger lie shame and humiliation. And consciously or not, he's still not comfortable exposing how very needy and out of sorts he feels about something seemingly minor.

Jake suggests that the reason for his lie is that he "wants to avoid confrontation." His wife is surprised by his communication shutdown "because she expects me to make an effort to tell the truth." Will she confront him? "Only a little bit," Jake reflects. "She knows. She's not stupid. She says, 'Sure there's not something you want to tell me?'" Notice how quickly she steps into a typical feminine role of taking care of their relationship. But Jake will have none of it. Instead he cops out and assures her that it's just business as usual: "No, I'm fine."

Guess what? Everything's not fine, not at all. That's the big secret that the lie of false harmony covers. For Jake to confront Christy means risking exposure to his own shame and helplessness as well as to hers. They would touch that soft spot of vulnerability that creates a potential for intimacy, self-knowledge, and mutual recognition. At this point in time, Jake still isn't ready. He declines her offer and retreats behind the mask.

Walking on Eggshells

You don't have to be married twenty years to don the everything's-fine mask that holds conflict at bay. For many men and some women it's a strategy that begins early and lasts long.

Consider Len, an information systems manager. He's good-looking, clean-cut, and just twenty-three years old. Now in the fifth year of a steady relationship with Ellen, he's no stranger to the long-term relationship. As we sit talking about the last lies Ellen has caught him in, he downplays them, saying he was "just caught in baby lies." I take the bait and ask, "What kind of baby lies?" *"Well, I have a bad habit of chewing tobacco, and my girlfriend asked me if I had done it. I said no. She later caught me. It was in my mouth."*

So why, I ask, would he lie about such an obvious habit?

Incredulous, he stares at me and patiently explains the obvious: *"I hid it to keep her from getting upset and having a nonproductive conversation. To avoid her upset, feeling the wrath of her yelling at me."*

Then he adds, "It's a five-year relationship," as if that will reveal the true weight behind his words. Hmmm. I ask, "Did you plan to hide it?" Yes, he did. But listen to how Len constructs his planned "baby lie" to Ellen: *"I saw my lie as caring for how she felt, unless the lie goes too far. For her, there's not much effect. Her asking me and her anger are just conditioned responses."*

So it would appear that Len sees Ellen's questions as reflexive responses, and his lie as more caring than self-protective. Then he reflects and adds: *"I tell my girlfriend the most baby lies when she's on her period because I don't want to do anything to rock the boat. No way in hell! She'll snap at me more than the expected amount. It's like walking on eggshells. I tell her lies to stay out of harm's way. They're lies of avoidance. I lie to avoid her wrath, disappointing her; I give excuses and I avoid saying yes, then not coming through."*

Len's pretty convincing. As he describes it, the relationship with Ellen is a lot like living under a reign of terror. So, of course, he tells "baby lies." Anything to stay out of harm's way. But, as you read his response, does he sound like he's talking about his experience with a girlfriend or with a demanding and angry mother who has the power to humiliate and shame?

Hiding His Feelings to Avoid Her Upset

It was a lie of omission to my wife, not saying how I felt about her business not making money. We need her income to prosper.
—Forty-four-year-old married male manager

Happily married Warren is talking about his journey during the past ten years of marriage toward becoming more truthful, observing that his wife "was absolutely honest with me from the start."

What secrets does Warren still hide from his honest wife? Just his feelings. He says: *"How I actually feel about something; I say that something's okay, not a problem."*

Why would he lie about his feelings when he's trying to be honest? *"I lie by omission to my wife because I don't want to hurt her feelings."* So he believes he is protecting her feelings by withholding his own. But won't she know how he feels anyway? I probe a little deeper, and the rhythm of the truth begins to emerge in his words:

"In marriage . . . you become more vulnerable. There's some open-ness between you. Something she does really bothers you, but you say: 'That's okay,' because you don't want to jeopardize the rela-tionship. You have a fear of being left . . . I don't want the confronta-tion that goes with it. I hide how I feel mainly to avoid confrontation; it's more possible to get hurt when you're more intimately involved, but for me it's more an issue of avoiding confrontation."

What's a current issue between them? Economics, for one. Warren explains: *"She's in her own business and that isn't support-ing our financial obligations. I want her to get out and go back to a job, so we can earn some money. What will I say? 'Why don't you earn $20,000 more?' I hate confrontation."*

Even though Warren says he is committed to honesty in his rela-tionship with his wife, he winds up wearing the mask of peace at any price. Why? Because he is an inveterate conflict avoider, afraid of offending and alienating his wife. So what? What's the harm in stifling his feelings because he fears confronting his wife?

Plenty. Research shows that the happiest couples bicker, argue, and complain. They regularly air their differences, rather than pre-tending things are fine by burying their anger, only to have it blow up months, years, or even decades later. In sharp contrast, the mask of "everything's fine" is the daily costume, the stock in trade of the smoothers and the avoiders who duck confrontation. These peace-at-any-price companions have a hard time working through the inevitable conflicts that come up in any close relationship. They are the master sweepers, who whisk anything unpleasant under the rug. There, hidden from view, all manner of hurts, slights, and humiliations accumulate. But nothing swept under the rug ever really disappears. One morning, arguing about who's going to make the coffee, he blurts out his unhappiness, vents the anger he still has about a remark she made two years ago at the office party, lets something slip out about the affair he had a year earlier. Unresolved issues keep festering, just waiting for their time and their place, their day in the sun.

And as these real and imagined insults fester unresolved, the problem for the relationship is:

When he pleases you at his own expense, you wind up paying for it.

Discontents and resentments rarely remain as hidden as we think. They leak out into the common spaces of our lives, from the bedroom to the living room and beyond—with corrosive effects.

Tales of Three Marriages

My husband stopped lying to me in my first marriage. It was after
three years of dating and two years of being married, when he told me
he was unhappy. He stopped living the lie that everything was okay.
—Thirty-three-year-old married female bank auditor

We've seen how the mask of false harmony works to hide shame
and anger and to avoid confrontation. Most of us have experienced
some variety of "everything's fine" in our daily relations. These lies
are especially hard to spot, since they are so often lies of omission,
the "not tells" rather than the blatant in-your-face lies of commission.

But what happens when the masquerade evolves into a whole
way of life, when the "not tells" pass as harmony rather than as the
temporary cessation of hostilities they really are? When we are wed-
ded to our roles and tasks rather than to each other as people? Have
we constructed a lie that serves to shield us from connecting with
another human being, risking rejection and facing our own fears?
Maybe this is just part of the human condition—to long for connectedness while rejecting the price we must pay for it.

Two Perfect Marriages

I once knew a couple who were universally admired for their
perfect marriage. Even as a busy physician Allison seemed to have
found time to fix Glen's lunches, replete with his favorite imported
gourmet delicacies. At parties they kissed and held hands, and she
sat on his lap. They always supported each other. No one who knew
them ever saw them disagree. Every movement, every exchange was
perfectly choreographed. Like championship skaters, they moved
with exquisite synchrony. Their careers soared. Their happiness and
their lives were seamlessly perfect. Then one day without warning,
Glen surprised her and all their friends. He left Allison for another
woman. She was shocked. He never gave her any warning that anything was wrong, that their sex life wasn't satisfying, that their life
together wasn't ideal. In that seamless perfection they created, they
had allowed no room for real differences to surface. The new
woman was gone in a few months, but Glen never came back, and
Allison never learned how something so seemingly perfect had
failed.

Or consider Susan, the perfect wife. She met Stephen during her senior year at a women's college in New England. He was attending a nearby engineering school and was the first man to ask her out. Before meeting Stephen, Susan had thrown herself into campus activities, but when Stephen courted her she allowed herself to be swept away. She married him just before graduation and became the perfect wife. She hand-washed and ironed his clothes, baked bread from scratch. She kept a spotless house and raised two children with meticulous care while Stephen worked his way up the ladder at a Fortune-500 company. Stephen sandwiched his attention to Susan between long hours at the office and countless business trips, but he seemed genuinely happy. For twenty years Susan busied herself being "everything I thought he wanted"—the perfect wife and mother. Then: *"One day he asked me to go for a walk with him in a park near our house. He took my hand in his, looked me in the eye, and said, 'I don't love you anymore, honey.' I never saw it coming. No build-up. Nothing. Whenever I had asked him, he'd always said, 'Everything's fine.' The following week he left and moved in with a twenty-eight-year-old woman. That was the end of twenty years. If he'd said something I would have changed, but he never said a word."*

These two tales illustrate a difficult point. No sound relationship survives unmarred by the imperfections of messy disagreement, conflict, and compromise. What these couples had was no perfect marriage, but a perfect division of labor—one that left no room for real emotional honesty, much less intimacy.

Both husband and wife in these perfect marriages allowed their respective roles to determine how their golden-sunset relationship played out. Accordingly, they performed their "shoulds" and "oughts" like real troupers. He did the breadwinner thing, she did the caregiver thing. Their marriage, in a sense, became part of communal life. But where was the private exchange, the airing of differences, the grappling with a shared and changing vision of life? These perfect couples forgot that the real business of relationships is to relate—to each other.

Tom, a business analyst, sums it up like this: "Women tell lies to bolster and pamper male egos, whereas men tell lies, commit deceits, and omit information to establish and preserve relationships, without checking on what's really needed." These couples lost sight of the personal, which, in its confusing disorder, truly allows two people to connect.

When the Hidden Truth Breaks Outs

This is an exceptional story of peace without harmony, denial without confrontation, and truth finally breaking out and demanding to be acknowledged. The players look and act on the surface of things like typical middle-class suburbanites anywhere in America.

Veronica, a Sunday school principal, is now divorced and living in the Southwest. Married for twenty-two years, she truly believed in happily-ever-after, but found none of it in her marriage. With hindsight, the signs were clear from the beginning, but Veronica didn't want to see them. The first sign of trouble came just after they had their first child. It seemed harmless enough. Jerry told her he had to go to the grocery store to buy something: *"It took him hours. He made excuses. It registered that he was lying, but he never 'fessed up. But about four months later it became obvious he was seeing several women. I felt scared, betrayed, but I never confronted him about his lying."*

Despite Veronica's fear that Jerry was having an affair with her best friend, she acted as if everything was fine. He did too. Then twelve years later he finally confessed the affair to her.

Why did he come clean after all those years?

It wasn't intentional. Veronica was looking through their Master-Card and Visa accounts at tax time when she found what looked like "a bunch of receipts from prostitutes on our MasterCard." Veronica describes what happened next: *"I knew he was troubled. I worried about his mental health. I feared pushing him over the edge. I consulted with a counselor. Then I called him up on the phone. I told him, 'I have some things on the MasterCard. Something is going on.' But I had a bigger problem than I knew. . . . He was on the phone with me a couple hours and told me he had been seeing prostitutes, having affairs. I thought maybe just one or two. But it was worse than I ever could have imagined. He was hiding a sexual addiction to prostitutes. He confessed."*

Veronica knew she wasn't in a perfect marriage. After all, she had suspected Jerry of lying for more than twelve years. But she hadn't confronted him. She had looked the other way. She hadn't asked; he hadn't told. Now the truth was demanding its day. How did she respond as the mask of "everything's fine" peeled away to reveal that indeed, nothing could have been farther from the truth? *"I was anxious. I couldn't breathe. I thought my life was over. I was devastated for a week. He kept telling me things. When he started telling me these things, I knew. Then, it clicked. It all registered.*

When you're lied to a lot you feel a little crazy. When he confessed, I didn't feel crazy or stupid. My fear hadn't let me verbalize. My fantasy was that my family would disintegrate."

What's particularly fascinating here is that Veronica, amidst all the pain and angst of discovery as Jerry poured out to her what he had kept hidden for so long, was viscerally relieved to hear the truth. Although she doesn't use this phrase, she finally feels whole. Her fear of losing her family and her economic security had overpowered her need to know the truth. The mask of false harmony that so thinly veiled a life-imperiling truth, shrouding not only their intimacy, but her own well-being and mental health had finally dropped away.

Still Veronica wasn't ready to let go quite yet. She lived with Jerry for another five years. She "wanted to believe we could work through it, that it would turn out okay." Then there were practical issues. Veronica had no full-time job and she was emotionally devastated. She, like Jerry, felt enormous shame. Jerry, she reported, "was surprised I wanted to stay and make it work." Like the heroine of Tammy Wynette's country-western tune, Veronica stood by her man, but she got professional help and she learned to be stronger and tougher: *"He went into a program for sex addiction. . . . I tried to understand why I would stay in a relationship like that. I set boundaries. I told him, 'You can't cheat on me or you're out.'"*

Veronica got involved. They "went to meetings, read books, went to therapy." They talked, and "he shared his thoughts about sexual addiction." She felt more connected to him. They agreed that neither of them would be sexually active outside their marriage. But what happened next pushed Veronica to the limit, where fortunately she found the strength to turn her attention to her own life and well-being: *"Then he called. He was arrested for picking up a prostitute. I wouldn't let him stay. We separated. . . . After I found out, I learned he'd been with people all year. He was lying. AIDS was a problem. I'd trusted him. He was not trustworthy. I turned to God when it happened. I took a moment. A voice said to me, 'Follow the light. Get out of the darkness.' No turning back. I was guided. . . . I felt a spirit guide me out of darkness . . . "*

When I asked Veronica what she would have preferred to have happened, what she would do differently, she said: *"I would change the way I managed things. I would trust my own instincts. Having enough courage to act. I would change not being able to say, 'This isn't right.' Even when we were dating I could have said, 'When*

*you're inattentive to me, it hurts my feelings.' But I was too busy tak-
ing care of his feelings, not my own. I denied a lot. I stuffed my own
feelings. I never learned to confront someone who is lying to you."*

Veronica suffered at the hand of the liar she had married, but
chose to use her experience to learn and grow. She offered this
advice to other women: *"Trust your gut feeling. If something doesn't
feel right, someone is continuing to lie to you. Don't feel crazy if
someone continues to lie to you. Some people are very clever, 'cause
they don't want to be caught."*

Three Marriages, Three Masks

The poet John Donne wrote, "No man is an island unto himself." Psychologists less eloquently make the point that all human
behavior is interactive. Our actions influence and are influenced by
others. Nothing we do occurs in total isolation from others. So it is
in a marriage or any relationship.

The partners in each of these three marriages you've read about
have colluded to hold in place the mask of "everything's fine" and
to deny the real problems brewing beneath the surface. The men
told only *what they thought* their partners needed to know. Then
again, the women made few demands for more information or for
more confrontation. The result was a flat, picture-perfect landscape
that had no room in it for the imperfections of real people who move
and breathe, grow and change.

In the first two marriages, Allison and Susan and their respective husbands each had a fighting chance to turn those relationships
around, had they only talked about what was happening to them as
a couple. To make that chance good they would have had to:

- Recognize that something was going wrong in paradise.
- Pay attention to their gut feelings, intuition.
- Start the uncomfortable process of communicating about what
  was hidden to one, but not the other.
- Confront their lies—both implicit and explicit.
- Schedule more time for intimacy.
- Move out of the narrow everything's-fine comfort zone to con-
  front their discomforts.

If they did these things, it's possible—no guarantees, but possible—that their pattern of "not tells" and other covert and more

overt lies would have been stemmed and replaced with more honest communication and eventually by earned trust.

In the third marriage, no matter what Veronica might have done, she would have been fighting a difficult and uphill battle. Her husband's chronic deception papered over a serious and life-jeopardizing sexual addiction that had probably kicked into place by the third year of their marriage. They both needed professional help to get through it. Veronica would have had to overcome her own insecurities to stand up to Jerry and demand the full truth. She needed to bolster her resolve to be strong, and to find the support she required every time he fell back into his addiction. Had she done this, regardless of how much or how little progress he had made, at least she would have taken care of herself sooner. They would have come to a fuller understanding of what they both were really up against, and perhaps she might have made a more informed decision to either stay or go fifteen or eighteen years sooner.

Even though she might have moved closer to Jerry in this process, she would have been foolish to trust a man who was obsessively driven by a full-blown sexual addiction. By shutting down and looking the other way, Veronica colluded with Jerry to jeopardize herself and her family. She was scared and probably doing the best she could. Yet by accepting his lies and suppressing her intuition that something was wrong, she denied her own right to health, intimacy, and real love, wasting precious years of her life. Although this tale has no happy ending, Veronica at least came away with a renewed desire to reach out to others.

Few couples will have to overcome the kinds of obstacles that faced Veronica and Jerry. Yet even when the road is far less rocky, something may still get in the way. Something far less unusual than Jerry's addiction and far more common to many men. And that's our tenuous relationship with the truth.

Are Men Afraid of the Truth?

Men tell lies to give themselves distance from us or to cover up their wanting to distance themselves, while women tell lies to get closer to men. Men need to be distant, not close, in order to cover it up.
—Veronica, a forty-five-year-old divorced Sunday school principal

Men lie about the truth in daily relations with women at home and at work, not because their lying breaks out as an aberration, but because it is part of how they have been enculturated to construct their daily world. In my interviews and my work with men, I have noticed a pattern of differences in the language men and women use in discussing truth and honesty. These patterns may reveal both power differentials and disparate underlying assumptions about truth's role and worth in communication.

Still, I was unprepared to hear so many men and so few women pair these words:

- Brutal honesty
- Unpleasant truth
- Constructive manipulation

The first few times I heard men use these words together and grasped the implications, I was dumbfounded. How is it that men coupled the words for the very qualities most of us claim to uphold as virtues, like "honesty" and "truth," with such negatives as "brutal" and "unpleasant"? And how is it that the Machiavellian "manipulation," a term most of us see as connivingly negative, comes out linked with that positive and upbeat word "constructive"? What's going on here? Do women make these same linkages? I haven't heard them yet.

Could it be that men's specific language here is a user's guide to their collective experience with truth-telling at home and at work? That it reveals their unconscious acceptance of the advantages of the lie and the riskiness of the truth? That beneath the facade of harmony are deliberately unspoken and unpleasant truths? These phrases reveal an interesting perspective—that truth and honesty inflict pain, or at least unpleasantness, while lies oil the wheels of daily life and maintain our ability to conduct business as usual.

As one man told me, "I don't think of it as lying. I think of it as problem solving."

How does this approach play out? Think of it this way. How likely would you be to tell the whole truth if "brutal" was your knee-jerk association with "honesty," and "unpleasant" was an automatic association with "truth"? And how deterred would you be from exploitation if you associated "constructive" with "manipulation," rather than, say, the more negative "self-serving" or "conniving"? You get the idea. Our thoughts influence our behavior, and if the truth is feared, wouldn't it make perfect sense to pretend that everything is fine?

Consider this. Recently I told Fred, a corporate client of mine, that he could count on Walt to tell him the real facts of the situation, to provide straight talk. My client's response was enlightening and fascinating. He interrupted me, asking, "But Walt's not *cruel*, is he?" I forced the issue by asking, "What was there about what I said that caused you to make that association?" He told me that the operative phrase that triggered it was "straight talk," just what most women say they want most from the men in their lives. Fred paired straight talk with a mental model of cruelty. Not what most women have in mind. Why did "straight talk," a colloquialism for telling the truth, trigger that connection in Fred?

The way we use words offers clues to how we think and how we manage ourselves in life. In your daily encounters, which of the three pairings are you most likely to reach for to get to your most immediate objective: constructive manipulation, unpleasant truth, brutal honesty? What does your choice tell you about yourself or about anyone picking one of these three phrases?

In the list below, you can see how many of the masks he wears privately can be worn publicly just as well.

HANGING ON TO FALSE HARMONY RATHER THAN GOING FOR THE REAL THING

1. He believes an airbrushed fairy tale and fears discord will mar it.
2. He has a "my way or the highway" intolerance for differences.
3. He's a denier: if it's not great, forget it—it isn't happening.
4. He's uncomfortable with conflict too close to home.
5. He fears losing you or the idea of you as the anchor in the relationship.
6. He fears losing the convenience of the relationship.
7. He sees admitting fears as putting himself in a weak one-down position.
8. He is the Dr. Strangelove of relationships and must maintain the manly illusion of control.
9. He's learned to put a positive face on doubts (big boys don't whine).
10. He uses false harmony to steer clear of time-consuming discussions.
11. He fears your anger and will make up anything to avoid it.
12. He avoids discussion because it stirs up his own ambivalence about the relationship and his commitment.

13. He uses "everything's fine" to plaster over his own disturbing feelings of inadequacy and neediness.
14. He is afraid of not being the rock, not immediately knowing or having the answers.
15. He suspects if you saw his insecurities and uncertainty, you would lose your respect for him.

The irony is that these masks wind up creating distance, not harmony—at work and at home. At work, he may believe that not rocking the boat and pretending that "everything's fine" buy him protection from vicious office politics and competing agendas. But even here loyalties are often forged from honesty and trust, not guesswork. At home, when one or both people won't risk revealing who they are in a relationship because they fear rejection or abandonment, the result is anything but loyalty and intimacy. All we gain is isolation.

From the "Damned If You Do, Damned If You Don't" File

A majority of women say they want the truth, nothing but the truth. What if he drops his mask of "everything's fine" or has never donned it in the first place? You've got a man in your life who is ready, willing, and able to tell it like it is. You said you wanted him to tell you whatever was playing in his head, and here it is in spades—feelings, reservations, a full panoply of doubts, insecurities, vulnerabilities. Are you up for it? Can you manage it? And, more to the point, do you really want to?

What's more, how will he handle your truthful and potentially angry reactions to his flat-out, no-holds-barred honesty?

One man in his late thirties who had just broken up with a woman risked just this. He told all on the first date in his new relationship with a woman he'd met at a singles dance. Here's how he summed up the result of his straight talk:

She used truth like a pry bar.

She thought he "had problems and that they should see her therapist together." This now defunct relationship achieved a record cool-down. His verdict: "Never again."

Maybe the problem wasn't honesty. Maybe it was timing. Hooks that entice you into seeing and admiring the other person's idealized self are often the essence of romance early in the relationship. But then, as relationships progress and become more stable and enduring, people want to discard these idealized presentations of self to reveal who they really are. That allows them to be loved and accepted for themselves and makes the successful long-term relationships comfortable.

Even though most women say they want the truth in their intimate relationships, the question remains as to how much of the truth they are ready to accept, and when and under what circumstances.

For example, Kim is not so sure the truth is always such a good idea. At thirty-three, she is twice divorced, running her own business, and dealing with her own set of issues around truth and honesty. Kim has identified herself as a partially reformed pathological liar, and her latest beau, Russ, as fate would have it, happens to be a relentless truth-teller. While this is helpful to Kim as she strives to figure out what is normal, she has more than a few reservations about Russ's truth-telling: *"I'm currently dating someone who tells me how he feels about me and the relationship every moment of the day. His words are like a barometer of his feelings and things are always evolving and changing. It hurts the relationship after a while. It feels like a weather report. I ask, 'Do I really need to know this much information?' Before, I thought, 'I deserve to be told this.' Now, I really don't want to hear this. I'm trying to feel good about myself. His negatives answer into my biggest fear about being real."*

Both Kim and Russ are exceptions and a study in absolutes. She uses lies to control an unpredictable reality by making it more manageable. He uses truth in the same relentless way. But control, not spontaneity and intimacy, is the hidden agenda here. So we can expect Kim and Russ to lock horns in their battle to manage each other no matter what the facts might be. Their arguments over truth are simply another arena where the battle of power and authority will play out.

The Man Behind the Mask

The mask presents a false image. Too bad, because what we crave is what we resist: real feelings, raw nerves, and the excruciating vulnerability of closeness.

Despite our best efforts, the particular facade we choose exposes the inner turmoil we seek to keep private. Masks reflect our cultural ideals and stereotypes—the ones we consciously or unconsciously use to measure ourselves against.

We all wear some masks some of the time. And that works for us as well as against us. From relatively harmless strutting to the most devastating deception, the mask distorts while it attracts—and shields. At first, our masquerades can be fun—charming games that let us cover a few secrets here and selectively parade a few there. But because its root is the false image, a steady stream of masquerades is guaranteed to distance and isolate the man or woman behind the mask.

In this and the last three chapters, we have looked at the deceptive masks that men and women wear to achieve sexual intimacy, to communicate commitment, and to hide feelings behind a facade that everything is fine. I believe that women, like men, feel at home in many of the masks we've discussed. But men's and women's choice of masks often differs dramatically. And because so many men conceal themselves behind the impenetrable shield of stoicism, it becomes a culturally acceptable mask that's harder and harder to pry off with each passing decade. Fathers pass this mask on to sons in thousands of subtle gestures and in overt admonitions to act like a man (don't show your feelings of vulnerability). Often fathers and sons become co-conspirators in keeping an unpleasant truth from the wife-mother, stifling their own feelings and any emotional residue in the process. For many men the mask of stoicism and the family of masks that hide feelings are as familiar as their own skin. Whether through unwillingness, inability, or laziness, they live encased in these masks. It's all too easy for men to be "suits," not only in the workplace, but in their own bedrooms and living rooms.

Leaving the mask in place is the path of least resistance, but doing that has high cost for intimacy. When the mask rigidifies to replace our true faces, *we literally lose face*—our own. Real feelings are buried and those that leak out feel mechanical and hollow when put to the test of time in relationships. He, and you, are truly deceived by the face you see before you. When the real person behind the mask can't access his feelings, his actions reflect a fragmented, externally defined self that primes him for the next set of even more dangerous lies—the lies of evasion.

Part 4
LIES AS
EVASIONS

Chapter 9
Away From
Your Prying Eyes

*I was dating someone for six months who said he had a platonic
female friend. I didn't question him. Then I caught them together . . .
He said he didn't think I could handle the truth. The truth wouldn't
have thrilled me, but at least I would have been able to decide.*
—Thirty-three-year-old divorced female entrepreneur

*When we moved abroad, what he didn't tell me was that his whole
family was coming to live with us and it was a permanent move,
planned with his family. First, after one month his mother moved in.
He said only to visit. Then came two male cousins. Then a sister-in-
law and three kids . . . The whole family immigrated and moved into
our tiny apartment.*
—Thirty-five-year-old separated female office worker

If you don't ask me, you don't need to know.
—Forty-two-year-old single male engineer

What is a man? A miserable pile of secrets.
—Andre Malraux

Now we are descending into the heart of darkness. Although lies of
evasion may begin innocuously, they often draw us deep into the
shadowy world of betrayal and subterfuge. Evasions include insidi-
ous lies of fidelity, addiction, split loyalties, and financial trickery.
At best, lies of evasion reflect a stunning lack of empathy and commitment, at worst a devious and dangerous bent for deception.

Lies of evasion make the hooks that initially drew us in, and the
masks that hold intimacy at bay, seem like mere child's play. Of
course they're not. Lies as masks set the stage for evasions by effectively distancing us from each other, creating an us-versus-them
mentality with the very people with whom we share our beds and

our lives. Evasions are the lies we dread most in our closest relation-ships. They are the lies that are harder to forgive and forget than any that preceded them, because they are intentionally designed to mislead or deceive us. No matter how sophisticated, experienced, or street-smart we have become, it's hard to be prepared for the eva-sive lie's trust-obliterating blow without crossing over into cynicism.

Martha still harbors resentment. After years of going to school part-time, while juggling kids and work, she had just begun student teaching and expected to have her degree by the end of the year. After she spent three months arranging day care for the kids and finding an assignment close to home, imagine her chagrin when her husband told her he had quit his job eight weeks earlier to accept an offer twenty-five hundred miles away. And oh yes, by the way, she would need to be packed and ready to leave by the end of the month.

Or what about Cynthia, who discovered that the man she had been supporting was using his free daytime hours to court the neighbors rather than to look for work? Or Ellen, who found that the man she had been living with for seven years hadn't been going to workouts at the gym, but to another kind of workout—in the bed of another woman. Or Lydia, whose first boyfriend told her he had to study rather than spend the evening with her, but when she vis-ited his apartment early the next morning, she found him in bed with another woman.

These women find it hard not to be bitter. Lies like these are the neutron bombs of intimate relationships, lies that destroy love and goodwill. They leave you physically whole but emotionally gutted. The only things they leave intact are the remnants of happier times—memories, photos, gifts, in-laws, children. Inevitably, eva-sions involve an orchestrated bail-out from a whole series of real and implied commitments, agreements, and promises. His intent? To dodge your scrutiny and disapproval so he can go his own way, undeterred by your judgments. The impact of his lies of evasion? They disarm, disillusion, and devastate.

Let's explore the nature of these evasions to get a handle on just what is being evaded, how it's done, and how being the target of the evasion affects us.

The Nature of Evasions

Hardly anyone goes out looking for lies of evasion. Most of us would rather spend a morning sitting in a dentist's chair getting our teeth drilled. Still, these lies have a way of finding us. And they do find us—usually remarkably unaware and complacent, given what is going on around us.

Lies as evasions have some of the same earmarks of lies as masks, with this critical difference. A mask makes his true thoughts and feelings inaccessible to you, whereas the evasion does that *plus* making his actions inaccessible to you. Because the masks he wears conform to our preconceptions, like the sex-role or cultural stereotypes that fit him and that you readily accept, the damage they do sneaks up on you. With masks, you collude in his masquerade to help him hide who he really is because his stoicism or secrecy or false commitment has come to feel so seductively normal that it fails to trip your internal alarms until it is too late. You're not asking, he's not telling. Lies as masks lay the groundwork for lies of evasion.

The *lie that evades* builds right on his masks and your unquestioning good faith and acquiescence. But then it moves far beyond those bounds. Evasions involve deliberate withholding, distorting, or falsifying of information so he can do whatever he wants without your knowledge.

He knows the score, and if there were no serious or dire consequences to his actions, he would let you in on it too. But if you knew or he told you, you'd get angry and hurt and maybe you'd move out and get on with your life. In short, he would have to deal with the real person his actions affect, and respond to the serious consequences of his actions. The name of this game would be truth *and* consequences, a game his evasive lies inform you he has flatly refused to play. He has no desire to be accountable to you. And he may even add insult to injury by framing his actions as being "for your own good," in your best interests!

What's Being Evaded?

This list of evasions is a ho-hum fooler. The subjects these lies evade evoke about as much passion as a page from a legal textbook. But don't be fooled by this list's antiseptic tone. Behind each of these terms lurks a daily soap opera of tragic and comic proportions.

The most common lies of evasion center on:

- Exclusivity
- Hidden addictions
- Finances
- Career matters
- Health issues

By and large, exclusivity, the "you are the only one" lie, is the hands-down winner for the number one spot on this sorry hit parade. This lie is mentioned four times as often as all the other lies of evasion combined, and we'll take an in-depth look at these lies of exclusivity in the next chapter.

Most everyone has been through the drill. He says you are the only one. But as the proverbial fly on the wall would tell you if only it could, you might as well be his wife or his lover, his old girlfriend or his new one, or the high school sweetheart he meets again at the twentieth reunion. His affairs and dalliances may be legendary, but chances are the boys at the bar or the gym know a lot more about them than you ever will. Count on learning about his office romance only when it gets him fired from his job, or when his former secretary or coworker files a sexual harassment suit with the EEOC.

Does all this sound unduly harsh? Maybe that's only because you haven't seen the tears, self-doubt, anger, and disappointment of the women who have told me those specific stories. Or maybe you've been lucky enough to avoid all this; or at least so you think.

A gay television producer I met told me two years before his death from AIDS about a documentary he had been working on. It began with the sight and sound of hundreds and hundreds of golden wedding bands being dropped into the lock-box at the local bath house. How many of these men's wives do you suppose suspected where their husbands had spent those stolen hours?

As a child, I used to watch an action-packed television drama called "I Led Three Lives," the tale of Herbert Philbrick, an FBI agent who infiltrated the Communist Party. More than a few of the married men I interviewed, and perhaps a few more we all know, would give old Herbert a good run for his money any day of the week, only their undercover work is centered on keeping two or more women, not foreign agents, in the dark.

Evasion's Golden Oldies: Addictions, Money, Work, and Health

His commitment and loyalties may not be divided between two women, like the dual allegiances a double agent professes to two countries. Instead, he may dedicate his discretionary time (which is also hidden from you) to a whole range of artfully camouflaged activities and goals. He knows their scope and depth, but intentionally keeps you in the dark.

Take addictions, for example. Alcohol, drugs, and sex combine to win second place in the evader's lineup, and they can be counted on to dramatically change the nature of any relationship. Go to an Alcoholics Anonymous meeting in any town to grasp the full range of deception to which addicts resort in order to keep their habit going. Your best strategy here is to understand that since his addiction is running the show, your relationship isn't really with him, it's with his addiction. And the nature of addictions is to hide, distort, and destroy. Him and you.

The evasion of addiction is followed, but at a fair distance in the lineup, by all manner of money issues, from stashing away unreported cash and bonuses to hiring lawyers to help him conceal and convert his assets so he can slip—miraculously maintenance-free—out of his marriage to you. Perhaps he merely tells you it's been a bad year financially, so there's no cash for remodeling the kitchen. But at the same time, he's skimming off greenbacks for a new Ferrari or a sailboat. Or maybe it's more serious. Maybe he's busily squirreling away your joint assets in secret accounts in anticipation of divorcing you. Or maybe his earnings are going toward the care and feeding of another woman waiting in the wings. Some money lies border on the pathological, but as long as money is equated with power and freedom, any man who has amassed a pile of it is likely to consider evasive maneuvers necessary to protect his self-interest. When he does this out in the open, as in a prenuptial agreement, it's not a lie of evasion. Both parties know what's up and go in with their eyes open. The pernicious quality of any trickery involving money comes when it's hidden, and when your perception of truth parts ways with the reality of your mutual finances.

But that's not all. What about those all-important career matters—you know, job change or loss, unhappiness, plans for the future, and, oh yes, sexual harassment suits—the ones that he knows about that you don't? And while we're detailing what you don't know, how's his health? Did he tell you that he is a borderline diabetic? Or that his doctor told him that if he doesn't stop drinking his liver and his brain cells will soon be indistinguishable? Or that he's being treated for genital warts?

If you have such a close relationship, how come you didn't know all this? Is it the male mask of stoicism or "everything's fine" that holds you at arm's length? Is it a weakening of commitment and the ties that bind? Or are we descending deeper into the treacherous and slippery slope of evasions? If his secrecy allows him to cover his tracks so he acts far beyond your range of vision in ways that harm, in ways you would reproach or reject as wholly unacceptable, consider it a full-blown evasion.

Plan for your self-defense, but not for your golden wedding anniversary.

Are Evasions the Most Common Lies of All?

Of course, men have no corner on the market when it comes to lies of evasion. I've heard many men tell me how their trust and lives have been shattered by a deceptive woman. As lies go, evasions are amazingly common among both men and women, outnumbering lies as hooks and masks by more than two to one for both sexes.

That becomes clear when we look at men and women's responses for two "last lies" questions I asked—the last lie you remember either telling or being told by a member of the other sex. Both the men and the women I interviewed showed amazing agreement. Based on their own experiences, their answers showed that approximately 80 percent of the "last lies" men told women were lies of evasion. How did women compare? Very similarly. For women (again, according to both men and women interviewed) lies of evasion accounted for close to 70 percent of their "last lies." However, these percentages hide a fascinating sex difference in these data. Only one-third of either men or women could remember a woman's last lie—either as the recipient or the teller. What about men? Eighty percent of men had no trouble providing the specifics of their last lie to a woman and 78 percent of women provided the nitty-gritty of a man's last lie to them.

Relative to types of lies men tell, where do evasions rank? They were the runaway winner for the men's category. Men used evasions seven times more than masks and fifteen times more than hooks in my analysis of both men's and women's answers to questions about the first and last times a man had lied to a woman.

If men lie more evasively than women, does this merely reflect their greater power and the more abundant choices that society bestows on them? When a man enters a relationship with a woman, he, not she, is generally viewed as having greater potential for earnings, status, influence, and accumulation of material assets. Does this leave some men feeling they have gotten the short end of the stick by giving up their deserved sexual and financial freedom while adding on responsibility and accountability? The evasive lie may become his wormhole to freedom, a way to restore lost equity, deal with his anger over being monitored, constricted, and controlled, and help restore his sense of masculine autonomy and entitlement.

Tools and Tricks of the Evader's Trade

How does he get away with it? That's the $64,000 question in the evasion game. In sifting through hundreds of tales of evasion, I discovered that evasion has its own methodology, its own rhythms. But the key to successful evasion is to make the strange seem familiar, to make the bizarre appear reasonable, to convert the unfathomable into the ordinary. That encourages you to see what you want to see or what he wants you to see, rather than the deception itself. It takes advantage of your need to believe the best, trust that people are good, and have faith that this man you care so very much about will extend you the courtesy of the truth. And that's why evasion, like any con game, can be so seductively successful and so remarkably devastating in the hands of a pro.

The checklist below will give you a quick overview of the tools and tricks that anyone seriously contemplating successful evasion is likely to use. You might have a few more to add from your own experience.

TRICKS AND TOOLS OF EVASION: A CHECKLIST

1. Denial

Denial is the most primitive defense mechanism according to Sigmund Freud. Also the most common, if that tells you anything. These lies of evasion range from the minor—he's been caught with his hand in the cookie jar, but says it's not his hand—to the kind of denial that heralds major infractions of trust. Just listen for his quick and resolute "I didn't do it," no matter what "it" turns out to be.

The first person I ever had sex with when I was seventeen and he was twenty-three lied to me. I got pregnant and drove to his house. His lie was "I know it's not mine—your 'thing' was loose when I met you."
—Thirty-one-year-old single female production manager

2. Rationalizations

He has a way with reasoning that explains it all, from his particular viewpoint and to his advantage. If you believe it, you get what you deserve. So take your time to sort fact from fiction. View him as a master rationalizer who could

---

be fooling himself as well as you. If you get confused, hire an objective third party to talk it over with. If you're in a serious relationship with this man, you'll need all the help you can get.

My husband said it hadn't been an affair. He said they had sex a couple of times, that he hadn't pursued it, but that she wouldn't let go.
—Thirty-nine-year-old separated female computer programmer

3. Secrecy

His secret could become yours, but in due time—his time. The problem here is that what you don't know will hurt you. Remember that no matter how hurtful the facts turn out to be, they are a lot friendlier than being blindsided by today's evasion months or years from now. So keep sleuthing. If your doubts are grave, hire a professional.

John's lie was that he was living at his sister's when he really was living at Nina's—the mother of his kid.
—Forty-year-old divorced female medical assistant

4. Broken Promises

This man is the master of asking for forgiveness, not permission. His promise was just a passing thought, not an agreement, and he'll say he thought you realized that. He promises anything, and anything is often just what you can expect. Count on his being unable to hold any position over time. Unreliability is his calling card. Remember the old saying the management gurus are fond of quoting: "Fool me once, shame on you; fool me twice, shame on me."

My second husband during our divorce settlement said, "Don't put anything in" about seeing his kids from the previous marriage. He said, "I promise you'll see them." His lie devastated me.
—Forty-one-year-old divorced female doctoral student

5. Anger

Whether it's his first or last resort, anger is the evader's ace in the hole. It converts his nervousness about being caught into instant rage, so his flush of shame becomes a flush of anger.

There's method to this madness: he lied because he's afraid of your anger and now he's counting on you to be just as intimidated by his. His righteous indignation and anger are tough counterpoints to your mere suspicion, so you're likely to be the one to back down. You might try anger yourself to see if he backs off. But do it publicly where you are safe and sound. And if he tends toward violence, get professional help—fast.

The last man I lived with would fly into a temper whenever I cornered him, shouting and screaming, "It's always me who fucks up, you never think you can do anything wrong. Well, let me tell you, you're not so perfect either." Then he would launch a missile of acerbic criticism my way, threatening to walk. Finally I did.
—Fifty-five-year-old divorced female journalist

6. Mind Games

This man literally knows how to drive you crazy. He sows doubt the way a farmer plants corn, and he gets a bumper crop in record time. He'll question your judgment and accuracy, poke fun at your memory, challenge your facts and IQ. Realizing he's just being self-protective may help, but this man is a big-time confidence destroyer, and quite possibly a confidence man to boot. So why not get a little self-protective yourself? Keep a journal with dates and quotes. He'll get the idea.

This summer I was dating a man and we were supposed to go out together. Was it seven o'clock or was it eight o'clock? I called him to check and he said we weren't supposed to get together. He said, "I didn't say that." But I had written it down in my book.
—Thirty-five-year-old single female interior designer

7. Excuses

As Hillary Clinton once framed it in a televised interview: "Coulda, shoulda, woulda." Whatever the excuses, they are designed to get him off the hot seat so he can continue to evade your knowledge and your censure. His excuses will get old long before they stop. Make this your relationship rule: *No excuses.* Then hold him to it.

*He said he stood me up because there was an accident on
the freeway and he stopped to help an injured woman. Next
he had to cancel our date for the symphony because he had
a flat tire and couldn't get the lug nuts off. Then at the last
minute he was too tired to go to a dance. I drove to the
parking lot of the dance and saw his car there. He had a
phony excuse for everything.*
—Thirty-six-year-old divorced female accountant

8. Technical Truths

The technical truth-teller is often smart and masterful. What
he says is absolutely true, so his conscience is clear. Too bad
it's what he doesn't say that's so critical. Just remember that
spin control is not operating in your favor. What you hear
will not resemble what you get. So take nothing for granted.
Keep asking for more information. Sure, he'll get testy. Just
ask yourself how much you really want to know, and what
the consequences of ignorance will be.

*A guy said he was going to work out with his buddies. I
wanted to see him that night so I called him on his car
phone. I heard a woman's voice say, "Who is it?" Later he
tells me, "It was a friend who needed a ride." It was a girlfriend who needed a ride.*
—Thirty-one-year-old divorced female physical therapist

9. Diversions

What a tangle of fake fires and fights he stages and fictions he
invents! Look for these and whatever else he is concocting to
distract you from noticing what's really going on. Just bet on the
fact that there's a lot going on. As soon as you get close to the
truth, he'll tell you a story about something that knocks you off-
course, banking on his ability to divert you. Don't take the bait.

*My husband Wade's last lie was about the affair with his
secretary at the office, telling me, "Someone at work is out
to get me."*
—Thirty-seven-year-old married female public relations
director

10. Bait-and-Switch

At first his words and actions seem to be in perfect synchrony
with yours. But these are temporary triumphs to be over-

shadowed by his later switch. This isn't parlor magic; this is
your life. You are a pawn in his grand scheme, and once he's
got you where he wants you, he's likely to deny the switch
ever happened and count on your stunned acquiescence.
Why not surprise him by saying no?

*We were getting married, I had sent my luggage to Hartford. He
calls and tells me, "It's best for us not to get married because
we're not from the same religious background." But five months
later he married someone from a very different background.*
—Forty-eight-year-old divorced female physician

11. Creative Disorganization

Good grief! He's so disorganized that you can easily believe he
got on the wrong plane, forgot your dinner plans or birthday,
lost track of time and stayed at the office until three in the
morning. But consider this: he may be more creative than disorganized. The ruse of disorganization buys him enormous
freedom away from your prying eyes. A pattern of unreliability could be a symptom of a serious personal problem, or a
just a very clever tactic.

*At first he was so charming I didn't even mind all the
changes and rescheduling. I'd run out to the airport to
spend thirty minutes with him before his plane took off.
Then he'd have me paged and say, "There's been a change
in plans." Later I realized it wasn't going to get any better
than this. He liked it that way.*
—Thirty-seven-year-old divorced female technical consultant

In the lies of evasion throughout this chapter, we'll discover how
men use these tools and tactics to keep the truth at bay. Stay alert
for the favorite evasive tricks of the men in your life, and while
you're at it, see if you can't identify a few of your own as well.

Why He Tells Lies of Evasion

Knowing the tools he uses to practice lies of evasion is the first
step in stocking your own arsenal of defenses against them. But the
idea here is not to play war games. It's to be prepared to protect
yourself from unnecessary pain and hurt. Knowing what many men
say about why they tell their evasive lies helps. Sure, his reasons
may seem patently obvious. They are *to him*. What's important is

that you too are aware enough to recognize them at close range. Here are some of the common reasons the men I've spoken with give for their lies of evasion.

SOME COMMON EXPLANATIONS FOR MEN'S LIES OF EVASION

- To get away with something temptingly forbidden that they want.
- To avoid disclosing the true facts of the situation that will lead to unwanted consequences.
- To achieve what's most convenient with a minimum investment of time and energy.
- To avoid a woman's anger and the powerlessness it evokes in them.
- To hedge their bets, so they're not left alone or the loser.
- To be in control of who ends the relationship and when.

What's especially intriguing here is the sizable proportion of men (slightly less than half) who in discussing their evasions adopt a particular way of rationalizing their evasive lies. *They claim honorable or protective intent and ignore the actual effect of their lie on the woman in question.*

Is this rationalization merely self-serving hype or is it a much deeper form of self-deception? That depends on the specific man and the specific situation. But in either case, this for-her-own-good stance reaps two immediate benefits for the evader. First, it allows him to affirm his own good intent in distinct contradiction to the real reasons for his lies of evasion (as listed above—getting away with the forbidden, avoiding her anger, etc.). Second, as a rationalization, it allows him to walk away whistling, feeling good about doing what he wanted, without burdening himself with undue (or even any) guilt. At the same time that you are suffering the consequences of his half-truths, lies, and betrayals, he may be sauntering toward the exit feeling quite good about his actions *and his lie.*

Evading Female Authority

The most galling part of these evasions is that he acts as if what he does has no effect on you whatsoever, that his infidelities, drinking, squandering of funds, lack of accountability, and career screwups are none of your business. But the truth is, despite his free-agent stance, his lies of evasion are often totally dependent on you.

How? Without you or someone like you, he would have nothing to escape from. If you weren't there he would have to invent you. You may be nothing more than the latest in a series of stand-ins, one among many in a long line of female authority figures reaching back from his mother and grade school teachers to high school girl-friends, ex-wives, and female bosses. If so, he will revel in defying, fooling, or escaping you and all the restrictions and constrictions you symbolize. How conscious is all this? Probably not very. Since his early experiences with female authorities took place so long ago, he probably wouldn't recognize this pattern if it bit him. And if he did recognize it, it's unlikely he'd say, "Wow. That's me." Too bad, because as long as he's unaware of the pattern, how can he change it? But before you feel too sorry for him, remember that his lies of evasion, understood or not, clear the path to his freedom. And to your betrayal. Without betraying you, how could he feel free?

His Evasion, Your Response

So far, we have been focusing mostly on him. What he does, why he does it. What about you? Where do you fit into this scenario, and where do you want to fit? What role do you play in making his evasions a reality or a pipe dream? You have your own patterns of response too. When a person you care about tells you a lie of evasion, you don't react randomly. You act in a way that reflects your own past, your own needs and motivations. And your own hopes.

Whatever your patterns of response, you also have choices. You can keep doing what you're doing. But if you don't like what's been happening in your relationships, that may not be the best decision. As one of my clients remembers his father telling him, "If all you do is what you're doing, all you get is what you've got." So consider that the most common response to the lie of evasion among the women I interviewed was *denial*. Then decide if denial describes your own pattern. If it does, you'll have to decide whether this is a pattern you want to hang on to.

Denial and Acquiescence: The Dance of Two

I was engaged for five years, but it didn't work out. He was having other relationships on the side. People tried to tell me, but I wouldn't listen to it. I said it couldn't happen.
—Thirty-six-year-old married female financial adviser

There are two key ways in which women aid and abet the process of maintaining a man's lies. The first is by outright denial of the signs and symptoms of his discontent, irritability, and distancing. These signs are usually none too subtle, and you should be able to spot them. For example, he's spending more time at work, on the golf course, off with the guys. Or he comes to bed later and is up earlier, while your sex life has gone the way of the old vinyl record. Or he looks at you less, responds to your comments with no curiosity and interest, initiates no interaction, and informs you only on a need-to-know basis. Any major change in behavior should command your attention, at least sufficiently to put you on yellow, if not red, alert.

The second way you can aid and abet his lies of evasion is by acquiescing to his denials, lame excuses, and counterattacks. He resents your questions and you just fade away. Too bad, because with your retreat into silent acquiescence the relationship is likely to fade away too.

Of course, you have your reasons for denying and acquiescing. And they are good ones called love, hope, trust, and fear. But by not taking a vigorous stance of intentional self-protection, you wind up partnering with him in the betrayal. Not a good idea.

Now before you beat up on yourself too much, remember that some men are accomplished masters of deceit and evasion. They could pass a lie detector test given by the CIA or the Secret Service with flying colors. They have no trouble looking you right in the eye and glibly distorting the truth. These men show no guilt, take no prisoners. But even though they can still fool you, most men who lie will be average, even ambivalent liars. So with the right approach you stand a chance of calling it the way you see it, getting to the facts of the situation, and ultimately clearing the air for a better relationship.

But many women miss this opportunity. Instead, they inadvertently worsen the situation by politely failing to confront, taking his first denial at face value. As one single thirty-six-year-old entrepreneur put it, *"My girlfriend correctly verbalized that I was seeing someone else. Then when I denied it, I was amazed how she let it drop so easily. And relieved. I just couldn't understand why she let me get off so easily."* He was amazed that she backed off so quickly! He couldn't believe his good fortune. *He denied it; she denied it.* From his perspective her failing to confront him was an irresistible invitation to lie even more outrageously. The result? He felt he had been given license to continue his lies of fidelity with impunity. And he did.

But why would she or any woman accept a man's quick denial so readily? Why not give him a run for his money by pushing him to the limit, by putting him on the hot seat and grilling him? Put yourself in her place. You rightly guess that he is seeing someone else. That means the clues and innuendoes you are picking up are registering, either consciously or subconsciously. Your intuition is screaming out that something is wrong. You ruminate endlessly, talk it over with your friends. But when you gather up your courage to confront him, he denies it in a heartbeat. Your response? Instant cave-in and retreat. Why? Why would you put your head in the sand?

Most women know the answer. We hope against hope that our perception and judgment are wrong. That there is no one else. No one wants bad news. We want the relationship to be wonderful, we want to be the only one. We want our fears to be allayed, not inflamed, so we grab at any bit of hope he offers. If he says we were wrong, that feels good. The last thing many women want is the unexpurgated truth. But since the truth will out anyway, it's just a question of *when* and on *whose timetable.* That's a lesson Heidi finally learned.

The High Cost of the Dance Marathon: Heidi's Story

Like so many of the women I interviewed, Heidi immediately came across as warm, articulate, and caring. It was hard not to like her right away. A recently divorced nurse in her late forties with four grown children, Heidi was brimming with stories and advice. Yet as I wrote down her answers to question after question, I couldn't suppress thinking: "How on earth could she have stayed with her man for twenty-seven years?" Then, looking back at my notes, I saw that Heidi actually started our conversation with the answer: *"When a man lies, all the signals are there. It was just that I didn't recognize them personally."*

The first part of her statement, "all the signals are there," was right on the money. The second part was both an understatement and a misstatement. The fact was that Heidi was determined to avoid seeing the laundry list of lies her husband Sandy perpetrated, day after day, year after year. She already knew all about the damage a relationship with other women posed to a marriage. Her father had cheated on her mother. His "not tells" had driven her mother crazy, and young Heidi had been "the one Mother sent out to check the mileage" on her father's car. Heidi had thought a great deal about her father early in her own marriage, "how he couldn't reach his dreams because he played around." How desperately she didn't want that history to repeat itself, "didn't want Sandy to be that way." Determined to give Sandy no cause to reject her, she worked hard to be an extra good wife, putting Sandy through college, doggedly "helping him reach his goals . . . doing everything to help him."

Then a few years ago the bottom fell out. Heidi realized that Sandy was running around with other women—lots of them—across the Potomac in Alexandria, "so many women he couldn't remember their names": *"He stopped coming home after work. He would say he was playing golf with the guys. He came home later and later. He would come home from playing golf with the guys at three in the morning."*

The dream of creating a marriage altogether different from her mother's was shattered as she woke up to the range and extent of Sandy's perfidy. And quite a range it was: from hidden caches of pornography to salary, earmarked for bills, squandered instead on topless dancers and clubs. And then there were the affairs. But the extent of Heidi's deep-rooted need to deny didn't become clear until she spoke to me about the secrets Sandy had kept from her: *"I didn't ever think Sandy kept any secrets from me before he started going to Alexandria with women. But back in the early 1980s he would go home with one of his secretaries. He actually got dismissed for doing this on the job. He was dismissed because he had a relationship with his secretary. I didn't learn the real reason for his being fired for eight years. At the time I'd gotten an anonymous letter about what Sandy and Claire [his secretary] were doing in the back room. But Claire was a good Christian woman. So I went to these people [in the office] and confronted them."*

The truth about Sandy and about Heidi's future had been apparent many years before Sandy finally flaunted his adultery. The truth had been staring her right in the face, but Heidi had squeezed her eyes shut. Reality, in this case, was the last thing she wanted to see. Even in our interview she still insisted that her husband hadn't lied to her "about the reason for his being fired." Rather she defended her man and her now irrational belief in him: *"He just didn't tell me everything he knew. He kept the grounds for his firing secret from me. That he wouldn't let Claire alone, that he kept her from doing her job. I found out about it later from his boss. I still do not believe anything was going on between him and Claire."*

Yet Heidi is no dummy. Her next comments show beyond any

reasonable doubt that Heidi is a world-class eyewitness: *"Sandy had a little wiggle he did in the shower. He'd move his penis back and forth to indicate he was feeling sexy. He had a hat from Old Town in Alexandria where she [his then current amour] lived. Someone complimented him on it and he said, 'Oh yeah,' then [fully clothed] he made the motion, his little wiggle."*

As an excellent observer of nuance, of subtle detail, Heidi had all the information she needed, just as most of us usually do. Heidi even offered this advice to help tip women off to a mate's adultery: *"Look for an improved way of dressing . . . He said, 'I've got to get a new suit.' Or making more long-distance phone calls from work or staying at work longer to get in long-distance calls."*

So how do we explain the intelligent and observant Heidi's collusion in Sandy's evasive lies of fidelity for so many years? Or any woman's willingness to go along with a program that is dangerous to her health and well-being?

For starters, Heidi felt dependent on Sandy for her self-worth. *"I was willing to pay any price to keep him. I didn't want him to leave me. He left me when I wouldn't have sex with him when our baby was four weeks old."* She was afraid to be left alone in life with their small children. She had learned and rejected the lesson of worried endurance from her mother. Now her denial let her continue with goodwill.

Second, she was anxious to prove that she wouldn't re-create her parents' troubled marriage. If she could just be good enough as a "mother, wife, and person," she felt she would deserve and get a better life. Through her own valiant efforts she could stave off the shame and distress of being married to a husband who cheated on her. But as Heidi herself acknowledged, in this process of trying so hard to be good, she neglected one thing: *"I wasn't good to myself."*

And Sandy wasn't easy to deal with. The few times she managed to confront him, he used evasive tricks and tools with a vengeance. Anger and mind games, plus a sprinkling of creative disorganization and diversion, were his tricks of choice. But any tactic likely to tap into Heidi's feelings of inadequacy and shame worked. Heidi told me how *"when confronted he would get angry and blame me for something else."* And sometimes, he turned both physically and mentally abusive: *"Toward the end of the marriage he wanted me to perform like . . . people at topless bars . . . He told me, 'You don't begin to measure up to other women.' I don't know if that is true."*

But here again, we see evidence of women's magnanimity and empathy, however unwarranted, toward the liars in their lives—a near constant in the long stream of women I have interviewed and seen as clients over the years. This is how Heidi appraised her ex-husband's lying ways: *"I think he was lying to himself. He was going out with other women to build his self-esteem. He's getting older, not performing as well in bed as he used to. I was getting a master's degree with a 4.0 average while he felt inadequate about his own life. . . . He was low on the totem at work."*

Listening to Heidi, Sandy's affairs sound more like a self-improvement course than the wrenching betrayals they were. Her comments and his actions expose a difficult truth: that she remained committed to him and the relationship, however dysfunctional, while his commitment was either stillborn or died somewhere in the middle.

How did it end? Heidi finally "got it." She "put all the clues together." She was angry and hurt, but still she didn't confront him. Why not? *"I'm not a confronter. I'm a protector. If it had come out that he was seeing another woman, he would lose his job. I felt I had done everything I could do. But even in bed he looked at me like he hated me. I was keeping him from doing all he wanted to do. He wasn't grateful for all I did for him."*

Heidi had paid a high price for her denial and acquiescence. Whatever feelings of shame and responsibility she carried from her parents' unsuccessful marriage drove her to try harder. If she were just good enough, she felt, he would at least show gratitude and appreciation. Instead, her determined endurance, her willingness to look the other way and not report or act on his trespasses, backfired. It won her emotional pain and depression, along with this man's contempt and even hatred. In the end, they divorced, but as the only responsible adult in this marriage, Heidi had to file for it herself.

Confronting the truth is tough. It's a real challenge for a lot of us, both male and female. And when we do, we may not always like the payoff. But the sooner we do it, the sooner we will have another opportunity to find the intimacy and trust we crave and deserve.

Women Who Don't Deny: Ripa's Story

Not all women deny, even when dealing with virtuoso liars. Ripa certainly didn't.

Ripa met Henry at a conference in Atlanta. It marked the start of a romantic and escalating year-long correspondence. She was a student in India and he was a writer at a university here. It was 1984 and a love story. The following year she came to the States to study because of him. Their relationship was idyllic: *"We meet in Raleigh-Durham, he visits me once a month, calls me daily, tells me he loves me, writes me letters, poetry. He dedicates a seven-hundred-page manuscript to me. He spoke of marriage. I was very interested."*

Then mutual friends showed her a few of his books. This is how Ripa tells the story of her discovery and disillusionment: *"In one of them he dedicated it to his wife. This happened just after one year of our relationship. He had told me he was single, when he was married. I guess I believed him because he's Indian too. I was shocked."*

Ripa refused to become his partner in the dance of denial and acquiescence. She immediately called him and confronted him with the evidence. She was greeted with a long silence, and then, "Let me explain when we meet, when we're together . . . " What could he possibly say that would right this grievous situation? Unfortunately, only more lies: *"Henry comes to visit, to explain. By then, I have found out that he's very much married, that he has a granddaughter. I refused to see him. He came to my apartment near the university. He still denied it. He said, 'Look at the publishing date [of the book dedicated to his wife]. We've since been divorced.' But his college confirmed he's married and that his wife taught at the same college . . . I returned his letters and his pictures."*

The relationship ended. Ripa had turned her life around to be with the man she loved and hoped to marry only to find out that, unknown to her, another woman had gotten there first, decades earlier, and was still holding her ground. Ripa had become "the accidental other woman."

What's particularly instructive here is how even in the face of Ripa's immediate confrontation with irrefutable evidence, Henry continued to deny, distort, and lie about his marital status. He pursued this young woman, courted her, and brought her halfway around the world for his own pleasure, but even at the bitter end he could offer her only more lies. Her verdict? A terse "I wish he would have left me alone." But then, like a majority of the women I interviewed, she too offered the precious gift of her goodwill and a face-saving way out. Her words may more accurately reflect her own need to see the world as a good and hospitable place than an assessment of his character: *"We made a good couple. He liked me. Maybe he was just going through a crisis in his life. I still try to put a positive spin on it."*

Perhaps because Ripa and so many women like her can't bear to believe that they have given their time and their lives to such scoundrels, they create their own personal revisionist history. These are lies of forgiveness, lies that allow them to decrease the dissonance between the painful facts as these women now understand them and the high hopes they held on to until the very end.

When I was researching lies, a flight attendant told me how she handled the bad and surprising news of her husband's infidelity. After receiving an anonymous letter about her husband's repeated infidelities throughout a fifteen-year marriage, she angrily confronted him, assessed his response, and then handed him a box of trash bags for his things before throwing him out. She recalls fearfully asking herself, "What am I going to do without him?" Then bounding back, answering, "I have a life, friends, children, work. He's the one who has nothing." Now happily remarried, she said her only regret is not responding to the now glaringly obvious clues of her first husband's evasions much earlier. When she looked back, the comments and habits that made no sense under the assumption of his fidelity were now startlingly clear. For example, sitting with their old gang, discussing friends' divorces, he volunteered, "I don't know why these guys want divorces. They think the grass is always greener—it's just different grass." At the time she remembered wondering, "How would he know?" Now she knows too.

Sometimes confronting is the first step in a long and rewarding process of rebuilding honesty and trust. But confronting doesn't always lead to a happy ending. Sometimes it just leads to an ending—which was in the cards anyway. Sleuthing in search of the truth often has the same mixed result. Women who creatively use their available resources—technology, government records, credit card statements, or even telephone directory assistance, phone redial, and telephone answering machine room surveillance—to confirm their fears and to catch him in the act may not like what they learn. But once they know the actual facts of the situation, they have wrested unilateral decision-making from his hands and taken back the power of informed choice. Now the decision to continue the relationship or not, and how, is as much their choice as his.

How Can You Defend Yourself?

Self-defense begins in earnest when you face, point-blank, whatever there is in you that compels you to trust the liar. Yes, trust the liar. That oxymoron my father warned me against so many years ago is still valid today, well preserved in the hearts and actions of many women. Your first job is to figure out just what it is in you that causes you to look the other way, to fail to confront his tres-passes, to dismiss that persistent rumbling in your gut that tells you something just isn't right. And your second job is to change your response and confront. Risk his censure, outrage, and denial. Recognize that it's unpleasantness now or later—after you've bet the ranch, the kids, and two or three decades of your life. We'll talk more about this at the end of the next chapter. But be assured that none of this is easy, so a certain amount of queasiness is, in fact, par for the course. And remember that you do not need to go it alone. You will need all the help you can get, so get it.

Now let's turn to a closer look at the many faces of the most common evasion of all: "Only you." This shattering betrayal of fidelity with its web of evasive deceit can invade intimate relations and trust at any stage—in the beginning, in the middle, or at the bitter end.

Chapter 10
Only You
(and You and You)

He allowed us to build our hopes, our dreams. He made me believe in them, that we'd move together to Florida. Then he told me he was married, that his family was coming here to Chicago.
—Forty-five-year-old divorced female executive director

He lied about his affair, that he was having a seven-year affair, even during my pregnancy. My last son was born in the course of his affair. I still have emotional scars.
—Thirty-seven-year-old remarried female finance director

I would have numerous affairs in both my marriages. It seems I made sure my partner would find out. But when confronted, I'd look deep into their eyes and tell them anything I wanted them to believe—and they believed it. I knew what they wanted to hear. They didn't want to hear the truth. I said, "Everything is fine . . . Nothing is going on . . . "
—Thirty-five-year-old married male film director

It's the old, familiar story. It's often hard to say when it started, but suddenly she notices an unexpected gesture, a new after-shave lotion, a preening fest before his mirror. Something feels different. Whatever it is, the soothing mask of "everything's fine" can no longer hide it. He's involved with someone else. Whatever happens next, chances are she's not going to like it.

Consider this scenario. Suspicious and distraught, she confronts him, pleading, "Tell me you are not having an affair." His response is textbook. He gladly obliges by telling her exactly what she wants to hear—that he is not. Still not entirely convinced, she rails, "I can't believe you would do this to me!" And he, seeing his opportunity, urges her not to. But the unpleasant truth hovers. Her gut is alerting her that something is wrong, and that has them both worried. He reaches deep into his bag of tricks and deftly deploys

denial, mind games, and diversions, the time-honored tools of evasion, to protect his cover. His response is predictable, as he vehe-
mently denies her allegations, accusing her of heinous thought
crimes. He reminds her of all he has done for her. He swears that
he'd never do anything to hurt her. Suddenly, he seems so vulnerable that she backs off. Then he buys her flowers, remembers their
anniversary, reassures her that "you are the only one." As her suspicion continues to escalate, he counterattacks, again finding her
guilty of distrust. She backs off, chastised, bewildered, and temporarily diverted from the truth.

"Only You" Packs a Triple Whammy

When there is someone else and a man denies it, his partner
encounters the baldfaced lie of exclusivity. But his infidelity rarely
stands alone as a breach of trust. Long before that lie surfaces, he's
created two related sets of evasive lies that support and hide what
he is really up to.

The first set of lies covers up what's really happening. These lies
provide alibis, explanations, and diversions to keep you in the dark.
They help you believe that nothing has changed, that you still are
the only one. Working late at the office, attending out-of-town business meetings, and visiting a sick friend are just a few of the easy
alibis that help make his case. These cover-up lies are sneaky, but
don't hit the issue of exclusivity head-on. In fact, their sole purpose
is to prevent you from being suspicious enough to pop the burning
question: "Is there someone else?"

The second set of lies involves direct denial. These are the outright
in-your-face lies ("No, honey. I swear there's no one else"), Or they
may involve partial denial ("It's not what you think. She made a play
for me. She's crazy. I swear nothing really happened. I was just trying
to let her down easy").

Infidelity and the two sets of lies around it pack a hard-hitting
one—two—three punch:

- **Punch 1. The infidelity itself.**

- **Punch 2. The cover-up lies.**

- **Punch 3. The lie of exclusivity.**

Here's how this triple whammy works. First, there's the infidelity. Maybe you know about it; maybe you don't. Then there are

the cover-up lies that follow close on its heels. These probably trip your sensors so you suspect something is wrong, even if you don't know what. Eventually there's the pièce de résistance—his overt lie of exclusivity that wrongly assures you that there's no one else.

Why be blindsided by any of this? In any relationship, why not be prepared to recognize and deal with all three? Let's start with the infidelity itself.

Punch 1. The Infidelity Itself

Cheating is as American as apple pie. Both men and women regularly violate both implicit and explicit agreements of exclusivity. That's hardly news. Alfred Kinsey, in his groundbreaking large-scale sex studies of the late 1940s and early 1950s, discovered that about half the men and one-quarter of the women surveyed had affairs outside marriage. Later works confirmed that while not all of us cheat, a sizable number of us do. Shere Hite's controversial 1987 report placed infidelities for men and women at 75 and 70 percent, respectively, while the conservative 1993 Janus Report estimated that one-third of men and one-quarter of women are extramarital players. These studies suggest that neither men nor women in committed relationships can take exclusivity for granted. But if you are a woman, according to the stats, you face a higher probability that your husband or lover will cheat on you than vice versa—although the gender gap for cheating appears to be narrowing dramatically. Of course, these statistics are based on what people are willing to admit, what truths they are or are not willing to tell social scientists. And since lying is more widespread than cheating, both sexes' frequency of infidelity could be much higher than reported.

Still, the roving eye is much more a male than a female sport. The fact is that men prefer a variety of partners. David Buss, in his 1994 book *The Evolution of Desire*, reports that in a study of unmarried American college students, men say they would ideally like six sex partners in the next year. Women say just one would do quite nicely. And all the sex surveys I've seen show men having more affairs with significantly more partners than do women. Why? Buss offers an intriguing explanation: the tendency of males, either beast or human, to be sexually rearoused when presented with new females, "giving them a further impulse to gain sexual access to multiple women." He succinctly captures what this means by citing the work of anthropologist Thomas Gregor on the Amazonian Mehinaku. For Mehinaku men, "Women's sexual attractiveness varies from flavorless (*mana*) to the 'delicious' (*awirintya*) . . . sad to say, sex with spouses is said to be *mana*, in contrast to sex with lovers, which is always *awirintya*."

Of course, some women crave variety too. As a former student of mine, a twenty-five-year-old married woman, once volunteered in a discussion of monogamy, "All any relationship really needs to keep it going is a hot new body." But suppressing women's desire for and willingness to pursue variety are a daunting array of foreboding social strictures. No matter which culture we look at, females who cheat on their partners face more severe punishment than do their male partners—from loss of their status or their assets to loss of their lives. Double standards reign supreme, and infidelity can be quite dangerous to a woman's health and safety.

That's the infidelity part. Now, what about the cover-up lies and the lie of exclusivity?

Punch 2. The Cover-Up Lies

If men promise exclusivity and don't uphold it, they face an immediate problem. It's called consequences. He wants freedom to see other women, but he doesn't want you to know he's exercising that freedom. He craves *awirintya* with someone new, not *mana* with you. It's what woman after woman I interviewed called the wanting-to-have-his-cake-and-eat-it-too syndrome. Dealing with your outrage, or even your suspicion, is the last thing he wants. So he lies about where he is spending his time, who he is with, and what he is doing. He hides his transgressions like Heidi's two-timing husband in the last chapter, claiming to be out playing golf, working late at the office, or going out with the boys. And maybe you fall for his alibis. For a while.

But lying isn't his only option. He is, after all, in charge of his own behavior. Let's not forget he can change his actions at will. Even after an affair he can revert back to exclusivity with you, or he can try to broach and negotiate a new nonexclusive agreement. Although both lying and cheating are tough, addictive habits to break, some men manage to do just that.

Why? Frequently because these men can no longer bear the betrayal and the pain they are causing or because they simply can't manage all the stress their daily dissembling creates. And sometimes because the demands of the other women have become untenable. I heard from, or about, only five such men in the course of ninety-five interviews, but I've worked with more than a few male clients who have stopped lying in their personal relationships, so such men are out there. Some men stop lying because they are confronted by a wife or lover who forcefully narrows their options to either stop and stay or continue and go. Other men choose to rev up or even flaunt their lies. They flirt with discovery. When a man's lies become too careless or too excessive, that's often his way of alerting you that your relationship is screeching to a halt. The dilemma this man may face is that he doesn't want to exit playing the bad guy. That means he wants you to take his hint and to end it for him.

But usually long before that happens, you will know the score. If you just stick around long enough you will make a startling discovery:

> Most people's hidden agendas are far less hidden than
> they believe them to be.

So, despite his intentional and self-serving web of cover-up lies, the truth leaks out. Then when you finally discover the infidelities, and the web of lies that hides them, you may realize that you've known the truth all along. Marriage counselors often report that when a man confesses he has been having an affair, even the most oblivious and unsuspecting woman manages to accurately name the other woman. More often than not, despite his diversionary tactics, subliminally we understand all too well what is going on. When that understanding brings us too close to what we don't want to see or accept, we work overtime to suppress our own intuition.

Punch 3. The Lie of Exclusivity

Intuition is a relentless and powerful internal radar system. No matter how you ignore it or try to shut it down, it miraculously keeps tracking whatever blips are out there. Even when we don't like what it tracks, intuition helps us avert personal disaster.

You sense something is wrong. Intuition is screaming in your ear. So you come in closer and open contact. At point-blank range you ask your partner, "Is there someone else?"

How does he respond? It depends on whether he's been unfaithful and whether he is truthful.

If he is *faithful and truthful,* he'll honestly say no. There's no problem with exclusivity, although your intuition may be picking up other sources of stress, like a work or health problem.

If he is *unfaithful and truthful,* he will honestly confess. You now have a lot to discuss, so this is no time to shut down communication. But remember, things may not be what they seem. His confession may capture only a partial truth, as with the twenty-three-year-old man who told me, "I 'fessed up to being with another woman. I conceded that we had spent one night together. In fact, we had been together for months." So do work out the issues between you, but don't forgive and forget prematurely.

If he is *unfaithful and untruthful*, he will lie about cheating and may pull every evader's trick to throw you off his scent. Should you decide to stick with him anyway, this man will give your intuition and capacity for trust a major workout every day of the year. Consider what this thirty-seven-year-old unfaithful liar had to say about his lies of exclusivity to his wife: *"My second wife would confront me with her suspicion of the lie, not with true knowledge of it. As long as I kept the difference between physical sex and love separate, I told myself, 'It doesn't affect her.'"*

If forewarned is forearmed, be so advised. Know what you are up against.

Most women would prefer their partners to be faithful and honest. But since many men are neither, you need to consider the question at the heart of the lie of exclusivity. If you were involved with a man who desired sexual and emotional liaisons with other women:

> Would you prefer to know the truth about his infidelity, or would you rather be fooled by his lie of exclusivity?

Sometimes women pay lip service to wanting the truth when, in fact, they prefer the lies that cover it or even his blatant denial. Where do you stand on this? To help sort through your reasoning, ask yourself the questions listed below. Then, if you're currently in an exclusive relationship, ask your partner how he'd answer if the hypothetical infidel were you rather than he. Remember, there are no inherently right or wrong answers, just revealing ones. The discussion could be an eye-opener.

WHERE YOU STAND ON UNFAITHFULNESS AND LIES OF EXCLUSIVITY

1. Is *exclusivity* an immutable, cornerstone condition of your intimate relationship with a partner? Just how important is it?

2. Is *honesty* about exclusivity an immutable cornerstone condition of your relationship with a partner?

3. Would you be more upset or hurt about discovering an infidelity, a web of cover-up lies surrounding it, or the blatant lie of exclusivity?

4. If you accidentally discovered that your partner was unfaithful, would you confront your partner more angrily about the infidelity or about the cover-up lies and lie of exclusivity?

5. What advantages does knowing about your partner's infidelities give you?

6. How would being aware of your partner's infidelity affect your future trust level?

7. How would being aware of your partner's cover-up lies and lie of exclusivity affect your future trust level?

8. Could you still justify loving your partner if you discovered years or even a lifetime later that this person had been unfaithful to you?

9. Would you love your partner less if this person were unfaithful to you and you knew about it?

10. If you discovered your partner's infidelity and cover-up lies that hid it from you, what, if anything, would have to change to keep you together?

What should you make of your answers? It depends. They may let you know which you view as more vile—the act of infidelity or the web of lies that covers it up, including the lie of exclusivity. For example, if you answered yes to question one, *fidelity* is essential. His breach of fidelity may be sufficient for you to head for the hills, whether he lies about it or not. The result? Suppose your partner knows this and is unfaithful anyway. From his perspective and yours, once he's had the affair his lie is the only way to keep you together. He and the other woman know the truth and you don't. You become the outsider.

Suppose you answered yes to question two. If honesty is the cornerstone of your relationship, then his *lie of exclusivity* may be as bad or worse than his infidelity. In any case, if you can talk honestly about the affair and what led to it, you stand a chance of reestablishing intimacy. But if he lies about an affair, or keeps lying about affairs, you may opt to pull the plug on the relationship and go forth in search of an honest man.

Infidelities and the lies that cloak them present serious breaches that build one upon the other to taint the closeness you feel and destroy your trust. First, you react to his unfaithfulness with an outraged "How could he do this to me?" Then, minutes later, you react all over again, exclaiming, "How could he have lied to me about it!" This enraging point-counterpoint can go on for years.

So what should you do? No one way is right for everyone. Once your relationship has been breached, arriving at an agreement of what's acceptable between you is key. Sexually open relationships, where both parties agree to other liaisons, work for some people as long as there's agreement. In some relationships, hiding infidelities may be the tacit agreement both partners are willing to live with, as long as there are enough other benefits to keep them together.

Discovering that a trusted partner is cheating can cause terrible pain. Yet seasoned marriage counselors will tell you that ongoing cover-up lies and lies of exclusivity pose a much larger threat to intimacy than the infidelity itself.

Why? Because without honesty in a relationship there is no touchstone of trust, no reliability, no assurance that what your partner says resembles what's real. Without honesty, how can you even acknowledge the infidelities, much less get to what's at their root? Only the most determined and thoughtful honesty between the two of you will create enough goodwill for genuine dialogue. Then, eventually, with patience, goodwill, and persistence, you may restore trust.

As you read the stories involving the many lies of exclusivity, keep your own answers in mind and think about how you would react in each situation.

Where Does It All Begin?

Lies of exclusivity can start at any time or age. No one is exempt. The roots of our lies of exclusivity and tacit acceptance of others' lies reach back into our own personal histories. An unfaithful father or mother can be a powerful teacher—someone to emulate or to shun. An alcoholic, abusive, or emotionally distant parent can sow the seeds of our adult behavior, whether it's lying and denial or hyper-responsibility and acquiescence to the lie. Our lies and acquiescence to lies may reflect the shame and fear many of us learned long ago. Men and women alike talked to me about the legacy they still carried from their fathers' or mothers' adulterous affairs and accompanying lies. They brought up the complicity and shame they felt so many years ago, which had stayed with them. These men and women feared they were doomed to repeat their parents' mistakes.

Many of the people I interviewed said their *first* remembered lies were lies of exclusivity that reached back to high school or to their first serious relationships. Their lies ranged from the touchingly awkward ("How could I tell my steady girlfriend I'd met someone I liked better when we were going to celebrate our third anniversary together?") to the blatantly premeditated ("He brought me all the way to Chicago to work with him and to set up a life together even though, as I later found out, he already had a wife and four kids back in Ecuador").

Others didn't dig that far back. Their *last* remembered lies were lies of exclusivity. Many were still playing out. Women told tales of disappointment and anger as men's lies of exclusivity peeled away to expose an unwelcome, often unanticipated truth. They described how another woman had gained entrance to their partners' lives, or how the man who had sworn exclusivity seamlessly shifted from purveyor of lies to expert at damage control. They described how he often found it necessary to rewrite history or expose the truth (as in "I never loved you"). Or how he reconstituted his "exit lies" as "lies of mercy," which ultimately proved less geared toward empathy than toward his own self-protection.

What binds all these baldfaced lies of exclusivity together is that they are universally painful to their victims and that each story contains a unique pattern of response that identifies it like a fingerprint. Although every story reveals its own characteristic pattern, many also share broader recurring themes. For example, you'll see how a number of the men and women most victimized by these lies of exclusivity inadvertently contributed to the problem by tacitly allowing the liars they loved to go entirely unchallenged.

How? By going along with the liar's program, by looking the other way, and by assiduously avoiding any point-blank questions that would expose the painful truth. For many victims of the only-you lie, the truth, not the lie, is what repels. They have so much at stake, it's hard not to sympathize. Who can blame the victims of these hurtful lies for wanting to cling to the belief that their partners still love and care for them and have their best interests at heart? But the truth lies somewhere else. Refusing to look at it won't make it disappear.

Don't assume that only-you lies just show up in the middle or end of troubled relationships. These hurtful lies of exclusivity often start early, gain momentum in the middle, and then entrap both liar and victim in a fiery end.

In the Beginning

It was freshman year when I was away from the girl I had dated for
two years in high school. We were like Brenda and Eddy in the Billy
Joel song. Three weeks before I was heartbroken about leaving her.
Then three weeks later I grew out of it. I found someone I liked better
. . . I figured I'd let it go as long as possible until she figured it out. I
told her I loved her at the end of every telephone conversation, when I
was going upstairs every night to be with the new girlfriend. I was
hanging on to the old because it was only two to three calls per week,
and it was little investment of energy. I was totally ready for the new
girlfriend. She was the most beautiful girl I'd ever seen.
—Thirty-year-old single male bond trader

In case you harbored any doubts, the preceding quote makes the
point quite nicely: You don't have to be married twenty years to
encounter the ubiquitous lie of exclusivity. Often such lies begin
early and gradually become a way of life. So if you encountered
them when you were dating, you have a good chance of seeing them
again in or out of divorce court. If you discover and confront this lie
of exclusivity early, congratulate yourself on your good fortune. You
may have saved yourself years of pain and suffering.

An Early Pattern of Lies

Lies of exclusivity and other lies of evasion are part of a pattern
that often shows itself early on and continues from one relationship
to the next. The first lies that men remember telling women yield
fascinating clues. For example, there's Chuck, still single at age
thirty-eight, who recalls telling a girl in high school that he couldn't
see her one evening because he was going to participate in his
cousin's confirmation. In fact, he didn't want to let her know that "I
was going out with another girl." Unfortunately, she saw Chuck
with his date at an amusement park, and despite his best efforts at
escaping her ire the next day, Chuck couldn't avoid her biting comment, "How was the confirmation?" That marked the end of that
relationship, but not of his pattern: *"It started my pattern. I like to*
see two different women and keep both in the dark. I lean toward
different personalities and looks . . . and I still keep getting caught."
The die was cast. Chuck had discovered his pattern. Lie to avoid
directly confronting a woman with information that she is not the
only one. Then fail to take sufficient precaution against being caught,

so that you can repeatedly move to higher ground without being entrapped in either relationship. For Chuck the lie of exclusivity is always botched. Barely adequate cover-up lies are the norm. Being discovered in two parallel relationships is his escape hatch, his wormhole to freedom. Until it begins all over again with the next and the next unsuspecting twosome.

Then there's Randy, now in his mid-thirties. Randy's first remembered lie was a lie of exclusivity. It was in high school with Anna Marie, early in the relationship, but there was already "implied exclusivity." Randy went out with someone else with whom he had been involved earlier. His friend Roger, whose own keen interest in Anna Marie overcame his loyalty to Randy, spilled the beans. Anna Marie, filled with fire and brimstone, gave Randy a run for his money. She confronted him with a vengeance, taking the silver bracelet he had given her and publicly dumping it into the bottom of a cup of Italian ice. Randy was one of those wants-to-have-his-cake-and-eat-it-too liars. His hope had been to "get away with it, to avoid disclosures, to avoid her 'out-freakage,' and to avoid the end of the relationship." By his own assessment, he had lied "brilliantly." Unfortunately, there were still consequences: *"I flat out denied everything. I looked her right in the eye and lied my ass off. 'What are you talking about?' She ended up believing me, but it was the end of our relationship. I broke up with her one month later. I felt embarrassed to be made a public spectacle of. Everyone knew."*

Randy, the successful liar, using classic evader's tricks of *denial*, *mind games*, and *anger*, had gotten away with the lie. But Anna Marie, even though she had allowed herself to be duped into believing his lie of exclusivity, proved too volatile, too hot for Randy to stay involved with. She was going to be hard to fool with a standard web of cover-up lies and she had embarrassed him publicly. He moved to higher ground by ending the relationship.

Randy's pattern is locked in place. He wants the freedom to do his own thing, go his own way, without having to account to a strong and angry woman. Creative lying, not infidelity, is his hallmark. When you get right down to it, Randy would rather shoot the breeze with the boys at the bar than play Casanova with down-and-dirty women. Randy may be a cheater, but it is dishonesty, not infidelity itself, that counts most. Randy, now married for ten years and a parent, is still up to his old tricks.

These reasons and patterns for lies of exclusivity don't change much over time.

Same Pattern Down the Road

You can take the boy out of adolescence, but you can't always take the adolescence out of the boy. Playing the field often remains the game of choice, whether he's sixteen or sixty. Edward is a case in point. A divorced and quite charming doctoral-level research analyst in his early sixties, Edward is brimming with stories of intrigue and infidelity. Evasion and Edward have had a long and satisfying relationship over the years—one that shows little evidence of winding down. His latest story has to do with the calculated way in which he misled a woman he was dating on the West Coast into believing she was the only one: *"I had a great many episodes where I needed to see my daughter in Vermont. Barbara would ask me where I was going to stay. I'd tell her how I stayed with the Carlsons—friends I'd known for a long time. 'They' were really Sally—a divorced woman, not the Carlsons. Telling the truth would raise the specter of 'What's going on here?' My lie is something that wouldn't present any problem to her, whereas staying with a divorced single woman would."*

Edward is the consummate avoider of confrontation. His subterfuges are both masterful and astoundingly effective. But when it comes to the lie of exclusivity, he doesn't give an inch. *"When Barbara asks, 'Is there another woman in your life?' I've steadfastly answered no even though there is. It would just lead to a lot more probing than I'm comfortable revealing. It would lead to questions of whether or not I'm sleeping with her. And I don't want to reveal this. She would find it distressing."*

Edward's stance is both *unfaithful and untruthful* with the various women in his life. His modus operandi is *secrecy, denial,* and *rationalization,* with a smattering of *diversion* and a liberal sprinkling of *technical truths and half-truths.* Like Chuck and the younger men interviewed, Edward wants to see two different women and keep them both in the dark. He wants to hold a tight rein on his relationships while avoiding women's anger and distress. He also wants to feel like a hero for saving them from *awareness of the distress he's inflicted on them.* He's a master at emphasizing his ersatz noble intent without acknowledging the damage he inflicts. Edward, having had thirty or forty years to rationalize his behavior, one-ups his junior colleagues for a special place in the liar's hall of fame by adding: *"I explain my lying to myself by saying it gets everyone out of the situation without causing pain. It saves her from doubt. A* Time *magazine article says everyone lies. My lies get everybody out of the situation without causing pain. Lying is a form of problem solving.*"

Edward manages to personalize lying by making it a moral imperative, something that saves people from pain. And at the same time he depersonalizes the lie into a problem-solving tool. He, of course, is an expert at lying as a "form of problem solving," and a hero of sorts, at least in his own mind. Lying, after all, is useful—like conflict resolution or debating.

Edward's unique pattern reveals an accomplished juggler of multiple relationships, balancing a series of half-truths, secrets, and lies of exclusivity. He plays well to his own applause. For Edward, lies of exclusivity are not a means to an end. They are part of how he defines himself, part of what helps him feel good about his role in the world. He does the women in his life a magnanimous favor just by lying to them. Maybe Edward should consider running for public office. We'll come back to Edward later when we look at lies that end relationships.

The Turbulent Middle

Lies of exclusivity at the beginning of a relationship disappoint. But at least you haven't devoted ten years of your life to the source of your upset. There are no mortgages, no babies, no long history to bind you together. Once it's over, it's over. But lies of exclusivity in committed relationships and long-term marriages cause endless cycles of pain and suffering. And their toxic residue can easily be carried by their victims from one relationship to the next.

After all, the two of you have made a life together. Maybe it's not storybook, but you think you're getting along. The mask of false harmony has held that illusion in place. But like corsets from days of old, masks of false harmony hold in a lot more than meets the eye. They provide a cover for all manner of evasions to develop and flourish—from leading a dual life to having small flings to evading you by spending long hours at the bar, at the club, or at work.

Both men and women can use lies of exclusivity with equally devastating emotional effects as they come to trust and depend on each other. Either partner's infidelities and the lies that surround them create the greatest fear and trembling in highly committed relationships, where partners share children and property, friends and relatives. But as they get older, women may proceed with far less certainty than men, who are still gaining status and power as midlife approaches and recedes. Women worry about how attractive they really are as they gain a few more years, a few more pounds, and fall further away from their own dreams. They begin to wonder whether they can still compete with the next and the next bumper crop of younger women. Such self-doubts provide fertile ground for even the most alarming lies of exclusivity to take hold, unchallenged. So it was with Laura.

When You Can't Even Trust Him With the Sitter

Laura was my first interview for this book. Late on a winter Saturday afternoon, Laura, divorced and in her mid-fifties, was dressed for an evening at the symphony. She made a point of letting me know she was still dating, still sexual, still viable. Intense and articulate, Laura had a definite edge. Having gone through the preliminaries, I asked the question: "Tell me about the last lie you caught a man in." Her tone was flat and matter-of-fact, as if she were reading a shopping list, but the pathos of what she was saying captured my instant attention. She told a story that was the first of many stories women were to tell me over the next year, stories that could break anyone's heart. *"The last big lie I caught a man in? When I was married, my husband said he would drive the babysitter home. When he didn't come home after a long while, I went out looking for him. I saw the car by the swimming hole. I opened the car door and I saw them in the act. I . . . found him in the car with the babysitter, making love. He looked stunned. He had said he would drive the babysitter home. Instead he took her to a deserted area and had intercourse with her. I [went home and] put all my kids in the car and headed for Chicago, drove in and subleased an apartment."*

Packing up her seven young children and going out into the world couldn't have been all that easy that dark night. "Was that the first time he had lied about his fidelity?" I wondered. No, turned out it wasn't. The assertive and confident woman before me apparently had not always been that way. Laura leaned back and sighed. *"I had found condoms in his briefcase from time to time, but I didn't talk to him about it."*

She didn't talk to him about it! Laura didn't even confront him the night she packed up her kids and left. She talked about these events as if they had been from another lifetime.

Why hadn't she confronted him? *"Our relationship was not healthy. He had a violent temper, and I acquiesced to it all the time. I did everything I could to keep him from yelling at me."* Her husband had used *anger* and *secrecy* to keep his bride, the mother of his seven children, in place. In response, Laura had submerged the assertive, sassy parts of herself beneath a victim's self-protective shield of fear and acquiescence.

Then, rising up from somewhere in the past, came the "good wife's disclaimer." Laura gratuitously added, *"He was a very well-meaning person. I don't think he planned it. He planned to take the babysitter home. He felt desire, lust. It was a spur-of-the-minute thing."* After all these years and all the pain and suffering, there she was, still alibiing for the old guy. Like his philandering, it was an old and dysfunctional habit.

Laura still had a lot at stake—in her words "my marriage, betrayal, and self-esteem." She planned to go back to Arizona where she had grown up, but she made a telling mistake. After her dramatic departure to Chicago, Laura called home the next morning. *"He was remorseful. He said it would never happen again. He said all the right things. Eventually, I went back with him. But I never trusted him again."* Having been caught by his wife in the act of sexual intercourse with a teenage sitter, Laura's husband took the *unfaithful and truthful* confessional approach. For a time that helped. Communication became a bit more open between them. Still the ending was hardly "happily ever after." *"Eventually he got a girlfriend who he was interested in. I figured it out and confronted him. I should have left and gone back to Arizona . . . "*

Laura learned the hard way. Old patterns don't just disappear because we decree that they will. This man was an unrepentant philanderer who did whatever he wanted to do, little of which bore any resemblance to his vows of monogamy. For him, the evader's tools of *denial, anger, secrecy, broken promises,* and *excuses* had become a required way of life.

Laura, by caving in, fearing abandonment and feeling responsible for holding her relationship with this scoundrel in place, had made it easier for her husband to cheat and evade without serious consequence. She made few demands on him and was every bit as anxious to avoid confrontation as he was. Because he didn't have to lie that much to get away with his infidelities, he didn't even bother to cover his tracks to remove telltale condoms from his briefcase. But on the one occasion when Laura did stand up to him, he turned remorseful and "said the right things."

Laura, as an active mother of seven, had a great deal invested in keeping even a dysfunctional relationship going. It was natural for her to rationalize that she was too busy, too dependent to cut her losses and strike out on her own. That led her to become his partner in their dance of intimidation and acquiescence. The pattern was set, until it became so futile and his actions became so blatant that she had to break out.

The *Glamour* Man

Some evaders are daring showmen. What they love is the risk of the high wire, going up against detection-defying odds, and they evade with their own cheeky brand of chutzpah. That's Stan, another master of the lie. A forty-something white-collar Walter Mitty Washington bureaucrat, Stan lives out his fantasies not with Mitty-like heroic rescues, but with a series of torrid fatal-attraction-style affairs.

Stan, unbeknownst to his wife of six years, has been carrying on a steamy affair with their jogging partner, Marlene. Bev knows that Stan takes significant liberties with the truth, but so far the fireworks his lies ignite have been more or less containable. As Stan frames it: *"My lies are front-end loaded. I come home sweaty or smashed. Bev says, 'Where were you?' I lie, 'I got out of the meeting early so I went and played racquetball.' She says, 'You're such a fucking liar.' It's not a big deal. But with the extramarital affair, I don't know. A friend told Bev, 'Stan is seeing other women.' She said to me, 'You're such a liar.' I said, 'What are you talking about. I can explain it to you.' Glib. Glib. Glib. . . . But I'm not threatened by her. I feel I can deny my way out of it."*

Stan seems to relish the opportunity to test his wit against Bev's need to know. So it comes as no surprise that he puts himself in unwarranted danger now and then, just for the sheer sport of it. Although Stan is both *unfaithful and untruthful*, his passion is for the lying and cheating, not the sex.

For example, Stan and Bev are flying back home from a San Francisco vacation and reading *Glamour* magazine together on the plane. They come across an article on how to tell if your man is cheating on you. Reading it out loud, Stan gratuitously offers, "Sounds like me and Marlene." Bev replies, "Do you think Marlene is a homewrecker?" Stan asserts, *"No, she's touchy-feely."*

What is Stan doing? Is he trying to get caught? He offers that he "set up Bev," but says he was just "testing the water with conversation," reasserting the fact that *"I'm not sexually involved with Marlene."* Did this lie just pop out of his mouth or was it planned? The answer is a frosty "Yes, it was calculated." It looks like Stan didn't fall off the high wire this time. But does he regret putting himself at risk by lying like this? *"Not really. I have symptoms of being a cheater. I'm hard to track down. I have the freedom to do what I want. I have the history of being a cheater."*

Stan uses the whole tool chest of *denial, excuses,* and *technical truths,* but he is a genius with *diversion, bait-and-switch,* and *mind games.* These help him evade his bright and pretty young wife's prying eyes. He has constructed a world for himself that compensates for the fact that *"I'm not able to do everything I want to do and maintain a relationship with Bev."* He feels he has to "make provisions for having such a scuzzy under-life, and the solution is to cover it up with lies."

Stan sounds smug, but he's a study in conflict over commitment and self-control. It's hard not to hear the turmoil he feels about what he is doing and whether to stay married or not. First he argues that he'd rather not cheat, that he'd "like to be Ward Cleaver," or "father of the year" to his two kids—then he back-pedals, making excuses for himself and distancing himself from any responsibility. He complains, *"I wish I found my wife so interesting I couldn't keep my hands off her. That I wanted to come home and rub her feet."*

So it's no surprise that in the next breath, when I ask him what he'd do differently, he totally abdicates responsibility by saying, *"I wouldn't have gotten involved in an affair or gotten involved with my wife."* But he can't hold that position either. He turns around to assume blame, cryptically adding, *"I screwed up bad at the end of my marriage."* The end of his marriage? Since he's still married, this slip reveals that he has given up on his ability to change his lying and cheating—behavior that has doomed his marriage as a union of trust.

Then there's fear of a woman's anger. Stan shows plenty of that, along with a well-hidden but genuine fear of losing Bev due to his increasingly risky and damaging actions: *"She asks me if anything has gone on between me and Marlene. I say no. Then I say something negative about Marlene. It's almost like Bev knows something has gone on. If I confirmed it, she'd have to divorce me. Our lives would be over. She says, 'Well, if I ever find out, I'm going to kill you.' A guy in my office was busted in a similar situation and his wife left him. He has to feel bitter."*

Yet as soon as Stan shows vulnerability and fear of loss, the macho mask of swaggering bravado clamps back into place: *"I can survive anything. In six months it wouldn't make a difference . . . I'm bullet-proof. If my wife woke up tomorrow and said, 'I don't* love you,' I wouldn't care . . . But I wish this [the affair] would really end. I think she's a psychotic little tramp. I wish she would leave me alone. I'd like to end things, get out, ignore her, but it's impossible to do. I've cooled off . . . If Bev did [know about it], I'd like her to be intolerant."

If you read Stan's stream of consciousness carefully, you'll see one of the clear markings of the evader's profile: ambivalence about commitment *and* vulnerability. Here's a man who can't commit to staying or to going. Here's a man who wants license to slip between the sheets of many women other than his wife or lover. But here's also a man who simultaneously needs and values his wife's or lover's righteous indignation. That proves to him, at least for the moment, that he is still valued. The paradox of the evasive liar is that he is both bullet-proof and ever so vulnerable. That's part of his charm. But his behavior has destructive emotional consequences that eventually compound, both for him and his many victims.

The problem here is that Stan's lying stands in the way of open and honest communication between him and Bev. Making matters worse, Bev has signed off on his lying and is focusing primarily on his infidelity. This creates a Catch-22 that shuts down important communication about his real problem, trapping him in his own lie of infidelity and all its accompanying cover-ups. What she is missing is that until he's honest they won't be able to solve the problems and infidelity in their marriage.

When Cheating Is a Red Herring

Tina is just twenty-six years old, but she's packed a lot of experience into those years. When I asked her about the last lie she had caught a man in, she laughed, saying, *"There are so many, I don't know which one to choose."* Too bad Tina wasn't kidding. The source of all these lies is Josh, the man with whom she's been living and fighting for several years, mainly over his drug addictions and episodic unemployment. The last serious lie she caught Josh in was when she was working at a new job and, as usual, Josh wasn't working at all. He had just successfully avoided participation in a drug rehabilitation program.

Trust between them had fallen to a new low. Since he regularly turned the ringer off the phone at home and refused to answer it, Tina compensated with technology. By using a room monitoring feature on her answering machine, she could tune in to whatever was going on in the apartment from her desk at work. One afternoon, when he didn't answer the phone, she heard his voice on the monitoring device. Apparently she didn't like what she heard because in her words: *"I went right home from work in a cab and asked the cab driver to wait. I found Josh with his ex-girlfriend. He had covered up everything I owned. I was angry. The look on his face was 'Oh, my God!' He was terrified when he saw me. He tried to physically push me out the door."*

The last thing she had expected was Josh's infidelity. But instead of venting her hurt and anger on Josh, she wound up displacing her anger onto his ex-girlfriend. *"If she was unfaithful to the sisterhood, I could deal with her."* The ensuing scene was pure sitcom pandemonium, with Josh's ex-girlfriend running out of the building and Tina only a few steps behind.

Tina packed her covered belongings and moved out. Then Josh moved out, and Tina moved back in. In the last frame of this soap opera they got back together, which, incredibly, they still are.

What are we to make of all this? Josh's lie was behavioral as well as verbal. By literally covering up Tina's belongings, he communicated in a visual flash to Tina just how conniving his lie of exclusivity was. Still, his evasive lies are generic Brand X. He wins points for lies in the multiple categories of infidelity, work, and drug addiction. He was pretending not to be home, to be out looking for work, when, in fact, he was with another woman.

But Tina knows Josh's cheating is just a red herring. It's a symptom of a much bigger problem. She gets to the heart of the matter when she identifies the real problem as the deadly game Josh is caught in—a game that combines *drugs, unemployment, and other women.* Tina says: *"With the other woman I can deal with it and act accordingly. But in drug use, if the person is in denial, nothing can work. He still lies about drugs. I told him to get in a program or 'I won't see you again.' It took all my strength."*

Tina understands she is emotionally committed to a drug user who can't be trusted with money or responsibility. Now she realizes his fidelity is also suspect. What's more, his word means nothing. Lies have become his way of life. If both his words *and* his actions are suspect, what's left? Josh is totally untrustworthy. And once again, we see that as long as there's no honesty, there's no solution.

The question remains: Why does someone as bright and responsible as Tina direct her time and energy to tracking, monitoring, and caring for someone committed, above all else, not to her, but to his habit? Apparently Tina wonders too, speculating that she may be "in a partial state of denial" and observing that she believes "what he says rather than what he does." Given her propensity for creative sleuthing, nailing the man in the act, and enduring the sleaze that his addiction brings into her life, Tina may make a better undercover cop than victim of Josh's careening and disaster-prone agenda.

For Josh, the game plan is set. Tina is just one more authority to defy. Tina's fighting a battle she can't win. Her pattern is to stave off this insight by getting caught up in the moment, continually fighting to put out all Josh's fires. That's a full-time job, with or without technological surveillance. Distracted from creating a decent life for herself, she throws herself into managing Josh's latest crisis and squanders her talents, believing in her power to bring him back in line.

No wonder she gains temporary relief by displacing her anger onto a real flesh-and-blood target like Josh's girlfriend. She watches her anger vie with her powerlessness as they both fight a losing battle against his addiction. It's one likely to sap his personhood and waste her years. For addicts and their partners, lies of evasion at any stage of the relationship are one more element in a destructive way of life.

The Dilemma

What a dilemma! In story after story we see women minding the family or the relationship while their men are out there playing to win their freedom to pursue other women. The lamentable result? Immediate and lasting conflict, with pain, sorrow, and misunderstanding as the natural consequences.

The dilemma is relatively simple. The resolution is not.

Each sex, locked in its own gender vision, sees the partner's role as they would play it from their own vantage point. This leads women to attribute their own characteristic mindset and approaches to men. And it leads men to project typically male assumptions and reactions onto women.

For example, women might expect men to do whatever it takes to preserve their relationship. After all, they would. And women who have a soft spot for believing a person's words—as much or more than they believe behavior—will expect a man's word to carry the same weight in a close relationship as their own. A man might expect women to play to win, to see through his scam and angrily confront him, or to bring the situation to a speedy resolution and move on. He is shocked when women don't. Over and over, as you have seen, men who lie about exclusivity seriously underestimate a woman's capacity to hold on to a devolving relationship. They are startled by the tenacity of the women who hang on, in spite of an ongoing saga of infidelities, cover-ups, lies of exclusivity, and the eventual wind-down and blow-away finish that is the topic of the next chapter.

This leaves each gender surprised and thrown off-guard by the other's reactions. That's been well documented by a host of researchers, including Deborah Tannen in her popular book *You Just Don't Understand.* Tannen convincingly documents the misunderstandings growing from men's and women's different use of language. But genderspeak is a reflection of our differing gender vision—not its cause. What we hold dearest doesn't take root from our words at all, but from the core of the self, from how we think about ourselves and see ourselves in relation to those we love. And here men and women have very divergent personal histories and experiences even when they grow up in the same families.

As a result, many women discover that the lies men tell women, particularly their wrenching lies of exclusivity, reflect a wholly different view of what is central in their lives.

Because men so often see lying as a game, one that goes with the territory of playing to win, it's easier for them to reduce even intimate relations to the level of the commercial transaction, like getting the best deal on a car or a contract. Listen to the language Bruce, an up-and-coming twenty-seven-year-old sales rep, uses in describing a no-regrets sex tryst he hid from the woman he is currently seeing. He says, *"Right after I started going out with Nancy . . . a woman I had known earlier who was unavailable became available."* He might have been talking about concert tickets or an upgrade on an airline. He has reduced the affair to a transaction. As many men see it, in these short-term transactions the lie, although not ideal, still holds a legitimate place. The lie oils the cogs that make the deal that allow him to play liar's poker for sport and profit.

This approach sets the stage for his personal lies to you. But, you might protest, business is business, while personal life is sacred. Sacred to you. When lying to outsiders is a knee-jerk reaction, lying to you may be far easier than you might imagine. Especially when his affair transforms you, sometimes literally overnight, from insider to outsider in the relationship. As you move from being a duo to a trio, you may be cut out of the transaction as the outsider who is no longer an essential player.

What about women? Women lie too, and the women I interviewed were not exempt from their own lies of infidelity. But for most of the women I spoke with, the love relationship remained central to their sense of self. So central that many were willing to look the other way, excuse his inequities, live with his lies. Finally, many even pleaded with the fleeing liar who had laid his transgressions on the line, to please, please, stay. They were more than willing to lie to themselves to protect the relationship that, rightly or wrongly, they had made the core of their self-worth. Some displaced their anger onto the other woman. Many were loath to confront the liar or show their real anger and hurt even after the relationship was over. Some of the women whose stories you've read continued to alibi for their now long-gone partner, explaining that he didn't really mean it, that his infidelities were just an impulse, an aberration, that he had been drinking, that he was such a good man. All that creates a dilemma.

The Resolution

Men are not children. They are accountable for their actions. Their behavior has natural consequences. And women do not have to collude with men in either their cover-up lies or their lies of exclusivity to protect these same men from dealing with the hurt they are causing.

Women are not fools. They don't have to throw their good sense and accumulated wisdom out the window just because they are in a romantic or committed relationship. Women need to heed their natural intuition, take responsibility for creating an atmosphere where they can talk frankly to their partners about what they sense is happening and how they feel about it. If a dedication to honesty and a few basic ground rules for straight talk aren't part of a particular man's repertoire, then this is a splendid opportunity for him to take the time to learn. Whether or not the relationship has a happy ending, both parties will be better off for the experience of communicating what's real, for understanding the other person's point of view, and for assimilating whatever nuggets of truth they can extract.

What if a woman suspects her partner is cheating? There's no formula for what to do, but in general, blaming and accusing are least effective. That approach just makes you an accomplice to the setup for the lies of ending, which we'll explore in Chapter 11. Taking responsibility for yourself and your own feelings is generally best. So calmly saying, "I sense that you're getting involved with another woman" is more likely to mark the start of a difficult but honest dialogue than asking, "Are you having an affair?" or "How could you do this to me?" This, however, is volatile territory, and many couples seem incapable of having any reasonable dialogue without a neutral third party to coach and keep them on track. There's no shame in needing a couples counselor either. In fact, that's probably the ideal way for everyone to safely get their cards on the table and to achieve the best results.

But the real issue here isn't necessarily his infidelity. It may be your own relationship with the truth. How willing are you to take responsibility for your own intuition, to keep your eyes open, and not to look the other way? How willing are you to serve him notice that you are willing to talk about the infidelity, the cover-up, and the lies as a problem you *both* need to solve? Consider this: If you were your own daughter or your best friend, what would you advise yourself to do that is different from what you are doing now?

Not telling your own fears and pretending everything is fine when you are crying yourself to sleep at night are also lies. These are your lies, your secrets, but these lies hurt you more than his. In the final analysis, you can't change his behavior any more than you could change your parents' behavior when you were a child. But you can change your own behavior.

In the next chapter we'll look at how lies of evasion and exclusivity can lead to an ending that destroys—and occasionally liberates.

Chapter 11
The Bitter End

They don't lie to end relationships. They tell you the truth, that they don't want to see you anymore. My husband wanted to move to Evanston to be nearer to his girlfriend.
—Fifty-four-year-old divorced female sales rep

I thought I was in a serious relationship. Then he said one day, "It's been fun." He was "moving to California with another female."
—Fifty-three-year-old divorced female business owner

He told me that his parents liked me when, in fact, they were plotting to end our relationship.
—Twenty-four-year-old single female bookkeeper

A man I had been dating for two months all of a sudden changed. He became very distant with me, then he told me he had gone back to an in-depth relationship, when in fact he had met someone new.
—Twenty-seven-year-old divorced female student

Welcome to the world of the brokenhearted. It happens to almost everyone at least once. But even the briefest stay here will convince you that endings are not for the faint of heart. In romantic and committed relationships, unless both parties want out, endings are bound to be hardest on the person left behind. Turn on the radio and count the number of songs that deal with the bitter end of relationships and the humiliation of the unceremoniously dumped partner.

Think back to your own experiences with endings, or listen to the gut-wrenching language of friends who have been rejected in a love relationship. They'll spill it out: How they've been *dumped, jilted, betrayed, misled,* and *abandoned.* How they feel *heartbroken, despondent, depressed, disillusioned, disheartened, shattered, angry, upset,* and *bitter.* Trust them, they're not joking. Endings hurt, and anyone who has been rejected and abandoned by someone he or she loves ranks that experience near the top of life's list of traumas.

Endings can also be hard on the person escaping the ties that bind. The Paul Simon hit tune of the '70s counted "fifty ways to leave your lover." Yet most of us remain clueless when it comes to how to end a relationship gracefully. We wonder whether we're doing the right thing as well as how to get on with it and get out the door. That goes for both male and female rejecters. There's no gentle and politically correct way to hit the road. Rejecters recoil at being the bearer of bad tidings. They don't want to be the target of tears and recriminations, *or even know about them*. Nor do rejecters relish long, guilt-provoking conversations that drag on for weeks or even months. Maybe they don't want to hurt anyone, but the fact is they don't want to stick around either. Some rejecters, particularly women, even fear being stalked by the one they are leaving behind.

The result? When it comes to endings, men and women both fly by the seats of their pants because they lack clear rules of conduct. They seek to avoid, deny, and disappear. Too bad the other person won't let them off the hook so easily, which means that they may yo-yo back and forth, trying to exit, being sucked back in, plotting to get out again. All that stress and strain only increases the appeal of the quick-fix, easy-out exit lie. Precisely what exiting partners lie about, or don't, depends on how uncomfortable they feel, what's at stake, and whether they're truly ready for a clean break. Some tell partial truths, opting to leave a trail of bread crumbs *just in case* they might want to find their way back. Others invent outrageous stories to set themselves free. Still others find themselves resorting to the most bitter pill of all—the unexpurgated truth.

No matter how it's done, the bitter end usually has two distinct, but often overlapping, parts:

- First comes the *setup* that paves the road to the ending.
- Next comes the *finish* that marks the end of that road.

On the pages ahead we won't cover "fifty ways to leave your lover" or all the nefarious setup and finish routines. Instead, we'll examine those endings that involve evasions and a breach of exclusivity. We'll look at how some men use setup lies to end one relationship, even as they move on to the next one waiting in the wings. We'll start with the setup, along with the broken promises littered along the pathway to the bitter end. Then we'll tackle the painful finish, including the deadly lies of mercy that paradoxically remove as well as preserve your last rays of hope. Last, we'll see how the truth makes its debut as a startling and amazingly effective last-ditch emergency exit.

The Setup

The setup is the exit plan. It leads you, willing or not, down the path to the dissolution of your relationship. It can be as well orchestrated as a space shuttle launch or as haphazard as Sunday's stop-and-go traffic. What characterizes the setup is that one member of the twosome, you or him, wants out and hasn't announced it to the other.

The setup accomplishes just the opposite of cover-up lies. Remember how cover-up lies hid his infidelity or other evasions? The *raison d'être* of the setup is to reveal the previously hidden signs of your partner's discontent—his infidelities, his addictions, his anger, his sleazy secret life. This sets you up so you will be more willing to let him go without protest. But no matter how bad this setup feels to you as the unwilling partner, make no mistake. It's not the end. During the setup, rejecters are consumed with laying bare all the reasons the relationship won't and can't work, all the flaws that now define their soon-to-be-left-behind partners. But unless you arrive there first and end it early, the actual end won't come until later.

When Harry Left Sally: Anatomy of a Setup

Let's suppose that Harry decides to end his relationship with Sally. To make a clean break, first he has to harden his heart against the possibility of working things out. Then he must painstakingly convince himself that ending the relationship is the right thing to do. That way he will be unmoved by Sally's pleas to stay and work it out. Next Harry must set up a chain of events that create distance and readiness to let go—both for himself and for Sally. This is where he allows hints or even evidence of his evasions and cover-up lies to slip out. Before they were hidden; now they are tactically placed clues that guide her along the path to the end.

Last, Harry must be ready to go quietly into the night *without* resurfacing. The purpose of the setup is to help Harry get away *and* stay away. Past and current infidelities, which let him bond with other women and move Sally to an outsider status, aid and abet that process.

But despite all his planning and maneuvering, something odd happens. Harry still feels stuck, and so does Sally. Why? Because endings are hard. Even if both Harry and Sally agreed to end it all, they could expect to have periodic misgivings and second thoughts. That's normal. It shows they're capable of empathy and bonding. Breaking any bond of attachment is painful for people who care about each other. But now Harry wants to get out. Maybe he fears hurting Sally, but that's secondary to his need to be free. Still, his misgivings hold him back. So in this process—and the setup is a messy process—Harry is likely to take two steps forward, one step back.

Sally, now totally bewildered, makes a fatal mistake. She tries harder. She blames herself, accommodates even more of Harry's bad behavior designed to create distance, and then tops the whole thing off by working overtime to forgive and forget his transgressions. Soon-to-be rejected partners may lose all sense of self in their efforts to hold on to the relationship.

Is there relief? Not for Sally. As she accepts more of Harry's distancing behavior as the norm, he turns up the volume. The result is mounting pain. Harry uses any means available to accelerate the break. As one thirty-year-old man explained, *"She couldn't believe we were breaking up, so I tried purposely to be hurtful."* Turning up the intensity of pain to get the woman to make a quick decision to bail out is one common tactic. One thirty-three-year-old man told his wife that if she kept asking questions her suspicion would cause him to leave. But leaving was already a foregone conclusion, and the infidelity that triggered her suspicion was part of his exit package.

Sally's best bet is to end the charade and open a dialogue by telling Harry what she sees him doing: *Harry, you seem discontented. All the things about me that you used to love now seem to irritate you. You're dropping clues that you're seeing someone else. The more I try to please you, the more fault you find with me. I have a feeling that you are trying to tell me something.*

He may still duck the issue because he's a coward and/or because he's not ready to make the break quite yet, but at least she will have gotten the issue out in the open. Keep in mind, however, that even the most frank discussions of endings may still lead to more lies. Even when you both agree to end it, there are no guarantees of honest or happy endings.

My Timetable, Not Yours

This is what happened to Brenda, a twenty-one-year-old elementary school teacher. She and Roy discussed their relationship and set a deadline for breaking up. Then he appeared to have a change of heart: *"He said he didn't want to. He started being extra nice, very sweet. He said he wanted 'to make love, not have sex.' He alluded to our future, said we'd 'be together for a long time.' He wanted me to meet his parents, his out-of-town friends."*

Brenda reconsidered. She took Roy at his word. That turned out to be a mistake. Nothing changed, she didn't meet his family or friends. Worst of all, *"one month beyond the deadline, we broke up."* Brenda is still bitter. She felt duped and controlled. *"I was angry. He misled me. He just wanted to go by his timetable, not ours."* Roy wanted to control the setup, and the timing of the finish.

Infidelity to the Rescue

For many rejecters, infidelity takes the lead as the number one setup tactic. His infidelity announces just how serious the breach has become. In one study, when researchers asked one hundred men and women which tactics they would use to get out of a bad relationship, having an affair or being seen with someone else both ranked high. More than one-third of the women I interviewed named a partner's lie of exclusivity, accompanied by his surrounding cover-up lies, as the most damaging lies to the relationship. And nearly all these lies of exclusivity were followed by a setup and an ending.

A twenty-seven-year-old divorced nurse I interviewed said that the most damaging lie her ex-husband told was "that I was the only one." She discovered his lie through a series of obvious clues her ex-husband had leaked to alert her that the end was in sight: *"There had been little clues. He didn't come home, the other woman called the house. Then I saw him with this woman. He walked away when I made a U-turn and drove up to them. When he came home his things were in boxes."*

He had started down the path toward ending a relationship that "was on the edge." Early on, men use a web of lies to cover up their infidelities. In the ending setup, they leave unmistakable clues that expose them. Her husband had left telltale signs, but was still too ambivalent and too guilty to pull the plug himself. But once his wife saw him with the other woman, she had all the confirmation she needed. She swung into action and moved him to the *finish* he desired but couldn't pull off himself. He lost control of the timing but got out without having to execute the dastardly deed of ending the relationship himself. He got lucky. His setup laid the groundwork; his wife did the rest.

How common is this? About 20 percent of the women I spoke with described a form of the setup in which a lover or husband fanned their suspicions with outrageously incriminating evidence.

Right on their own turf, they encountered a philanderer's well-stocked lost and found: hotel receipts, credit card charges, love notes, phone bills, lipstick marks on shirts and shorts, even underpants in the glove compartment!

Julie, a forty-three-year-old divorced restaurant manager, said her third husband, Mack, got her attention when he left the other woman's "letters lying around in a drawer you'd normally open." When Julie confronted him, "at first he denied it," but "when he couldn't deny it anymore, we openly talked about it." Then the dance began. Julie realized that "I didn't want him anymore at this point, but I didn't particularly want anyone else to have him while we were still married." They had been arguing over whether to have children, and she felt his cheating and lying stemmed from that. Mack was sure of one thing: he wanted out of his marriage. So consciously or not, he began preparing his exit with provocative behavior, cover-up lies, and finally eye-catching evidence of his infidelity designed to grab Julie's attention and move her to action.

The setup turns out to be as much fun as recreational bathing in warm hydrochloric acid. Breaking up is truly hard to do. But still, "It ain't over till it's over," and that may take more time, more effort, more heartache.

Broken Promises as a Means to the End

In the early stages of the relationship they determine what you want, then they promise it.
—Fifty-four-year-old divorced female account executive

Early in relationships, promises are hooks that draw us in. There are also promises that come later, once the relationship has evolved. Some are showstoppers that capture our best hopes. They set our expectations so we can plan our future, feel loved and secure, and get on with our lives together. When that works out well, it leads just where he said it would. Other times, these promises are meant to be broken. They are just another part of a confusing two-steps-forward-one-step-back exit strategy.

Of course, there are many other reasons for broken promises. Some people just blow in the wind, incapable of holding any position over time. For them broken promises are par for the course, not personal to you at all, not meant to lead you to the end. (Although sometimes the accumulation of broken promises becomes so grating that you opt to engineer your own setup and final ending.)

It's disheartening enough when he promised that if you got that job offer in Des Moines he'd go with you in a minute, but now that you're talking to Des Moines real estate brokers he acts like a move around the block is way too far. Is he stubborn, or is he slowly and manipulatively turning down your faith in his reliability and commitment as part of his exit plan?

Suppose he says he loves you and wants to marry you. That's a promise. When you feel the same, it's bliss. But what if it's part of a setup that's more exit ramp than main highway? Ask Leslie, a forty-nine-year-old divorced entrepreneur and one of ten women I interviewed who traveled a path of broken promises to a bitter finish. She learned that "with this ring . . . " can be the ultimate faux promise.

Leslie loved her man. She must have, to have given up her small but successful medical supply business and her comfortable home to follow Frank halfway across the United States. Generous to a fault, she even lent him the money she had in the bank so he could pay his taxes. Why? Because Frank said he "wanted to marry me, that he loved me." They'd been together two years.

The story doesn't get better. After they moved to Boston, Frank and the relationship began to unravel: *"Frank drank, changed, became self-absorbed. I was working for him. I was under his thumb. Then he decided we weren't going to get married. I left after six months and went back to Chicago. Then he begged me to come back."*

For six months Leslie had been denying the damaging news her husband-to-be was broadcasting. He drank and didn't pay attention to her needs. Having been in control of her life in Chicago, she in turn was beginning to feel hemmed in by him. That should have told her something. Even without benefit of tea leaves, the signs were not auspicious. Then Frank reneged on his promise of marriage. From an outsider's viewpoint, lovely Leslie had gotten lucky. Frank's setup was starting to work. She still might have avoided wasting any more of her life with this boorish, alcoholic, self-centered, and erratic man. She'd been saved by the bell after all.

Not quite. Leslie was too heavily invested in the relationship. She wanted to force-fit the bleak reality of life with Frank onto her illusion of a life with Frank. Still in love with the pleading Frank, she returned to Boston, where, in Leslie's words, "the same old pattern started." But with a hopeful difference. Frank this time made his promise good with an engagement ring, which, as Leslie explained it from a safe distance a year later, did its job "to get me back to Boston."

Once back, Leslie accidentally found a note that fell out of Frank's pocket. The setup was in full gear. Written on the back of a receipt from a service shop where he regularly hobnobbed and did business, it simply stated, "Nice seeing you again. Good luck in your search for Mrs. Right." For Leslie things began to add up. Despite his engagement to her, the good employee, money-lender, lover, and companion, Frank was letting the world know that he hadn't stopped looking for a wife. Leslie reacted appropriately to the setup: *"It made me real sick. I loved him. I was devastated. We screamed at each other. He loved me, he didn't love me, he wanted other women. Finally it exhausted me—I couldn't take it anymore."*

She got it and, in a moment of lucidity, left him. She went home to Chicago. But remember, the setup is a messy process that isn't over till the painful finish.

Still not ready to let go of Frank and his cheating heart, Leslie gave him one more chance. They met for an oceanside rendezvous. By this time the result was predictable to everyone but Leslie: *"He dumped me, left me in a motel in Bar Harbor. He said, 'I'm going back to Boston. I'm not ready to get married. I'm through with this.' He said days later, when I called him, 'I still love you.' But he took out another woman and she's living with him now."*

It's easy to see Leslie as the fool, but look at what she'd put at stake in believing Frank's empty promises. She'd given up her home, her business, and her cash to her fiancé. This wasn't just any man, but a man she loved and had been with for three years and was all set to marry. She wanted him to deliver on his promise. But all he could deliver was his ambivalence. And he used that ambivalence like a weapon to push Leslie away, then bring her back.

In the meantime he was plotting his route to his next relationship with new candidates for the "Mrs. Right" position. Frank, despite the engagement ring, was doing his best to fire Leslie.

But Leslie, instead of wearing down and out, kept coming back for more.

The setup wasn't working. Frank, like many men, had seriously underestimated the amount of pain a woman is willing to endure to hold on to a relationship to which she had pledged herself. Finally Frank was backed into a corner. He had to do what he hoped Leslie would do for him—put an end to the relationship. When the setup of his erratic behavior, drinking, cheating, and lying didn't drive her away, Frank ultimately had to play the heavy and do it himself. His broken promises were part of the setup. But sometimes broken promises are part of the painful finish.

The Finish

Often devastating, the finish is the final chapter, the bitter end. Now it's really all over. Any hope for a shared future is forever erased. Ambivalence, from one or the other party or both, has played itself out. The tie is severed. Relief or grief, sometimes both, become the dominant reactions.

After all the going back and forth, all the painful separations and reunions, someone finally pulls the plug. Maybe it's the original rejecter, like Frank. Frustrated by Leslie's ability to ignore the setup in favor of holding on to her dream of their life together, he finally ends it. Or maybe it's the spurned and exhausted lover, like thirty-year-old Holly, who could no longer bear the roller-coaster emotions of repeated breakups and reunions. She explained, *"I was in a four-year relationship with a man who lied and kept breaking up with me. Finally I told him it was all over."* But he was still determined to have the last word when it was clear they'd reached the painful finish. Once Holly told him it all was over, he took pride of ownership by driving the last nail into the coffin, confessing he didn't love her anymore anyway.

The painful finish pits truth against fiction, fact against fantasy. The only question that truly matters at this stage is which door provides the quickest and surest way out. For many men this is the last-ditch, anything-goes effort to disengage. Love turns into war and all becomes fair.

Diversionary lies, which throw you off the scent of his infidelity or other evasions, are legion here. Maybe he takes a cruel shot at some attribute you can't easily change, one that you are sensitive about—like your age, religion, family background, height, weight, or personality. Religion was a favorite among the men and women I interviewed. Or take family background. Suppose he says, "Look, my family just can't hack it that you are from the wrong side of the tracks." That is actually a fairly clever, if cruel, finish routine. Why? First, because it may sound enough like the truth to pass muster, even though he's just grasping at any plausible reason to end the relationship and get himself out. Second, because it's tough to argue with something that shames and embarrasses you or that you know you can't change. He has defeated your will to keep pursuing him.

A Typical Finish

Gary, a forty-five-year-old single male tax accountant, ended his relationship with Fran with hurtful information—more out of desperation to become unstuck and put closure to the relationship than because the information was either relevant or true.

"I used Fran's weight and background, revealed to me under confidential circumstances, to end the relationship in two to three arguments."

As a blow-away finish, this was extremely effective. Gary reported that "Fran was *very angry* at the time. She didn't speak to me for a couple years." How did Gary feel about doing this to someone he once had cared about? He admitted that he was unhappy that he "would have stooped to this level to end a relationship." But then he also confessed to "reacting with a certain inward glee," confessing that "I have a mean streak in my makeup that got out." It sounds like Gary is feeling vindictive, like he's getting back at Fran for something. Was her weight the real reason for ending it? According to Gary, she was struggling with a weight problem, but the real reason for the breakup had nothing to do with her weight or the authenticity of her credentials, as he had charged. Rather, it was that "I was unable to perform sexually to her expectation." Fran had made sexual demands that Gary couldn't meet, striking a serious blow to his self-esteem and leaving him feeling inadequate to please her. The relationship had become too difficult psychologically for him to maintain. Apparently it wasn't enough for Gary to say, "Fran, things just aren't working out for me in this relationship." Instead he struck back as he bolted for the door, taking careful aim at her self-image by targeting her appearance and integrity as the reason for his leaving. Maybe it wasn't honest, but in Gary's mind, at least, he had restored equity.

Broken promises, as you remember, are an essential part of the leave-taker's armament. At the bitter end, as the relationship shuts down, these broken promises often linger to disillusion, infuriate, and render their victims powerless to act in their own behalf. Even worse, these broken promises may gravely impair the victim's ability to trust someone else the next time.

That's what happened to Charlotte, now forty-seven years old, with a war chest of stories of cheating lovers and husbands. But she still smarts when she thinks about the painful and unanticipated finish to her relationship with Chico, the man she planned to marry. Chico was a navy man from a wealthy family in Houston. The family had a large home in Miami, where Charlotte and Chico were going to move after the wedding. They'd seen the priest and she'd bought a wedding gown. When Chico said he'd "go to Miami to have the house fixed up and that we'd live there," it sounded fine to her. Unfortunately, "until this day, I haven't heard from him." Chico's broken promise was not the setup; it was the finish, an abrupt finish with major impact on Charlotte: *"It woke me up. Now I don't take words for granted. I don't take loving actions for granted. I don't take anything for granted."*

Charlotte's story is extreme, but it is a variation on a theme echoed by several women interviewed, women whose relationships ground to a mysterious and unanticipated halt when they were jilted or dumped by the men with whom they had been eager to spend the rest of their lives. From these women's perspective there appears to have been no discernible setup. Could be they were so in love, they missed it. More likely, however, these men wore the masks of false commitment and "everything's fine" right to the bitter end. Like the hidden Houdinis in Chapter 6, these liars said and did whatever they had to while planning their escape route. Even at the finish line, they chose to slink out into the night with a hit-and-run, a major and devastating "not tell." Their broken promise is *behavioral*, not verbal. This evasion, which allows them to avoid giving their partners both the courtesy of the truth and the closure of the lie, is pure and simple cowardice. Because it comes without any explanation at all, many women who have been jilted mentally replay the scenario for years in search of an answer.

Even in long-term marriages, some men squeak out to their final ending on the strength of a "not tell." These are the consummate and successful avoiders. Often their partners are among the last to discover the real reasons for their defections from the relationship. Grace, now divorced and in her mid-forties, was talking about the end of her marriage. Her husband, Vic, had been unhappy, and they agreed to a divorce. Shortly after she moved out: *"I was out with a friend and I said, 'Let me show you where I used to live.' I drove by and Vic and Ruth were out on the front lawn raking leaves. Ruth had moved in right away. I'd never asked him if he was having an affair."*

Grace is shocked and hurt. She learned that: *"While my father was dying, my husband started seeing another woman and concealed it. I didn't consciously suspect anything when we were living together. I had too much to deal with."*

She didn't suspect or catch him until right after she moved out.

She knew her "ex-husband would lie whenever under pressure and make up stories," but she never thought he would either have or conceal an affair. His setup consisted of not rocking the boat, resting on his laurels as a faithful husband, while amplifying his general unhappiness in life. He used the diversion of Grace's father's illness to start a relationship and a new life with someone else. Grace's inattentiveness helped Vic keep his cover-up lies in place. All he had to do was exhibit his unhappiness, withdraw his affection, and allow her own assumptions of who he was to take their course. That would be more than enough for the relationship to glide to the smooth finish he desired. Not smooth enough, though, for Grace to be spared the pain.

Then there are men who get to the finish line using a highly evolved form of avoidance, the saintly lie of mercy. Too bad this lie so often masks their real motives and fears, leaving their former partners still hoping and wondering *when*, rather than *if*, they'll be getting back together. Lies of mercy are pure avoidance for the liar and pure hell for the women who believe them. Even though some lies of mercy reflect a liar's genuine intent to spare his victims from pain, the effect of the lie is to disinform—to rob a woman of the real information she needs to make intelligent decisions in her own best interests. In essence, the liar presupposes he knows what's best for the woman he is leaving, and then acts—without consulting her.

Lies of Mercy to His (Not Your) Rescue

I always want to know the truth. I'm glad to be told. I know I'm going to be hurt now, rather than later.
—Thirty-six-year-old single female entrepreneur

Some men avoid the unpleasantness of endings by not showing up, others by not telling. Some tell quick and dirty lies that injure and push you far, far away. Others avoid your rage and control by telling lies of mercy that frame the bad news in a way they hope you will accept, as they secretly set up housekeeping with someone new. That way these leave-takers won't be subjected to your anger, upset, or frustration, or the host of other raw feelings that accompany the bitter end. By telling you lies of mercy they rationalize that they won't hurt you. Instead they kill you with kindness. It doesn't occur to them that an unpleasant truth may be much kinder than a pleasant lie.

But it should, and eventually will, occur to you.

With lies of mercy, he may believe he has severed the knot and arrived at a noble finish to the relationship, one that short-circuits pain. But rest assured, the pain he has short-circuited is his own. He is so tactful, so ingenious, and so evasive in his lies of ending that you may not even realize it's truly and irrevocably over until years later. Years of waiting, years of wondering! Do lies of mercy ever work? Sure. When neither party is heavily invested in the relationship, or when both are avoiders who prefer things light and easy.

Let's go back to Edward—the research analyst from Chapter 10, who regards lies as a form of problem solving. He sees nothing wrong with ending a relationship with a lie of mercy. He told Lonnie, his close companion with whom he "had a very good relationship for a long time," that he had been fired from his job, that he was under more stress than he really was and that he had to move to a small high-tech company in the Southeast because it was the only job he could find. Unfortunately, it also looked like that would end their relationship. Circumstances, not Edward, dictated the move. But the truth, as it turns out, was much more complicated: *"I was uncertain about how to end it . . . I didn't want to upset her. I didn't confess that why I wanted out was that I had another relationship waiting in the wings. I manufactured a crisis to get out of my job and relationship. I wanted the possibility of a new relationship. The new one was very stormy. She was in the process of a divorce . . . There was a fair amount of lying all the way around, lying mostly to avoid pain on my part and hers."*

Edward wanted to break out of his relationship with Lonnie "without causing pain or having to 'fess up to the embarrassing business of saying I wanted out because I wanted out." He wanted freedom without accountability to Lonnie, but he couldn't bring himself to say that. Although his company had plenty of political machinations, it was neither politics nor being fired that propelled him hickety-split across the country and out of the relationship. Instead, it was the possibility of someone new, someone married, someone who had promised to divorce her husband. As Edward put it, "There was something much more satisfying beckoning me," and he wanted to pursue that opportunity.

But Lonnie, like so many women during the setup and the finish, refused to accede to the separation and a break in intimacy. Based on the inaccurate and misleading lies that Edward had fed her, she was still committed to her man. You can guess what happened next. Lonnie's expectations that their relationship would continue forced Edward to turn up the volume. His lie of mercy had hit a hard and painful stop, causing Edward to take remedial measures.

"I refused to communicate with her. She took this very hard."

In the meantime, hidden from Lonnie's prying eyes, he struck up a relationship with the new woman who was still married and was in the process of divorcing her husband. Unfortunately, it didn't last since she went back to her ex-husband and remarried him, leaving Edward heartbroken and lonely. But his lie of mercy had allowed him to leave a trail of bread crumbs to find his way back to Lonnie, should he need to. By telling her that he had been forced away by work issues, rather than hot pursuit of a brand-new and highly charged relationship, he had invited her to keep her hopes alive, maintaining her like a low-premium distant insurance policy—"just in case." So: *Two years later I sent a note saying I was sorry that I hurt her, that I should have handled it better than I had. I was not asking for resumptions of anything. Then she insisted she wanted a resumption of friendship, but long-distance and with no sexual intimacy.*"

The result? Lonnie, his faithful woman friend, now writes him regularly. Edward is still avoiding her and not telling her the truth. For Edward the relationship "now lingers like a distant cloud, but it doesn't get in the way of a good time and talk or relaxation between the two of us." He sees Lonnie "twice a year, not often." Edward, it turns out, is still pining over the remarried one that got away, while keeping the faithful and patient Lonnie peripherally in the picture. His tactics haven't changed.

Why didn't Edward just level with Lonnie when he left and say that it wasn't working out for him and that he'd met someone new? He seemed to feel badly about deceiving Lonnie, but not bad enough to avoid doing it again. He rationalized his brand of finish— a lie of mercy, followed by cessation of communication, by saying, "I am the kind of person who dislikes confrontation and will avoid a fight. So I would do the same thing again." Who could blame him for not wanting Lonnie to know how easily he had dumped her for the gossamer hope of a relationship with a married woman he barely knew? Edward felt his lie was justified.

Too bad poor Lonnie, kept in the dark, had wasted three years of her life writing and calling the elusive Edward, who never bothered to mention that he had someone else in mind from the beginning of his deception.

Edward's so-called lie of mercy served to protect him from Lonnie's hurt and rage while leaving the home fires burning, "just in case" his new flame turned cold. The continuing lie of mercy, stringing Lonnie along, exposes more of a lack of courage than a beatific surge of mercy. By framing his choices in simplistic black-and-white thinking ("I must tell her either the brutal truth or the lavish lie"), he ensures that he wins, while Lonnie and the truth are the losers. Note that Edward made no tough either/or choices for himself. Instead he chose both the lavish lie *and* the just-in-case trail of bread crumbs back to Lonnie. Self-interest, not mercy, reigned.

Later in our conversation, Edward exposed the raw nerve of the truth, a truth that could have been part of a real dialogue between them: *"I never really discussed the real reason it wouldn't work out between the two of us. It would have hurt her too much. She's much too controlling of my life. I've never told her that."*

So Edward knew all along that their relationship was doomed. That in part is what made him so eager for a new one. But even if Lonnie didn't make a good main act, she was good enough for a safety net.

Edward, like most of us, wants to see himself as a good and caring person. But every time Lonnie called or wanted to visit, Edward was beset with guilt and reminded of his deception. If only Edward had had the courage to frame the truth in the same caring way he says he had framed the lie—responsible, empathic, tactful—he might have done the right thing.

Let's Be Friends

It's hardly seductive. How could it be? The words signal a final evasion before he disappears into the night. In the context of a sexual relationship, "Let's be friends" are fighting words, at least for the partner who's still hanging on. Whether one is male or female, how positively or negatively this "finish line" is seen often depends on whether you're on the initiating or the receiving end.

In fact, "Let's be friends" is the generic escape clause that usually shows up at the end of a difficult relationship, when getting out is the primary objective of one member of the twosome and hanging on is the primary objective of the other. It's a last-ditch attempt to swim for freedom without capsizing the boat. Most of the women I spoke with saw the parting salvo "Let's be friends" as no more than a high-end version of that other time-honored but meaningless escape code, "I'll call you."

But there's more to it than that. When you make a seamless transition from jilted lover to friend at his request, he successfully circumvents your anger at being rejected. After all, how could you vent your rage and upset at this very nice man who is now your trusted friend and good buddy? But what about you? Do you feel judged as not good enough for a love relationship with him, but just fine as a drinking buddy or confidante about his career ambition or his ambivalence about the new woman he is dating? And will that friendship keep you from getting on with your life?

It's no surprise then that more men than women in my interviews felt they had successfully ended romantic involvements with a "Let's be friends" strategy. After all, he still has the pleasure of your company without having to endure any obligation or pressure from you for anything more. He gets what he wanted—freedom from whatever constraints you represent and freedom from you as a mate.

A few men even pointed out that their former lovers turned platonic friends were the only women with whom they were able to maintain no-lie relationships. After all, they'd never lie to a friend. So what were you before?

Yet none of these men would consider resuming a committed relationship with their former lovers who had become trusted friends. Which doesn't mean that it couldn't happen, but it does suggest that you shouldn't stake your future on it. If you really like this person and want a friendship with him, it could work out to everyone's benefit. But when you fall for "Let's be friends" as a crumb, thinking you are buying time and an opportunity to restore your exclusive love relationship, recognize that you are desperate and let go.

I know this is hard, because in love relationships it's natural to become bonded and attached. Even when your partner has lied and cheated or treated you badly, you still may face loss and grief over severing the bond of attachment. As many women have told me, they can't believe how long they have grieved for "jerks," even blaming themselves, not him, for the loss of the relationship. The problem is that by staying in close proximity to a former partner who has rejected you, particularly after a history of evasive lies and infidelities, you just delay the process of healing and getting on with your life.

Friendship under these circumstances, even when sincerely offered, is his lifeboat—not a vessel that will carry you to where you want to go. When the offer of friendship is just a formality that keeps him from feeling like a complete heel, regard it as more of a condolence than a solution.

Remember the idea of parity that we applied to lines? With parity both parties are operating on the same wavelength, with similar, matched agendas. At the bitter end, without parity one partner pushes toward friendship while the other pushes toward restoring romance. Parity is especially critical to a successful "Let's be friends" ending. If both of you agree that you care enough about each other to embark on a friendship without long-term romantic commitment, there's lots of room to make things work. It's when "Let's be friends" is a lie—either in its offer or in the other partner's false acquiescence—that trouble sets in.

The Truth Will Set Him Free

Most of my relationships were ended by the truth. The lies kept them going.
—Thirty-nine-year-old married male television producer

Look at it from his point of view: He wants out, so he begins his leave-taking with an infidelity. Then his ambivalence and guilt about leaving usher in a host of cover-up lies, as well as the lie of exclusivity. Now he is sick of the life and the lies he has crafted, fearful of her anger and suspicion. He desperately wants his freedom. He has done everything he can to clue her in so she'll be the one to bail out. That's part of the setup. He's used a full repertoire of transparent excuses, lame denials, smoking-gun evidence to announce and proclaim to her that his affections have taken a hike, that she's not the only one.

In his mind this is what he is telling her, pure and simple: *"Repeat after me: This relationship is over. I am not going to see you anymore. We are not an item, not a couple. No forever, no tomorrow. You go your way, and I'll go mine. Your lawyer can talk to my lawyer."*

But what does she do? She stands by her man. She denies anything is wrong. She asks him no questions. She looks the other way. She dutifully buys spray stain remover to get the lipstick off his undershorts. She refuses to confront. She says his job is too stressful, that they ought to spend more quality time together. Maybe, she offers, a little counseling would help.

And why *should* she change her tune now? She's been his willing partner, colluding in his cover-up all along. But remember, the truth leaks out, and they both know that. As you may recall, a woman confronted with irrefutable evidence of her husband's infidelity often can name the other woman even though she's been denying the affair. It's taken enormous energy for her to continue to suppress her natural intuition day after day. She's drawn the blinds on her normal curiosity and analytic approach. Something hasn't felt right to her for a long time, so down deep she probably knows the score.

But she doesn't want to *see it now*, any more than he wanted to *tell it then*. The only difference is that now he's anxious to get to the finish. Now he wants to make the break and move on to his new life without her.

Yet *her* pattern of nonconfrontation is part of *their* emotional landscape. Often silently she has been enduring the pain of his distancing and his evasions, even before he lied about exclusivity. Chances are, depending on what she has at stake, she's ready and able to endure a lot more pain, more than he had ever imagined, before giving up and calling it quits. Like a lioness protecting the sanctity of their relationship, their pride, she'll steadfastly hold her ground. Not likely what he had hoped for at this point.

So in his mind he responds: *"Uh oh . . . She still can't hear me. What do I have to do to get her to hear me, so we both can move on with our lives?"*

Call it a teachable moment, when life has become unwieldy enough to force us to be open to a new way of doing things. Or call it the end of hope or the dawning of a new day. But sometimes at this point, an inner voice suggests to him, "Why not try telling her the truth?"

What should he do? Consider his imaginary dialogue with Truth:

Him: Are you kidding? Why not just keep telling her what she wants to hear?

Truth: Because that isn't working. If you want to get out, you have to tell her what she doesn't want to hear.

Him: You mean the truth?

Truth: Right. It's the only way to reach her that you haven't tried yet.

Him: Okay. But do you think she can stand it? I don't want her to self-destruct on me or go ballistic.

Truth: The facts, even if she hates them, are friendlier than the lie. She won't feel crazy anymore. She'll be able to get on with her life.

Him: If you say so. Here goes.

Honey, there's something I've been meaning to tell you. Listen, this is the truth:

(Pick any two)
__*I'm married.*
__*I never loved you.*
__*I found someone else who really turns me on.*
__*I can't stand the way you always try to control me.*
__*I want a divorce.*
__*I'm not going to leave my wife.*
__*I'm not going to marry you.*
__*There's no romance, no chemistry in this relationship.*

Her (pleading): Wait a minute. Slow down. There's no need to jump to conclusions. Sure, I'm disappointed that you felt you had to lie to me when all I wanted was the truth. But now that I know what is going on, don't leave me. We'll work things out, get counseling. You know how much I love you.
Her (angry): You are the biggest lying, cheating scumbag! I can't believe anything you say. You don't know the difference between the truth and a lie. Where do you get off? How could I ever have wasted a minute of my life with you. I don't even want to look at you!
Honey—

(Pick your favorite response category and answer)

1. Hanging on
__I'll always love you.
__We can work it out.
__Don't leave me.

2. Venting anger
__How could you do this to me?
__I knew you were lying, you jerk!
__Get out. This is the last straw.

3. Reclaiming sanity
__The truth hurts, but it's better than a pack of lies.
__I thought so all along.
__It's a relief to know what's really happening.

When he takes the truth out of its plain brown wrapper, it only seems obscene because he's kept it secretly hidden for so long. Now it's his path of last resort, the one that gets him out. But the gnawing and uncomfortable truth is what they've both been living with all along. So now what do they do with it?

How did you react to this dialogue? What advice would you give to each of them? Would you urge him to have more empathy? Would you urge her to hang tough?

Consider the real people who shared how their partners ended a relationship with a truth that would set them free.

THE FREEING TRUTHS THAT FINISHED WHAT HIS LIES STARTED

- "I told this girl that there was no romance in the relationship. That I couldn't go any further."
—Thirty-year-old single male

- "I told her that I wasn't going to break off my relationship with another woman."
—Forty-four-year-old married male

- "In ending a relationship, I told the partial truth. I said, 'This isn't working for me.' She started crying on the phone. I told her a couple little things, but some major things I couldn't tell her."
—Thirty-five-year-old single male

- "The truth revealed was like a bomb. That my ex-husband was not really happy."
—Thirty-one-year-old remarried female

- "He said, 'I don't think I love you anymore. I think I'm in love with the other person.'"
—Thirty-three-year-old separated female

- "He said, 'I love my wife. I'm not going to leave her.'"
—Forty-five-year-old divorced female

- "I asked my husband, 'Is there someone else?' He said yes."
—Fifty-year-old divorced female

Some of these truths are blunt, even brutal. The men who told them were often more skilled as liars than as truth-tellers, and their parting truths reveal that. Some held on to their unspoken truths far too long, so when they finally burst forth, they conveyed a startling vengeance and lack of caring. But before you condemn an unwelcome truth, remember that the truth, like the lie, has many faces. And remember that the intent of the truth, like that of the lie, can be noble, while the outcome can be searing.

Still, the truth with all its potential for causing pain is real and enduring—it won't go away. Unlike the confusing and ephemeral lie, the truth informs, clarifies, and teaches. The truth *feels* right because it *is* right.

Even if the particular relationship they were in didn't have a happy ending, the women who were told the truth were given a powerful gift. They finally had a chance to understand what was really happening. They had won another chance to build their future on more solid ground. Although they had feared the truth, it was the lie and all it represented that had caused them and their partnerships the most grievous damage and robbed them of choice.

Endings and Beginnings

Endings bring mixed blessings. There's loss, plus a bittersweet chance to sort out what you've learned along the way—a chance to try all over again. Let's face it, when you've traveled a path strewn with evasive deceptions, lies of exclusivity, broken promises, and a deliberate avoidance of straight and honest talk, it really *is* time for a change.

However, changing partners won't be enough. If you're sick of what you've been putting up with, you have to consider changing the only person you truly can change—yourself.

Once you realize this, endings can be as liberating as you allow them to be. The trick is to stop trying to please the liars in your life to win their love, and start concentrating on respecting your own wants and needs.

That's one of the lessons that woman after woman I interviewed shared with me. Many of the women in the stories you've read so far have elected to give away their power to the liar—the man who cheated on them and covered it up, the same man who, when confronted, lied head-on. And the man who, when it suited him and his timetable, found a convenient way to be free of her.

How did these women give up their power? They looked the other way, didn't confront, hoped things would get better (generally, they got worse). They let things go that mattered to them, acting as if their own lives were scarcely as important as the act of pleasing the liar, the cheat, and the evader. And by not confronting, not standing up to be counted, they became co-conspirators in the lie.

Ironically, none of this created great happiness for either party. Most of these relationships characterized by lies of evasion ended in a setup and a finish that left one or both partners bitter and estranged. Quite a few of these partnerships are still in progress. But without major changes, like saying what will and won't be acceptable and trusting themselves to talk about what they sense and know, the end is predictable—even if not in sight.

In these tales of evasive lies and endings, sometimes the truth came out. Even when this happened at the bitter end and at a high price, woman after woman and man after man called the truth a relief.

Freed from debilitating partnerships, these women won another chance to take back their own power to do what was right for them. And for the men who have lied, evaded, and cheated, it wasn't too late to decide to become as comfortable with the truth as they were with the lie.

After all, the truth these men and women feared sometimes created terrible disappointment, but it also liberated. It won them a chance to try again, with greater self-respect and integrity. That's a gift. They have another opportunity to create a more open and intimate connection the next time around.

For some men and women, the truth will require heroics. For them, the lie has become a way of life. Moving toward honesty will require a drastic and unsettling departure from deeply ingrained habits and patterns.

Part 5
RECOGNITION AND DEFENSE

Chapter 12
Extraordinary Liars, Disrupted Lives

It took me seven years to realize that he was a habitual liar, that they weren't just little white lies.
—Thirty-nine-year-old divorced female school teacher

My husband lied about everything. That he was shot, handcuffed, and dragged off. That he had cancer.
—Forty-seven-year-old divorced female department manager

There are two kinds of people in the world—liars and non. Two liars can't stand each other. Neither can two people who tell the truth. The ideal packaging is the liar and the non. There are two kinds of liars too. Sleazy liars who lie for their own gain and recreational liars like myself. One has no code of ethics. They don't understand right from wrong. . . . Liars are very charismatic people. People like being around them. You need charisma to bring off the lie.
—Thirty-two-year-old married male financial analyst

Imagine this. You're piloting a plane and suddenly your electrical systems fail. No radio, no lights, no radar. Throw in a cloud cover and you can't tell which way is up and which is down. In aviation this pilot's nightmare is called "black cockpit." Speeding blindly through time and space, you are forced to rely on your own instincts to get you safely back down to terra firma.

The outrageous liar, the liar who steals your faith and trust in your own ability to discern what is truth from what is not, creates a different kind of black cockpit—a black cockpit of the heart for anyone who innocently and lovingly trusts him. Whenever you trust the extraordinary or pathological liar, you risk knocking out your own internal guidance systems, the ones that keep you safely out of harm's way.

When I first began researching *101 Lies*, it wasn't the extraordinary but the ordinary liar that caught my eye. Since even the most dedicated truth-tellers among us are bound to slip up some of the time, I figured that everyone I interviewed could contribute an experience or two, and their insights about lying and being lied to. All I had to do was ask the right questions.

What I failed to anticipate was the urgent need of black-cockpit survivors to tell their story.

Survivors of the Black Cockpit

Bursting with nervous energy, they poured their hearts out. A torrent of words, punctuated by hand-wringing and sighs, detailed how they had been drawn into the world of a smooth-talking liar.

What had shattered their equanimity was personal, invisible, and shame-inducing. How, they wondered, could they have allowed themselves to have been taken in by such a person? Their ability to fully believe in another person, as well as their ability to respect and trust in their own judgment, had been compromised.

Connie, a warm and lively thirty-seven-year-old divorced professional account executive, began her story, still astonished that anyone as normal as she would have such a yarn to tell: *"I'm wondering how I wound up believing him. It amazes me—the things I believed. I want to warn other people. Women are very gullible. If you're an honest person, you don't even think of men lying. The first time it happened, I said I'm not going to be that stupid a second time. And then I met Lenny."*

Then there was Marisa, the fifty-three-year-old divorced interior designer who, with a mix of pathos, humor, and cynicism, drew me into her story before I could get my pen uncapped: *"I want to talk about an experience I had in the last couple years with a skilled liar who got a large amount of money from me. This man I was dating conned me out of $105,000. I've gained fifty pounds and I doubt my own judgment. I'm here to help get rid of the experience by talking about it."*

Even in the vast kingdom of deception, with its endless expanse of lies and "not tells," the outrageous lies that fooled these women were the outlaws. They left in their wake stunned and angry survivors who asked, "How could he, how dare he?" Outrageous lies don't just bend the truth, they eclipse it.

Eclipsing the truth is a way of life for the habitual perpetrators of the extraordinary lie. These are not occasional liars, driven to defend themselves in dire circumstances, but men and woman addicted to the lie as a preferred mode of communication. Two of them, one male and one female, labeled themselves "recovering pathological liars." They wanted to explain their past lies. Jessica, already familiar with the benefits of public confession, introduced herself by saying: *"Trust and deception are a big part of my life. I thought I would like to meet you. I was interviewed and was the subject of a magazine article on pathological liars. I was nervous about volunteering. I'm not as nervous now. I was on a talk show about my lying."*

Jake may have been a recovering pathological liar, but he also qualified as a recovering Don Juan. His lies centered on, but were not limited to, his multiple affairs: *"I just recently have gone through the end of a marriage and through counseling. . . . I have modified my lying behavior, but it's still one of my biggest problems. I have two failed marriages. I have been a pathological liar . . . Most problems in my personal relationships have been because I lie . . . I'd like to help others avoid the mistakes I made."*

They wanted to tell their stories, explain how their lying had evolved past even their own outer limits, and talk about how hard it was to stop.

The Extraordinary Liar

Jessica and Jake called themselves "pathological liars," a term used for many years by psychologists and psychiatrists to describe dangerous or compulsive liars, but no longer favored as a diagnostic category despite the public's continuing use of it. Throughout this chapter, I substitute the term "extraordinary liar" instead, to capture the extreme nature of these lies.

So who are these people I'll call extraordinary liars? And why do they behave the way they do?

Extraordinary liars are extremists. They lie more frequently, and often with greater credibility about more aspects of life than the ordinary liar. Some are predatory liars on the lookout for an easy mark, who know how to ingratiate themselves to you from the first moment you meet. Many are habitual liars. But you won't know that until you've been around them long enough to feel the cumulative weight of their lies.

They may lie for sport or profit or both. The con artist lies for profit, while the extraordinary liar falsifies as a way of life. Some are "two-fers." They qualify as both con artists and extraordinary liars. Whatever their goal, count on them to feel little or no remorse or empathy for the pain and suffering they bring you.

The lie for them has a life of its own, well beyond what a particular situation may require. The lie becomes their end as well as their means. They lie when they think they have to *and when they are sure they don't.* They become experts of the liar's craft. Self-interest is their *raison d'être,* no matter how tempted you may be to believe otherwise. Since most people will extend a liar the benefit of the doubt when they shouldn't, the extraordinary liar enjoys enormous short-term success. That reinforces and primes them for their next encounters. Since they tend to be rolling stones, always moving onto their next sting, many of these masters at deception enjoy near serial success, far removed from their last target's anguish. Even after they swear off their lying ways, they may be so hooked on the heady control and freedom the lie brings that they keep heading back to the liar's trough for just one more drink.

The hallmark of the extraordinary liar is a stunning failure of empathy for the targets of their lies. Interestingly, that lack of empathy may astound the liars as much as it astounds their friends and partners. If you don't recognize these extreme liars at the front end, you'll certainly recognize them at the back end by the trail of broken promises and hearts they leave strewn behind.

Ordinary liars are more likely to respond to their own lies with a broad range of feelings, including remorse, shame, and guilt. Their falsifications are more specific to a situation, rather than free-floating or deeply ingrained in their personality. Ordinary liars falsify to impress someone they've just met, to avoid a particular consequence, to protect their privacy from an intrusive friend, to avoid being the bearer of bad tidings or to get away with something. Every now and then, nearly all of us lie gratuitously. We don't have to, but we do anyway. That's ordinary. But for the extraordinary liar, gratuitous lying is a natural way of life. Extraordinary liars are likely to falsify freely and frequently, even if there is no particular end in sight. Lies gradually become their life work.

By taking a closer look at the extremes, we also gain a new perspective on our own more familiar turf—white lies, lies of convenience, and excuses. The extraordinary lie makes clear how the hooks, masks, and evasions that we come to silently expect as an integral part of daily life prime us to overlook and rationalize the symptoms of the lie, even when it's hardly in our own best interests to do so.

Will You Encounter the Extraordinary Liar?

How likely is it that you or someone you know will hook up with one of these distorting, dissembling, and finagling extraordinary liars? Hard to say, since no one really knows how many there are. One thing's for sure. Extraordinary liars are *not* beating down therapists' doors seeking treatment. In fact, it's well known that the serious liar usually won't seek help unless forced.

The newspapers tell us about the ones that land in prisons or who have lied and cheated in corporations and government—at least the ones who got caught *and* who did something illegal. So, all things considered, your chances of encountering the extraordinary liar in the workplace, at a conference, living next door to you, or in a personal relationship might be higher than you would imagine.

Not long ago Carolyn, a fast-track friend of mine, spent a week at an executive training workshop where a quiet fifty-year-old psychologist, who had just moved to the area, won the group's sympathy by sharing his grief over a daughter's debilitating health problems. Several months later, an aghast Carolyn showed me a news clipping with the headline "Man Who Acted as Psychologist Charged as Fraud."

The "psychologist" the group had so warmly embraced had no license to practice, had served in prison for grand theft, and had posed as a medical practitioner in another state. How did this man get away with it? And how did people react?

Carolyn was shaken. Single and pressed for time, she had seen conferences as safe places to meet interesting professional men and to let her guard down. This man had seemed insightful and vulnerable, but a good con artist can fool anybody. Even the director of the town's Alcoholism Council was quoted as saying, "People have commented that they trusted [him] and that there was no reason not to . . . I've heard people refer to him as a visionary."

Still, most women fail to translate what they read in the newspapers to the men they meet on their own turf. They fail to believe that these liars and cheats are people they'd be likely to meet, much less date or marry. Consider a 1995 newspaper headline that proclaimed, "Man With 4 Wives Gets 5 Months in Jail." This man had married four women in three states and had to make detailed notes to himself to keep his stories straight! Do you suppose that any of those four women would have rushed to meet this man at the altar and disrupt their lives, had they suspected that he was an extraordinary liar and polygamist?

Most women quite naturally don't suspect a new love or a part-ner would qualify as an extraordinary liar. Because many of these extreme liars develop "specialties" in financial or matrimonial or identity lies, they will lay their traps in these areas early in the rela-tionship. That single-minded focus may help you spot them. But whatever their modus operandi, if you're not aware that these liars are out there, *and* that they could be a coworker or a 'friend of a friend, you're not likely to recognize one. They are pros at hiding who and what they are.

Some are dangerous, some are not. It's unlikely you'll be able to tell the difference at first blush. One key characteristic of the psy-chopathic personality is that its extreme and pervasive pattern of lying is often coated with a thick veneer of instant charm. Some of these charmers gravitate toward careers in fields like sales and act-ing, allowing them to take advantage of their natural charisma. But many don't. Some are good enough to fool the experts or even lie detector tests. It pays to remember that *while all extreme liars will not be psychopaths, most, if not all, psychopaths will be extreme liars.* Although we won't be focusing on the psychopath per se in this chapter, keep in mind, should you encounter one, that they can pose a serious threat. So stay alert and don't minimize the danger.

With that said, let's begin our journey into the world of extraor-dinary liars and ordinary women. When Connie met Lenny she unknowingly undertook a black-cockpit voyage that temporarily disabled her internal navigational system.

Truth and the "Single" Man

Connie's saga began shortly after her divorce when she started playing the dating game. She met a nice man at the safest spot and time she could imagine—her family's synagogue on the high holi-days. They dated, she slept with him, and only accidentally did she learn that he even though he had said he wasn't married, his wife thought otherwise. Naturally Connie felt duped: *"I had no clue if I asked a man a question, he would lie about the answer, or that if he volunteered information, it would be a lie. I was upset. . . . And I never heard from him again. I started thinking all men are scum."*

Determined not to be fooled again, she decided to meet new men at singles functions where everyone had been prescreened. That was where she met Lenny, who she mistakenly thought was part of the singles group. In fact, he just happened to have wandered into the hotel bar to watch a game on television: *"When he said he was from*

out of town, I asked him point-blank, 'Are you married?' He said
no. No! No wedding ring. He said he was from New York and he
asked me out the next night ... It was perfect. There was nothing
out of his mouth I didn't like. He was so charming you could just
die. He was such a gentleman. Older, in his fifties, he called me from
the airport to say goodbye. "

Not willing to play anybody's fool again, Connie researched
Lenny to verify that he was a Manhattan lawyer. When she called
New York telephone information and found nothing, she discussed
this with her father, who said, "This man is probably married." That
pushed Connie to persist. After locating her man in a Connecticut
commuter town, she went one step further: "I called his number to
see if I got a woman. I just got an answering machine for a couple
weeks. So I decided he was safe. Later I confronted him on saying he
was from New York when he really was from Connecticut. He said he
didn't think I'd know where his little town was, so he said
Manhattan. I was willing to suspend disbelief. "

Connie had satisfied herself that Lenny was telling the truth.
She suspended her disbelief and moved back to her natural level of
trust. Their long-distance relationship was on and thriving. He came
to Phoenix on weekends and for Connie's birthday. They went to
Miami together.

Then, about six months into the relationship, Connie's internal
radar flashed a red alert. It was nothing she could put her finger on,
but she called information to see if there were any other phone list-
ings at his Connecticut address. Indeed, there was another. *In his
wife's name.* The earlier number turned out to be his son's, a number no one ever picked up: *"I had done my 'due diligence,' but it
hadn't worked. I called him at the house number and confronted
him. 'So you're married!' 'Yes.' I yelled and screamed, bitched,
moaned. I wrote his wife a letter. Men, when they hear this, go
totally black. Their eyes widen, their jaws drop. They drool. I said I
was really sorry I went out with her husband. I didn't know he was
married. "*

Later she confronted him again on the phone. "He tried to be
decent." He said he "didn't enjoy having an affair or lying, but he
was too much of a coward to hint." She had become so emotionally
hooked that they started seeing each other again, despite his marriage. At this point Connie began to lose her ethical radar. She
shifted toward trusting a liar and justifying that trust. So when
Lenny told her this wasn't his first affair, instead of seeing him as a
serial adulterer, she felt vindicated: *"When he told me this, I didn't*

feel like I was a homewrecker. I just wanted to feel appreciated and loved for me. I told him I had written his wife. He seemed surprised, not angry. If she got the letter she didn't do anything about it."

As the relationship became more serious, Connie came back to her senses and "decided to tell him to forget it." Then Lenny had a change of heart: *"He is acting strange. He tells me that he is going to divorce his wife. So I decided to keep going. He found out his wife was having affairs. He said he found a diary of hers."*

That was enough for Connie to throw her hat back in the ring. She cared about him. She couldn't believe how well suited they were. Then money problems began to crop up in paradise. They went to Puerto Rico, but Lenny asked Connie to put the rental car on *her* credit card. She learned that he was thousands of dollars in credit card debt.

Then the bombshell hit: *"One week after a trip to New Orleans he calls me from the Phoenix airport. He wants to kill himself. He had been caught embezzling money—$35,000 from an old lady. He says, 'I let everyone down, my son, my family.' I spent the night with him at an airport hotel. He's in hiding. The embezzlement was a secret. I never knew why he did it."*

Let's get this all straight. Connie just wanted a nice single guy to hang out with after her divorce. Instead she wound up falling in love with a married embezzler who's running from the law! Despite her attempts to detect his lies, he dissembled from day one about being married and about where he lived. Later he began to borrow money from her. Gradually he played on her need to be loved and appreciated, and drew her deeper and deeper into his lying, cheating life.

Connie's cockpit had gone pitch black. She tried to do three things. Stand by her man, be his adviser and lifeline, and deal with her mounting anger toward him over the totally unacceptable situation he had put her in.

She advised Lenny "to go back" and "face the charges." But courage, as you may recall, was not one of Lenny's strengths. So he ran. Their situation pitched out of control. Here is Connie's verbatim account of what happened: *"His attorney tells him he's going to do two years in prison. He resigns from the Bar Association and goes on the lam. He came to see me . . . I was the only one who knew where he was. I advised him to settle somewhere, to get a job, to make money. Go to New Mexico, Wyoming. My biggest fear was he'd move in with me and I'd have him in my house the rest of my life. His world was collapsing. I was the only one he was involved with. He asked me for money for medical care. This was hard for* *him. I sent him $150. He had no money, no car. Only a bicycle. He broke a leg. Then he couldn't ride a bike with a cast."*

In the end Connie found her way out. She turned him in: *"The FBI came to see me at work. They took me into a room. 'Do you know where he is?' I said yes. I'm not going to lie to the FBI. The FBI said I couldn't tell him about talking to the FBI. We had a hard phone conversation. He got picked up that evening late. He called me collect from jail. I concealed the truth. I didn't tell him I was the one who turned him in. When I did tell him two to three phone calls later, he said, 'I never wanted to get you involved in this.'"*

"They shipped him back to New York. . . . It's still going on. He still calls me from jail. He told me he stole $35,000 over four years before he knew me. He called me on New Year's Eve and all New Year's Day. I had a hard time. I ask him in a tirade, 'Why did you ruin everything?' He's in jail. Why? He said, 'I just didn't think you'd love me if I didn't take you on trips.' I don't know how it will end."

How did Connie feel? At the time of the interview, she was still trying to assimilate the astounding turn of events and figure out how she got drawn into them. You can hear the anger bristling in her words: *"He apologized for involving me. Men think it's okay to do something really awful, so long as you apologize. Or tell you, in fact, that they were a jerk. Then that entitles them to be one."*

But Connie blamed herself as well. With piercing hindsight she had come to realize how little she heeded his early lies that flashed clear warning about who he really was. Early in the relationship, when she still believed he was single, she had noticed that his passport age was fifty-four rather than the forty-eight years he claimed to be. At the time Connie dismissed this as "a little white lie," explaining, "My mother lies about her age!" But with chilling insight, she added what nearly all victims of the outrageous liar eventually understand:

"Later I realized he lied about everything."

The experience had left its mark. Connie said, "He's still lying to me about how much money he really did take." She justifiably claimed she'd never be able to trust him again. But there was more fallout than that. Not only was a relationship with Lenny no longer possible, Connie now felt she couldn't "trust men in personal relationships anymore." Her whole approach to expecting and seeking intimacy has been seriously damaged.

What would Connie do differently? She says, *"As soon as I*

wrote his wife the letter, I wouldn't have seen this man again." She would have set firm boundaries and stuck to them. She wouldn't have suspended her disbelief so early or easily.

When she is asked what Lenny regrets about what he has done, Connie's answer is as revealing as it is terse: *"He regrets he got caught by the law."*

Pick up any newspaper and you'll read about people like Lenny. That Lenny is a liar who broke his ethical vows as an attorney to uphold the letter and spirit of the law, while perturbing, is not big news. What's alarming is that Connie, in her second postdivorce relationship, would allow herself to trust and be taken in by this extraordinary liar.

Believe It or Not

At heart, most of us are believers. We want to have faith in what people tell us. That, in fact, is what the liar counts on.

If our parents were reliable, and we weren't abused or otherwise traumatized, we've learned two things: to trust people we love *and* to trust our own senses. In a world of honesty, that works just fine, but in a world of guile, it spells serious trouble.

Connie's first postdivorce dating experience had put her on serious notice. She discovered that a woman can't automatically trust the words of a man she's just met. Lots of women learn that. And Connie took the lesson seriously by checking Lenny out.

Satisfied with her investigation, she then "suspended disbelief." That suspended disbelief rendered her defenseless to the *modus operandi* of a predatory liar. But, even if Lenny weren't an extreme liar, it would have been a mistake for her to suspend disbelief too early. That's fine when you go to a play or a movie, but not in intimate relations. After all, suspending disbelief too early would have made her prey for an ordinary liar as well.

Like Connie, most of us are totally unprepared for extreme liars. They look and act like anybody else, except often they are more charming, more irresistible. They are the candy men who offer you whatever you crave as a draw not because they love you, but because that is the game they so expertly play. To gradually lure you into their world, against your own better judgment, is their challenge. That requires solid skill in discovering what you most desire, what you need. Then these liars promise you your dreams. They carefully hone their competencies in saying and doing just the right things to overcome your doubts. For the naive subject, the outrageous liar, who promises everything and delivers just enough to convince, is hard to turn down and even harder to give up.

Connie had flashes of insight about Lenny on several different occasions. But each time Lenny unerringly helped her shut down her intuition. That disheartening experience with an unethical liar is part of what Connie, and all the other Connies out there, carry forth into their future relationships. It will take time for Connie to rebuild faith in her own judgment about men.

Let's consider one more such experience. Marisa was the victim of a sting with Saul, a far less charismatic liar than Lenny, but unarguably effective as a con artist.

The Con Artist

Her friends certainly couldn't understand what she saw in him. They thought she'd lost it, but they politely kept their mouths shut until it was over. When you came right down to it, Marisa was puzzled too. She hadn't found him all that attractive, his health was poor, and he was awful in bed. He lied when he didn't have to and made promises he didn't keep.

Then why did she endure an eighteen-month relationship with Saul? And why on earth, in the last three of those months, did she decide to hand over to him all the money she had, all $105,000 of her savings? These are questions that Marisa now has had ample time to ponder, and her insights are right on the mark.

As a busy interior designer interested in meeting men, Marisa liked to answer the personal ads. That's how she met Saul. He picked her up at her new townhouse in a nice part of town and immediately began touting his financial successes. Marisa recalled how, at the onset, *"He told me, 'I have more money than Donald Trump.' He said he owned his own house, that he had a successful chain of camera stores in malls, a couple of grown kids who were doing well. He talked big, said he kept a couple tuxedos in his closet."* Saul promised a lot, but his delivery, like his sexual performance, left Marisa waiting. According to Marisa, he was especially skilled at adjusting his promises to whatever she thought was important. That chameleon-like quality should have been a tipoff: *"Saul started out with promises, lies. He created expectations, plans that never happened. He claimed to be extremely wealthy. He'd say, 'You have to free up a weekend this summer so we can go to Charleston,' but then if I said, 'Okay. Which weekend?' he'd say, 'Don't pin me down. Don't rush me.' Then he'd turn around and sweet-talk me. He'd call me up and say, 'This is your number one honey.' I liked the attention, the promise of what could be. He knew what I wanted; he observed me to a fine degree to find out what I wanted, what was important to me. Then he promised it. I had met a lot of men who didn't have two dimes to rub together. I saw Saul as a hardworking, successful businessman."*

When they talked about finances, Saul was an attentive listener. Marisa liked that and found herself revealing more and more. She talked to him about a bad real estate deal she had made and "he was very sympathetic." And as Marisa wryly noted, "He also found out I had assets." Eventually, after a year or so had passed, he sprang the trap that he had so carefully set: *"He asked me for a short-term loan to help his businesses. He said it was a fantastic investment. He'd get an over-the-counter promissory note. 'Then if anything happens to me, you'll be rich. With the kind of interest I could pay you—you wouldn't need to work.' I had to go through quite a bit to get the money—it was in a tax-deferred annuity. He was on the phone with me every day. He said he needed a check. He was remodeling a store in Charlotte.*

"I gave him $105,000 that he never paid back. After he got my money, he paid me some interest. He dribbled $200 at a time . . . Then he stopped . . . Only then, I began to suspect. After the last check he said, 'I don't think we ought to see each other socially . . .' After the first of the year he had a going-out-of-business sale. I filed a suit and won. I have a judgment against him. But I can't collect, even with an attorney. He disappeared. Later I found he had twenty-five lawsuits against him."

Operating in a black cockpit, Marisa had lost her sense of direction. Up became down. Now, well beyond damage control, she was just trying to sort through the wreckage to make sense of what had happened to her.

First, Marisa discovered Saul's "facts" were all wrong. He did live in a house; it just wasn't his. The name he used may not have been his real name, since he went by at least two. His "successful" stores were really in bankruptcy. As Marisa sorted through the charred remnants of her relationship with Saul, it dawned on her that she was probably set up from the start. He was not the successful businessman she had thought he was, but a true "con artist, sleaze, and failure." He "may have lied about everything" from square one onward. When it came to truth, Saul's role was pure makeover artist: *"His first lies were white lies. He lied about everything—his age by six years, his height by three inches, his weight by twenty pounds. Everything was wrong. He even lied about his birth date. He said he was a July 4th baby and was born in October—and this was just the beginning."*

Looking back, she saw his white lies "as part of a pattern I should have caught." But that wasn't obvious to her until she "saw the larger lies." Even then she hung in there, failing to confront him. Most alarming of all, she was beginning to realize her own role in allowing his scheme to play out. When Saul told these white lies, Marisa had been predisposed to feel "sorry for him." *"I rationalized for him. I gave him the benefit of the doubt, when it was premature to do so. I thought he looked older than his years and felt sorry for him. I thought he was unattractive, and was trying to make himself feel better. I thought, 'The poor thing.' He thinks he weighs 190 pounds. I couldn't see him for what he was."*

The result? Marisa, like Connie and countless other women and men duped by an extraordinary and predatory liar, wound up fearful of trusting her own judgment, "afraid of another relationship." She saw all too clearly how her need for companionship and his plot to bilk her fit together. Her post-disaster analysis of what happened is brilliant. At the same time Marisa was being taken in, she was also taking in all the information she would have needed to whisk herself safely out of harm's way. But instead, she chose to ignore her internal navigational system. She'd temporarily disconnected her intuition. Why? *"I was vulnerable. He was saying what I wanted to hear. Even though he was physically unattractive to me, I settled. . . . Now I can see he was too smooth. He was ornery and selfish. He used me all along. He'd call and say, 'I made reservations at some great place.' Then he'd be one to two hours late. With excuses. 'I couldn't get away from the store.' He was doing exactly what he wanted to do.*

"There was no end to what he would ask me for. His car broke down on Saturday. He'd call and say, 'Could you let me use yours for four to five hours?' Then it became seven or eight. I had to rearrange my day. He put me down. He created doubt. At my brand-new townhouse, he said, 'If I lived here, I'd be claustrophobic.'"

Saul was no amateur. He did what the ordinary liars among us do—but he lied more, better, *and* to an extreme and unrelenting degree. That's what made him an extraordinary liar and a successful con artist. Saul began with exaggerated frog-to-prince hooks and lines to draw Marisa in. Like any good liar, he told her what she most wanted to hear. Then he made just the right promises to fan her expectations. He played her. The airtight masks he wore hid who and what he was. His evasive lies allowed him to do what he wanted, undetected, while keeping Marisa tantalized and anticipating what he knew would never be. At the same time, he began to play a subversive form of mind game where he questioned her beliefs, disarmed her defenses, disempowered her, and created doubt. All that was calculated to make her more receptive to whatever he might propose next.

Saul, in fact, was engaging in a mild form of brainwashing. By undermining Marisa's beliefs and creating chaos, he was robbing her of her power and creating psychological dependence on him. He played an escalating form of bait-and-switch that cut deep into her self-esteem. During eighteen months he introduced just enough turbulence into Marisa's life for her hold on reality to start unraveling. That made it easier for him to achieve his goals.

What amazes most is not that Saul was a lying and thieving con artist. It's that Marisa, even as she was being pulled into his topsy-turvy world, quietly observed and recorded what he was doing with the accuracy of a camera. Her cockpit may have gone black, but her intuition was working overtime. She still failed to bail out. In her own words here, she chronicles how insidiously Saul gained power over her: *"I'd spend two to three days with him, then think, 'Why'd I get myself into this?' I gave him power over me. My friends couldn't believe it. He got cheaper and cheaper. He took me to cafeterias for dinner. He said he had a cleaning service for his home. Then I'd come over and he would ask me to vacuum. We'd go to his business after hours to deliver paint and he even had me carry the paint. He tried to have sex and he was impotent. He said, 'She [his former wife] did this to me.' He'd go out of town and say, 'I want you to come over right now. This is the only time I'll get to see you.' He lied about everything, but at no point did I say, 'This is enough.'"*

At first, he told her what she wanted to hear and she believed his promises. Then he tore her down. Besides the loss of her savings, Marisa suffered the humiliation and shame of being seen as so needy that she, a successful businesswoman, would associate with and believe a swindler like this.

Marisa never confronted his fraud directly—only through her attorney.

When I asked Marisa what she had at stake in this relationship, she answered, "Hope." But when I asked her what she would do differently, her extensive answer made it clear she'd been pondering that for a long time.

First she'd look for clues to *spotting the liar*. Here in condensed form is Marisa's hard-won advice that applies just as well to the ordinary as the extraordinary liar.

> ### MARISA'S BEST ADVICE FOR SPOTTING THE EXTRAORDINARY LIAR
>
> *These things should raise a red flag:*
>
> **1. Little White Lies**
>
> "When he lies about his age and his weight, that may be part of a larger pattern."
>
> **2. Brags Too Much**
>
> "Be extremely suspicious of anyone who brags about his material possessions."
>
> **3. Lone Ranger, No Tonto**
>
> "Not meeting any of his friends, family, or children—that's a clue."
>
> "Ask to meet his friends."
>
> **4. Promises Not Kept**
>
> "We're going to do this and that; but when you get to that point the guy can barely buy a green banana."
>
> "Or when he's all talk, no action, that's a sign too."
>
> **5. Cash Only Purchases**
>
> "Watch out for a man who pays for everything in cash."
>
> **6. Incongruities, Oddities**
>
> "He went into the hospital for an angioplasty and didn't want me to visit."

Second, Marisa would do a few things differently as a result of her experience with Saul, the con artist:

> ### WHAT MARISA WOULD DO DIFFERENTLY
>
> **1. Verify and Detect, Aggressively!**
>
> • "I would use all the methods I have in business."
>
> • "Get a credit report verification."
>
> • "Hire a detective."

---

2. Go for a Second Opinion

- "I'd talk to my own friends about how they see him."

3. Put Him in a Context

- "Ask to meet his friends, family, business acquaintances."

At the end of our interview I asked Marisa, "What question should I have asked that I didn't?" Her answer was a question I had heard more than once.

"Where are all the honest men? I'd just like to know where they are."

Who Is Dumb Enough to Trust a Liar?

How is it that bright and articulate professional women like Connie and Marisa would trust such lying, finagling, thoroughly unethical men? We would never do that, would we? *Or would we?*

In fact, when most people hear stories like Connie's and Marisa's and the many others in this book, they long to blame *not* the liar, but the *liar's victim!* It helps them separate the kind of people who would believe liars and thieves from the kind of people they are, or think they are. You know, the safe and sensible sorts. That lets them go on believing that bad things happen to other people, stupid and gullible people, not people like themselves, that *they* would never fall for the ordinary or the extraordinary liar's scheme.

Yet, they do. What could be wrong with them? Look at it this way. Throw a frog in boiling water and it will leap out of the pot. Smart frog. But look what happens when you put a frog in cold water and gradually turn up the heat, degree by degree. The frog stays and is cooked. That's just what happens when an unsuspecting person hooks up with a serious liar.

The serious liar eases his target into the water using all the normal conventions—flirtations and lines that are 50 percent technical truth and 50 percent wish fulfillment. No one bats an eyelash. It's just the usual. Then there are the masks worn by serious liars. They do such a fine job of covering feelings, background, intent, and problems that the well-maintained carefully crafted mask of serious liars may seem identical to everyone else's lying masks. They give no cause for undue alarm. Stay in the water, they say—it's just a little warmer now. Evasions? Sure there are a few evasions. We expect a few. He lies about money. Well, so do a lot of people. Did you notice how the temperature is rising? You think he's seeing someone else? But when you ask, he says, "No, you're paranoid." He manufactures a gold-medal cover-up. He denies, gets angry, accuses, makes excuses, diverts, plays mind games. You are getting confused? Could it be that's because the water's so hot?

You get the idea. It could happen to anyone, *with any liar.* But in the case of the extraordinary and predatory liar you stand a much better chance of being cooked.

So pack a rudimentary understanding of the extraordinary liar as well as the outlandish lie in your self-defense kit.

From the Liar's Mouth

We've heard from two victims of extraordinary liars. What about people who are the tellers, not the victims of extraordinary lies? From more than three hundred hours of interviews I've culled some of their thinking about their own lies. Among these liars were three self-identified extreme liars and two recovering "pathological" liars (Jake and Jessica) who were articulate and willing to share their viewpoints. We also hear from Randy, a thirty-five-year-old medical sales manager and Will, a twenty-five-year-old entrepreneur. Their verbatim comments are eye-openers.

Charisma

Who hasn't been taken in by a charismatic liar? Engagingly friendly and warm, he knows how to create instant rapport, the kind that encourages you to lower your defenses. Research shows that such an extrovert's lies are more immediately believable than an introvert's. The extroverted liar, who flashes a confident smile and feels little anxiety about the lie, is a natural at deception. This liar has probably been lying and getting away with it since the age of five. That's when children first realize that Mommy and Daddy can't read their minds to know what really happened when they were out of their parents' sight. Their early successes at lying breed confidence and a seductive sense of superiority and control. That confidence reduces their anxiety about being caught and frees them to try again and again. Practice makes perfect, and the result is even greater skill in lie-telling. By the time you meet them at age twenty-five or thirty-five or forty-five they're old hands at the lying game. Here is what Jake, the film producer and reforming Don Juan, had to say about his own charisma with women: *"I've been told by many women that I have a certain charisma, an attraction for the majority of females. I have the ability, when nervous, to react the opposite way, to become calm. This is confused with confidence. Women sense confidence and respond."*

But if you read his statement closely, you'll see that Jake is telling us that his charismatic confidence is fake, yet another lie. When Jake is inwardly nervous he has learned to appear confident. He wears the liar's mask of bravado. Whatever they've fallen for, it's not the real him. Although he sees it as more of a quirk in his makeup than the result of a long history of perfecting his "good liar's demeanor," he creates a lose-lose situation for everyone. Like many liars, he doesn't feel he has earned either the right to be loved for himself or to tell other people how he really feels without being rejected. To win approval and affection, he lies and promises more and more. In the long run he is destined to disappoint.

Secrecy and Freedom From Control

Secrets are one way of establishing personal boundaries around our private space. They begin in childhood as a way of eluding the control of a powerful parent to develop a separate and stronger sense of self. Extreme liars get hooked on the control and independence that the secret brings. They love the exhilarating freedom of doing their own thing, undetected. Many men who lie keep secrets from the women in their lives, as if these women were surrogates for their powerful and controlling parents. Randy, a married thirty-five-year-old medical sales manager, could write the book on it: *"I don't find it necessary to give out information. It starts with a mother or a first girlfriend. She wants to know where are you, so you can be tracked down. So she would have control of your time. One thing successfully married men learn to do is withhold information from their wives. I don't like full disclosure. I don't ever tell anybody the full story. It's not anyone's business. I see most women as not really wanting to know unless they absolutely have to. They won't press."*

No question, ordinary and extraordinary liars agree that full disclosure cramps their style. Both may feel that the women in their lives exert a stifling control that robs them of their freedom, and maybe their manhood. Randy conspiratorially offers his bullet-proof formula for total freedom: *"I cover up cheating on my wife, drinking, taking time off work, all behavior unbecoming a person of my stature in the community. You have to be totally untraceable. No way you can be found out by any reasonable means. You have total freedom. You can make up any pattern. At nine I go fishing or to sit in a bar. I tell my boss I have an appointment with a customer. I will lie to my boss or wife, but I wouldn't lie to a customer. That would really hurt someone. I wouldn't steal, but I would cheat on my wife."*

Randy says he would lie to his wife and his boss, but not to a customer. Why? Because both his wife and his boss represent a powerful authority with a license to intrude, control, and contain him. His lies allow him to strike an angry blow at the female authority of his wife and at the societal authority of his boss. The customer, in contrast, is Randy's way out, his alibi and passage to freedom. But then again, he may be lying about *not lying* to a customer. With a serious or extraordinary liar it's hard to tell.

Jake, the recovering "pathological liar," has found his own less elaborate shortcut to secrecy and the freedom it brings—the half truth: *"One of the reasons I was such a good liar is because I didn't lie. I just didn't tell the whole truth."*

The beauty of Jake's approach is that his half-truth or technical truth is not only effective, but it gives him the two-edged satisfaction of complying with the letter of the truth, while he secretly violates its spirit. Jake and only Jake knows and retains the rights to the hidden truth.

A New Improved Fictional Self

Who needs Pygmalion? Don't like your family, your background, your social status? Invent new ones. Make a wish come true by pretending that you are someone else! Both ordinary and extraordinary liars exaggerate and embellish. The question is: How much is too much? Some liars reengineer their whole identities. But no matter who outrageous liars say they are, they know inside it is still them. Look at the similarities here between two extreme liars.

Will
"My lies were all part of my packaging. I went to high school in Lake Forest, Illinois, where there are lots of mansions. I lived on the edge of that, but I assimilated into the North Shore money culture . . . I paid lots of attention to things like silver patterns and china. I took on a blasé attitude. People got the impression I lived better than I did. I was posturing, passing. It was a status thing. Where I wanted to be, where I wanted to be from."

Randy

"I lie because as a child I was trying to make myself more interesting to other people. What if I told the truth? I'd no longer be interesting. Now my life is so interesting I don't have to lie . . . I created myself as fiction. I tell 'more than anyone' lies. More intelligent, more worldly, richer, more experienced, more drug use . . . Hell, I'm thirty-five years old. I made $130,000 last year. I bought a beach house. I had an affair. I'm a fucking interesting person."

What about the woman who is an extraordinary liar? Jessica habitually reinvents herself. Like many "pathological liars" and a lot of ordinary ones, Jessica is especially convincing because she ends up believing her own stories. As clinicians know, these extreme liars share three characteristics: (1) they repeat their own story so many times that it begins to feel true, (2) they are heavily invested in denial and in defending themselves against an unacceptable reality, and (3) they are desperate for the psychological payoff that their fabricated schemes bring. As a result of all three factors, *they suspend their own disbelief!* They believe their own lies. Jessica undertakes a far more extreme level of reinvention than Randy or Will, lying about her education, her college degree, her finances, even a large inheritance she will be getting. Eventually it all seems real: *"I say I went to private school, that I graduated from college, that things are more together than they are. I say I'm financially better off, more successful than I am. That's what men want to hear. They are afraid of dependence. I don't let them know I have a lot of debt."*

All that is a mere prelude to the pure fiction that erases years of her life and includes the invention of an evil twin alter-ego, the repository of all Jessica's shameful deeds: *"I was involved in four adult films and in phone sex. I was married too. At eighteen for eight years. We lived as a couple for only two years. It's easier to say I was never married. I invented a lie of a twin sister so I could say she did it. She became the repository of all the bad traits. I didn't have them anymore."*

Jessica even lied about having leukemia, telling her husband that it had been in remission, and "had come back." She invented an elaborate scheme of going to the hospital for treatment. When I asked her why she did this, Jessica simply said: *"He took care of me. I wanted to be taken care of and have a legitimate reason to be taken care of. I thought he kind of knew it was a lie, but didn't really want to know. I would like to tell him I am sorry."*

For some outrageous liars, the lie is a preferred tool for getting their needs met. Those needs might be for love, admiration, and dependency, like Jessica, or for power, superiority, and control, like Randy. Once shorn of their fantastic make-believe, these liars often feel little sense of entitlement to be loved and accepted on their own merit, or even to get their own needs met. They constantly play for the approval of a widening audience, but their own relentless inner critic is likely to be much harder to placate than the targets of their lies.

A Lying Way of Life

For extraordinary liars, lying is a familiar old friend. Resorting to the lie gives old-shoe comfort, a way of reassuring themselves that all is right in the world. For them, pulling out a familiar lie is like turning on the night light after a disturbing dream. The lie becomes a plumb line for determining the tilt of any situation. The lie dictates what feels normal. So when nothing much is happening, they're tempted to set new lies in motion. As one man I interviewed explained, "Lying is a form of social communication." Randy understood that early on: *"I lie just to keep the conversation going. A friend and I in high school started a game of lying to people using each other as references—lies with minute details. It was playful. It's a habit. I started young so I'd sound more worldly. Now I've done a lot, but I still lie a lot."*

That quick sense of superiority and control the habitual lie brings is nothing less than addictive. But when a confirmed and addicted liar steps back from lying, he gets a strikingly different perspective. Jake, for example, is trying to change, but is finding that's not easy: *"I even found myself striking up conversations with strangers and lying to them. How do I change? What steps do I need to go through? What are the warning signs? Are there any tricks, like in a twelve-step program?"*

Telling Right From Wrong

The ordinary liar, even the naturals, seem to distinguish right from wrong well enough. As we move to the extreme cases, like Connie's experience with Lenny and Marisa's with Saul, we move farther into the world of antisocial and psychopathic liars whose pressing egocentric needs may blur the more conventional distinctions between right and wrong.

While that should make it easier to distinguish them from an ordinary liar, it doesn't. Despite the fact that extreme liars are often impulsive, thrill-seeking manipulators, who like to live at the edge and who, therefore, should stand out in a crowd, their highly convincing lies and superficial charm create instant camouflage.

Even worse, although few extraordinary liars are likely to be life-endangering psychopaths, most criminal psychopaths, like serial murderer Ted Bundy, are highly skilled liars who show a characteristically callous lack of empathy and lack of remorse or guilt. Paul Ekman in his 1992 edition of *Telling Lies*, a landmark book on recognizing clues of deceit, cites Ann Rule on this issue. Rule, the author of five books on serial killers, happened to work with Ted Bundy, but did not realize at the time that he was a serial killer. She is quoted as saying that "the anti-social personality always sounds sincere, the facade is absolutely perfect. I thought I knew what to look for, but when I was working with Ted there wasn't one signal or giveaway." Although we don't know how true that is, we can appreciate that he fooled her. That capacity to fool the experts gives warning to anyone who seeks to easily peg a psychopathic liar.

What does all this have to do with the extraordinary liar's sense of right or wrong? It underscores that they probably won't see right and wrong the same way you do. Consider recovering "pathological liar" Jake's comment on the ethics of his lie: *"It's not wrong, unless I get caught. I got caught, but I could lie and get uncaught. In the first marriage I got caught with what became the second wife ... I'm not sure I explained my lying to myself in great detail. The logic I used was 'So, I slipped ... '"*

He has a sense of operating outside normal conventions of right and wrong—he's wrong *only* if he gets caught. The wrong here is not a moral wrong, but the wrong of making a mistake, that gives him away. But even then, Jake sees himself as sly and powerful enough to slip off the hook and swim to freedom. He even presents himself as clever enough to use his moral infraction to create a brand-new life for himself. Notice how he depersonalizes the object of his extramarital affection as "what became the second wife." Unfortunately and predictably, history repeated itself with "what became the second wife." He cheated on her too. Jake's extreme philandering and cover-up lies defined him far more than any particular relationship did. No wonder he used the phrase, "So, I slipped," to explain away his habitual lying. You can almost see him shrugging his shoulders.

Or consider Will's approach to the ethics of lying: *"I didn't think about it until I was caught; then I justified it. It's a preservation thing. I lie to preserve my own best interests. I don't think about it . . . I have an honesty-is-the-best-policy doctrine, but I still slip from it."*

In theory, at least, Will understands right and wrong well enough. He even lays claim to a personal code of honesty. But when his behavior deviates from the code, he just ropes it off and ceases to think about it. When he's caught and is forced to confront his lying, he justifies it in two ways. First, he defines it as crucial to his best interest, the way a government justifies a heinous bombing by saying it was in the national interest. Then he grants himself leniency by using a cover we're all likely to agree with, that people do make mistakes and that no one's perfect. Both Jake and Will, in different parts of the country, use the identical idea of "slipping" from the truth to excuse and explain their frequent and recurring pattern of intentional lies.

The Feelings Were Real (Just Don't Count on Anything Else)

Their stories are fake but the feelings are real. Extreme liars may fabricate lies or stories that match their feelings. In the moment their stories and embellishments feel real to them because they mirror the emotions they are paying attention to. This makes what they tell you convincing because it sounds heartfelt. Unfortunately, it's still a lie. Psychologists call these *affective lies*. Here is how two real liars explain the way they do this:

"I am honest about feelings. But I lie to flatter, to prevent conflict now."

"I guess you could say I made it all up and caused terrible heartbreak. I never really planned to leave Judy and live with Beth. Just my feelings were real—anger at Judy and affection for Beth."

Look at it this way if you can: Their lies are a guide to their feelings, not to real events or any joint reality. Affective lies may capture the feelings of the teller, but they clearly ignore those of the victim.

A Failure of Empathy

Extraordinary liars are abysmally low in empathy. That's also the mark of the habitual liar as well as many an ordinary dissembler. In fact, much of what goes wrong in personal relationships and the world at large could be ascribed to a failure of empathy. The result? Even if these low-empathy liars didn't lie, their low capacity for empathy would eventually render them unsatisfying friends, inconsiderate lovers, and shallow soulmates. Not a good prognosis for a relationship. Even Will, in a moment of self-reflection, finds himself disturbed by the short-term, transactional focus of his various maneuvers and lies with women. First he describes how he denies his current woman friend's accurate perceptions and accusations about another woman. Like most extreme liars, he takes enormous pride in the effectiveness of his denials. He knows he can rely on the just-at-the-water lie—the lie he pulls from his pocket at the very moment of being caught to achieve a dazzling recovery. Note how Will adopts the take-the-hill language of a military maneuver to describe his victory over Marcy: *"I have a fair sense of humor, so I can slip out of it, turn it around. When confronted, it's a blitzkrieg of denial and changing the subject. I used to plan it out. It's a barbaric way of doing it. The sheer force of words. It throws me out of harm's way. You hope you'll come over the top with sheer strength and win them over and stop the accusations—as opposed to confessing and working it out. You deny before they start asking questions. Take the over-the-top approach. 'Listen, I was by myself last night.' I give them the propaganda. I love confrontation."*

When I asked him how he explained his lying to himself, he became thoughtful: *"It's shocked me in the past, how little remorse I have. Lately, I tell myself . . . what goes around comes around. I should at least be empathetic."*

Will's insight about his lack of empathy is a good one. If he becomes dissatisfied enough with himself and his relationships he could change, but that's likely to be a long journey. It's not one that a woman can or should count on in her relationship with the extraordinary liar—even one with insight into his behavior.

The liars in your life can't be counted on either to recognize their lack of empathy or to change it. Nor can you hope to turn them around with your love and support. That would take enormous commitment from both of you and years of your lives. If you're emotionally attached to a liar, this is not what you will want to hear, but your best bet is not putting yourself at the liar's mercy at all. Your best bet is to recognize the identifiable markings of the liar before you commit, and then to walk away whistling and unscathed. That way you protect yourself against the heartbreak and damage he'll surely bring into your life, before moving on to his next gig.

Pegging the Extraordinary Liar

How do you spot an extraordinary liar? First, you have to remember the obvious: they are out there, but they won't stand out in a crowd. That's part of the game they play that lets them get a toehold in your life. Second, you need to know what characteristics to look for.

The questions below will help remind you what to keep in mind to peg the extraordinary liar. Try out these questions by going through them with a known liar in mind. You be the judge of how accurate they are. Then apply these same questions to someone who you are sure lies very little, if at all. You should see a difference. If you're satisfied, try applying them to someone whose honesty you have under serious scrutiny.

Two caveats. First, you're likely to award even ordinary liars more than several positives on this checklist. That's exactly what should happen. But for the extraordinary liar there will be a thunderous clap of yes's. When it comes to the extraordinary liar, if each question here were a mousetrap, you'd catch a lot of mice.

Second, if you suspect you are dealing with a psychopathic personality or dangerous liar, go over the questions on this checklist with someone else who knows him well and who will be honest in making an evaluation. As we learned from Connie and Marisa, it's hard to be objective when you truly want the relationship or once you're emotionally hooked.

A CHECKLIST FOR PEGGING THE EXTRAORDINARY LIAR

Yes	No	Questions
___	___	1. Does he lie even when there's no apparent reason to lie or nothing to gain from the lie?
___	___	2. Is he always ready to lie as a natural knee-jerk reaction, rather than planning the lie?
___	___	3. Does his self-worth rise and fall on other people's perceptions of him?
___	___	4. Have you caught him consistently lying over time?
___	___	5. Does he lie as much about the trivial aspects of life as about the big ones?
___	___	6. Did you notice that he lied about two or three small things at your first or second meeting?

7. Does he set up your expectations with enticing promises but fail to deliver, time after time?

8. Has he structured his life and his time so he doesn't have to be accountable to you or people in authority?

9. Does he show a consistent pattern of exaggeration or creative embellishment as if reality is never enough?

10. Does he fictionalize accounts of events even where you were present and know it didn't happen that way?

11. Does he always have a ready answer that gets him off the hook or excuses him?

12. Does he fabricate tall tales about his past, his occupation, or his finances and sometimes wind up believing them himself?

13. Does he make a point of guarding his privacy, keeping secrets, and giving you very little information, or giving you information only on a need-to-know basis?

14. Does he show an insatiable need for approval and praise?

15. Does he brag about his material possessions well beyond their actual worth?

16. Does he offer fantastic excuses for even small infractions?

17. Does he show little remorse or empathy for the past or current victims of his lies or schemes?

18. Does he keep the various parts of his life partitioned off from one another, so you don't see his friends, coworkers, or family?

19. Does he feign major or frequent illness or disease in order to be taken care of or get sympathy?

20. Does he have one specialty that he lies frequently about, like money, other women, the price of his clothing, how he spends his time, his business dealings?

21. Does he have a history of antisocial behavior that includes two or more of the following: cheating on exams, taxes, or applications; violating professional ethics; repeated pattern of traffic violations or trouble with the law; shady business deals?

22. Does he habitually treat rules as if they apply to other people but not to him?

		23. Does he come from a family where lying, cheating, or breaking the rules was the accepted norm?
		24. Does he have a history of alcoholism, drug addiction, sexual addiction, or workaholism?
		25. Does everything in his world have to be perfect?

Remember the story of the frog. Thrown into a pot of boiling water, it jumps out and saves itself. Put it in a pot of cold water that is slowly heated, and it stays and is cooked. This checklist was designed to keep you out of hot water.

If you found yourself checking *yes* for more than four or five items, beware. The water feels tepid, but it could be heating up. This is no time to tread. Suppose you checked *yes* for six to nine items. If it gets any warmer, it's time to jump out of the pot. If in doubt, hire a professional counselor and get a second opinion. If you've checked *yes* for ten to fifteen items, this man's problems are fast becoming yours. The water is getting uncomfortably hot and you may need someone to pull you out. If you've checked more than fifteen items and you are in a relationship with this man, call 911. If you're too exhausted by all his shenanigans to get out on your own, enlist the help of friends, family, and professionals in the community. You are worth it.

Your best strategy is to stay alert and know what to look for early, before the water begins to gradually heat up. That way you can jump out of the pot before you, like the unfortunate frog, get cooked.

Defending Yourself

If lying is a way of life in and outside our relationships, then self-defense should be too. Conscious and deliberate self-defense affirms your worth and guards your well-being. For starters, you'll want to know everything you can about how to spot the lie and the liar, and then what to do once you have done that.

What else do you need? First, how about a few general principles and tactics for protecting yourself? They will allow you to do three things:

- Gain the power and control you need to feel good about yourself and your relationship.
- Keep you on track for attaining the love and intimacy you seek.
- Help you retain your energy for all the other areas of life.

When you get right down to it, you'll need a whole bevy of self-defense techniques and principles to protect yourself from both extraordinary liars and the more common garden-variety types.

So let's move into the heart of self-defense. In the next chapter we'll look at how to spot the ordinary lies that men tell women, as well as the all too ordinary liar who tells them.

Chapter 13
Self-Defense

I've caught quite a few liars . . . I probably have a 10 percent hit rate.
—Twenty-two-year-old married female business owner

It feels good to have your suspicions confirmed. It's stressful to be in a position where you think he's lying to you, but you're not sure. As a result of this . . . I have chest pains, I was bitter, I had weight gain. I felt evil. I hated him. I wanted to hurt him. He was jerking me around and I was tired of it. I thought we were partners.
—Thirty-nine-year-old single female office manager

I'm not the shrewdest person in the world when it comes to detecting lies. He says, "I'd like to have you over for dinner." Then I'm surprised when he never calls.
—Thirty-nine-year-old single female sales manager

I look for evidence. Anything in his possession that is new, like panties in the glove compartment, tampons in the medicine cabinet, lingerie in his drawers.
—Thirty-year-old single female commercial artist

Most people try not to lie. They use language imprecise enough to allow them to tell the truth, like "I'm seeing a friend." It's technically accurate, but it's not a random choice. I could have said, "girlfriend."
—Thirty-year-old single male bond trader

We've come a long way and heard a lot of lies—far more than 101. We've peered behind the hooks and masks and evasions in the worlds of both ordinary and extraordinary liars. Any way we cut it, it would be hard to deny that there's a whole lot of lying going on—not just out there in tabloid land, but right in the midst of our own private lives.

In earlier chapters we discussed tactics and tools you could use to defend yourself against specific types of relationship lies and against extraordinary liars. Now you'll get what you've been waiting for: a generic, all-purpose primer packed with information to help you recognize and defend yourself against the everyday lie and the everyday liar.

The road to successfully detecting what is and what is not a lie will not be a smooth one, but don't be discouraged. Just because it's a hard road that requires more focus each step of the way makes it no less worth traveling. Of course, some men's lies will be obvious. Then the main question becomes what to do about them, and when and how to confront them. Other lies raise tougher questions because they are more subtle mixes of half-truths, technical truths, and "not tells." These will demand your intelligent sleuthing and analysis.

Beyond the lies, there's the issue of the liar himself. Some liars rival Laurence Olivier's talent in the realm of make-believe. They require you to be on perpetual guard to avoid being dazzled and duped by their stellar performances. Others are such bumbling dolts it's tempting to feel sorry for them. Don't! Left to their own devices, they'll only improve. Lying, particularly clever lying, may be an adaptive survival skill—even if it's not one you relish in close quarters. Research tells us that the more often a person tells an untruth, the better that person becomes at suppressing the obvious cues that advertise the lie—and at fooling you. And not coincidentally, the more often a person tells a given lie, the more likely that person will actually begin to believe it. That smooths the way for his oft-repeated lie to become a familiar and plausible substitute for the truth. Once he believes his own deception, he can pass it on to you very convincingly. Even if you could read his mind (which you can't, as he well knows), he might fool you. So by default you will become either a behavioral detective who ferrets out the lie or the lie's passive victim. Although neither is sexy, each is a choice that you may have to make and remake every day.

Maybe you are one of those women who don't want to know the whole truth all the time. Still, wouldn't it be useful to know *enough of the truth to take care of yourself*?

If you came equipped with a built-in lie detector, you would know immediately if someone was putting you on or telling the truth. But you don't. No one does. When it comes to detecting the lie or the liar, we're all at a disadvantage. In psychological experiments, people's success rate in detecting lies is roughly the same as it would be if they had guessed by flipping a coin. With a well-practiced liar, even the experts succeed only a small percentage of the time. It's far easier to get someone to believe an outrageous lie than to correctly identify whether someone is lying. It's as if we have been preset to believe, not to doubt, the information, words, and promises even strangers offer us. So detecting the lie, the impostor, or the fraud plays to our weaknesses rather than to our strengths. Human nature has thrown the advantage to the liar! Even worse, real lie detectors, the kinds of devices used by law-enforcement agencies like the FBI and the CIA to screen and test their own employees, aren't foolproof either. Among my clients are a few good liars who have fooled lie detectors and the experts who interpret their findings.

Nonetheless, most people don't feel helpless against the lie. They develop their own favorite methods for sorting liars from truth-tellers, lies from realities. You probably have, too. Suppose you suspected your husband, your newest love, or a family member of lying. You're not quite sure, but something doesn't ring true. What would you do? Which clues would you look for to decide if you'd heard a lie or the truth? How would you check it out?

Improving Your Lie Detection IQ

How good are you at telling if someone is lying? Let's check your lie detection IQ. Picture this: A man in your life has told you a lie about something important—could be his background, his intentions, his health, his level of commitment, his exclusivity. We've covered a lot of territory, so you have a lot to pick from. Which clues will he inadvertently communicate that provide a dead giveaway that he's fibbing? Read each of the questions below and choose the answer that best fits your own hunches and detection strategy.

ASSESSING YOUR LIE DETECTION IQ

---

1. **If the eyes are the mirror of the soul, they're a dead giveaway that he's lying if:**

   a. He turns his head away and avoids eye contact.
   b. He keeps shifting his eyes.
   c. He blinks a lot.
   d. He looks directly into your eyes.
   e. His pupils dilate.

2. If you listen to his voice, without tuning in to the words, you'll be able to tell he's lying if:

a. He talks louder and faster, speeding to get through.
b. He stutters or hems and haws.
c. He ends statements with upward inflections, as if asking a question.
d. His voice is more high-pitched than usual or has a whiny tone.
e. He pauses for a long time between his words or before replying.

3. His facial expression is the key to detecting his lie if:

a. He smiles too much.
b. His smile is a little crooked.
c. He wears a totally blank poker face.
d. He smiles for too long a time.
e. He smiles with his mouth, but not his eyes.

4. If you watch him closely, his body language will tell all if:

a. He gets fidgety or acts nervous or keeps shifting his posture.
b. He makes too few gestures to illustrate his point.
c. He shrugs his shoulders and sighs a lot.
d. He makes peculiar hand gestures or movements.
e. He plays with his watch or shuffles papers.
f. He folds his arms, crosses his legs.
g. He rubs his hands together, scratches, touches his body.
h. He gesticulates all over the place.

5. His attitude is the key to detection if:

a. He becomes angry or argumentative when asked questions.
b. He looks sheepish or guilty.
c. He overreacts, is too animated, or protests too much.
d. He answers questions a tad too thoughtfully or too carefully.

**6. It's the things he can't control that give you the best
cues, so you know he's lying when:**

a. His pupils dilate.
b. His rate of breathing changes.
c. He keeps swallowing.
d. He sweats, his palms are sweaty.
e. He blushes or gets red in the face and neck.
f. Color drains from his face.

How did you do? Let's take each item and separate your
favorite myths from what research shows about lie detection.
There's been much ado in the popular press about what body language and nonverbal clues reveal. What about shifty eyes, fidgety
behavior, hand movements, voice quality? Are these really valid
indicators that you can use to trap the liar and catch the lie? Or do
they merely pad the list of false reassurances we use to deny how
powerless we are at lie detection before being confronted with the
tangible and trust-shattering evidence?

Item 1. His Eyes Will Give Him Away

The eyes have it. They are the all-time favorite method of lie
detection. Nearly 30 percent of the women I interviewed named
some clue related to a man's eyes as their favored method of lie
detection, and 22 percent regarded any form of averted eye contact
as a definitive clue.

Too bad they are wrong. And you will be too, if you rely on a
man's lack of eye contact to spot his lie. Some liars will look you
right in the eye and say, "I love you" when they know you'll be history in the morning. Some truth-tellers are so painfully shy that
they can scarcely speak a word while looking you in the eye. So
don't count on his averted gaze as proof of his lying heart.

No less an expert than psychologist Paul Ekman, who researches
clues to deception, concurs that most people see the eyes as the "mirror of the soul" and have faith in their ability to read them. However,
he points out that while a gaze may be diverted down or away with
shame and guilt, most liars won't avert their gazes. Why not?
Because they're too smart. They know that's what everyone expects
and that eye contact, unlike facial flushing, is a snap to control.
When liars are questioned about their deceptions in psychological
experiments, they actually increase their eye gazing! Only the most

naive liars avoid eye contact and even then not for long. What researchers of deception know that every woman also should know is:

Liars will vigorously regulate any nonverbal behavior
they believe people identify with deception.

Eye contact is at the top of the list. So give yourself points if you answered that a liar will stare directly into your eyes (answer *d*). Just be aware this is not a foolproof method for catching a liar, since a truth-teller may look you in the eye too. Use it to help you, but don't count on it.

Can you count on the eyes to provide any clues to help you spot the liar? Luckily, there are two reliable clues. Liars tend to blink more than nonliars (answer *c*). And, if you watch closely enough, you can see the liar's pupils dilate (answer *e*).

Item 2. His Voice Tells All

Well, it tells some. Only 11 percent of the women I interviewed used voice cues to detect a man's lies. That means 89 percent missed one of the more reliable indicators of a lie. According to Ekman, in about 70 percent of people studied, pitch becomes higher when they are upset. So if a man's lie involves strong emotions or if he is worried about being caught, his pitch may go up. Since level of pitch is hard to control even for a skilled liar, once alert to this clue, you stand a good chance of spotting it.

Also, he may talk louder and faster when he is stressed or apprehensive, so if you circled answers *d* and *a*, you are on to two reasonably reliable tipoffs to the lie. Unless, of course, his stress is related to something else.

Suppose his pitch only goes up at the end of a statement (answer *c*). A rise in inflection that ends a statement usually indicates uncertainty or a sense of powerlessness in a situation. It may or may not signal the lie.

The problem is that none of this is simple, since pitch and rate of speech can reveal emotions as well as a lie. For example, if he is feeling morose about his lie or the circumstances surrounding it, his pitch may become lower and he'll talk more slowly, not less slowly. So while high *or* low pitch yields telltale signs, each only helps distinguish a particular emotion. That still falls short of telling a lie from a truth. More confusing, if he is telling the truth but fears you are wrongly accusing him, he's likely to exhibit the same high pitch, loudness, and fast clip of speech as the apprehensive liar. All this may show you is that he's afraid. His voice, like yours, reveals stress. Some women hear men who sound stressed and uncertain as whiny. Although they are correctly identifying the whiny sound as indicative of stress and fear, it's not necessarily a sign of lying.

What about stuttering, hemming, and hawing? Bingo! If you circled answer *b*, you're on the right track. Stumbling over words and repeating himself are valid clues that may betray his lie—as long as he's afraid of being caught and is feeling anxious. But before you get too smug, consider that some studies show just the opposite. They find that even casual liars are adept at monitoring and controlling what they say and how they say it. Their lie-protecting strategy is "Less is more," so they say less and use fewer gestures. That allows them to stay out of detection's way. And these savvy controllers also have fewer speech errors and pauses because they know that's exactly what you will be looking for.

Item 3. His Expressions Reveal Him

They may, but in micro-bursts that you are unlikely to catch by watching. His real emotions flash across his face and are gone in less than a quarter of a second. Too bad you need a stop-action video camera to see the show. Still, that may be enough for you to intuitively pick up that something is wrong, so pay attention.

His smile, on the other hand, is observable and may tell you something if you've known him long enough to have a mental baseline for his characteristic smile. Ekman, in his extensive research on the smile, found that asymmetry in facial expression is a reliable clue to deception. When the expression on one side of the face doesn't match that on the other side, it's a tipoff that the emotion shown on the person's face isn't truly felt. In right-handed people the expression is often stronger on the left side of the face. The crooked smile reveals a gap between what's shown and what's felt. Yet this flash of emotional insincerity doesn't necessarily mean he is lying with his words. It's just another useful clue. Among the women I interviewed, only one identified the crooked smile as a lie detection cue. Interestingly, she was one of the few women I interviewed who admitted to being a skillful liar herself. So if you circled answer *b*, you're up there with the experts.

For the liar, the smile is very effective as a foil. It immediately puts people at ease. That gives the liar an added boost, since most people have a hard time distinguishing a genuine smile from a fake one, and with good reason. Although we think about the smile as a signal of happiness, researchers have identified eighteen distinctive *nondeceptive* smiles that flash everything from happiness to contempt, from fear to misery.

So how do you tell a false smile from the genuine article? First, watch for the asymmetrical smile. Second, regard smiling oddly or too long as another clue to deception (answers *a* or *d*). Look for either a crooked or mouthy smile that *doesn't* involve any lowering of the eyebrows. With the fake smile, the eyes may not be involved at all (answer *e*). These smiles may come on too abruptly, fade too quickly, or last too long. Something about their timing will seem peculiar and catch your attention. Although false smiles indicate a feeling is being concealed, they won't reveal if there is a verbal lie or "not tell." They are merely a hint that something is off. Now you'll have to figure out what.

How about a poker face? At its best, its purpose is to relay no information at all. Poker players wear their impassive masks to avoid giving away their hand, *or their delight in bluffing their opponents*. They suppress negative and positive emotions, since both leak valuable clues. In my experience, the poker face is more characteristic of introverted analytical personality types than personable and glib liars. Among the people I interviewed, it was the dedicated truth-tellers, not the liars, who wore wooden poker faces. The poker face is more likely an indication of a lie when it is markedly uncharacteristic behavior for the person suspected of lying. So once again, the message is clear: establish what's usual for him before taking his poker face as the mark of a liar.

Item 4. His Body Language Will Reveal the Truth

Maybe. Among the women I interviewed, 20 percent identified reading a man's body language as an integral part of their lie detection efforts. No question, body language, including posture, gestures, expressions, positions, and movements, is a rich source of hidden information. With the exception of facial expression, body language remains ever so slightly outside conscious control for most people. Although liars like to control their words and facial expressions, when it comes to body language it's hard to know exactly what to control. That makes the body language of an unsophisticated liar a veritable storehouse of leaky information waiting to be raided.

However, there's a small problem. The liar doesn't have to

tightly control body language because, like the Dead Sea Scrolls, it hasn't yet been fully deciphered. Sure, we've all seen articles that say crossed arms and legs mean a person is closed or hiding something (answer f). But that person may also be cold, tense, or tired, or use gestures in an idiosyncratic way. The only way to fully understand body language well enough to detect the lie is to carefully observe how a man in question normally moves, sits, and gesticulates. That is your baseline, and any deviation from that standard should grab your attention. Any glaring discrepancy between what he says and what his body is doing may be reasonable evidence that he's at war with himself or isn't being honest. But it's not foolproof.

If you want to read his body language to discover telltale signs of the lie, what should you look for? Suppose he's fidgety or nervous, drumming his fingers against a table or fiddling with his watch. Ten percent of the women I interviewed took that as a clue that a man was lying. Ekman says, "Everyone thinks that liars will fidget, that restlessness is a deception clue." True or false? The average as well as the sophisticated liars usually know people believe it is true, so they will squelch a bad case of the fidgets if the stakes are high. Remember that even an average liar is likely to suppress any clues that would permit his detection. That's why your answer a wins you no lie detection advantage. But what happens when a liar works hard to quell his squirmy movements? Instead, he displays tight and unnaturally controlled body language with few gestures or movements. Interpretation, please? If he makes too few arm or hand gestures to illustrate his point, he may be lying. Then again, he may be bored, tired, distracted, reflective, or fearful. The problem here is that when a man shows too few illustrating gestures, it may suggest any number of underlying causes. That's why you must be cautious in interpreting them as a sign of a lie. And even to get to the point of saying "too few gestures," you need to know his normal standard for talking with his hands. For an excitable extrovert, few gestures may have a different meaning than for a phlegmatic introvert.

People who appear to be grooming themselves publicly by scratching, picking at their skin, rubbing their hands together, or touching their bodies are more likely to be judged as liars. But again, according to Ekman, there's no evidence that's so. While some people do this kind of thing when they're stressed, paradoxically, others do the same thing when they're relaxed. Baseball players scratch and touch themselves all the time, even on national TV. You have to know the person before you make your judgment, so scratch out answer g as being generically helpful.

But if you circled answers *c* and *f*, you're right on the money! These odd gestures and shrugs are the "tells" of the liar's game. Veteran poker players watch for the "tell" in their opponents. What is a "tell"? It's the revealing and idiosyncratic sign of deceit—the subtle tipoff that turns a poker player's opponent into an open book. Back in Chapter 9, "Away From Your Prying Eyes," Heidi encountered a "tell" that exposed her husband's affair. Her husband Sandy always made a little back-forth wiggle in the shower when he was feeling sexy. Remember how, when he was complimented on a hat he was wearing, he made the same gesture? The hat happened to come from the same neighborhood where his woman friend lived. For Heidi that gesture, even when he performed it fully clothed, was a "tell," a clue to Sandy's adultery.

A "tell" can be personal like Sandy's, or more universal, like a slight head shake indicating no when making a promise. Then again, it might be a subtle shrug of a shoulder along with a sigh that betrays a person's sense of powerlessness to carry something out. It might even be an odd hand motion, or obscene gesture unconsciously performed during a stressful conversation. Some of these "tells" are done consciously; others, like slips of the tongue, may be a wholly unintentional revelation of his true intent or feeling.

Item 5. He's Got "Attitude" and You Get Truth

His attitude gives you a readout on three important factors. First, how fearful is he of getting caught? When he overreacts with anger and argument, that may be a fight-or-flight high-adrenaline reflex coming into play. As such, it may reflect his fear that whatever his lie may have been, you will discover it. It also may be a way of getting you to back off so you don't come close enough to find out what he is really keeping from you. Possibly you may have pushed some other hot button hidden deep in the recesses of his personality that has nothing to do with his honesty. Whether or not he turns out to be lying, it's good to know his hidden hot buttons. For example, he hates his word to be questioned or anyone to pin him down. Knowing his flash-points gives you another advantage: you can assess whether you want to live with them or not. So if you circled answer *a*, and you pursue the source of his anger, you could learn quite a bit. Just remember that his anger won't necessarily reveal a lie.

The flip side of this coin is that he may overreact or get angry because he feels wrongly accused, because he is having a bad day, or because he is going through a serious life crisis. His emotions and immediate reactions give us far too little information to judge the lie or the liar. When we judge someone to be lying based on his attitude or emotion, we run the risk of making a mistake that Ekman labels the "Othello effect"—mistakenly interpreting emotion as proof of a lie when it may just be proof of emotion, unrelated to any lie or deception. So answer *c* takes us back to flipping a coin.

Next, how much guilt or shame does he feel about lying? He may look sheepish because he feels sheepish. Maybe he protests too much because he is ruminating about his deception and incubating his shame, grievously lying to himself as well as you. But before you congratulate yourself for choosing answer *b*, consider the next point. He may be pleased as Punch that he has put one over on you. His problem is that he feels guilty for enjoying himself too much. Then again, he may be feigning anger or sheepishness so *you* will feel guilt and he will gain an even stronger one-up position. So as a lie detector, looking sheepish or guilty may be misleading, even as it informs.

What if he answers your probes just a little too carefully, using slow and deliberate speech with lots of pauses and "ums" and "ahs"? Suppose he thinks long and hard before answering, measuring every word very thoughtfully. What if his speech is more like stop-and-go rush-hour traffic than his normal seventy-mile-per-hour clip? If you circled answer *d*, you could be on to something. He might well be lying—but only if his long pauses and verbal traffic jams are different from his normal way of speaking *and* you'd expect him to be well-informed on what he's talking about. Be careful, though: he could be proceeding with caution because he knows the topic is important to you, because he feels you're scrutinizing him for something, or because he is distracted by something else going on.

I have found that if I ask someone who is hiding something a direct but unexpected question about it, there's likely to be a longer pause (generally five to six seconds) before the answer than the one- to two-second pause one might expect. This is what psychologists call "response latency." It's as if the liar is saying, "I'm thinking, I'm thinking," and buying time before coming up with an answer. But this works as an indicator only if the answer hasn't been well-rehearsed and only if this isn't the person's usual style, so separate the myths from the realities and proceed with caution.

Item 6. Only His Autonomic Nervous System Knows for Sure

Now we're down to the wire. Autonomic reactions are pure, unadulterated physiology: pupil dilation, patterns of breathing, sweating, frequency of swallowing, and blushing or blanching (turning pale). Since these involuntary reactions can't be easily controlled or inhibited by anyone short of an elite group of pulse-regulating swamis, they're good indicators of the lie. These same factors, plus skin temperature and heart rate, are what sophisticated lie detection equipment picks up in minute detail. So if you checked any or all of the answers *a*, *b*, *c*, or *d*, you are on the right path.

How will autonomic cues help you detect the lie and catch the liar? First, you have to know what they will and won't tell you. They flash, to anyone observant enough to notice, that this person is experiencing strong emotion. But, according to Ekman, the scientific jury isn't in yet on whether these responses tell that a person is experiencing just any strong and negative emotion or whether that emotion happens to be grief, fear, anger, embarrassment, or some mix of them all. Right now all we can say is that someone who displays dilated pupils and flushed skin, blinks and breathes rapidly, or sweats heavily is reacting emotionally. Because people can't exert control over these reactions they're reliable signs of strong negative emotion. That's a boon to your lie detection, so pay close attention to these indicators. But remember, just because someone is experiencing strong emotion, that doesn't mean he is also lying. Some well-practiced liars, as well as actors, fool lie detection equipment by training themselves to relive an emotionally charged past experience. That way they can substitute their past joy or serenity for their true but negative emotions, like anxiety or anger. And there's one more exception. Even if they are not actors or well-practiced liars, people who truly believe their own lies will not show strong negative emotion when lying. Tripping neither their own autonomic systems nor sophisticated lie detection equipment, these lucky liars are the foolers.

What if you divested yourself of all your personal myths and practiced lie detection until you got good at it? You'd still do only slightly better than you would by guessing alone. You'd drive yourself crazy trying to catch the micro-expressions that are the "tell" of the lie. Try it out yourself with anyone you suspect of lying. Try catching the asymmetrical smile, the pupil dilation, and the quick gesture. It's tough. Many years ago I worked with a compulsive and havoc-wreaking liar. He lied so well that I could only tell his lie by confronting him or asking him a probing question, then carefully watching for his pupils to dilate or for a characteristic flush on his neck. The problem was that many of his lies were told in window-less meeting rooms with dim lighting. Sometimes I strained so hard to see his pupils dilating, I lost track of the normal ebb and flow of conversation. His pupils did dilate. His neck did flush. That was supportive evidence. But in and of itself, these signs still did not prove he was lying.

You Watch the Liar—The Liar Watches You

As you become more vigilant in your self-defense, realize that liars are vigilant too. Count on them to be scanning your behavior for any sign that you suspect what they are up to. If they think you're on to them, they're likely to step up their own spin control. That includes keeping a tighter lid on any nonverbal signs that might give away their deception. Liars who have a lot at stake are tireless observers of your suspicions and consummate performers. Managing their own behavior and your perceptions is their stock in trade. And remember, the lie detection techniques we just discussed work best with the ordinary, unpracticed, occasional liar who is nei-ther pathological nor compulsive.

My advice? Be an informed observer, but understand what your observations will and won't tell you when you suspect a man in your life is lying. Successfully detecting a lie relies heavily on your having a good understanding of how the suspected liar normally acts and what's at stake for this person. The more you understand about him and his motivations, the higher your probability of putting all the clues together. At the same time, be aware that a liar will be watch-ing you, whether or not you watch him.

Refer to the quick reference list below to remind yourself of the myths and realities we have just discussed that help you focus on how to spot the lie and the liar.

QUICK REFERENCE LIST OF LIE DETECTION MYTHS AND REALITIES

Myth 1: A liar can't look you directly in the eye.

Realities: The liar compensates for your expectation by look-ing you in the eye.

Eyes and facial expression are most easily controlled by the liar.

Myth 2: A liar's voice betrays the lie by its high pitch, fast delivery, loudness, speech errors, and pauses.

Realities: Voice is a fairly reliable indicator of emotion, but having an emotion isn't in itself evidence of a lie.

Liars and truth-tellers both experience similar emotions for different reasons. That makes lie detection harder.

Fear and sadness sound different but both may be associated with the lie.

Even experienced casual liars can suppress most expected cues, except for pitch.

Myth 3: The smile is just a polite social grace and should be taken as such.

A poker face usually hides a lie.

Realities: A smile is a disarming piece of ammunition in the ordinary liar's armory, but is not incontrovertible evidence of the lie.

Fake smiles that are crooked, involve the mouth more than the eyes, last too long, come on too quickly, and fade unevenly, may reveal not a lie, but a gap between emotions shown and felt.

A poker face reveals more about personality than lying, except when a normally expressive person abruptly shifts to a poker face.

Myth 4: Body language reveals damning information that identifies the liar.

Certain body language can be read for meaning like a dictionary.

Liars' fidgeting and restlessness give them away.

Folded arms and crossed legs show a person is hiding something.

Realities: Interpreting body language is complicated. Even crossed arms and legs mean many different things.

To understand body language you must observe the person to establish a standard. Knowing the context of the behavior as well as the person's physical state (tired, bored, cold) is essential.

Liars suppress any behavior they believe gives their deceit away, including fidgeting.

Reliable nonverbal clues to detecting lies include intentional and unintentional nonverbal "tells" (shrugs, hand signals, and head shakes, as well as totally personal movements).

Myth 5: Disproportionately angry or overactive responses to questions show that the liar feels defensive and guilty about the lie.

Looking sheepish or guilty is proof perfect of his deceit.

Too much reflection or hesitant answers show he is buying time while thinking of his answer or alibi.

Realities: His lies reflect his personality and how he manages stress. He must be understood within the context of his background, work life, and motivations.

"Attitude" reflects complex feelings and reactions to everything going on in his life. His anger, guilt, or procrastination may or may not expose his deceits.

Myth 6: Autonomic nervous system responses like flushing, breathing rate, perspiring, and pupil dilation give the liar away, just like a polygraph.

Realities: Autonomic nervous system responses are solid indicators of strong negative emotions like anger, fear, distress, shame, and guilt.

A person can feel and show strong negative emotions without lying, so even involuntary indicators are not foolproof.

Some skilled liars and experienced actors can fake or inhibit involuntary responses by remembering and reliving a specific emotion.

Liars who believe their own lies will not show strong negative emotions when lying.

Now play it safe by backing up these techniques with a solid understanding of the principles behind relationship lies.

Some Truths About Self-Defense

The way to detect a lie is to detect a liar. We have been talking about this throughout the book. Now let's look at eight principles that will provide you with information, clues, and self-defense tactics that flow naturally out of your relationships and the situations you are in.

Self-defense starts with you. So have a clear and nonnegotiable vision of what is and is not acceptable to you. That way you're less likely to give your power to the liar and become a victim. Then be willing to stay alert to the lie and the liar, dispassionately monitoring what he is doing without forgetting your standards—and reminding yourself what is at stake if you don't.

Not very romantic? Maybe not, but neither is being blindsided by deceptions that were apparent to everyone but you. Even in the best possible scenario, why assume two people will automatically see things the same way? People are different, men and women are different, you and he are different. For starters, we vary in the minutiae of our personal backgrounds, life experiences, and expectations about trust and intimacy. These differences are more than inevitable; they make relationships exciting. But because there are so many differences, it's not likely that you and he will be in perfect accord on when it is and isn't acceptable to shade a truth or substitute a falsehood. The two of you may not even agree on what is or isn't a lie or whether it's okay to conceal the truth. So if getting the facts is important to you, don't presume that will happen magically. You'll both have to set standards as part of what's important in the relationship and get mutual buy-in. Then you both must decide how to enforce your standards for honesty.

The following eight defense principles will help keep you on your toes:

- **Principle 1. Even Liars Get to be Who They Are.**

- **Principle 2. It's Easier to Lie to "Them" Than to "Us."**

- **Principle 3. Some Men Lie for Short-term Victory.**

- **Principle 4. Hold on to Your Disbelief for a While.**

- **Principle 5. Men Tell You What You Want to Hear.**

- **Principle 6. You'll See It When You Believe It.**

- **Principle 7. He Who Lies to Himself Is Hardest to Detect.**

- **Principle 8. The Facts Are Always Friendly.**

Principle 1. Even Liars Get to Be Who They Are

He lies to you. Then the clever devil manages to escape your anger and your detection of his lies. Too bad the one thing he can't escape is being who he is. Even though you were initially fooled into believing that the frog was a prince, that the liar was a truth-teller, it is a given that eventually his behavior will reveal to you exactly who he really is—not because he wants to, but because he can't help it. All you or anyone else has to do is stick around long enough. Eventually, his mask will crack, his evasions will become obvious, and in some unguarded moment he will inadvertently reveal to you his true but not particularly pleasing colors.

Why? Because our behavior is both consistent across situations and as unique to us as a fingerprint. There's a certain economy to being who we are, day in and day out, rather than in constantly hiding ourselves. A master liar can pull off a deception for extended periods of time, but it takes tremendous focus and energy that the ordinary liar doesn't usually have the wherewithal to pull off unless the stakes are extraordinarily high.

So if you wait long enough, he will show you who he really is. Just as the onion peels itself to reveal each new layer, if lying is part of his makeup, it gradually will show itself. But if you're too busy assuming or slumbering, you won't catch the show. And if you're trying to remake him to fit your own ideals, you will have disconnected your ability to detect the obvious. No matter. He'll reveal himself anyway, but passively waiting for the process to unfold could rob you of years of your life.

No matter how he initially appears to you, chances are very high that he will revert to original form, because the he-gets-to-be-who-he-is rule is always in play. The hooks are no longer necessary—he got what he wanted. His masks take too much effort to hold in place, so they slip. His characteristic evasions are too ingrained, too tempting to put on ice for long. His ethics and morality were cast years before he ever met you. Years after the fact, as you look back, you'll realize all the signs were clearly there from the beginning, if only you had been clearheaded enough to see them.

Tactic 1. Take a behavioral snapshot.

Lies have short legs.
—German saying

About fifteen years ago I stumbled onto a valuable trick I call the "behavioral snapshot." The first time I meet someone I instruct myself to observe and remember every detail I can of this person's behavior, personal expressions, likes and dislikes, and statements, and the way I feel when this person says or does certain things. I am absolutely attentive. I try to miss nothing. Then I store it in my mind. Sometimes, if the person is a client or someone I know I'll be dealing with in the future, I jot down a few detailed notes to jog my memory. Then I file them away.

Later, I pull that first snapshot out of the memory box and recapture what I saw in that first meeting. Amazingly, it is filled with useful information that, with Janus-like hindsight, I now understand. Sometimes I talk to the person about that first meeting and what I saw then.

The behavioral snapshot has three benefits. First, it focuses you on observing and developing a baseline for this person. You'll never be this objective again, so what you see now will be more and more revealing as time goes on. Second, this person will reveal much of who he is in that first meeting: passive or active, charming or withdrawn, changeable or steady, argumentative or agreeable, centered on self or other. And third, just in case you are dealing with a liar, this person may expose many of the markers, the signs and signals of the lie, right in the first meeting.

Try it out. Or dig into your past to think about a first meeting with a man who lied to you. Conjure up all the details. Even without doing it intentionally, it's amazing how much we take in. Were there any signs of what was to come? What can you see now looking back with 20/20 hindsight?

Your behavioral snapshots become convincing evidence that behavior is consistent, and the clues we need to protect ourselves are often far less hidden than we think from the start. Even if he successfully hides who he is from you in the first few rounds, eventually he, like you, will get to be who he is. And if he is a liar, you will be far better off without him.

Principle 2. It's Easier to Lie to "Them" Than to "Us"

A number of years ago I was flying across the country and happened to sit next to the son of a southern legislator. We were discussing men's lies to women when he told me a story. He said, "When I was a just a boy on my daddy's knee, my daddy said, 'Son—there's two kinds of people in the world. There's the 'thems' and the 'us's.' You can say whatever you want to a 'them,' but you never lie to an 'us.'"

His daddy's point was a good one. All groups constantly sort people into members and nonmembers, insiders and outsiders. Loyalty—fierce loyalty—is awarded to the insiders, the "us's." They are trusted and valued. The "thems" have no such luck. "Thems" become second-class citizens. There's a code of honor even in a den of thieves. It doesn't matter whether we're talking about a street gang in Chicago, the U.S. Congress, the AFL-CIO, or a Wall Street brokerage. The real code of honor applies strictly in-house. As an outsider, expect whatever spin of truth suits the insiders' objectives. You won't be valued in the same way. That makes you a potential and unwitting pawn in their game, whatever it is. Unless you know it.

What does this have to do with men lying to women? Quite a bit. Many men tend to see other men as "us" and women as "them." They didn't come to their viewpoint overnight, so you can't expect it to disappear overnight either, just because you happen to be sleeping together, living together, or having children together.

After all, boys and girls prefer to play in same-sex groups until early adolescence. That promotes the separation of the sexes—the boys against the girls. When boys and girls begin co-mingling in their preteens, girls often find themselves depersonalized as objects to be won. The goal? To "get to first base." The guys, not the girls, remain the defining club—the "us's" with whom he will swap his war stories, bond, and promise to tell the honest-to-goodness unexpurgated truth. What about girls? In this scenario girls, like parents, are often cast as "thems." The same kind of "thems" you can tell anything while still retaining your honor—as long as you remember not to lie to an "us." A single man in his early twenties told me he was a great liar, but never lied to his "friends." Who were these friends? Not the woman in his life with whom he's been involved for two years, but his male drinking buddies and old high school chums.

Male privilege and power bonding often maintain an us/them situation between men and women in work, play, and family. Watch any executive meeting that includes both men and women. You'll quickly discover how who is an "us" and who is a "them" can be based on gender or other us/them sorts like race and age. Observe how often men look at men and address each other by name as compared with how they interact with women. Men tend to include one another. Women are often treated like movie extras hired in for the day—inconsequential bit players, outsiders, "thems."

When men's strongest allegiances and honor codes are with other men, it becomes easier to depersonalize and discount women, thereby distancing themselves sufficiently to impede empathy. That paves the way for the lie. Then once he begins lying to you, that pattern of lies will distance him even further from full capacity to empathically connect with you.

Tactic 2. Refuse to be blindsided by us/them sorting.

Be aware of us/them sorting. Notice if he is visibly less at ease talking to you than to his men friends. Do you disappear from his radar when you and he are with two or more of his male friends? Do you become a low priority when he has a choice about how to spend his time? Does he choose to spend large portions of his free time in postadolescent male groups at the bar, the gym, the club, the golf course, the lodge, the union—in short, in activities from which you are excluded?

Even more important, does he consistently create and maintain male-female barriers when he doesn't have to, using cultural stereotypes to make his point? For example, does he hint that you wouldn't understand the economics or the math or the blueprint he's concerned with because women don't get that kind of thing? When he compliments you on something you've done well, does he add a gratuitous tag of "That's pretty good, for a woman"? Does he rarely miss an opportunity to point out your gender, as in "You are a really successful (rich, smart, clever, hardworking) *woman.*" If so, regardless of his motivation, he is putting you in a box labeled "different." And that supports us/them sorting and its accompanying power games.

How can you bridge the us/them distance between the two of you? Begin by stressing your commonalities, minimizing your differences. Tell him your point of view and help him see you as a complex person with a full range of feelings, interests, and abilities. Become friendly with his pals. Let them get to know you and see you as a real person so that you can become as much of an insider as they are capable of letting you be.

In the final analysis, us/them sorting won't convert a nonliar into a liar. When he sees you as a "them," it just makes you easier to lie to. And once he begins lying to you, that reinforces your status as a "them," creating greater distance. If you feel you can manage his degree of us/them sorting, accept it as a cultural reality. If not, bail. Many men have made a conscious and successful effort to rid themselves of this us/them behavior. At the same time, remember that not engaging in us/them sorting is no guarantee he won't lie to you.

Principle 3. Some Men Lie for Short-Term Victory

All he wants is short-term victory. In his mind, he's a general conducting a military campaign to reach a goal or to avoid a setback. Forget long-term intimacy and commitment. This man is thinking with a strictly tactical take-the-hill mindset. Applying principle 2, you are a "them" to be wooed and won, or to be fooled into thinking something that's not true (such as that he's working late when he's really out with the guys or with a new love interest). Somewhere he might have learned that all's fair in love and war and has equated the two. The cunning lie is part of his weapons armory, but sometimes it's not clear whether he sees you as a love to be won or an enemy to be tricked, or as both.

Maybe he's not playing to you at all but to his buddies or his view of himself as adventurer-hero. His language of love is the vernacular of military maneuvers and espionage thrillers, but he's talking about you. In any case, one thing's for sure, when he acts as if his love manual has been lifted from *The Art of War* rather than the *Kama Sutra*, it might be time to pull up camp and head out.

Tactic 3. Spot his tactics and slow things down.

Speed is often of the essence here. The problem is not a single lie, but a whole approach that reduces his relationship with you to a win-lose maneuver in which he's justified in doing whatever it takes to win. You have to spot what he's doing and take quick countermeasures. If you don't, either your love relationship will be over before you know what hit you, or you will be involved in a relationship that has been reduced to a series of tactical campaigns and short-term transactions. You will be left feeling like you ate Twinkies for dinner.

But when in doubt, forget speed. Drag your heels. Just because he is pressing for victory, you don't have to make it easy. Take your time. If this is a new relationship, suggest lunch next week. Put him off. If this is someone you are already involved with, talk longer term. Help him get past his view of you as the next hill to be taken by talking about how that makes you feel. See what he is willing to commit to and how he follows through. Gather information. Set a standard of honesty as a ground rule of the relationship, get his agreement, and then enforce it. Every army has its rules and regulations. Let him know what you want and that you find his short-term approach a barrier to the relationship. See if you can find common ground, or a battle you can fight together where you are part of his team rather than an object to be won or an enemy to be outsmarted.

Principle 4. Hold on to Your Disbelief for a While

This principle has more to do with you than with him. You've heard it throughout this book. Bright, perceptive women who should know better get into a relationship with someone they like, and after an all too brief period of intense scrutiny, throw caution to the wind. Why? Because they found no reason *not to* trust him. They suffer from a condition I call *premature suspension of disbelief.* As a result, they do precisely what no woman should ever do: they believe a liar. Sometimes, aside from a bruised ego, the effects aren't devastating, but other times they can do serious harm to life, health, or finances. Just remind yourself that you don't have to suspend your disbelief because you've slept with someone a few times or even because you married him. Informed and gentle skepticism is a virtue that countless women wish they had exercised more persistently.

There is compelling evidence that women are indeed more trusting than men in close personal relationships and show a greater disposition toward trusting the people they like. Confusing liking and trust isn't a problem if someone you like also happens to be trustworthy, but in the first six months of a relationship, trustworthiness is merely speculation. Give it time.

Tactic 4. Manage your expectations and apply gentle skepticism.

Manage your expectations.

Even though you want to believe everything he says, allow yourself to entertain the idea that a man you would like to trust might be lying to you. Maybe he's keeping a stack of critical relationship-stopping "not tells" under wraps ("I'm married," "I'm interested in another woman," "I'm having an affair at the office," "I'm planning to divorce you as soon as the kids graduate"), or maybe he's telling outright lies. Expect that building trust from scratch or rebuilding it after a meltdown will take time and experience together. One part hope mixed with two parts chemistry is not enough.

Successful expectation management rests on knowing and communicating what you are willing to overlook and where you are going to draw your line in the sand. Decide what your standards are and tell him. Just as he gets to be who he is (principle 1), so do you.

Which values cause you to lose your equanimity when they are violated? For some it's reliability, for others exclusivity, for others emotional commitment. For some it is breach of trust. Talk together about your mutual expectations for critical values you each hold.

Manage your expectations about liking versus trust. To earn your trust he's going to have to keep his word and consistently come through on something of importance, and I don't mean just showing up for dinner. Watch how he manages the biggies. Track where he has promised something and now has encountered competing demands, clashing opinions, or added responsibilities. How does he treat you and the other people involved? Does he treat you like an *us* or a *them* (principle 2)? Does he make you feel important only as long as you are part of his short-term victory plan (principle 3)? Be a broken record, reminding yourself over and over that liking is an instant response to someone, the kind of decision that travels like a reflex through your spinal column, not your cerebral cortex. Base your decision to trust a man on the real facts of his reliability—observed over time. And remind yourself that keeping the difference between liking and trust in mind is a natural antidote to being blindsided by a liar.

Apply gentle skepticism.

Why let someone else create a model of reality that may or may not be right for you? Such a model will be based on that person's experiences, beliefs, needs, and a host of hidden agendas as well. At first, challenging someone's story or perception might feel wrong—especially if you're used to believing most of what people tell you (remember how woman after woman said she believed a liar because there was no reason not to believe him?). Pretty soon you'll wonder how you ever got along without it. Applying gentle skepticism to question someone's stance is different from assigning blame or guilt. It just takes your natural curiosity and pairs it with two parts creativity and one part skepticism to ask a few tough what-if questions.

Is there another way to look at what he is saying or doing? Suppose you were a newspaper reporter. You'd ask who, what, why, where, when, and how questions at every juncture, not because you're a difficult person, but because you want to get the facts of your story right. Apply those questions to understanding who the man in your life is. See yourself as curious, not rude. Check his number in the phone book. Find out about his background, his motivation, and his commitment. Ask to see where he lives, works.

Meet and talk to his friends. Corroborate his stories with his family. You're just substituting your healthy gentle skepticism for a head-in-the-sand suspension of disbelief. If a lie of exclusivity and accompanying cover-up lies come into play, ask him for more information, then check the details.

One of the extraordinary liars I interviewed offered this advice: "Listen for inconsistencies in his stories. Watch for incredible amounts of detail, followed by pockets of vagueness. Ask if he is trying to tell you too much too soon."

Finding out that he is telling the truth won't hurt you in the long run. Discovering the lie early on may disappoint you now, but save you grief later.

Principle 5. Men Tell You What You Want to Hear

To some men, telling women exactly what they want to hear is a time-honored ploy. Granted, there are days we'd all like to hear it, but when what you want to hear has no remote resemblance to the truth, expect trouble. Your choice will be to grieve on the front end of the relationship for what will never be, or to grieve on the back end of the relationship for what never came to fruition. Either way, you'll grieve because what he said wasn't true, and you acted as if it was.

Remember the principle of synchronicity from Chapter 4? The basics are easy: He "interviews" you to find out what you want and then provides either a rough approximation of that, or future promises of it—to get what *he* wants. He promises and you believe. He takes his short-term wins and he's history. You wonder what happened and what is wrong with you. He seemed so nice, so promising. Only the last part is true. He was promising, but not in the way you had hoped.

Tactic 5. Map your soft spots.

Get down on paper and file your wish list of everything you hope a man will say to you and promise you. Then rank the items on your list in order of importance. This is the map to your vulnerabilities. If you have never had anyone take care of you, and he offers to rub your head when it hurts, make you tea when you're tired, or take you away from it all when you're at the edge, how could you doubt him? That's the point. Doubt him. The proof is not today or tomorrow, but in three or six months or years.

If he offers everything on your wish list, enjoy it, but slow down and smell the roses. Learn more about him. Don't be seduced by your own hopes, by your own words fed back to you as promises. Let a few of those promises play out before granting him the gift of your trust.

Principle 6. You'll See It When You Believe It

Women, it seems, are more adept at reading nonverbal cues than men. For example, we pick up on a slight movement that someone makes and make sense of it. A man is more likely to miss it. This ability suggests that women should be more able to detect nonverbal leakages, the subtle signs and symptoms of the lie. Oddly enough, something peculiar happens to the feminine advantage in reading nonverbal signs when a person is lying rather than telling the truth, and when that person happens to be a man! As lies and deceptions increase, women lose their edge in decoding the same kinds of nonverbal cues they could read so easily when he was telling the truth. Hmmm. What are we to make of this?

Two Australian psychologists, Kerryn Hurd and Patricia Noller, found that women go about decoding men's deceptions by attending to obvious rather than covert emotions. Other researchers like Bella DePaulo found similar results, and concluded that women are more likely than men to view a deception so politely that they overlook what is true. It would appear that many women deferentially accept the lie. They deny what they see with their own eyes. For example, they pay attention to the most obvious facial cues, like eye contact, rather than the more subtle cues they read so well when the truth is being told. Again, this isn't merely a laboratory finding. In chapter after chapter, you have heard stories from women who have done just that, almost always to their own detriment. They've politely accepted the lie at great cost to themselves. Maybe you have done the same. Sure it's uncomfortable to call someone on his lie. Your early training may have hammered home that you're supposed to see no evil, hear no evil, speak no evil, or that, above all, it's important to be "nice." But let's face it—there's nothing nice about being duped by a liar, especially when you possess the skills to detect the lie. Whether or not women are more prone than men to being deceived, *you* don't have to be.

Tactic 6. You'll *believe* it when you *see* it.

Is it that some women don't see the deception or that they choose to ignore it? Too many women are trapped into the "power of positive thinking," especially their own, when the situation isn't all that positive. Don't do it! Let yourself get in touch with the negative possibilities as well as the positive ones. We may be conditioned by our socialization to maintain relations by looking on the bright side. Because we are so overly socialized that we paste on our smiles and politely accept the lie, failing to question the liar, we pave the way for our own unhappiness down the road. Why limit your scope of reality because you're expected to be nice? Why not allow yourself to imagine that someone can be lying for his (or her) own gain, and that you have the right, privilege, and duty of calling it as you see it? That way you protect yourself and cut your losses early. Why stick around for more? Behavior is remarkably and boringly consistent after the first four or five dozen times.

Principle 7. He Who Lies to Himself Is Hardest to Detect

We all like to see ourselves as good and honorable people. The liar is no exception. Maybe it's just wishful thinking, maybe it's selective attention to whatever facts support our own position. Maybe it's just self-serving bias. Whatever it is, liars who believe their own deceptions are the hardest to detect. They don't leave a trail of nonverbal cues or the common symptoms of fear that average liars, who know they are lying, leave behind. They make up detailed stories and repeat them so often to so many people that they become real perceptions or memories both for them and for the deceived.

When he truly believes his own deception, he is a tough number to detect and an even tougher number to confront. Even worse, his obvious sincerity may pull you deep into his lie, his shame, and the problems behind his self-deception. When you confront him, denial is the order of the day.

Tactic 7. Get help.

What's important here is not convincing him that he is lying, but instead keeping yourself from being sucked into the complex and elaborate set of defenses he has built to keep his lie or lies intact. It's fair to assume he is lying to himself in a major way if he says, "I don't have a drinking problem," when he does, or "I just borrowed a little money," when he embezzled cash from his employer. In such cases you can assume that there is a long history of subterfuges he's invented to hold his lies and their underlying pathology in place and that it will take someone with considerable skill at confronting them to break through his defenses. Your job is to focus on you and your needs, not his. Not becoming part of his dysfunctional system is a favor you can do for both of you.

If his lies are less severe embellishments, exaggerations, or white lies that he believes to be true, it's tempting to call them minor and overlook them. But even here, it is the pattern rather than the individual lies (was it a lake or a swamp?) that matters. One of the women I interviewed, thirty-four-year-old Millie, a creative director, said that her husband Les "lies about unimportant things that don't carry weight." If he lies about things that don't matter on a routine basis, and you don't call him on it or get help for the two of you, he's getting plenty of practice for the big ones. You're giving him the tacit message that (1) it's okay to lie, (2) when he does lie, you won't notice or confront him, and (3) he doesn't have to be honest to build trust with you.

In her answer to another question, Millie noted that no one particular of Les's lies was most damaging to their relationship. Rather, "it was a whole series of little whites" that damaged the relationship "by eroding trust." Millie, who has said she is willing to overlook little white lies if Les's intent is honorable, nonetheless sees the cumulative effect of his "little whites" as quite damning.

The moral of the story: Don't rationalize. Maybe you can help him change a pattern of lying, maybe not, but you'll need help to make that determination. Insist that he get help and you might save the relationship. If he refuses, get help yourself so you will make an informed decision about your best course of action.

Principle 8. The Facts Are Always Friendly

It may not seem like it at the time, but the facts are always friendly. It's what you don't know that will hurt you. When someone tells you a lie, that person has decided what you are and are not entitled to know. That takes informed choice away from you and puts your future in someone else's hands. Perhaps into the liar's hands.

Some men interviewed said they withheld information or falsified the facts because they didn't want to hurt their wives, lovers, or friends. From their perspective their intent was honorable. Many felt their partners couldn't handle the bad news. So they became the keeper of the secrets. That may sound like Father-knows-best protectionism, but more often than not it's pure cowardice. They are protecting themselves from a partner's anger and sorrow. And instead of making plans to take care of herself, she may believe his soothing but false assurances that everything's fine. Without knowing the truth, she's shooting in the dark. She'll have no idea how to deal with the real situation. Yet man after man told me how his lies were exactly what the woman in his life wanted to hear. What's the right solution?

Tactic 8. Be satisfied with nothing less than the facts.

Aggressively and actively seek feedback and information. Talk to him. Tell him not only that you want to know the facts of the situation, but that this is the fair and principled thing to do. Tell him how important his honesty is to you. Impress on him what being in the dark about your relationship is doing to your ability to take care of yourself and plan intelligently. Let him know exactly what you're in the dark about: your sexual risk, your finances, his addictions, his job, or your future together. Be calm but persistent. Describe how you feel and tell him what you would like to know. If he refuses to talk to you or gives you what you suspect are more lies, use other resources. Talk to his family, friends, coworkers. Look at phone and travel expenses, receipts, or whatever else is legal, appropriate, and available. Remind him that the facts are always friendly. It's what is known to one person and hidden from the other that destroys and incapacitates. Heed this "reality check" advice from Harry, a forty-six-year-old consultant: *"Investigate. Take nothing for granted. A person is known by the friends he keeps, so check with people who know him. Who introduced you to him? Investigate what he says, the places he's been, the people he says he knows. Pay attention to whatever doesn't feel right. People don't deliberately lie to me much anymore because I ask more questions, make it harder to lie to me. I interrogate them and keep on going."*

Harry also offered some parting advice that, while crude, sums up succinctly a point of view many women can benefit from hearing:

My behavioral principle is simple.
Don't deal with assholes, with people who lie to you.

A Short Primer of Self-Defense Rules

The first rule of the road is to decide what you will and will not tolerate. Cliché or not, you are in charge of you. He, likewise, is in charge of himself. You are neither his keeper nor Pygmalion. Once you get that straight, the rest is easier. It's also easier to become a good chooser at the outset than to convert a bona fide liar into an honest man. He and only he is capable of changing himself. When you both value honesty, it's easier to speak up and point out how a lie affects you and the relationship. Once you've agreed on your operating standards, you're more likely to weather even a jarring confrontation. You're on the same wavelength.

You'll still have to choose your battles. Some lies are trivial, some are more devastating. Some lies are polite lies ("No, I don't think you're too fat"). You'll need to differentiate and confront him on any lies that get in the way of whatever is important for you. Just keep in mind how you'll feel if you don't tell him how his lying affects you and what you would like him to do instead. If honesty isn't as important to him as to you, why not know it, before you take one more step toward the future?

In the day-to-day emotional ups and downs of a relationship, you may forget self-defense. Here is a chart to jog your memory. Make a copy of it and keep it at hand.

RULES OF DEFENSE AGAINST THE LIAR

1. Set your own standards, then communicate them to him.
2. Ask him to agree to honesty as a priority between you.
3. Refuse to suspend your disbelief.
4. Pay more attention to his behavior than to his words.
5. Listen to what he says, then verify it through investigation.
6. Like him, but withhold trust until he's earned it.
7. Realize that you will not change, rescue, or transform him.
8. Refuse to ignore smoking guns.
9. Don't make excuses for his lies or bad behavior.
10. Pay close attention to your intuition, what you sense.
11. Put him and his life in a context of friends and family.
12. Confront the lie even if it's uncomfortable for you to do so.
13. Recognize the family of lies that are hooks, masks, and evasions.
14. Recognize the signs and symptoms of an extraordinary liar.
15. Know when to pull the plug and when you need outside help.

Now let's go over a few more principles to help guide you as you confront the lie and the liar.

How to Confront a Liar: The Quick Confronter's Guide

I toss off small lies as someone's insecurity. I excuse it in that way. But big lies, they have more importance. How to confront them is a problem for me.
—Forty-three-year-old divorced female Sunday school principal

Confronting poses a problem for lots of women. Once you've detected the lie, what do you do? Do you confront the lie and the liar head-on? And how? It's a lot like catching a mouse. Now that it's thrashing in the trap, what are you going to do with it? You'd like to get it out of your sight and deal with it, but you'd rather not get your hands dirty. One thing's for sure, it won't go away by itself.

My best advice? Get over it and deal with it, but realize you have many choices when it comes to how to handle the lie. Reframe that old choice of "truth or consequences" as truth *and* consequences. No matter what you opt for—the truth or the lie—consequences will be the order of the day, so you might as well drive the process rather than be the victim of it.

It's important to confront a man's lies in a way that's right for you and your values. But however you do it, learn to become a better confronter. Not confronting just gives him license to keep on doing what he's doing. If that's lying, he'll keep lying. By failing to confront the liar and trying harder and harder to please him, you make it easier for him to lie, harder for him to stop lying. There's no incentive. The lie gets him what he wants without negative consequence. Just be careful to let the consequence fit the crime. Don't overreact. Behavior should have natural consequences. The idea is to clear the air for honesty and intimacy, so choose your battles and calibrate your reactions to the magnitude and effect of the lie.

Talk About Outcome, Not Intent

You don't know what his intent was in telling a lie. But whatever it was, it's a safe bet that he'll transform it into something far more noble and altruistic than the actual reason. Most of us are self-serving and want to be seen in the best light possible. Why should he be any different?

Your best bet is making no assumptions about his intent and refusing to point the finger of blame. Instead, talk about the outcome of his lie and its effect on you. Describe the situation first. Be matter-of-fact. Don't rant and rave. (You can always exercise that option later.) Since men tend to interrupt women, and he is likely to deny or trivialize the whole incident, ask him not to interrupt or respond until you finish. Specifically, tell him what you're saying is important to you and you want him to listen carefully to what you have to say *before he responds*. Tell him how you feel, and be clear and concrete about what you would like from him. Do you want him to simply acknowledge how you feel? Do you want an apology? Is there a problem exposed or exacerbated by his lie that you need to resolve together? Do you want his pledge and commitment to do something differently? When you know what you want and state it, you exponentially increase your chances of getting it.

See Persistent Lying as Serious

Lying may be normal and adaptive, but if he lies frequently, persistently, and gratuitously even when he doesn't have to, you'll be the one doubting your own sanity. Remember, he knows the truth; you don't. Why let anyone play mind games on your time that affect your well-being?

When this happens, it's time to get help—not for him, but for you. He may or may not be amenable to help. That's his problem. But why you are sticking around? If you are not getting what you need from the relationship, the problem has become yours.

Confronted With His Own Lies

Confronting him about the effect of his lies in a way right for you sets the course for developing intimacy based on greater honesty and trust. But that's not the end of it. He will respond. He's probably not used to being confronted. And he may feel guilty, shamed, accused, and blamed, or all of the above.

Based on my interviews and work with clients, here are a few ways both genders say men are likely to respond when confronted. Keep in mind that men and women often respond differently to being caught in their own lies. Women tend to be more apologetic and to offer complex explanations. Men tend to shut down, deny, justify, or blame their accusers.

Forewarned is forearmed. He's not likely to respond in the same way you would. Don't take this personally. Just acknowledge whatever he may be doing. For example, he says it never happened, he trivializes the lie, he refuses to talk about it, or he blames you. Acknowledging what he says *is not* the same as agreeing with it or condoning it. Yet it creates breathing space for dialogue. Matter-of-factly talk to him about how what has happened is affecting you. Be careful to neither blame nor shame. Let him see that his actions have had consequences in your life. Refuse to argue about it. Simply tell him you want him to listen. What he does next will tell you a great deal about who he is. One man I know likes to talk about what he calls the "law of unintended consequences." This is his way of saying he is an honorable person who sometimes lies and makes decisions that hurt others in ways he didn't intend. But he still stops short of taking responsibility for the pain he causes.

The list below identifies a man's likely responses to being confronted. Be prepared to hold your ground, talk it through, and get help if needed.

HOW MEN RESPOND WHEN CONFRONTED ABOUT THEIR LIES

1. **Denial.**
2. **Minimizing the lie's importance.**
3. **Arguing that this lie is an exception.**
4. **Making excuses.**
5. **Justifying the lie.**
6. **Blaming you.**
7. **Discrediting your ability to tell fact from fiction.**
8. **Accusing you of being irrational.**
9. **Emphasizing their honorable intent.**
10. **Reframing the lie as purely pragmatic, or as a half-truth.**
11. **Insisting their feelings were real.**
12. **Ducking behind "Everyone makes mistakes" or "I slipped."**

The lie goes with the territory of personal relationships. It is neither an aberration nor an exception, but part and parcel of everyday life. Defending yourself against the lie's grievous consequences is no armchair exercise. It requires your full readiness to identify, confront, and make decisions that will protect your own interests—not those of the liar.

Every Woman a Detective?

All of us have read detective stories and watched whodunits where we've tried to solve the murder mystery before the truth unravels. Whether your favorites are the British mysteries populated by literate sleuths, or the hard-boiled American thrillers where private eyes bust drug kings, or the new wave of stories featuring savvy women detectives, for each and every one of them, two things count:

Evidence and instinct.

The same two things count in self-defense. The difference is that when you apply these two concepts early enough, there is no victim.

In this chapter and throughout this book we have looked at how you can gain enough insight to protect yourself and stay alert to the evidence you need to detect the lie. You've heard how you can sharpen your skills in ferreting out both nonverbal and verbal clues, distinguishing them from the foolers and false leads that whisk you away from the truth. You can get better and better at detective work by simply remembering to do it and not missing an opportunity to practice your skills. Like any good detective, your job is to put *all* the clues into the broader context of both the person *and* the situation and to resist jumping to conclusions.

Every murder mystery fan knows, however, that the facts aren't enough to crack the case. Great detectives seem to have a feel for things, a nose for clues and behaviors that count. Great reporters, like sleuths, also seem to have a nose for news. They can smell the story before it breaks. You can develop the same kind of intuitive sense for the lie and the liar. How? The same way detectives and reporters learn it. They weren't born with this skill, and neither were you. First, you must identify and focus on the problem to be solved. Then it takes time and dedication. Trial-and-error experiences, listening to hunches, and being open to learning, as well as a history of terrible mistakes and failure, can and will shape your capacity for brilliant success—if you let it.

The eight principles outlined in this chapter can help you become a better spotter of the liar's behavior. Following these principles and the fifteen rules for general self-defense summarized here won't guarantee you success every time. But they'll move you in the right direction. Use these principles and rules like a bullet-proof vest. Then, once you've fully satisfied yourself that you are not dealing with an inveterate liar and that your trust is justified, put the vest in a drawer where you'll have it ready whenever you need it again.

At a deeper level we are all truth-seekers. Your intuition is continuing proof of that. So tune in to your intuition, your sense of what feels right or wrong, and award your sixth sense the respect it's due. To effectively defend yourself against lies and liars or any threat to your well-being doesn't require you to become paranoid or distrustful of the goodness of human beings. Watchfulness, alertness, and a dose of healthy skepticism paired with the natural curiosity you were born with should do just fine.

Let yourself follow your nose for truth and your best instincts to take care of yourself, not the liar.

CONCLUSION

To Tell the Truth

I don't want the confrontation that goes with telling the truth.
—Forty-six-year-old married male manager

I never think about my lying. Like all my lies, I say it's the way you handle a situation.
—Thirty-five-year-old single male financial analyst

It seems like it just happens. Lying is a natural thing to do to keep things alive.
—Twenty-five-year-old single male account manager

The truth hurts but it hurts less than a lie. At least you're dealing with something real. If two people were on a desert island, how could they lie? They would have to live with it.
—Thirty-two-year-old single male administrator

I'm intolerant of lying. I don't care what the reasons are. I want the truth. You can't get close to someone when they lie.
—Forty-one-year-old divorced female school teacher

So it seems men do lie. Not just in the public world of profit and politics and business and sport, but in their private lives as well. We've heard from the liars *and* from the victims of the lie. Yet, if you're like most people, you don't really think that believing the lie, trusting the liar, and having your faith in the integrity and honesty of someone you care about shattered, are what will happen to you. That's what happens to other people—people you read about in books like this.

Even when we've been lied to by a father or a husband or even a man we've just met, it's easy to view it as the exception or to make excuses for the person who violated our sense of fair play and faith in the goodness of people. We miss both the pattern of the lie and our own reactions.

Nonetheless, at some level, conscious or not, we do tune in. Over and over women ask me the same telling question: "How common are lies in close relationships?" I suspect their unstated question is "could the devastating lie happen to someone as ordinary as me?"

Although I can't answer that question, let me tell you about my experiences in the space of one week as I finished writing this book. Since publishing deadlines and client emergencies had me on a treadmill, I'd neglected the basics like getting my eyes checked, having my hair cut, buying new luggage, etc. So one sunny day in Washington, D.C., I cleared my calendar and out I went.

I'd known the nurse at the opthamologist's office for years and although I hadn't seen her in a long time, she remembered that I was writing a book. She asked what it was about, and when I told her the title, she burst into tears. It turned out that her husband of twenty-three years had been having a five-year affair with another woman whom he had been bilking to support a gambling habit— the magnitude of which Marnie hadn't even suspected. Making matters worse, he'd used their marital assets, including their home and savings, to pay his mounting debt. Through her tears she said, *"Dory, this happens to other people. People in a book. Not to me."* And that's the point. If we expected something like that to happen, wouldn't we safeguard ourselves against it?

Then I went to get a haircut. Suzanne, who has been cutting my hair for a couple of years, said, "Dory, could you talk to my business partner?" Why? Turns out her partner had lost her wedding ring and couldn't find it anywhere. Her partner's husband had said he'd look for it and would let her know if he found it. Later, she went to a video arcade with her son. Waiting in line, she spotted her husband holding hands with a woman. She raced across the mall and confronted him. Horrified, she saw her wedding ring on the other woman's hand. What was going on? Her husband of two years had married someone else! "A bigamist," I gasped. "When did this happen? Where is your partner?" Suzanne softly said, "two weeks ago," pointing to the young woman cutting hair at the next station. I had seen this woman for years and even knew who her husband was. And as the three of us talked, Bobette said, *"I can't believe this is happening to me. This is the kind of thing you read about in the newspapers, the kind of thing that happens to other people."* Right. But down deep most of know that the good faith that allows us to suspend our disbelief to trust another human being can be destroyed by a liar who seems as close and known to us as our own skin, yet acts like the stranger on the six o'clock news. As we work so hard to excuse him, to explain his bad behavior, to blink away the distressing news, and to pretend that it is just business as usual, we miss the point.

The point is compelling. We need to defend *ourselves, not the liar*. It is time to take a stand, refuse to be afraid to confront the lies, and stop perpetuating the mindless gender scripts that allow men to lie and women to deny. It is time to realize that the lies that abound in public life don't stop when the door shuts behind him and he says, "Honey I'm home." It's time to understand that if we don't take a stand, we contribute to the conditions that allow the lie to succeed. How? By denying our intuition, failing to confront, backing down when challenged, making excuses, and hoping for the best while settling for the worst.

Later that week I went to buy some luggage. I couldn't find the style I had purchased in the store just a few months earlier. When I inquired about when they would get it in, the salesman told me they'd *never* carried that style. But *I knew* differently. And so did he. I'd bought it *from him*. Challenged, he held his ground. I escalated. He denied, got angry, blamed me, the customer, for making him look bad. He was so convincing that I could see how incredibly easy it would be to believe him, *to trust him rather than my own experience and the undeniable facts*. So, with *101 Lies* in mind, I thought, "Here it is: 'Men lie, they just do.'" I told a friend about the incident. "Well," she hedged, "maybe he was just having a bad day." *He* was having a bad day!

The pattern is hard to duck once you see it.

He lies. She excuses. He lies. She confronts. He denies. She doubts herself, not him. He gets angry and accuses. She backs down. She reframes his actions in the best possible light, privately still trying to make sense of what she suspects isn't and can't be real. Friends and family help us doubt ourselves and believe the lie. The dance goes on. The lying and the hurt continue. But we're no longer talking about the people out there. We're talking about you and me and the men you long to trust and love.

What is the answer? It's self-defense. It's truth. It's refusing to fall into the trap of positive thinking when your intuition is broadcasting that, truly, there is nothing to be positive about.

But let's not get confused. Men are not the enemy, nor are women. One part of the problem is the long and rigorous gender socialization that leads men to see women first as objects to be won and eventually as authorities to be eluded in their quest for freedom. That same socialization process also drives men to shut down expressing their feelings and uncertainty. Women, too, feel the consequences of gender socialization. Women learn to accommodate and smooth conflict, to stifle their independence and feel inadequate rather than strong without a man. When they come together, these gender scripts create conditions that breed distance and failure of empathy—even before the lie works its reverse magic.

That men lie doesn't necessarily mean they desire intimacy any less than women. Sure, they may be more ambivalent about it as they wage their attachment battles. But men, like women, value close, warm, and secure relationships. Nonetheless, the ease and high payoff of the lie get them what they want, and if left unchallenged, creates a lasting dilemma. He lies to protect himself, to avoid humiliation and punishment and to achieve his immediate goals. As soon as he lies, his attention is diverted from building the relationship to covering his tracks in order to prevent discovery. And if confronted, he faces the challenge of convincing the confronter that she has suffered a temporary but undeniable lapse of sanity. That's a pretty tough climate for intimacy to thrive in.

Think about the times you have lied in a trusting relationship. As you lie, you distance yourself from the people to whom you lie, turning them into impersonal objects. You wall them off. That makes lying and covering your lies all the easier. You protect yourself against empathy, lest their pain become yours.

The lie thrives in us/them relationships, in which differences, not similarities, become the order of the day. But the lie also exacerbates any existing differences by creating a new invisible barrier. You can still see the other person, but you cannot touch their core and they cannot touch yours when deception stands in the way.

So what can we do to change this dynamic and end the lying game? Should we look for a perfectly honest man? Or do we have to accept a man who will lie some of the time? And if we are in a relationship with a good man who nonetheless lies to us (and to others), can we help him to change in the direction of more honesty?

IN SEARCH OF THE HONEST MAN

There are honest men, so should you decide to search for one, it's hardly a case of "abandon hope all who enter here." But the *perfectly* honest man, the *relentless* truth-teller, may pose other problems. Men (and women) who *never* lie may be poorly equipped to adapt and to survive the rugged terrain of work, politics, and love. When they insist on telling nothing but the facts in painstaking detail *no matter* what the other person wants to hear, we encounter the polar opposite of the liar who tells what he thinks the other person wants to hear no matter what the facts may be. The relentless truth-teller is an extremist who does his damage by being locked into his own rigid system, which is fitted with as airtight a failure of empathy as that of the extreme liar.

Such men may tell the whole truth, and that's commendable, but flaunting their own brand of near fanatical "truth-seeking" can make them difficult and discomforting partners.

So what are the alternatives? How about the *imperfectly* honest man? The man who lies some, but not most, of the time? The man who lies, but who can still agree that in his personal relationship with you he will abide by certain standards that you both will take responsibility for enforcing? The good news is that nature has created an abundance of such men. So if we can hold our own, insisting on an explicitly defined no-lie relationship, we might just get what we want. Women and men who have established no-lie relationships talk about them with reverence, even when they are not permanent and, in fact, even when they are not romantic. Why? In the no-lie relationship there is acceptance of who each partner is, rather than a shallow idealization. There is a genuine commitment to the relationship beyond the immediate. You each act as though you are in a real partnership that will last. Add romance and love and you've got what a lot of people say they want in life.

But if lies are what we're used to, how do we begin to tell the truth?

TO TELL THE TRUTH

Is it possible for anyone to be one hundred percent honest all the time in personal relationships? Maybe if people were honest all the time they would hate each other. My mother is two-faced, politicians lie. It's confusing. We're all used to lies.
—Thirty-six-year-old single female office worker

Is telling the lie easier than telling the truth? Could be. After all, the lie is often the quick and dirty maneuver of choice. It gets us from here to there and lets us win and move on. Because lying as a way of life often generates results, both men and women have opportunity after opportunity to become well-practiced, even highly skilled lie-tellers in a world that values and rewards short-term victory over longer-term commitment.

In this scenario, truth and intimacy, connectedness and caring, are the losers. When the lie becomes our preferred form of communication, we have little trouble shading the truth and telling the lie to achieve our objectives. Talking straight becomes a dying art. We end up knowing many ways to lie but few ways to be honest.

Yet our challenge is precisely that—to become skilled truth-tellers. For many men and some women this is uncharted terrain. Just as not all lies are heinous, not all truths are brutal. Truth is brutal when we lack skill in framing our truths in a caring way that the other person can hear, when we can't walk in the other person's shoes to understand his or her viewpoint. Truth is brutal when we wait far too long to tell it and then use the truth to set us free from the relationship rather than to make it stronger. Truth is brutal when it is used as a last-ditch hit-and-run tactic—as in "I don't love you and I never did"—as he (or she) disappears into the night.

If we gave the same careful consideration and energy to making the truth as acceptable to the other person as the lie, we would find that there are many ways to tell a difficult truth. We could describe the facts of the situation without editorial comment and let the other person see the facts as we do. We could set the situation up as a thorny issue that we must discuss together with goodwill, making it clear that no matter what the outcome, we value the other person. When we risk being held accountable and being confronted, we are solidifying our bonds of caring with the other person, no matter what the outcome. When we speak frankly about our inherent contradictions—our needs to connect and be separate, to feel secure and free—we forge a real partnership. By communicating our fear and discomfort in being honest, we paradoxically find new strength where we felt weakness and deeper alliances where we anticipated rifts. Honesty strengthens our bonds, whether we are talking about a brand new romance or ending a particular phase of an important relationship. It's no accident that men and women who had established no-lie relationships—even those with former lovers or spouses—see them as central to their well-being.

Yet, despite all the benefits of honesty, the lie continues to gain ground. Getting every bit as comfortable with the truth as the lie remains a challenge for men and women in private and public life. But it is a worthy one. The truth is rarely as glamorous or enticing as a well-told lie. Still, when we are able to accept ourselves and our own truths, we find ourselves better able to embrace another's truths. And in those moments when we and another human being open our hearts to each other, we also open ourselves to something of immense worth. In that connection, *us* and *them* disappears. We begin to wrest "winning" away from the self-interest that dominates the lying game. Winning is reframed in a new context—one of a partnership in which two people seek lasting trust. Winning is transformed into the ability to open and sustain channels of honest communication, even when one partner or the other slips. *Winning is defined as saying no to the lie and the lying game.*

These three simple, but powerful, principles will help you move in this direction:

- *Respect*: Regarding yourself and your own personal history as a source of wisdom; valuing your feelings as a source of empathy.
- *Intuition*: Heeding your intuition as a wellspring of insights that rarely misguide you.
- *Boundaries*: Setting well-defined boundaries around whatever levels of truth and falsehood you will and will not tolerate in a relationship.

It has been many years since my father warned me, "Never trust a liar." Although the meaning of his advice had eluded me at the time, it stuck with me. Yet, something hadn't felt quite right. One piece of the puzzle was still missing. Like you, I had to find that piece for myself. So as you go forth seeking closeness and intimacy with the men in your life, here is my father's advice, amended by what I found. With the collective experience and wisdom of the women and men we have come to know so well throughout this book, the puzzle now includes the missing piece:

> Never trust a liar. *Do trust yourself.*

APPENDIX

Women's and Men's Interview Questions

WOMEN'S INTERVIEW QUESTIONS

1. What made you volunteer for this interview?

2. What's the very first lie you remember being told by a man in a personal relationship?

Probe Questions:
How did you discover it was a lie?
Why do you think you believed him at the time—if you did?
How did you feel about it?
Did you confront him? (When?)
What was the outcome?
What would you have liked him to do instead?
What's the first lie you ever remember telling a man?

3. At what stage in a relationship with a man are you most likely to be aware that he has lied about something important?

Prompts:
Is it at first meeting, in the early stages, in the middle, in the end?
What are the clues, the giveaways that he is lying?
In your opinion, what purpose do lies at this stage of the
    relationship serve?
How likely are you to confront him with your knowledge of the lie?

4. What's your immediate gut reaction when you suspect you've been lied to?

Probe Questions:
When you're positive that you've been lied to?
To what extent do you ruminate over (keep thinking about) the lie?

5. What's the most recent line, trick, or fabrication a man used just to get you interested in him?

Probe Questions:
Did you know or suspect it wasn't true at the time?
How successful was his approach?
What lines, ploys, tricks, or fabrications have you used to get men interested in you?
How well did they work?

6. Tell me about the last time you actually caught a man in a lie or deception—some misrepresentation of the truth.

Probe Questions:
How did you find out it was a lie?
Why do you think you initially believed him?
What was at stake for you?
Did you confront him about the lie? (What happened?)
Why do you think he lied to you? What do you think he hoped to accomplish?
To what extent do you think his lie was planned?
How did this lie affect you?
What was the outcome for the relationship?
Do you think it was what he wanted?
Do you think he "lived to regret" it?
Did you ever try to even the score?
With hindsight, if you had your part to do over again, what, if anything, would you do differently?

7. Over the past five years, what would you say are the three most frequent variations or misrepresentations of the truth you've ever heard from men?

Probe Questions:
That you most often told men over the past five years?
What differences, if any, do you see between the lies men tell you and the lies you tell men?

8. In a relationship with a man, typically what clues make you suspect he might be lying to you?

Probe Questions:
How do you define a lie?
Is concealing the truth a lie?
What methods do you have for detecting lies, deceptions, a liar?
How successful have these methods been for you?
Do you apply the same approaches for detecting lies women tell you?

9. Tell me about the last time a man told you the truth about something important, and you felt sorry he hadn't shaded it.

Probe Questions:
What were the circumstances?
Why do you think he told you the truth, rather than shading it?
How did you react to his telling the truth?
What was the outcome?

10. What kinds of things would you say you are most likely to lie to a man about?

Probes:
Background, intentions, feelings, commitment, sex, money, trivia, etc.

11. From your own experience and the experience of friends, what kinds of things would you say men are *most likely* to lie to women about?

Probes:
Background, intentions, feelings, commitment, sex, money, trivia, etc.

12. What's the last or a typical bedroom lie you suspect or know a man has told you?

Probe Questions:
What made you suspect it was a lie?
How did you react at the time? (Later?)
Did you believe him at the time? Why or why not?
Did he know that you thought it was a lie?
What purpose do you think his lie served?
What would you prefer him to have done instead?
What's the last bedroom lie you told a man?

13. Think about a time when a man you were involved with deceived you or omitted a crucial fact involving money or finances.

Probe Questions:
What made you realize it was a deception? (When did you realize it?)
How did you react to it? (Did you confront him?)
What do you think he hoped to accomplish with the lie?
How did it end?

14. In your last serious relationship or marriage, what was the most damaging lie to your relationship that your partner (husband) told you?

Probe Questions:
How did it damage the relationship?
How did you react to it? (How did this leave you feeling?)
What lie that you told him was the most damaging to the relationship?
Why did you lie about this?
How did he react to it?

15. What's the most hurtful lie—or a truth finally revealed—a man has used to end your relationship?

Probe Questions:
What made it so hurtful?
How did it affect you?
What would you have preferred him to do?
Did the relationship then actually end?
What's the most hurtful lie you have told a man to end a relationship?
How did he react to it?

16. What about white lies? Think about the last time you were aware of a man fibbing to you about something inconsequential—something that didn't seem worth lying about.

Probe Questions:
What led you to believe it was a lie?
What did you make of him lying about this?
How did you react to this lie?
Did you confront him?
Do you think he intended or planned to lie to you?
What's the last white lie you told a man?
What do you make of your lying over things that don't matter
    much? Were you surprised by your own white lie?

17. What secrets are you most likely to keep from the men in your life?

Probe Questions:
Why do you keep these things secret?
Do you think they know about them?
What secrets are the men in your life most likely to keep from you?
How do you know?

18. How about the most outrageous or unbelievable lie a man has ever told you? What comes to mind?

Probe Questions:
What do you think prompted him to lie in such an outrageous way?
When and how did you become aware it was a lie?
What happened? (Probe: Did you talk with him about it?)
How did you feel about it?
What's the most outrageous or unbelievable lie you ever told a man?
What did you hope to accomplish with this lie?
What was the outcome?

19. Think about the very last time you remember lying to a man.

Probe Questions:
How did he react?
Was he aware that you were lying at the time?
If not, how did he find out?
Did he confront you about the lie? (Probe: What happened?)
How did this affect your relationship?
How do you think he felt about it?

20. Think about a time in the past five years when you were lied to by another woman.

Probe Questions:
How did you know it was a lie?
How did you react?
Did you confront her about it?
How did you feel about it?
How did it affect your relationship?

21. Was there a time in a close personal relationship with a man *who had been lying*, when you felt he *stopped lying*?

Probe Questions:
When did he stop?
What happened?
What made you realize he had stopped?
How did you react (feel)?
Why do you think he stopped lying?
How did this affect the relationship?

22. Have you ever had a close personal relationship with a man where you're pretty sure he didn't lie to you or deceive you at all?

Probe Questions:
What made you think he wasn't lying?
How did this affect the relationship?
How do you explain this?
Did this ever happen in a close professional relationship?
In a relationship with another woman?

23. What should I have asked you about lies that I didn't? (What did you want to talk about in this interview that we didn't get to?)

24. How many times would you say you lied, or exaggerated the truth today in this interview?

25. Has the interview today changed the way you view the lies that men and women tell each other?

26. What, if anything, would you say you've learned over the years from your experience with lying and being lied to?

MEN'S INTERVIEW QUESTIONS

1. What made you volunteer for this interview?

2. What's the very first lie you remember telling a woman in a personal relationship?

Probe Questions:

Why did you lie about this?
What outcome were you hoping for?
Did she discover it was a lie? How?
Did she confront you?
How did it end?
How did you feel about deceiving her in this?
With hindsight, what, if anything, would you do differently now?
What's the first lie you ever remember a woman telling you?
How did you know it was a lie?
Did you confront her?

3. At what stage in a relationship with a woman are you most likely to shade the truth, or lie about something important?

Prompts:
Is it at first meeting, in the early stages, in the middle, in the end?
In your opinion, what purpose do lies at this stage serve?
How do you explain your lying or shading of the truth here to yourself?
How likely is she to confront you with her knowledge of the lie?

4. What's your immediate gut reaction when you suspect you've been lied to?

Probe Questions:
When you're positive that you have been lied to?
To what extent do you ruminate over (keep thinking about) the lie?

5. What's the most recent (or typical) line, trick, or fabrication you've used with a woman used just to get her interested in you?

Probe Questions:
Do you think she knew or suspected it was a lie at the time?
How successful was your approach?
What ploys, tricks, or fabrications have women used you to get you interested in them?
How well did they work?

6. Tell me about a time when a woman actually caught you in a lie or some deception.

Probe Questions:
What were the circumstances?

How did she find out it was a lie?
Do women usually know when you are lying?
Did she confront you? (What did she do or say?)
If she believed you at first, why do you think she believed you?
What was at stake here for you?
Why do you think you lied or shaded the truth? What did you hope to accomplish?
To what extent did you plan the lie?
At the time, how did you feel about lying to her?
How did this lie affect the relationship?
What was the outcome?
Was this what you wanted? (What she wanted?)
Did she ever try to even the score? How?
With hindsight, what, if anything, would you do differently?

7. Over the past five years, what would you say are the three most common variations on the truth you have told women?

Probe Questions:
The lies that you have told?
That women have told you over the past five years?
What difference, if any, do you see between the lies you've told women and the lies women have told you?

8. In a relationship with a woman, typically what clues make you suspect she might be lying to you?

Probe Questions:
How do you define a lie?
Is concealing the truth a lie?
What methods do you have for detecting lies, deceptions, a liar?
How successful have these methods been for you?
Do you apply these same methods to detecting lies other men tell you? (If not, why?)

9. Tell me about the last time in a personal relationship you told a woman the truth about something important, and you felt sorry you hadn't shaded it.

Probe Questions:
What were the circumstances?
Why did you decide to tell the truth here rather than shading it?
What did you expect her to do?

How did she react to your telling the truth?
What was the outcome?

10. What kinds of things would you say you are most likely to lie to a woman about?

Probe:
Background, intentions, feelings, commitment, sex, money, trivia, etc.

11. Tell me about the last time you remember lying or conceal-ing the truth from a woman in a personal relationship.

Probe Questions:
What was at stake for you?
Did you plan to lie or conceal the truth?
Did she find out? If so, when and how?
What was the outcome?
Did you have any regrets?

12. From your own experience and the experience of your friends, what kinds of things would you say women are *most likely* to lie to men about?

Probes:
Background, intentions, feelings, commitment, sex, money, trivia, etc.

13. What's the last or most typical bedroom lie you've told a woman?

Probe Questions:
Did she suspect it was a lie? (Why/Why not?)
How did she react at the time? (Later?)
What purpose do you think this lie served?
Did you think about the lie in advance of telling it?
What's the last bedroom lie a woman told you?

14. From talking with other men and your own experience, what would you say are the three lies that men are most likely to tell women?

15. Think about a time in a personal relationship when you somehow deceived a woman or omitted a crucial fact about money or finances?

Probe Questions:
What did you hope to accomplish with this deception or omission?
Do you think your partner realized it was a deception or omission?
  (If so, when did she realize it?)
How did she react to it?
Did she confront you?
How did it end?

16. In your last serious relationship or marriage, what was the most damaging lie to your relationship that you told?

Probe Questions:
How did it damage the relationship?
How did she react to it? (Probe: How did this leave her feeling?)
How did you react to it? (Probe: How did this leave *you* feeling?)
Why did you lie about this?
What lie that she told you was the most damaging to the relationship?
How did you react to it?

17. What's the most hurtful lie—or truth finally revealed— you've ever used to end a relationship?

Probe Questions:
What made it so hurtful?
Why did you choose to end the relationship in this way?
How did she react to it?
Did the relationship then actually end?
How satisfied were you with the outcome?
What, if anything, would you do differently if you could do it
  over again?
What's the most hurtful lie—or truth revealed—that a woman has
  ever told you to end a relationship?
How did you react?

18. What about little white lies? When was the last time you remember fibbing to a woman about something inconsequential—something that didn't even seem worth lying about?

Probe Questions:
What led you to lie here?
To what extent did you intend or plan in advance to lie?
What do you make of your lying over things that don't seem to
  matter much? Were you surprised by this white lie?

Did she confront you?
Did you ever clear the matter up by telling the truth?
What's the last white lie a woman has told you?
Do you think that telling white lies is wrong?

19. What secrets are you most likely to keep from the women in your life?

Probe Questions:
Why do you keep these things secret?
Do you think they know about them?
What secrets are the women in your life most likely to keep
   from you?
How do you know about them?

20. How about the most outrageous or unbelievable lie you remember ever telling a woman? What comes to mind?

Probe Questions:

What do you think prompted you to lie in such an outrageous way?
What did you hope to accomplish or gain?
Was she aware it was a lie? (If yes, when and how did she
   become aware?)
What was the result?
How did you feel lying to her at the time?
What's the most outrageous or unbelievable lie a woman has ever
   told you?
When and how did you become aware it was a lie?
How did you feel about it?
What was the outcome?

21. Think about the very last time you were lied to by a woman.

Probe Questions:
How did you react?
Were you aware that she was lying to you at the time?
If not, how did you find out?
Did you confront her about the lie?
How did this affect the relationship?
How do you think she felt about it?
What would you have preferred her to have done?

22. Think about a time in the past five years when you were lied to by another man.

Probe Questions:
How did you know it was a lie?
How did you react?
Did you confront him about it?
How did you feel about it?
How did it affect your relationship?

23. Was there a time in a close personal relationship with a woman when *you had been lying* and *you stopped lying* to her?

Probe Questions:
What happened?
Did she realize you had stopped?
How did she react (feel)?
Why do you think you stopped lying?
How did this affect the relationship?

24. Have you ever had a close personal relationship with a woman where you didn't lie to her at all?

Probe Questions:
Why do you think you didn't lie in this relationship?
Could you briefly describe the relationship?
Did your honesty or the fact that you didn't lie ever become an issue?
How did your truthfulness affect the relationship?
Did this ever happen in a close professional relationship?
In a relationship with another man?

25. What should I have asked you about lies that I didn't? (What did you want to talk about today in this interview that we didn't get to?)

26. How many times would you say you lied, or exaggerated the truth today in this interview?

27. Has the interview today changed the way you view the lies that men and women tell each other?

28. What, if anything, would you say you've learned over the years from your experience with lying and being lied to?

DORY HOLLANDER, PH.D., is a psychologist, organiza-
tional consultant, and career coach. She is president
of New Options, Inc., a St. Louis-based consulting
firm specializing in workplace communication and
executive coaching for companies. Dr. Hollander also
conducts seminars on gender-related issues and has
taught university courses on sex roles. She has published a book on career management and has served
as president of several professional organizations
including the Missouri Psychological Association. Dr.
Hollander divides her time between St. Louis and
Washington, D.C.

To share your stories and insights about lies and
lying with Dory Hollander, write:

Dory Hollander, Ph.D.
P. O. Box 42671
Washington, D.C. 20015-2671